Praise for *Kitchen Witchery*

"Laurel has here delved into the subtle enchantment of ... ...ounter daily, the food we eat, leading us to see food as not just energy, but a path."

—Cliff Seruntine, permaculturist, shaman, and author of *The Wildwood Way* and *Seasons of the Sacred Earth*

"What an inspiring and informative read, offering us an opportunity to revive a nature-based and natural perspective to what has become another chore for living: cooking. This work is a beautiful weaving of physical, mindful, and spiritual knowledge and teachings that we may use to enrich our own lives, the lives of those we care for, and the natural world."

—Daphne Seruntine, herbalist specializing in primitive food storage, preparation and usage

"*Kitchen Witchery* is a fabulous mix of practical knowledge and magickal application that invites you to step into your kitchen with mindfulness and purpose. Sometimes a wooden spoon can be as powerful as a wand!"

—Deborah Blake, author of *Everyday Witchcraft* and *The Eclectic Witch's Book of Shadows*

"Far more than a recipe book (though it is packed full of wonderful recipes), *Kitchen Witchery* encourages magickal mindfulness of the nutrition we put into our bodies…Laurel Woodward provides a resource that helps us consider the source, energy, and impact of what we consume, including magickal correspondences for ingredients. Food is fundamental to our existence and, with the knowledge provided in *Kitchen Witchery* at our disposal, we can build a strong and healthy foundation for life by cooking with intent, wisdom, and power."

—Emily Carding, author of *Faery Craft* and *So Potent Art*

KITCHEN
WITCHERY

About the Author

Laurel Woodward (Portland, OR) has been a witch for twenty years and is also a tarot reader. She has written for magazines and ezines on the subjects of healthy living, organic gardening, sustainable living, and the magick of tapping creative energy.

To Write to the Author

If you wish to contact the author or would like more information about this book, please write to the author in care of Llewellyn Worldwide Ltd. and we will forward your request. Both the author and the publisher appreciate hearing from you and learning of your enjoyment of this book and how it has helped you. Llewellyn Worldwide Ltd. cannot guarantee that every letter written to the author can be answered, but all will be forwarded. Please write to:

Laurel Woodward
℅ Llewellyn Worldwide
2143 Wooddale Drive
Woodbury, MN 55125-2989
Please enclose a self-addressed stamped envelope for reply,
or $1.00 to cover costs. If outside the U.S.A., enclose
an international postal reply coupon.

Many of Llewellyn's authors have websites with additional information and resources. For more information, please visit our website at http://www.llewellyn.com

LAUREL WOODWARD

KITCHEN WITCHERY

Unlocking THE *Magick* IN Everyday Ingredients

Llewellyn Publications
Woodbury, Minnesota

FIRST EDITION
Second Printing, 2021

Cover design by Shira Atakpu

Llewellyn is a registered trademark of Llewellyn Worldwide Ltd.

Library of Congress Cataloging-in-Publication Data
Names: Woodward, Laurel (Cookbook writer), author.
Title: Kitchen witchery : unlocking the magick in everyday ingredients /
  Laurel Woodward.
Description: First edition. | Woodbury, Minnesota : Llewellyn Publications,
  [2021] | Includes bibliographical references and index. | Summary: "A
  collection of magical correspondences for a variety of cooking
  ingredients and recipes"— Provided by publisher.
Identifiers: LCCN 2021015239 (print) | LCCN 2021015240 (ebook) | ISBN
  9780738767840 (paperback) | ISBN 9780738768045 (ebook)
Subjects: LCSH: Cooking. | Magic. | Witchcraft. | LCGFT: Cookbooks.
Classification: LCC TX715 .W8996 2021 (print) | LCC TX715 (ebook) | DDC
  641.5—dc23
LC record available at https://lccn.loc.gov/2021015239
LC ebook record available at https://lccn.loc.gov/2021015240

Llewellyn Worldwide Ltd. does not participate in, endorse, or have any authority or responsibility concerning private business transactions between our authors and the public.

  All mail addressed to the author is forwarded, but the publisher cannot, unless specifically instructed by the author, give out an address or phone number.

  Any internet references contained in this work are current at publication time, but the publisher cannot guarantee that a specific location will continue to be maintained. Please refer to the publisher's website for links to authors' websites and other sources.

Llewellyn Publications
A Division of Llewellyn Worldwide Ltd.
2143 Wooddale Drive
Woodbury, MN 55125-2989
www.llewellyn.com

Printed in the United States of America

Contents

Recipe List

Disclaimer

This book is not intended to provide medical advice or to take the place of medical advice and treatment from your personal physician. Readers are advised to consult their doctors or other qualified healthcare professionals regarding the treatment of their medical problems. Neither the publisher nor the author take any responsibility for any possible consequences from any treatment or advice to any person reading or following the information in this book.

Please avoid any foods you have sensitivities to. Confirm a recipient's dietary restrictions and allergies before feeding or otherwise exposing them to prohibited foods.

INTRODUCTION

It starts with knowing and then willing what you know ...

A kitchen witch is crafty and clever. She sees potential in even the most common ingredient as she applies her very own flavor to this most functional form of magick. Her home is a sacred space, and she plies her craft in the kitchen using everyday items to brew potions, make teas, and cook up tasty treats for those she loves. She is attuned with the tides of the natural world, and she reflects them in seasonal dishes. Her power is in the clearness of her intention, the focus of her energy, and the force of her will as she employs the magickal properties of herbs, spices, vegetables, fruits, roots, and greens to empower her workings. Most of us have a bit of kitchen witch in us.

I embrace kitchen magick in my own nature-centric practice to transform chore into ritual. I may be a busy wife and mother of four, but I have found that when a task is approached mindfully, it shifts from mundane into an intense, meaning-filled moment that makes life magickal. When I integrate mindfulness into my everyday activities, I become engaged, awareness heightens, and I become pointedly conscious of myself right there in that single moment. Perception shifts and suddenly the moment transforms as if I stepped out of time and into another reality in which all sensations are heightened. The light is brighter, the colors richer, time deeper. All that is meaningless falls away until there is only me there in the bubble of that single moment, and as I witness the shift, a delicious lightness shivers across my skin and sinks down into my bones as the moment swells and expands and becomes transformative. It is truly magickal. Whether I am making breakfast, kneading bread, or pulling garden weeds down on my knees, fingers dark with soil, when the task is approached with mindful clarity, it becomes not just a meditation to get the task done, but a ritual to manifest a fully formed act of creation.

This book is a cookbook designed to elevate the way you approach cooking, shifting it from a half-hearted attempt into a powerful, fully conscious action that sets energy in motion to nurture, heal, or compel, to manifest your dreams. It is not tied to any one religion but enriched with the teachings of many. I have included the foundations of spellwork, basic concepts, and examples to help you grasp the techniques and apply them to your practice. For when you approach a task as ritual, it pulls your thoughts from the world and focuses them on the singular moment. It allows you to be there with it, to feel whatever it is that you are feeling. It makes space and expands your horizons, turning what seemed impossible possible.

Chapter 1
Why Food Matters

Not that long ago the act of providing food dominated people's lives. Each community had to produce their own food. When they did well, their families ate well. When they did poorly, they died. Diets were seasonal. In the spring and summer months, the people ate lots of fresh organic fruits and vegetables. During the colder seasons, they ate meats, nuts, beans, roots, and porridge. Cooking dominated village life. There were no markets, no grocery stores. When a family needed food, they grew it, foraged for it, or hunted it.

Today we have a whole industry telling us what and where to eat. We think it's normal to grab a meal at a drive-through and eat it on the go, and when we do shop, we fill our carts with premade products wrapped in glorified packaging proclaiming "All Natural" and "Healthy Choice" when most of the things we are selecting are not even classified as food but as "foodstuffs" that are loaded with sugar and chemicals and hold very little nutritional value.

Unhealthy diets and lack of access to nutritious food are two of the driving factors behind what a new report from the International Panel of Experts on Sustainable Food

Systems describes as the "ballooning costs of health impacts in food systems."[1] Food has changed.

Fruits and vegetables grown decades ago were much richer in vitamins and minerals than the varieties most of us get today.[2] Family farms around the world are disappearing as factory farm corporations are taking over food production.[3] Most of today's food has been processed, showered with pesticides, sprayed with Roundup, treated with chemical solvents, and stripped of most of its goodness.

But facts have not changed. You are still what you eat and as a society, we are paying the price with low energy, poor health, and weight problems. It is common to wake feeling tired and groggy, and most compensate by gulping down coffee and grabbing ready-to-eat meals on the go. And we snack and snack on empty calories made of salt and sugar and unpronounceable chemical ingredients. Unhealthy dietary patterns have become increasingly prevalent over recent decades—a trend that has been accompanied by increasing rates of overweight, obesity, and noncommunicable diseases worldwide.[4]

We need to return to our roots, filling our menus with produce from the local farmer's market, garden grown vegetables, and organic supermarket choices. With just a bit of attention and effort, you can swap out the junk food for healthy, better-tasting fare and regain your health and vigor in the process. Make a choice to fill your pantry with empowering supplies. Sadly, today the buyer has to be aware and choosy to avoid the cheap, the fake, and the altered. When you are at the market, make it a habit to read each label before you put an item into your basket. Avoid the choices that contain a lot of additives. Put back the products that have been highly processed. Avoid the packages and choose real food whenever possible.

....

1. Olivier De Schutter, "Towards a Common Food Policy for the European Union," IPES-Food panel, February 2019, http://www.ipes-food.org/_img/upload/files/CFP_FullReport.pdf.

2. Roddy Scheer and Doug Moss, "Dirt Poor: Have Fruits and Vegetables Become Less Nutritious?" *Scientific American,* April 27, 2011, https://www.scientificamerican.com/article/soil-depletion-and-nutrition-loss/.

3. Chris McGreal, "How America's Food Giants Swallowed the Family Farms," *The Guardian*, March 9, 2019, https://www.theguardian.com/environment/2019/mar/09/american-food-giants-swallow-the-family-farms-iowa.

4. Cecilia Rocha, "Unraveling the Food–Health Nexus," Global Alliance for the Future of Food and IPES-Food, October 2017, http://www.ipes-food.org/_img/upload/files/Health_FullReport(1).pdf.

The Importance of Buying Organic

Many foods contain harmful chemicals that you won't find in the ingredients list. More than 1.1 billion pounds of pesticides are applied annually to crops in the US alone.[5] These applications are being done solely to increase crop yields, not to make your food better for you. This is big business at work. Poisons and herbicides are sprayed on food crops, and the produce is sent off to market with a blind eye to what harm it may cause to your health. And there is harm. In 2015 the International Agency for Research on Cancer (IARC) published a report that the herbicide glyphosate and the insecticides malathion, diazinon, tetrachlorvinphos, and parathion are possibly "carcinogenic to humans."[6] The insecticide chlorpyrifos has been associated with developmental delays in infants.[7] Studies have also suggested that pesticide residues—at levels commonly found in the urine of kids in the US—may contribute to ADHD prevalence and are linked to reduced sperm quality in men.[8]

Glyphosate, the active ingredient in Roundup, is the most widely used herbicide in the world. Its use has been linked to cancer, autism, severe food allergies, and autoimmune disease.[9] Studies from the World Health Organization Specialized Cancer Agency have shown that long-term exposure to glyphosate has been linked to potential development of non-Hodgkin's lymphoma and other serious health issues. In 2015, both the state of California and the World Health Organization declared glyphosate a probable carcinogen.[10]

5. Donald Atwood and Claire Paisley-Jones, "Pesticides Industry Sales and Usage: 2008-2012 Market Estimates," Environmental Protection Agency, 2017, https://www.epa.gov/sites/production/files/2017-01/documents/pesticides-industry-sales-usage-2016_0.pdf.

6. International Agency for Research on Cancer, "IARC Monographs Volume 112: Evaluation of Five Organophosphate Insecticides and Herbicides," World Health Organization, March 20, 2015, https://www.iarc.fr/wp-content/uploads/2018/07/MonographVolume112-1.pdf.

7. Michael Biesecker, "States Sue Over EPA Decision to Keep Dow Pesticide On the Market," Associated Press, July 06, 2017, https://fortune.com/2017/07/06/states-sue-epa-dow-pesticide/.

8. Alice Park, "Study: A Link Between Pesticides and ADHD," Time, May 17, 2010, http://content.time.com/time/health/article/0,8599,1989564,00.html; Mandy Oaklander, "A Diet High in Pesticides Is Linked to a Lower Sperm Count," Time, March 30, 2015, https://time.com/3763648/pesticides-diet-fertility/.

9. Anthony Samsel and Stephanie Seneff, "Glyphosate, Pathways to Modern Diseases III: Manganese, Neurological Diseases, and Associated Pathologies," Surgical Neurology International 6, no. 45 (March 2015), https://www.ncbi.nlm.nih.gov/pmc/articles/PMC4392553/.

10. International Agency for Research on Cancer, "IARC Monographs Volume 112: Evaluation of Five Organophosphate Insecticides and Herbicides," World Health Organization, March 20, 2015, https://www.iarc.fr/wp-content/uploads/2018/07/MonographVolume112-1.pdf.

In 2017, California listed glyphosate in its Proposition 65 registry of chemicals known to cause cancer. Since then "more than 42,000 people have filed suit against Monsanto Company (now Bayer), alleging that exposure to Roundup herbicide caused them or their loved ones to develop non-Hodgkin lymphoma and that Monsanto covered up the risks."[11]

Glyphosate exposure is not good for you, yet since 2012 it has been used in California to treat almond, peach, cantaloupe, onion, cherry, sweet corn, and citrus crops.[12] Peas, sugar and beetroots, carrots, potatoes, and onions have been found to contain high levels of glyphosate, as do quinoa, tea, beer, and wine.[13] Tests have found glyphosate on wheat, barley, oats, and bean crops that are not genetically engineered because it is becoming a more common farming practice to spray the crop just before harvest to desiccate the field, or kill the crop and dry it out so it can be harvested "sooner than if the plant were allowed to die naturally," writes Ben Hewitt, which means glyphosate is in a lot of the things we eat. In fact it is this practice of preharvest desiccation that "accounts for over 50 percent of dietary exposure" to glyphosate.[14]

We are being exposed to harmful chemicals. They are in many of the products we are eating, and no one knows the damage this exposure is doing, though some are beginning to wonder. Corn is a big offender. Monsanto spliced Bt into corn genes. Bt is *Bacillus thuringiensis*, a naturally occurring bacterium found in the soil that breaks open insects' stomachs when they eat it, causing them to die. Big Food claims GMOs are safe, that the Bt would never be absorbed into humans. However, a study by the physicians at Sherbrooke University Hospital in Quebec, Canada, discovered Bt toxin was present in 93 percent of

....

11. Stacy Malkan, "Non-Hodgkin Lymphoma: Glyphosate Fact Sheet: Cancer and Other Health Concerns," US Right to Know, last modified April 12, 2020, https://usrtk.org/pesticides/glyphosate-health-concerns/.

12. Elizabeth Grossman, "What Do We Really Know about Roundup Weed Killer?" National Geographic, April 23, 2015, https://www.nationalgeographic.com/news/2015/04/150422 -glyphosate-roundup-herbicide-weeds/.

13. Jihad Aldasek, "Updated Screening Level Usage Analysis (SLUA) Report for Glyphosate," United States Environmental Protection Agency, October 22, 2015, https://paradigmchange.me/lc/wp-content /uploads/2019/03/GLYPHOSATE-use-EPA-HQ-OPP-2009-0361-0064.pdf; Kara Cook, "Glyphosate in Beer and Wine," CalPIRG Education Fund, February 2019, https://uspirg.org/sites/pirg/files/reports /WEB_CAP_Glyphosate-pesticide-beer-and-wine_REPORT_022619.pdf?_ga=2.33097086 .1581849178.1551185850-857148262.1551185850.

14. Ben Hewitt, "Why Farmers Are Using Glyphosate to Kill Their Crops—and What It Might Mean for You," Ensia, December 19, 2017, https://ensia.com/features/glyphosate-drying/.

the pregnant women they tested, and it was in 80 percent of umbilical cord blood of their babies.[15]

In 2018 a group of scientists from the Environmental Working Group purchased more than a dozen brands of oat-based breakfast cereal, instant oatmeal, and snack bars from grocery stores in the San Francisco Bay Area and Washington, DC, area to give Americans information about dietary exposures that government regulators are keeping secret. Glyphosate was present in every sample, and "all but two of the 28 samples had levels of glyphosate above EWG's health benchmark of a daily exposure of no more than 160 parts per billion, or ppb."[16] The highest levels of glyphosate were found in Quaker products. Quaker Oatmeal Squares Honey Nut cereal had 2,837 ppb of glyphosate. Quaker Oatmeal Squares Brown Sugar was second with 2,746 ppb. General Mills came in fourth with 1,171 ppb of glyphosate in their Cheerios Oat Crunch Cinnamon cereal. Large amounts of glyphosate were also found in snack bars, with Quaker Breakfast Squares Soft Baked Bars Peanut Butter the highest at 1,014 ppb.[17]

Quaker's response was reported by Fox KTVU, CBS News, the *New York Times*, and *People*: "Quaker does not add glyphosate during any part of the milling process. Glyphosate is commonly used by farmers across the industry who apply it pre-harvest. Once the oats are transported to us, we put them through our rigorous process that thoroughly cleanses

....

15. Aziz Aris and Samuel Leblanc, "Maternal and fetal exposure to pesticides associated to genetically modified foods in Eastern Townships of Quebec, Canada," *Reproductive Toxicology* 31, no. 5 (May 2011): 528–33, https://pubmed.ncbi.nlm.nih.gov/21338670/.

16. Alex Formuzia, "Roundup for Breakfast, Part 2: In New Tests, Weed Killer Found in All Kids' Cereals Sampled," EWG, October 24, 2018, https://www.ewg.org/release/roundup-breakfast-part-2-new-tests-weed-killer-found-all-cereals-sampled.

17. Alex Formuzia, "Roundup for Breakfast, Part 2: In New Tests, Weed Killer Found in All Kids' Cereals Sampled," EWG, October 24, 2018, https://www.ewg.org/release/roundup-breakfast-part-2-new-tests-weed-killer-found-all-cereals-sampled.

them (de-hulled, cleaned, roasted and flaked)."[18] So if your oatmeal, oat cereal, granola, or snack bar is not organic, then chances are it contains a hefty dose of glyphosate.

If you are choosing non-organic wheat or oat products, you are choosing products with hidden chemicals, and the truth is we know very little about the long-term effects of glyphosate or any other pesticide in our food. The harm may take ten to twenty years to become evident. We do know glyphosate is bad for the environment, and it persists in the soil and the groundwater.[19] The National Resource Defense Council writes that it has caused a "steep decline" in monarch population, "over 80% in the last 20 years," due to loss of milkweed.[20] Glyphosate-based herbicides can "harm all facets of an ecosystem, including the soil biology and composition, water, and non-target plants, aquatic organisms, amphibians, reptiles, invertebrates, animals, and humans."[21] Its toxicological effects have been traced from lower invertebrates to higher vertebrates. A 2017 environmental study observed toxicological effects "in annelids (earthworms), arthropods (crustaceans and insects), mollusks, echinoderms, fish, reptiles, amphibians and birds. Toxicological effects like genotoxicity, cytotoxicity, nuclear aberration, hormonal disruption, chromo-

....

18. Leslie Dyste, "Study: Weed Killer Found in Oat Cereal and Granola Bars," Fox KTVU, August 16, 2016, https://www.ktvu.com/news/study-weed-killer-found-in-oat-cereal-and-granola-bars; "Weed-Killing Chemical Linked to Cancer Found in Some Children's Breakfast Foods," CBS News, August 15, 2018, https://www.cbsnews.com/news/glyphosate-roundup-chemical-found-in-childrens-breakfast -foods/; Mihir Zaveri, "Report Finds Traces of a Controversial Herbicide in Cheerios and Quaker Oats," *New York Times*, August 15, 2018, https://www.nytimes.com/2018/08/15/health/herbicide-glyphosate -cereal-oatmeal-children.html; Shay Spence, "General Mills Responds to Report of Cancer-Linked Chemical Found in Its Cereals," People, August 16, 2018, https://people.com/food/general-mills-cheerios -weed-killer-chemical-glyphosate-quaker-oats-response/.

19. W. A. Battaglin, M. T. Meyer, K. M. Kuivila, and J. E. Dietze, "Glyphosate and Its Degradation Product AMPA Occur Frequently and Widely in U.S. Soils, Surface Water, Groundwater, and Precipitation," *Journal of the American Water Resources Association* 50, no. 2 (April 2014): 275–90, https://onlinelibrary.wiley.com /doi/10.1111/jawr.12159; Eva Sirinathsinghji, "Widespread Glyphosate Contamination in USA," Institute of Science in Society, August 2014, http://www.i-sis.org.uk/Widespread_Glyphosate_Contamination _in_US.php.

20. Sylvia Fallon, "Report: Monarchs, Other Species Endangered by Pesticides," Natural Resources Defense Council, October 30, 2019, https://www.nrdc.org/experts/sylvia-fallon/report-monarchs-other -species-endangered-pesticides.

21. Sharon Rushton, Ann Spake, and Laura Chariton, "The Unintended Consequences of Using Glyphosate," Sierra Club, January 2016, https://content.sierraclub.org/grassrootsnetwork/sites/content.sierraclub.org .activistnetwork/files/teams/documents/The_Unintended_Consequences_of_Using_Glyphosate_Jan -2016.pdf.

somal aberrations and DNA damage have also been observed in higher vertebrates like humans."[22]

You can avoid the exposure by feeding your family organics. Fruits, vegetables, and grains labeled organic are grown with the use of safe natural pesticides. They are treated with natural herbicides and, infrequently, with limited, highly regulated synthetic pesticides. Eating organic food eliminates daily doses of pesticides, toxins, and herbicides from conventionally farmed foods and keeps the food on your plate good for you. And recent studies have confirmed that organic foods often have more beneficial nutrients, such as antioxidants, than their conventionally-grown counterparts. The *British Journal of Nutrition* published a study that concluded that due to different soil management practices used in organic agriculture and non-organic agriculture, "organic crops and organic-crop-based foods contained higher concentrations of antioxidants on average than conventionally grown foods."[23] In a six-year study published in the *Journal of Agricultural and Food Chemistry*, researchers found that organic onions had about a 20 percent higher antioxidant content than conventionally grown onions.[24] The bottom line is, sure, organic produce is more expensive, but forgoing a dose of poison makes it so worth it.

Magickal cooking applies the same principles as any magickal ritual. The energy of an object is greater the closer an object is to its natural state. In kitchen magick we choose the cleanest source of energy, avoiding unnatural pollutants, and align these natural energies with intent as we work the ingredients into a food to nourish the mind and body and set an intention in motion.

Kitchen magick is alchemy, for through heat or cold or with brute force by stirring, smashing, or kneading, we empower a substance with will and intent as we change its

....

22. Jatinder Pal Kaur Gill, Nidhi Sethi, Anand Mohan, Shivika Datta, and Madhuri Girdhar, "Glyphosate Toxicity for Animals," *Environmental Chemistry Letters* 16 (December 2017): 401, https://www.researchgate.net/publication/321822115_Glyphosate_toxicity_for_animals.

23. Marcin Barański, Dominika Średnicka-Tober, Nikolaos Volakakis, et al., "Higher Antioxidant and Lower Cadmium Concentrations and Lower Incidence of Pesticide Residues in Organically Grown Crops: a systematic literature review and meta-analyses," *British Journal of Nutrition* 112, no. 5 (September 2014): 794, https://pubmed.ncbi.nlm.nih.gov/24968103/.

24. Feiyue Ren, Kim Reilly, Joseph P. Kerry, Michael Gaffney, Mohammad Hossain, and Dilip K. Rai, "Higher Antioxidant Activity, Total Flavonols, and Specific Quercetin Glucosides in Two Different Onion (*Allium cepa* L.) Varieties Grown under Organic Production: Results from a 6-Year Field Study," *Journal of Agricultural and Food Chemistry* 65, no. 52 (June 2017): 5,122–32, https://pubs.acs.org/doi/10.1021/acs.jafc.7b01352.

form. A stick of butter is mixed with sugar and flour and worked with love to become a delectable treat filled with nurturing energy and kind intent. A pan of broth is filled with vegetables to become a healing elixir. Spices are ground and herbs are crumbled to stir a lover's passions.

Kitchen magick is green magick. When we mindfully prepare a meal, the kitchen becomes sacred space. Everyday actions become powerful when we turn a mindless routine into a mindful ceremony. When we cook, grounded in the moment, aware and vested, we are able to focus intent, direct energy, and make the mundane an act of magick!

Chapter 2

THE MAGICK OF
EVERYDAY THINGS

Everything, including you, is composed of vibrating atoms. It is this action of vibrating that emits a frequency, and it is this frequency that produces an electromagnetic field. Your electromagnetic field holds your atoms together. It is the interface that allows one part of your body to talk to other parts of yourself. In fact, every process keeping you alive can be traced back to an electric field that some component of your body is creating.[25] So it is with every leaf, root, fruit, nut, and seed you consume. Each bite vibrates with a unique brand of its own energy that you take within to bond with or collide with.

There is amazing energy in the food we consume, both metabolic and magickal, or at least there can be if you choose to consume the right foods. Fruits like apples, apricots, avocados, beets, and pomegranates are anti-aging and increase beauty. Roots brim with a hearty, grounding energy to support health and stability. Seeds hold encouraging, positive energy to nurture cells and fuel acts of creation and beginnings. Leafy greens are associated with

25. Jack Fraser, "How the Human Body Creates Electromagnetic Fields," Quora, November 3, 2017, https://www.quora.com/Is-it-possible-for-the-human-body-to-create-an-electromagnetic-field/answer/Jack-Fraser-11.

money and growth, and when you include them in your diet, they boost your vitality and well-being and make your energy sparkle.

Foods provide nutrients for our daily meals and medicine when we are ailing. Food items also possess energy for magickal work. Kitchen magick works by correlating the natural energies of food items, aligning them with an intention, while you work them into a dish to nourish the mind and body and set intent in motion. By learning this craft, it becomes possible to make magick while you cook up tasty, nutrient-rich, nurturing fare for your friends and family.

You too can be a kitchen witch. It just takes practice and know-how. For example, let's say your best friend is coming for tea. It's been a while since the two of you have spent any quality time together but you really miss your relationship. You know your friend loves avocados, so you decide to work with their loving energy to energize your relationship. You toast a couple of pieces of organic whole-grain bread (wheat to nurture and renew) and top it with smashed avocado (to foster affection). You drizzle a generous amount of olive oil over the top (to heal and bless your friendship), and then you squeeze a fresh lemon over it (to brighten the energy) and add a generous sprinkling of crushed red chili flakes (with energy to warm and energize). As you prep the meal, you say,

Fruit of Venus, with each bite
bless this friendship with delight.
With each bite our bond strengthens
and as our relationship lengthens,
your loving energy flows
to grant many more joyous episodes.

That is how it works. The kitchen witch looks at the natural energies of produce, plants, herbs, spices, and oils and infuses them with energy and intent to manifest the working. Avocados are a food of love associated with Venus and the element water. They are rich in antioxidants that nourish skin cells to help reverse aging. An avocado is a good fruit to use in attraction, beauty, or love magicks. It holds energy to rekindle affection or ignite passion. If your lover likes avocados, you can feed him guacamole to deepen his feelings or inspire romance.

Lover's Guacamole

Exposure to the oil in chili peppers may cause skin irritation, so wear gloves when handling peppers. Avoid direct contact. The oil can cause a very uncomfortable burning sensation that, depending on how sensitive you are to it, can last for hours.

You will need:

2 ripe avocados

½ cup diced onion

2 tomatoes, diced

handful fresh cilantro, chopped

1 jalapeño or serrano pepper, seeds removed, finely diced

1 clove garlic, minced

juice of 1 lime (add to taste)

salt

Slice the avocados open and remove the pits. Scoop the flesh into a bowl, set your feet, draw your energy in, and focus on the bowl before you. Fix your intention in your mind. Then mash the avocado, and as you work, focus your attention on the task and tell it what you want it to do. You might say something like,

> *Fruit of Venus, bless me with your power.*
> *With each bite, I am empowered.*
> *He loves me. He loves me. He loves me.*

When the avocado becomes creamy with small chunks, add the remaining ingredients and stir together. Serve with chips or a quesadilla while you personify your most charming self.

Adding the Magick

The effects of magick have been debated down through the ages, yet magickal practices persist in cultures around the world. In his book *The Triumph of the Moon: A History of Modern Pagan Witchcraft*, Ronald Hutton writes that many of the people he interviewed had no idea how their rituals actually worked. Then one shared, "The first stage is when you totally believe in witchcraft. The second is when you realize that it's a complete lot of rubbish. The third is when you realize that it's a complete lot of rubbish; but somehow it also seems to work."[26] And it does. When one applies attention and intention to a task, the results are, well, magickal.

Spellwork is approached like a recipe. This + this = this. When a potion maker created a brew that proved effective, he noted the process and passed it down, making it possible for us to take that knowledge and apply it today. For each plant, flower, shrub, and tree contain a unique magickal signature, an enormous potential stored within that, when aligned with intent, not only enhances a magickal working but causes the results to be more predictable. Knowledge is power. When you learn and understand the behavior of an object, you gain the ability to predict a magickal response. To empower your work, do your research. Get to know the energies you are working with.

Kitchen magick is all about aligning like energies and approaching a task mindfully to pour energy into the creation process through a concentrated effort that is molded with an intention into an edible creation. Here is another example: Let's say your husband has a big interview and if he gets the job, your family will be set. So you help him get ready. You make sure he has everything he needs and he looks his best. Then the morning of the interview, you light a green candle that you've anointed with olive oil (for blessings). You sprinkle it with a pinch of ground nutmeg (for luck), cloves (luck and prosperity), and cinnamon (to draw prosperity). You set it in the center of the table and light it as you cook up a hearty bowl of oatmeal (wealth and prosperity), which he finds comforting and grounding. You carve up an apple (the apple holds the energy of love, wisdom, and enchantment) and sprinkle the bits over the steaming oatmeal. Then you add a splash of maple syrup (the real stuff from the tree, which is associated with riches) and a sprinkle of cinnamon (luck, strength, wealth, and a dash of psychic power so he has the wisdom to say the right things). And the whole time you are working, as you stir, as you chop, and as you sprinkle, you are putting the intention for him to succeed into the food, like a secret message that programs the dish. As you take up the knife to carve the apple, you place your feet and come to center to pull your mind from the distractions of the world, drawing your focus inward, and as your perception heightens and the moment swells, you draw a breath and direct all your attention into the food prep. Then you add the power of the spoken word by telling the apple what you want it to do. You can whisper, sing, chant, or even just think as you center your laser focus on chopping the apple. Then when you have all the ingredi-

26. Ronald Hutton, *The Triumph of the Moon: A History of Modern Pagan Witchcraft* (Oxford, UK: Oxford University Press, 1999), 396.

ents assembled, you can voice your petition or say a prayer to direct the energies to work together.

> *Today is his day.*
> *Success is his.*
> *With a bite of apple and a bit of oat,*
> *Joe finds favor and claims the prize.*
> *The job is his,*
> *the job is his,*
> *the job is his!*
> *With the sweetness of maple,*
> *Joe finds favor.*
> *He is at his best.*
> *Joe wins and the job is his.*

Or something like that. The phrases can rhyme, but they don't have to. A rhyme is easier to repeat and finds a rhythm that makes it easier to raise energy. And that is what you are doing. You are creating a meal, but your actions are also raising energy as your thoughts align with the energy of the ingredients to create a mold for the universe to manifest your goal. You set the dish at the table and repeat your petition. When you feel ready, you can draw a breath and blow it out through your mouth in a long slow gust to activate the energy and send it off into the universe.

The rest is up to Joe. You have encouraged him, prepared him, and put him in the right mindset for the encounter. Before he leaves, you tuck an acorn into his pocket as you kiss him and wish him luck. Then you let the candle burn until the interview is over.

While half of the magick of food is in the ingredients, the other half comes from you during the food prep. You are raising energy and molding it with your intent every time you make something, whether you mean to or not. Through focus of will and conscious action, you can mindfully multiply that energy and imbue your labor with intent to manifest what you desire.

Here is another example: Let's say you are having two new friends over for lunch and you want to make a good impression. You clean and prepare your home in honor of their visit. You know that mandarin oranges, mint, passion fruit, pine nuts, pineapples, pistachios, tarragon, and tangerines all have sociable qualities, and when added to a dish, they foster feelings of welcome. You just happen to have a fresh head of lettuce, some mandarin oranges, and a package of pistachios on hand, so you decide to whip up a welcome salad. You gather your items, and as you wash and chop and put together the dish, you hold the intention that the afternoon will be fun, that your friendships will gel, and that your guests will go away feeling good about you.

Goat Cheese, Mandarin, and Pistachio Hospitality Salad

This recipe makes 3 servings.

You will need:

1 head romaine or butterleaf lettuce

1½ cups orange segments (mandarin, tangerine, or clementine)

6 ounces fresh goat cheese, 2 ounces for each serving

⅓ cup chopped pistachios

Wash, blot dry, and chop the lettuce before dividing it onto three pretty plates. Add ½ cup orange segments to each. Top with crumbled goat cheese and pistachio pieces.

Shallot Dijon Dressing

Serve the salads with a batch of this brightly flavored dressing. It utilizes the energies of lemon for happiness and friendship, honey to sweeten, and mustard and a shallot to guard against negativity.

You will need:

1 shallot, chopped

½ cup lemon juice

1 cup olive oil

1 Tablespoon dijon mustard

1 Tablespoon honey

salt and pepper to taste

Add the ingredients to a large-mouth jar and allow it to stand for 30 minutes before serving. Shake and pour the dressing over salads or serve it alongside them. Store any left-over dressing in your refrigerator for up to 1 week.

∞

Back to your guests. You serve up the salad with a loaf of fresh baked bread and iced tea. Your visitors are wooed. They feel welcome and honored. They both notice your efforts, and as a result, both open to your friendship. The mood lightens. The conversation becomes easy. The afternoon is a success. Your new friends leave happy, and all it took was a little time and attention to detail.

Setting an Intention

When approaching any magickal act, the first step is setting forth a clear intention. Magick in its simplest form is an intention that is honed and focused on before being acted on so that it will come to fruition. When you begin a project, think about what it is you hope to achieve. What are you working toward? Your answer is your intention.

For example, let's say you are going to bake a loaf of bread. Why are you baking this loaf? Is this a spiritual act? Bread is a favored offering of many deities, household spirits, woodland spirits, and other spirits of the land. Is this an act of love or nurturing? Are you working to empower yourself or someone else? Or perhaps you are hoping to compel a response from someone? The intention, or the reason you are mixing up this loaf, is the very thing that gives it power. An intention is a clear desire, expressed as simply as possible. So figure out what you want to achieve and put it forth into a clear, concise statement. Your intention might be a statement that is self-empowering. It can be positive thoughts of love and healing nourishment to present to your family. It could be happiness and joy to share with your friends or any other desire you wish to manifest.

For a magickal act to be successful, you must know what you want and believe that you can have it. Decide what you want and simplify your desire into a clear concise statement as though you have already gained it. An intention to heal would be stated as "Sam is well" or "Sara is healed." An empowering intention: "The job is mine," "I am blessed," "I am happy," or "I am whole." Or "I gain the reward. Success is mine." A compelling intention would be something like "He loves me," "She has this," "They accept this," or "We all get along."

State your intention and then pour positive energy directly into the loaf as you make it. In spellwork an intention is voiced or written or simply held in the mind and fueled with concentrated attention and energy of action so that it can manifest. In kitchen magick a recipe is worked through with a goal in mind. A cake is baked to honor a loved one. A bowl of soup is cooked and fed to a sick child to heal them. A cup of tea is brewed and drunk to calm the spirit. No matter what you make, you are creating it for a purpose. In magickal cooking it is this purpose that is emphasized, meditated on, and fueled with energy (while we gather ingredients, stir them together, or chop them into bits) so that it will manifest.

Successful magick is achieved through force of will and concentrated thought. Control of the mind is one of the most important attributes of a spellcaster. Control of the mind, or moving your thoughts from the past or from the future and setting them on the present moment, is a simple and powerfully liberating action that you accomplish through practice. Learning to be present in the moment grants you the power to shut off the chattering of your "monkey mind" and allows you to be fully present in the moment.

With the mastery of this next exercise, you will learn to quiet your mind, focus your thoughts, and be present in the moment.

Meditation to Come to Center

The act of coming to center is a form of mindfulness. It is the process of drawing in your attention and flooding it with the here and now. To do this, we pull our mind from the world and fix our thoughts on our centers so that our focus and perception can intensify as it floods with the immediate moment. By drawing in our focus, we draw scattered thoughts into a single sharp focus that consists only of us there in that moment. And as perception shifts, it expands and sharpens into a wondrously exhilarating experience of being right there, awake and alive, and oh so aware of being there in your own skin. Through the act of coming to center, you can step out of the mundane world and channel your focus into your intention to fuel your recipes and gain a desired outcome.

Learning to come to center changes the way we perceive things, as it increases our powers of perception, the ability to naturally observe and correctly interpret the world around us. By mastering this exercise, you will gain the ability to gather your energy and attention at your core, sharpen your focus, and expand your senses, allowing you to open your perception and notice things you were missing before. With practice you will be able to let your awareness expand to encompass a larger and larger area as the ability of each of your senses becomes sharper and more focused.

Let's begin. Get into the meditative position that best suits you. You may sit or stand. Just make sure you are in a comfortable position and your spine is straight. Slowly draw a deep, even breath. Focus on your breath following as it enters your body. Notice how your chest expands and rises. Notice how your body feels. Don't allow other thoughts to distract you. Keep your mind solely focused on what it feels like in this moment. When your lungs are fully expanded, hold the breath for the count of three. Then slowly release it, exhaling out to the count of three. This is the meditative breath, the mindful or "conscious breath."

Breathe, and as you draw a deep breath, close your eyes. Bring your focus to the area behind your breastbone. This area is known as your center. (Some of you may feel it lower in your belly and that is fine too.) Focus on your center as you breathe. Draw a slow, deep breath in to the count of three, hold and pause to the count of three, then breathe out to the count of three. Breathe, and as your breath moves through your body, visualize a light growing, glowing brightly within your center. Breathe and be present as you focus on the lovely inner glow. If you need to, you can add the sense of touch by pressing your hand over the area as you follow your breath. Breathe deeply as you hold your focus on the glow.

Breathe and feel the energy expand with each breath. Hold your focus inward so that there is only you, your beautiful glowing center, and your breath. Sit with your breath until you experience a shift as the moment grows sharp. Your perception will open and intensify as you become intensely aware of how it feels to be there, in that moment, within your skin. Sit with your expanding perception and witness the shift as your senses fill and swell with the delicious presence of the moment.

Timing Your Work with the Energy of the Moon

The moon hovers above us, a beacon in the night sky, influencing more down here on Earth than we will ever know or suspect as she rhythmically passes through the twelve signs of the zodiac, connecting with each of the cosmic energies in turn. Not only does the silver orb influence the tides, but it is suspected that she also influences the behaviors of all life on this planet, be it plant, animal, or human. Indeed, in stories and lore the moon's influence has been blamed for changes not only in a human's behavior, but in the behavior of the seas, the fish, and even the plants in the field. Gardening by the phases of the moon "is an idea that has been around for as long as humans have been growing their own food."[27] More recently it has been observed that plants not only absorbed more water at the time of the full moon, but that cuttings are more apt to root at this time. Pliny the Elder, the first-century Roman naturalist, noted in his *Natural History* that the moon "replenishes the Earth; when she approaches it, she fills all bodies, while, when she recedes,

27. Jaime McLeod, "Why Do We Garden by the Moon?" *Farmers' Almanac*, April 6, 2015, https://www .farmersalmanac.com/why-garden-by-the-moon-20824.

she empties them."[28] It is because of this cause-and-effect relationship we work to draw things to us when the moon goes from new to full and push things away when it goes from full to dark.

The shifting moon influences many things seen and unseen. While it is recognized that the gravitational attraction results in tidal forces that affect both the oceans and Earth's crust, it is suspected that it affects much, much more. Understanding the shifting qualities of this power will give you the ability to supercharge your magick. To take advantage of moon energy, we look to the work of those before us, practitioners who observed different cause-and-effect relationships and recorded the results of their workings, and we are able to take what they learned and apply it. It is for this reason we work spells for gain and increase during the waxing moon and decrease during the waning phase.

Do you know what phase the moon is in? First and foremost, determine if the moon is waxing or waning. This will define how to word your intention so that it aligns and is supported by the powers that are present.

During the waxing moon, craft intentions for …

- Blessing
- Protection
- Good luck
- Love, attraction, and friendship
- Fertility
- New job and career advancement
- Fast money, wealth, and abundance
- New opportunities
- Healing and good health
- Communication, inspired creativity
- Happiness and harmony spells

During the waning moon, craft intentions to …
- Cleanse or purify
- Bind or banish
- Clear energy or return a hex

28. Pliny the Elder, *Natural History: The Empire in the Encyclopedia*, trans. John Bostock and Henry T. Riley (London: H. G. Bohn, 1855; Perseus Digital Library), bk. 2, ch. 102, http://www.perseus.tufts.edu/hopper/text?doc=Perseus%3Atext%3A1999.02.0137%3Abook%3D2%3Achapter%3D102.

- End a relationship or repel attention
- End a barren phase
- Banish behaviors, obstacles, and obsessions
- Banish debt and end scarcity
- Unblock energy flow
- Banish sickness, end indulgence
- Support self-examination, proofreading, study
- End grief, soothe negative emotions, banish discord

Like a great mirror, the moon reflects the light of the sun as it rotates around Earth, and as it moves, its appearance from Earth changes. Approximately every twenty-nine days the moon cycles through its phases: it appears to wax from a thin crescent, growing until it brightly glows full, and then wanes as it goes back to a thin crescent before becoming completely absent. When the moon is dark, it is at its lowest energy point. When the moon is full, it is at its apex. Each phase of the moon supports a different action or inaction based on the increasing or decreasing of the light.

Our modern minds have lofty ideas about who we are and our place in this modern world that ignore our physical natures and the fact that we are beings of flesh and bone and blood rooted in the ancient tides of the natural world. Like brother bear and caribou and even monarch butterfly, we respond to the pulse, mostly unaware, ignoring the physical response and accompanying reactions. Just as our bodies respond to the seasons, we also react to the moon, reflecting its shifting form in our emotions, energy, and mood. Science has explained how the gravitational attraction of the sun and the moon creates the tides, that it affects the waters of the Earth and the plants of the field. Why wouldn't we suspect that we too experience a reaction?

Tracking the lunar cycle allows us to forge a connection to this flux of energy. It creates an awareness of the magickal tides and fosters a relationship with the natural world, of which we are a part of it. Just as you know what season and what day it is, you should be aware of cycles of the moon. The moon's cycle continuously ushers energy though our lives as it rises to arc across the sky before setting again. Every month it waxes and wanes, shifting from new to full, affecting more of life on Earth than we will ever know.

Go outside and look at the sky. Get to know the moon's schedule. The new moon rises around sunrise. Each day, the moon rises fifty minutes later than the day before so that the first quarter moon rises around noon and the full moon rises near sunset. The last quarter moon rises near midnight.

The Dark Moon

As the moon moves around Earth, its appearance from Earth changes in relation to its position to the sun and Earth. When the sun and moon are aligned on the same side of Earth, the moon is not illuminated. The night sky is dark. Old World witches defined this conjuncture as the dark moon. Today there is a lot of confusion about this phase due to different definitions from modern-day astronomers and scientists, who have made the terms *dark* and *new* interchangeable. But energetically the dark moon and the new moon are not the same.

The dark moon is the period opposite the full moon: the time when there is no moon visible in the sky and when energetically the moon is at its lowest point. The energy is quiet and very receptive. The dark moon is a deeply magickal liminal phase associated with the womb. It is a time to pay homage to ancestors, a time for mediumship, a time to hide what needs to be kept secret or to seek what is hidden or lost. The dark moon offers energy for shadow work. It is the night to gaze into the void, to communicate with the denizens of the underworld. A time for banishing, binding, curse-breaking, and hex work.

Perform a Dark Moon Meditation

The night of the dark moon is a powerful time to go inward and check in on yourself. Fill a bowl with water and set it so that you can see the dark sky in the water's reflection. Settle into a comfortable position where you can gaze on the surface of the water. Come to center and engage your intuition by moving your attention to the spot in your head between your ears. Sit quietly and listen. Watch the surface of the water and see what comes up. Take note of every word, sound, image, symbol, smell, feeling, or thought that comes up. When you are finished, write it down, in as much detail as you are able, to read again later. You will be surprised by what you find.

The New Moon

The time of new moon is when the first crescent of the moon is visible, signaling the very beginning of the waxing moon cycle. At the new moon the energy is beginning to build for increase, making this a time to cast spells for new beginnings and new projects. Its influence can also boost ambitions and careers. This is the time to plant seeds for things you wish to manifest.

Greet the Moon as It Rises

Like the sun, the moon also rises in the east and sets in the west. When the moon is new, it rises at sunrise. Each night afterward it rises later so that on the first night of full moon, the moon rises around sunset. Research what time the moon is going to rise in your area. Go outside and find a place with a clear view of the horizon. Watch for the moon to crest and greet it with a shout, a song, or a bow. Lift your arms and say hello. This is your practice. Make it a power time. Smile and open your heart, and the moment will become powerful.

The Waxing Moon

Look at the moon. Did you know you can always tell if the moon is waxing or waning simply by holding up your hand? (Right hand for those in the Northern Hemisphere; left if you are in the Southern.) Hold your hands up with your thumbs extended and palms facing the moon. If the shape of the moon appears similar to the shape of your right hand, it is waxing.

As the moon waxes (the illuminated surface as seen from Earth is increasing), the energy that is present supports increase. Work to bring things to you. Now is the time of action, a time to build and create. Look back at the intention you set at the new moon. Do the work needed to move your plan forward. This energy will support all spellwork to draw love, luck, abundance and prosperity, and positive opportunities.

The Full Moon

The full moon occurs when the moon's entire hemisphere facing Earth is illuminated. At this time the tide of energy swells and surges to its apex. It beams down upon us, heightening our emotions, sharpening our intuition, and clarifying our focus. Emotions swell and moods deepen, causing some people to act erratically. Crime often spikes around the full moon. The oceans too respond to the pull of the moon with high tides. Trees and plants drink up more water. Seeds wake and sprout. Cuttings send out roots.

The period of full moon lasts for three days. It is a power time for ritual work to manifest desires. It is a time for wish fulfillment, a time to finalize projects, to manifest what was set in motion at the beginning of the cycle. The energy of the full moon fuels our magickal work, making us capable of more. In its light we can build, we can summon, and we can work defensive and protection magicks. The three-day period of the full moon is also a valuable time for spiritual growth and practical magick.

Throw a Full Moon Celebration

Organize an inspirational get-together. Have a group of friends over. This does not have to be your magickal group, only people you wish to be a part of your metaphysical tribe. Host an outdoor party. You can have a fire. There is something bonding about fires that always boosts the energy of a gathering. You can gather around it and sing or dance and drum. You might want to tell stories, lead a group meditation, or form a circle and make a wish to the moon. No need to freak anyone out—you can keep it low key or make it more upbeat depending upon everyone's comfort level.

Bake a Moon Cake

On the first night of the full moon channel your inner kitchen witch to make an empowering moon cake. Use your favorite recipe. Channel moon energy as you gather, measure, mix, and stir. Mindfully mix in a magickal ingredient or two to boost its mystical powers: a sprinkle of arrowroot to deepen the mystical, a spoonful of lavender to promote happiness, or a crumble of rose petals or a dash of rosewater to inspire affection. Decorate your cake with flowers and herbs, or cut out a stencil of the moon's cycle and place on the cooled cake's top. Sift powdered sugar over the top of the stencil until the cutout pattern is filled in. Remove the paper and eat or share over the next three days to infuse your energy with the energy of the moon.

The Waning Moon

As the moon begins to wane, it passes from full to third quarter, to crescent, and back to dark, completing the cycle. Through this part of the cycle, the energy recedes, making it possible to push away or banish things you want to be rid of. Instead of drawing prosperity, do work to banish want. Instead of drawing love, do work to end loneliness. Instead of manifesting opportunity, do work to unblock energy flow. The moon now grants energy to release, cleanse, and clear away. Work rituals to purge negative influences, banish what is unwanted, or reverse other magick. Use this energy to remove obstacles that have stalled your progress. Now is the time to remove, banish, and bind. Do work to remove curses, change ill luck, or break a cycle you would like to end. The waning moon will support magick to end unwanted behaviors of both yourself and those around you. Work to deal with troublemakers, end gossip, or compel someone to leave.

Timing Your Magick with the Days of the Week

Have you ever had one of those moments when everything just clicked? When it felt as though the energy of the universe was at your back, that you were "in the flow," and that the universe itself was aiding you in your efforts? You can make those moments more frequent by aligning intention with the energy of the universe. When we time ritual so that it is supported by the moon's cycle and the energy of each day, our intention is energized by the powers that be as we sync our hearts and minds with the greater universe.

Just as the moon holds energy to support our magickal work, so does each day of the week. Long ago when humans were creating the calendar, they gazed out into the heavens and named the days after the seven luminaries, which are the sun, the moon, and the five planets that were visible to the naked eye: Mars, Mercury, Jupiter, Venus, and Saturn.

Sunday: Named after the sun god Sol or Helios, Sunday holds strong masculine energy to increase health, happiness, and general prosperity. Use this energy to manifest your dreams, advance your career, and fortify personal achievements.

Monday: The day of the moon goddess Luna or Selene, Monday's fertile feminine energy can be used to grant clarity and fuel aspirations of the heart. Work today to expand your intuition, instill harmony, attract love, or inspire your inner muse.

Tuesday: Named after Mars or Aries, Tuesday brims with strong masculine warrior energy for leadership, strength, courage, passion, and defense. Use this energy to fix problems or deal with trouble. This force will also stimulate action and launch something new.

Wednesday: Belonging to the messenger Mercury or Hermes, Wednesday's energy will benefit any work of expression. Do work today to send, enhance, or fix any communication. It will empower all work regarding messages, study, and travel.

Thursday: Jupiter or Zeus's day, Thursday brims with benevolent energy to manifest abundance and growth. This day's energy will support increase for good health, prosperity, expansion, success, and luck.

Friday: Belonging to Venus or Aphrodite, Friday brims with love energy for relationships, family, attraction, beauty, affection, friendship, trust, healing, and
protection.

Saturday: Holding the karmic energy of Saturn or Cronos, Saturday has a reputation for healing through tricky life lessons. Use this energy to aid the sick,
restore what is blocked, find peace, or deal with issues that are restricting you.
Saturn will support work for self-preservation. Use this energy to fuel work for
protection, to remove obstacles, or to bind a troublemaker.

We look at the work others have done before us and apply their findings, knowing that
joining like energies to intent will make a spell become more predictable. If the day is Saturday and the moon is waning in Scorpio, working a fast money spell would most likely
fizzle, as the energies available are not suited to the intention, but cast a spell on that same
day to uncover what is true and the energy would fly to the heavens. To supercharge your
efforts, determine what energies are available before doing any sort of magickal work.

Cleanse, Consecrate, and Charge Your Magickal Tools

When a new magickal item comes into your practice, chances are it changed a lot of hands
and passed through a lot of different energies as it made its way to you. A good energy
cleanse is advisable before you consecrate it. If it is an item that will tolerate being soaked
in water, a ritual bath is the ideal cleansing method. If it is an item that will not, burial
in a bowl of earth or a dish of salt will neutralize the energy. If the item is delicate, you
could light a stick of sage and pass the item through the smoke to cleanse it of the residual
energy.

If you are not sure what process you should use, ask the item. Hold it in your dominant hand and come to center. Open your mind and listen to the object. It will most likely
let you know what you need to do with it to welcome it into your practice. When you
have settled on the method, cleanse your item.

After you have washed, buried, or smudged it, it is time to consecrate it, or make it
sacred by dedicating it to a magickal action. This is an act of blessing the item in the name
of the deity or the energies you work with in your magickal practice. You may do this
any way you like. You might hold it in your dominant hand and ask your deities to bless
it. You might light a stick of incense and pass the item through the fragrant smoke. You

might anoint the item with a blessing oil or baptize it in moon water. You might ask for an elemental blessing, naming each element as you anoint it with each of their forms.

I let the item lead me and perform the ritual depending on what is required. For example, to consecrate a new candle, I rinse it in water, dry it, and hold it in my dominant hand while I tell the candle what I want it to do for me. Then I cover it with my other hand as I visualize white light cocooning it. After the visualization, I hold the item up to my lips and blow out a long slow breath over it, knowing my breath is linked to spirit and that it works to activate my intention.

If it is a new wand I am consecrating, I use a more elaborate practice inviting each element to add their blessing, for I work most often with the wild, raw energy of the elementals in my magick. To do this, select something to represent each element and set it at each respective compass point. Place the item you wish to bless in the center. Invite the elements to add their blessing. Begin in the north or the east, and anoint your object with the representation of the element as you ask for it to bless the item for your ritual work. North might be sand, soil, or salt. Take a small amount of it and sprinkle it over the item as you ask for its blessing. East might be smoking incense, a feather, or a bell. South might be a candle flame. West a dish of water.

Move to the next element and continue until you come to spirit. At this point lay the item back in the center and blow over it. Then say,

By earth and air, by fire and water, and by breath of spirit, you are now blessed.

Thank the elements and release them with a "hail and farewell."

Most importantly, keep in mind this item is now a magickal item. Treat it with respect. Keep it for magickal use only. Store it in a place that houses your consecrated items.

We each work with energy a bit differently. What is natural to me might not feel right to you. This magickal routine is a very personal part of your craft. Listen to your intuition and trust it to lead you to your place of power. When your item is blessed for magickal use, it is time to charge it, and the method I find the most magickal is a charge under the light of the full moon. Stand in the moonlight. Hold the item out in your dominant hand, exhale long and slow over the item to infuse it with your breath, and then tell the item what you are going to use it for. Hold it out to the moon and ask that it be filled with power. Lay it down in a puddle of moonlight to soak up the energy.

The Magickal Energy of Kitchen Ingredients

Magick in its simplest form is an intention that is honed and focused on before being acted on so that it will come to fruition. When we attempt a magickal working, we work with the energy that is present to fuel our intention. Magickal energy is everywhere, in every aspect of the universe. It is in objects. It is in the hour. It is in the day of the week. Magickal energy is in the moon, and the sun, and the stars. It is in the earth, air, fire, and water. Learning to sense it, to name it, and apply it is magickal knowledge that will fuel your magick and make it predictable.

Science holds that everything in the heavens and Earth is made up of energy and that energy can be neither created nor destroyed: it can only be transformed from one form to another.[29] As magick workers, we identify each energy as a magickal force, and when working a spell, we select objects by their corresponding energies and match them to intent, aligning the correspondences, before we raise energy, mold it with intent, and release this energy to manifest an outcome. Scott Cunningham once wrote, "Attuning and working with these energies in magick not only lends you the power to affect [*sic*] dramatic changes in your life, it also allows you to sense your own place in the larger scheme of Nature."[30] And while we might not understand exactly how it works, the simple knowing that it does is all we need to gain the results we desire.

Every ingredient in your kitchen holds a unique magickal energy that can be used in your magickal practice. Each energy corresponds with an intention, and each can be aligned and magnified and released to produce a willed result.

....

29. James E. Girard, *Principles of Environmental Chemistry* (Sudbury, MA: Jones & Bartlett Learning, 2013), 21.

30. Scott Cunningham, *Earth Power: Techniques of Natural Magic* (St. Paul, MN: Llewellyn Publications, 1983), xii.

Chapter 3

WHEAT AND OTHER FLOURS

Open most pantries and you will find a stock of staples. Along with the basics of rice, beans, oatmeal, lentils, pasta, and the soups and canned goods, the shelves usually hold a supply of dried herbs and spices and a variety of baking supplies, and each and every ingredient holds its own unique brand of magickal energy.

Flour is made by milling wheat. Wheat holds magickal energy for abundance, fertility, prosperity, and protection. It is one of the sacred grains. It was the cultivation of grains and cereals around 10,000 BCE that allowed hunter-gatherer groups to transition into permanent agricultural societies.[31] Calendars were created centered around the planting, growing, and harvesting of the grain. The cultivation formed entire cultures and religions around the world, with rituals practiced at each part of the agricultural year.[32] A good harvest meant good health, good luck, and overall abundance. A bad year meant hunger, loss of strength, and possibly the defeat of your army and hostile takeover by another country.

....

31. History.com Editors, "Neolithic Revolution," History.com, last modified August 23, 2019, https://www .history.com/topics/pre-history/neolithic-revolution.

32. Beth Hensperger, *Bread for All Seasons: Delicious and Distinctive Recipes for Year-Round Baking* (San Francisco: Chronicle Books, 1995), 6–8.

Most cooks think of flour as flour, the result of milling kernels of plain old wheat. What they don't realize is that there are many varieties of wheat, each with its own flavor, color, texture, and aroma. In the United States alone, there are eight official classes of wheat: durum wheat, hard red spring wheat, hard red winter wheat, soft red winter wheat, hard white wheat, soft white wheat, unclassed wheat, and mixed wheat.

Wheat varieties are divided into two main categories: spring and winter. Spring wheat is planted in spring and harvested in the fall. Winter wheat is planted in fall and harvested the following summer. Both varieties are further divided into two types of grains, hard wheat and soft wheat. Hard wheats are higher in protein, or gluten, resulting in dough with an elastic texture, making them best to use in recipes for bread and pasta. Soft wheats have less protein and a higher starch content. Soft wheats are used for making pastries.

Use wheat for magick involving abundance, beginnings, fertility, money, protection, and rebirth.

Common White and Whole Wheat Flours

White flour is the finely ground endosperm of the wheat kernel. It is made by removing the bran and the germ, leaving only the endosperm of the wheat kernel behind. Unfortunately, the process reduces the fiber content and strips the flour of most of the healthy fats and phytochemicals, leaving it mostly empty. Sadly, most white grocery flour is also bleached or treated with chemical agents to speed up the aging process. Bleached flour has a whiter color, a finer grain, and softer texture, which make it the favored flour for commercial baking. However, this is a cheap foodstuff that has been stripped of most of its goodness. Avoid bleached flour. Unbleached flour is white flour that has been left to bleach naturally as it ages.

White Flours

Some common white flours are all-purpose flour, bread flour, pastry flour, cake flour, and self-rising flour. The primary difference between each of these flour types is the percentage of protein, or gluten, they contain. It is this percentage that makes one type of flour better for a recipe than another. Protein is the molecule that binds the ingredients together, which means the higher the protein content, the denser and stickier the dough. When we wish to produce a sturdy loaf, we use a flour with a high protein content. When we wish to produce a light, airy product, we use a flour with a low protein content.

All-purpose flour is the staple you will find in most kitchens. It is made with a combination of hard and soft wheats, usually a composition of 80 percent hard red wheat and 20 percent soft red wheat. It has a midline protein content (10 to 11 percent) to provide lift and structure to a yeasted bread as well as lightness to a layer cake. However all-purpose flour is made in a process that strips away the germ and bran and removes most of the nutrients and fats. It is available both bleached and unbleached.

Bread flour, or strong flour, is also milled only from the endosperm. Most varieties are made from hard red spring wheat. Bread flour contains the highest level of protein (11.5 to 13.5 percent) to bind the flour and allow it to trap the carbon dioxide released by the fermenting yeast. It is this action that gives lift and structure to the dough and produces a loaf that is wonderfully chewy. Bread flour also tends to be bleached and enriched.

Pastry flour is milled from soft wheat. It has a slightly lower protein level than bread flour (8 to 9 percent). It too is made from the endosperm of the wheat berry. The germ and bran have been stripped away, along with most of the nutrients. Baked goods made with this flour hold their shape and have a tender crumb.

Cake flour is milled from soft wheat and also is made only from the endosperm. Cake flour contains the lowest amount of protein when compared to other flours (5 to 8 percent). Baked goods made with cake flour are light and airy and have a tender crumb.

Self-rising flour is a combination of all-purpose flour, salt, and baking powder (1 cup of all-purpose flour plus 1½ teaspoons of baking powder and ¼ teaspoon of fine salt). It is convenient but unreliable, as the amount of salt and baking powder it contains becomes an unknown variable when using in recipes.

When choosing one of these, empower your food by skipping the bleached options and buying organic.

Whole Wheat Flours

Organic whole wheat is brimming with earth energy. It is both nurturing and grounding. It symbolizes rebirth and renewal and is associated with the Goddess, the harvest, all agricultural gods, prosperity, and protection. To tap into this energy, you are going to have to buy organic flour, the fresher the better. Flour contains volatile fats in the germ and bran. Some varieties will spoil faster than others. Most mills will stamp or write the milling date right on the bag. For best results, use flour within three to six months of milling.

Some common whole wheat flours are whole wheat, white whole wheat, stone-ground, and graham flour.

Whole wheat flour is made from the whole kernel of red wheat. It contains all of its nutrients, fats, and fiber. It has a high level of protein (14 percent). Because it produces heavier, denser baked goods, it is often combined with a white flour in recipes for breads, cakes, and muffins.

White whole wheat flour is milled from the whole kernel of hard white wheat. Even though it is a paler color, it contains the bran, the germ, and the endosperm of the white wheat kernel and all the goodness to produce a loaf with a heady aroma and mildly nutty flavor. White whole wheat flour has a lower level of protein (12 to13 percent) than whole wheat, making it a good choice for most bakery goods, particularly for those who don't enjoy the hearty, coarser texture of whole wheat flour. Just be sure to buy organic.

Stone-ground flour is made the old fashioned way with stones grinding the wheat berries instead of steel mills. As a result, nothing is stripped away, and nothing is added later in the process. Stone-ground flour retains more nutrients than steel-milled because the heat generated from the steel mills destroys some of the delicate vitamins and antioxidants. This flour retains all the grain's fats and oils so that it bakes up into chewy aromatic breads that bring comfort to the body and soul. If you like a hearty loaf, give stone-ground flour a try.

Graham flour is a coarse-ground whole wheat flour. It is made from dark northern hard red wheat that is not sifted during milling and thus retains all the germ, oil, and fiber from the wheat kernel. It was advocated for in the 1830s by Sylvester Graham, an evangelist for dietary reform, as an attempt to divert people away from the popular white flour.[33] Graham flour has a sweet, nutty flavor and is used to make graham crackers. I love the flavor of this flour and often mix it with white whole wheat and sweeten with molasses to bake a hearty winter loaf.

Wheat brims with Earth energy. Its life cycle symbolizes rebirth and renewal. It is associated with Leo, Venus, Pluto, Demeter, Siva, and all the Corn Mothers—not to be confused with the New World corn crop, *corn* is an Old World word meaning cereal grain, explains Stephen Harrod Buhner in *Sacred and Herbal Healing Beers*. When the American settlers named maize *corn*, they were actually just calling it cereal.[34] The Corn Mothers embodied wheat, rye, pea, flax, and barley and were the harvest and the agricultural gods.

When you are shopping, select products that are as close to their natural state as possible. Organic whole wheat holds energy for abundance, beginnings, fertility, money, pro-

33. Karen Iacobbo and Michael Iacobbo, *Vegetarian America: A History* (Westport, CT: Praeger, 2004), 26.

34. Stephen Harrod Buhner, *Sacred and Herbal Healing Beers* (Boulder, CO: Siris Books, 1998), 156.

tection, and rebirth. Read the label. If it doesn't say "certified 100 percent organic whole wheat," then you are not getting the best quality product. Remember that much of the magick of food is in the quality of the product.

Other Types of Grains and Cereals
Barley
Health, love, money, and protection

Barley is a member of the grass family. It originated in western Asia, where it was one of the first grains to be cultivated. The Greeks and Egyptians called barley "the sacred grain."[35] Evidence from as long ago as 10,000 BCE indicates it was used in the brewing of beer.[36] Barley is associated with the harvest, Saturn, Cronus, Demeter, and the full moon of the month of August, the Barley Moon. Barley is used in love, healing, wealth, and protection spells. Add a cup of barley to stews to make them hearty and boost healing powers. Cook up a pot of groats to help end money troubles. Add barley flour to recipes to change negative feelings into positive ones or to ground or cancel out any negativity that originated from an outside source.

Einkorn
Fertility, health, love, protection, riches, vitality

Einkorn is an ancient hulled wheat, whereas modern wheats are not hulled. It was domesticated in Syria more than 7,000 years ago.[37] It has never been hybridized and is easier to digest than modern wheat for those with gluten intolerance, possibly because it has a simpler structure, containing only fourteen chromosomes compared to modern wheat's forty-two.[38] Einkorn is loaded with nutrients. It contains four times more beta-carotene than modern wheats, which boosts the immune system and helps prevent cancer and heart disease. Einkorn has two times more vitamin A and three to four times more lutein, which helps prevent macular degeneration and cataracts, and four to five times more riboflavin,

35. Dale Pendell, *Pharmako/Poeia* (San Francisco: Mercury House, 1995), 214.

36. Buhner, *Sacred and Herbal Healing Beers*, 147.

37. Buhner, *Sacred and Herbal Healing Beers*, 147.

38. Raymond Cooper, "Re-discovering Ancient Wheat Varieties as Functional Foods," *Journal of Traditional and Complementary Medicine* 5, no. 3 (2015): 138–43, https://www.ncbi.nlm.nih.gov/pmc/articles/PMC4488568/.

an antioxidant that slows aging and increases energy. Add einkorn to recipes to add health-boosting positive energy for abundance, growth, and vitality.

Dough made with einkorn flour tends to be sticky, and the fiber absorbs more liquid than the all-purpose flour. When using einkorn in a recipe, start with less water to see how the flour works with it.

Kamut
Fertility, health, spirituality, and wealth

Kamut, also known as Khorasan wheat or Oriental wheat, is an ancient wheat species native to Iran and Central Asia. It is a large grain, twice the size of modern-day wheat, and like einkorn and spelt, it has not been hybridized or genetically modified, which makes it easier to digest than modern wheat. Kamut is nutritious. It is a good source of fiber and protein. It has 40 percent more protein than modern wheat and contains more amino acids, vitamins, and minerals. It is a good source of selenium to help prevent inflammation, manganese to promote strong healthy bones, and phosphorus to boost kidney function. Kamut also contains zinc to boost the immune system, reduce cold symptoms, and help prevent illnesses.

Sheaves of kamut are a well-known symbol of prosperity. Substitute whole wheat with kamut flour cup for cup to boost positive energy and create a dense, golden loaf with a sweet, nutty flavor.

Rye
Fidelity, love, and prosperity

Rye is a grass related to wheat and barley. Rye is one of the seven sacred grains cultivated in Europe around 2000 BCE. It is associated with Venus, Earth, the Goddess, harvest rituals, celebration baking, good health, love, and prosperity. While all grains can be used to make grain dollies, wheat and rye are favored. Rye is known for its love-drawing abilities. Add rye to your recipes to encourage the ability to give and receive love. Serve your lover toasted rye bread to warm their feelings toward you. Note that this grain is not related to the ornamental grown as lawn known as ryegrass.

Spelt

Communication, divination, fertility, love, immortality, protection, riches, and spirituality

An ancient wheat that originated in Iran around 6000 BCE, spelt is also known as dinkel wheat, dinkel grain, and hulled wheat.[39] The Greeks held that spelt was a gift from the goddess Demeter and named it *zeidoros*, or "life giving."[40] The Romans left it as an offering to the spirits of the dead.[41] It was a staple grain in Europe in the Middle Ages and was introduced to the United States in the 1890s but was replaced in the twentieth century by the modern bread wheat cultivar. As spelt is a wheat, it is not gluten free, but it is much closer to its natural state. It has never been hybridized but remains an heirloom grain that has retained all its whole-grain nutrition. It is a popular grain used in the making of beer and ale. Spelt flour has a sweet, nutty chewiness. It is high in fiber, a good source of iron and manganese, and easily digested.

Spelt carries earth energy and symbolizes rebirth and renewal. It is associated with all the harvest and agricultural gods and is used to attract prosperity. Use spelt in bread recipes and muffin recipes. Spelt is not a one-to-one replacement, as it has higher levels of gliadin, the protein that makes dough stretch, which means spelt cookies tend to melt into a globby mess. For this reason, spelt doughs and batters have less internal structure and do better when baked in loaf tins and cake pans. Also spelt flour is more water-soluble than wheat, so you will need to cut back the liquid when substituting for whole wheat flour.

Spelt is associated with Mercury and will infuse a recipe with energy to lift communications and empower the ability of speech. Make spelt muffins with dates and walnuts and serve at any money-making project to increase success.

The Art of Bread Making

The art of baking is a time-honored tradition. Every time an art is learned and practiced, it is inherited and infused with new life. By learning this ancient art, one can reach back through history to reconnect to our ancestor's way of life.

A good loaf starts with good-quality flour. It is the wheat that determines aroma, flavor, texture, and appearance. And unlike most other recipes, each bread recipe is merely a guideline, as the amount of water needed to reach the ideal consistency is always

39. S. Padulosi, K. Hammer, and J. Heller, eds., *Hulled Wheat: Proceedings of the First International Workshop on Hulled Wheats* (Rome: International Plant Genetic Resources Institute, 1996), 71.

40. Rolf H. J. Schlegel, *History of Plant Breeding* (Boca Raton, FL: CRC Press, 2018), sec. 7.3.1.1.

41. Jörg Rüpke, ed., *A Companion to Roman Religion* (Malden, MA: Blackwell Publishing, 2011), 264.

unknown because every variable—the type of flour, where the flour was grown, and even the weather conditions during its development—contributes to the flour's ability to hold water. Some flour is thirsty. It is not something that can be determined until you are mixing and working the dough.

When mixing your dough, always start with half the amount of water called for. If the dough is too dry, slowly add more water until the desired texture is reached. If the dough is too wet, add a sprinkle of flour and work the dough until it loses its stickiness and becomes firm, smooth, and elastic.

The Magick of Yeast

There is magick in using yeast. It is the yeast that holds the energy to activate or initiate action. There are four essential ingredients in every yeasted bread recipe: flour, water, salt, and yeast. Mix them together and reactions begin. Enzymes in the yeast and the flour break the starch molecules down into simple sugars that the yeast then consumes and converts into carbon dioxide and ethyl alcohol bubbles. These bubbles cause the dough to rise and gives a loaf its lift and density.

Yeast is a living, single-celled fungus. It lies dormant until it comes into contact with warm water (100 to 105 degrees Fahrenheit), so temperature is also important. The temperature of your kitchen, as well as the temperature of the liquid in your recipe, either encourages or hampers the way the yeast reacts. Too cold and your yeast will remain dormant. Too hot and it will die.

Yeast also dies if it has been kept dormant too long. If you suspect your yeast is old, you can test it, or proof it. Stir 1 teaspoon of sugar into a ½ cup of warm water. Stir in your yeast and allow it to set for 10 minutes. If the yeast is still good, it will activate and the liquid will become frothy as bubbles develop. If nothing happens, your yeast is too old.

The Importance of Salt

Salt is an age-old protective aid strewn across thresholds and windowsills, cast over the shoulder, thrown over footprints, and added to baths and washwaters to cleanse and purify. It is used to set magickal barriers and to absorb, break down, and neutralize negative energy. Salt is a natural preservative. It kills bacteria. It is a natural desiccation agent. It is corrosive, or causes things to rust, and when mixed with water, salt will conduct electricity. Salt is magickal.

In cooking we think of salt as a seasoning, and while it does add flavor, in the science of bread making salt has a much bigger role because it stabilizes the action of the yeast by controlling the amount of water it releases, slowing fermentation and enzyme activity. Salt gives structure to the loaf by tightening the gluten structure and strengthening the dough. Too little salt and your dough will be sticky. It will not come together well and will resist becoming elastic.

All types of salt work in baking. The type you use is up to you. However, if you are using a flaky salt such as kosher salt, sea salt, or pink salt, you will need to increase the amount a bit. For example, if the recipe calls for 1 tablespoon of salt and you are using a flaky or coarse salt, add 1 heaping tablespoon.

Choose the Right Pan

In the past loaf pans were a standard size of 9 × 5 × 2½ inches. Today you can find a range of sizes from two-pound loaf pans to minis. To find the size of your pan, measure across the top, or fill with water to find volume. For best results use the size of pan specified in the recipe. The dough should fill ¾ of the loaf pan. If using a glass pan, reduce the temperature by 25 degrees.

Common Loaf Pan Sizes

Mini: 5¾ × 3¼ × 2 inches

4 Cup: 8 × 4 × 2½ inches

6 Cup: 8½ × 4½ × 2½ inches

8 Cup: 9 × 5 × 3 inches

Basic Bread Recipe

You only need four ingredients to make basic bread: flour, salt, yeast, and water. This recipe makes one loaf with delightful taste and texture. I added a spoon of sugar to feed the yeast.

Note: Bread making is easier in a warm kitchen.

You will need:

9 × 5-inch bread pan

about 1½ cups warm water

1 Tablespoon sugar

2¼ teaspoons yeast, or 1 ¼-ounce packet if you bought it this way

4 cups flour, plus more for dusting

2 teaspoons salt

Lightly grease the bread pan and set aside. In a small bowl, add 1 cup of water and the sugar. Sprinkle yeast over the top of the water mixture and whisk. Set aside to proof (10 minutes). In a large mixing bowl, mix together the flour and salt. Make a well at the center and pour in the yeast liquid. Stir until the dough becomes ragged.

Arrange two small bowls, one filled with water and the other filled with flour, next to your work surface. Sprinkle a bit of flour over your work surface and place the dough on it. Place your feet and root them to the floor. Come to center. This means you are to switch into quiet mode and draw your attention inward. When your thoughts have become quiet and your perception has expanded, move your attention to the dough.

Mindfully begin to work your dough by pushing your palm down into it. Press the dough away from you with the heel of one, or both, of your hands. Lift the edge of the dough that is farthest from you and fold the dough in half toward you. Focus on the work you are doing and channel your intention into the dough as you work it. Engage your full body as you work the dough. Use the muscles of your hands, arms, shoulders, and back. Be present and aware of each push, fold, and roll.

When we fuel the dough with intention, it becomes a vehicle to manifest our desire. Know exactly what it is that you want. Have a clear, concise image of what you desire. Words have power. Whisper your intention as you work the dough. If you feel inclined, you can chant or even sing as you mindfully channel your intent into the dough. Feel the dough under your palms. Watch as it changes structure. You are creating a loaf of bread but your actions are also raising energy as your thoughts align with the energy of the ingredients to create a mold for the universe to manifest your goal.

The motion of kneading dough not only fuels your intention, but it also strengthens the strands of gluten, which gives your bread structure. Press your palm down into the dough and roll it, standing it on its end to press again. At this point you can add more water if the dough is too stiff or more flour if the dough is sticky. Just reach into the bowl next to your workstation and scoop up some water or flour and sprinkle it over the dough as you work it with your other hand. Add the addition little by little until the dough is smooth but not sticky. After 10 minutes of kneading, the dough will become smooth and elastic. Place the dough in an oiled bowl. Cover the bowl with an oiled piece of plastic wrap and set aside in a warm place (a sunny countertop is perfect) to rise until it has doubled in size, about 2 hours depending upon the temperature of your kitchen.

When the dough is twice the size it was, punch it down and turn it out again onto your floured work surface. Roll the ends under to form a loaf shape. Place the dough in the bread pan and cover with the oiled plastic wrap. Set aside for a second rise of 45 minutes.

After the second rise, the bread dough should be above the pan. Take a sharp knife and slice the top of the loaf down the center. Heat the oven to 400 degrees Fahrenheit. When the oven is hot, slide the loaf into the middle and bake for 10 minutes. Then turn the oven temperature down to 375 degrees Fahrenheit and bake 40 minutes more.

When the bread is done, an amazing aroma will begin to waft out of the oven and fill the room with a heavenly scent. Open the oven and check to see if your loaf is done. It should be golden brown. Turn the loaf out and tap the bottom. If it sounds hollow, it's done. If it doesn't pass the thump test, return it to the oven for 10 more minutes. Let the loaf cool on a wire rack.

Add Some Pizzazz

You can vary this recipe by sweetening it with honey instead of sugar or by adding ¼ cup of fruit or vegetables or 2 Tablespoons of herbs. Some nice combinations include the following:

- Raisins and cinnamon to sweeten and warm
- Walnuts and dried cranberries to encourage bonding and bolster communication
- Olives and rosemary to add energy for love and protection
- Pepper jack cheese and green chilies to energize a beginning, prompt an action, or inspire creativity
- Parmesan, basil, oregano, and thyme to stir affection and nurture love
- Sun-dried tomatoes and sautéed onions to promote healing and boost protection

Baking as a Magickal Art

As you consider adding ingredients to your recipe, begin with your intent. Write it out as clearly and concisely as you can. Then align like with like. Keep in mind it's all about the energy. Each and every ingredient in your kitchen contains its own unique magickal energy, an enormous potential, that when aligned with intent not only enhances a magickal working but causes the results to be more predictable. Knowledge is power. When you learn and understand the behavior of an herb, fruit, or vegetable, you gain the ability to predict a magickal response. To empower your work, do your research. Get to know the energies you are working with. And don't forget to set an intention at the start of each project. Whisper your intention as you add each ingredient. Tell it what you expect it to do. Then as you engage in the action of measuring, mixing, and kneading, you will program the dough with your intention.

Keep a written record so that you can duplicate your successes. Your notes will act as a guide to help you identify what worked and what fizzled. Write your intention and the recipe you used at the top. Make note of the date, the time, and the phase of the moon and list each ingredient. And later, as events unfold, record the results in as much detail as you can. It is this data that enables a magickal practitioner to evolve.

Farmhouse White Bread

This recipe makes 3 loaves.

You will need:

3 bread pans, 8½ × 4½ inches

¼ cup honey

1 Tablespoon salt

⅓ cup butter

1½ cups boiling water

4½ teaspoons yeast, or 2 ¼-ounce packages if you bought it this way

1 teaspoon sugar

¼ cup lukewarm water

2 eggs

8 cups flour, plus more for dusting

Set your intention and come to center. Begin programming your loaf as you engage in the action of gathering your ingredients, measuring, and mixing. Measure the honey, salt, and butter into a bowl and pour the hot water over it. Set it aside to cool. In a measuring cup, add the yeast and sugar to lukewarm water and set aside to activate. After 10 minutes, add the yeast mixture to the liquid in the bowl and stir in the eggs. In another bowl, measure out 4 cups of flour and make a well. Pour the liquid mixture into the flour and stir the flour in from the edges of the bowl until the dough is smooth. Add 4 more cups of flour and work the dough until the flour is incorporated. Cover the bowl with oiled plastic wrap and put in the refrigerator to chill for at least 3 hours or overnight.

Lightly grease the bread pans. Cut the dough into three parts. Rub your hands with butter and place a piece of dough on a lightly floured work surface. Place your feet and begin to work the dough, squeezing and kneading until it becomes smooth and elastic (about 10 minutes). If the dough is too stiff, add a sprinkle of water. If it is sticky, add a bit of flour. Channel your intention into the dough as you work it. Be present. Work each piece of dough until it changes structure. Then shape each into a loaf and put each into a prepared bread pan. Cover with oiled plastic wrap and let it sit in a warm place until each of the loaves has risen to the top of the pan (about 2 hours).

Preheat the oven to 400 degrees Fahrenheit. Remove plastic wrap. When the oven is hot, place the loaves into the center and bake for 25 minutes. Remove the loaves from the pan and let cool.

Overnight Brioche

This recipe makes one brioche. The high egg and butter content gives this rich yeast dough a lightly sweet and intensely buttery texture and fills it with a nurturing energy for happiness and abundance. To reach desired consistency, the dough must rest for at least 10 hours or overnight.

You will need:

7-cup brioche mold

2¼ teaspoons yeast, or a ¼-ounce package if you bought it this way

½ cup warm milk

½ teaspoon salt

3 cups bread flour, plus more for dusting

3 eggs, plus 1 more beaten for glaze

½ cup butter, softened

2 Tablespoons sugar

In a small bowl, add yeast to the warm milk and stir. Let the yeast sit for 10 minutes. In a large bowl add salt to flour and sift together. Make a well at the center for wet ingredients. Pour the yeast mixture into the flour and salt. Then mix in the eggs. Cream the butter and sugar together. This whips air into the butter so that it will mix more evenly into the dough. Gradually add the butter mixture to the dough, kneading until the dough becomes smooth and shiny. Cover the bowl with oiled plastic wrap and let it rise until doubled (about 2 hours). Lightly punch down the dough, cover the bowl again, and place in the refrigerator overnight.

The next morning, turn the dough out onto your work surface. Cut off ¼ of the dough and set aside. Shape the larger piece into a ball and place it in the brioche mold. Press down in the center to form a hollow. Shape the smaller piece into an egg and press it, small end down, into the center of the larger piece of dough. Brush the dough with beaten egg. Cover and let the dough rise for 2½ to 3 hours, until it has doubled in size and looks very puffy. Bake at 400 degrees Fahrenheit for 10 minutes, reduce heat to 375 degrees, and bake for about 20 to 25 minutes more or until golden.

Cheddar, Olive, and Rosemary Rolls

Olive and rosemary carry energy for love and harmony. Serve them to foster affection or strengthen familial bonds. This recipe makes 13 rolls.

You will need:

baking sheet

2¼ teaspoons yeast, or 1 ¼-ounce package if you bought it this way

2 Tablespoons sugar

¾ cup warm water

2½ cups flour, plus more for dusting

½ teaspoon salt

¼ cup olive oil

1 cup shredded cheddar cheese

½ cup minced olives

2 Tablespoons minced fresh rosemary

Sprinkle the yeast and sugar over the water and set the mixture aside to proof. In a large bowl, combine the flour and salt. Stir in the water mixture and mix until incorporated. Add the oil, cheese, olives, and rosemary. Mix to create a soft dough, adding additional flour if needed.

Turn the dough out onto your lightly floured work surface and knead until it becomes smooth and elastic (about 7 minutes). Oil the bowl and return the dough to it. Cover and let it rest for 30 minutes.

Divide the dough into 13 balls. Arrange the balls on a baking sheet. Cover the pan with oiled plastic wrap and let the rolls rise in a warm place until doubled (about an hour).

Preheat the oven to 375 degrees Fahrenheit. Bake for 13 to 15 minutes, or until the tops are browned.

Perfect Pizza Crust

Pizza is a comfort food. The luscious scent of it baking and the way it tastes and feels to sink your teeth into it is deeply comforting. Align your intention to the energy of the toppings and the combinations become endless. Traditional pizza sauce is rich with uplifting tomato energy to protect health, inspire creativity, and draw love into your life. Add the nurturing energy of cheese and handful of mushrooms (to bolster courage or amplify psychic awareness) or bell peppers (to foster growth and prosperity). Or instead of a tomato-based sauce, top with a generous amount of pesto and mounds of mozzarella and sliced tomatoes and you have a tasty pie brimming with positive energy for romance and harmony. This recipe makes 2 large or 4 individual-size pizzas.

You will need:

2 baking sheets

2¼ teaspoons yeast

1 Tablespoon sugar

1 cup warm water, plus ½ cup more for sprinkling

3 cups flour, plus ¼ more for dusting

½ teaspoon salt

¼ cup olive oil

a light sprinkling of cornmeal to cover baking sheet

In a 2-cup measure or a small bowl, mix the yeast and sugar together. Stir in 1 cup of warm water and set aside for 5 minutes. While the yeast is activating, set up your work surface. Place ½ cup of warm water and ¼ cup of flour in easy reach. In a mixing bowl, combine flour and salt. Make a well in the center and add the yeast mixture and the olive oil. Stir with a fork until combined. Then turn the dough out onto a lightly floured work surface and knead. Add a bit of the flour or a sprinkling of water as needed until the dough is soft and slightly sticky. It should pull cleanly away from your fingers. Knead the dough until it is shiny, smooth, and elastic. Spray the bowl with cooking spray and place the dough inside. Cover with oiled plastic wrap and leave to rise for 1 or 2 hours or until doubled in size.

When the dough has risen, remove it from the bowl and punch down. Divide it into 2 balls and cover with oiled plastic wrap. Set aside for a second rise.

When the dough has doubled in size, rub your hands with oil and work it into the desired shape. Roll the dough out on a lightly floured work surface into a thin disk. Lightly sprinkle cornmeal over the baking sheet and place the pizza dough on top. Top with desired sauce and toppings.

Wrap any unused dough in plastic wrap and freeze for future use.

Bake in a very hot oven (450 degrees Fahrenheit) for 12 to 15 minutes or until the crust is lightly browned. Do not overcook or the crust will be hard.

Soft and Flaky Biscuits

This recipe produces a perfectly light and unbelievably flaky biscuit with soft buttery layers. Serve at meals to encourage, pamper, or impress. This recipe makes about 12 biscuits, depending upon the size of your cutter.

You will need:

baking sheet

2 cups flour, plus more for dusting

2 Tablespoons baking powder

1 Tablespoon sugar

1 teaspoon salt

6 Tablespoons cold butter

1 cup milk

Preheat the oven to 425 degrees Fahrenheit. Sift flour, baking powder, sugar, and salt into a large mixing bowl. Cut butter into the flour mixture until the dough resembles rough crumbs. Add milk and stir with a fork until it forms a ball. Turn the dough out onto a well-floured work surface and press into a rectangle, about 1 inch thick. Fold it over and gently pat it down again. Repeat twice. Cover the dough loosely with oiled plastic wrap and allow it to rest for 30 minutes.

Gently pat out the dough again into a 10 × 6-inch rectangle. Cut the dough into biscuits using a floured glass or biscuit cutter. Place biscuits on a baking sheet and bake until golden brown, 12 to 15 minutes.

Spelt Muffins

Spelt is associated with Mercury and will infuse a recipe with energy to speed communications and empower the ability of speech. Its positive healing energy will heighten awareness and boost vitality.

You will need:

muffin tin

2½ cups spelt flour

1 Tablespoon baking powder

½ teaspoon salt

3 eggs

1 cup milk

1 Tablespoon butter, melted

¼ cup honey

Preheat the oven to 425 degrees Fahrenheit. Grease and flour a muffin tin. In a large bowl, combine flour, baking powder, and salt. In a separate bowl, beat the eggs. When the eggs are frothy, beat in milk and butter. Pour wet ingredients over dry ingredients. Pour honey over the top and mix until just combined. If desired, fold in 2 Tablespoons of any herb or ¼ cup of a hard cheese to empower. Do not over mix. Fill muffin tin with batter and bake for 20 minutes or until lightly browned.

Pita Bread

This flatbread has roots in the Mediterranean and the Middle East and is often served with hummus. As it bakes, the soft dough fills with air and puffs to form a pouch, making it an ideal luncheon bread to stuff with salad, vegetables, or any other sort of savory filling. Bake up a batch to encourage stability in life.

You will need:
baking sheet

2 cups flour

2¼ teaspoons yeast

1 Tablespoon salt

⅔ cups warm water

2 Tablespoons extra virgin olive oil

In a large bowl mix together the flour, yeast, and salt. Add water and olive oil. Mix well. Turn the dough out onto a floured work surface and work it until it becomes slightly shiny and elastic, about 10 minutes. Place it in an oiled bowl and cover. Let it sit in a warm place until the dough has doubled in size. When it has doubled, punch it down and divide it into 8 pieces. Roll them flat into ovals. Place the ovals on a baking sheet and allow them to sit for 30 minutes. Bake at 450 degrees Fahrenheit for 6 to 9 minutes. Do not over bake. Your pita should puff but not brown. The bread will turn hard if it bakes too long. Remove the pitas from the baking sheet and cover with a cloth to keep the bread soft.

Pancakes, Waffles, and Crepes

My dad was the cook in our house, especially when it came to breakfast creations. He would stand over the stove and craft some lovely morning treat with a good-humored smile. He became known for his waffles and "hot cakes," which he would serve up with a different twist each time he made them, but whether they were topped with sliced bananas and peanut butter, covered in whipping cream and maple syrup, or poured in the image of Mickey Mouse, they were always delicious and the most requested by us kids, our friends, and eventually our children.

Pancakes, waffles, and crepes are comfort foods that can be served up both sweet and savory. Top them with maple, apple bits, strawberries, or raspberries and they become a food of love. Cover them in peanut butter and they will fortify endurance. Slather them in almond butter to boost communication.

Basic Pancake Recipe

This recipe makes about 8 pancakes.

You will need:

2 cups flour

2 teaspoons baking powder

1 teaspoon baking soda

2 Tablespoons sugar

¼ teaspoon salt

1½ cups milk

2 eggs

2 Tablespoons butter, melted

¼ teaspoon vanilla extract

In a bowl, whisk together the dry ingredients. Add milk, eggs, melted butter, and vanilla and mix until smooth. Spray and heat your pan. Drop in a pat of butter and when it has melted, spoon in ¼ cup of batter. Cook until the underside is golden and the top is speckled with bubbles. Then flip and cook until lightly browned. Serve immediately or warm in a pre-heated oven while you make the rest of the batch.

Berry Pancakes

If you are lucky enough to live where berries grow wild, this recipe is a fun and easy way to serve them up for a snack or any sort of meal. They carry the berry's energy plus the gentle nurturing energies of milk, eggs, and flour to sweeten, protect, and foster happiness. This recipe makes about 8 pancakes.

You will need:

2 cups flour

2 teaspoons baking powder

1 teaspoon baking soda

2 Tablespoons sugar

¼ teaspoon salt

1 cup milk

2 eggs

½ cup sour cream

2 Tablespoons butter, melted

¼ teaspoon vanilla extract

½ cup fresh berries, tossed with a spoon of flour

In a bowl, whisk together the dry ingredients. Add milk, eggs, sour cream, melted butter, and vanilla and mix until smooth. Fold in berries. Spray your pan and heat. Drop in a pat of butter and when it has melted, spoon ¼ cup batter onto griddle. Cook until the underside is golden and the top is speckled with bubbles. Then flip and cook until lightly browned. Serve immediately or warm in a preheated oven while you make the rest of the batch.

Pumpkin Pancakes

Pumpkin holds energy to attract the positive. Make a batch of pumpkin pancakes and serve to elicit fondness. This recipe makes about 10 pancakes.

You will need:

2 cups flour

2 teaspoons baking powder

1 teaspoon baking soda

2 Tablespoons sugar

½ teaspoon cinnamon

½ teaspoon ginger

½ teaspoon nutmeg

½ teaspoon salt

1 pinch clove

½ cup pumpkin puree

1½ cups milk

2 eggs

2 Tablespoons butter, melted

¼ teaspoon vanilla extract

In a bowl, whisk together the dry ingredients. In a large bowl, whisk the pumpkin and milk together. Add the eggs, melted butter, and vanilla and mix until smooth. Stir the dry ingredients into the pumpkin mixture and mix until incorporated. Spray your pan and heat. Drop in a pat of butter and when it has melted, spoon ¼ cup batter onto griddle. Cook until the underside is golden and the top is speckled with bubbles. Then flip and cook until lightly browned. Serve immediately or place on a baking sheet and keep warm in the oven while you make the rest of the batch.

Crepes

A crepe is a very thin French pastry similar to a delicate pancake. It is served filled or topped with a sweet or savory mixture. This recipe makes about 10 crepes.

You will need:

1 cup flour

1 teaspoon baking powder

1 Tablespoon sugar (omit for savory option)

¼ teaspoon salt

1½ cups milk

3 eggs, beaten

2 Tablespoons butter, melted

1 teaspoon vanilla extract (omit for savory option)

In a bowl, whisk together the dry ingredients. Set your feet, come to center, and fix your intention as you whisk in milk, eggs, melted butter, and vanilla. Whisk the batter until it is well blended. Refrigerate the batter for an hour or overnight. This allows the flour to absorb the liquid, which results in crepes that are soft and tender.

After the batter has chilled, check its consistency. At this point it should look like cream. If it seems too thick, stir in another spoon of milk. Spray an 8- or 9-inch nonstick sauté pan with cooking spray and heat over medium heat. Pour ⅓ cup of batter into the hot pan and tilt the pan to spread the batter evenly over the bottom. Cook until the corners bubble and the bottom turns a light golden brown. Flip and cook the second side until spots appear on the bottom. Transfer to a plate and cover with a towel to keep warm. Repeat the process, stacking the crepes to keep them warm.

My Favorite Crepe Fillings

Crepes are versatile, as you can fill them with sweet or savory fillings. Sweet fillings are lovely for breakfast or dessert, while savory crepes can be paired with a salad and served as a main course. Classic crepes are filled with berries and whipping cream, but there is really no limit to what you can fill a crepe with. Peanut butter and jelly make a nice simple spread. Apricot jam pairs well with goat cheese. Or you can keep them simple and top with a dollop of fresh whipped cream or a sprinkling of powdered sugar. Match your intention with the filling to make a crepe to empower protection, draw prosperity, or inspire friendship or affection.

Cheesy Apple Pie Crepe Filling

This filling boosts affection and inspires romance. Halloumi cheese is a grilling cheese from the Eastern Mediterranean island Cyprus. When cold, it is tough and rubbery, but when it is heated, it holds its shape and transforms into a lovely, salted caramel–flavored treat.

You will need:

2 Tablespoons butter

1 apple, cored and chopped

halloumi cheese, cut into ¼-inch slices, 1 for each crepe

2 Tablespoons sugar

½ teaspoon cinnamon

¼ teaspoon nutmeg

1 batch crepes (see page 49)

honey or maple syrup

Melt butter in a large skillet. Add apple pieces and cook until soft. On the other side of the pan, place halloumi slices and cook on both sides, until the cheese turns a caramel color, about 2 minutes. Pour the sugar and spices over the apple bits and stir until syrupy. To assemble, place a slice of grilled cheese on each crepe. Dollop a heaping spoon of apple mixture over the cheese. Fold the crepe into quarters. Set on a plate and finish with a drizzle of honey or maple syrup.

Lemon Ricotta Crepe Filling with Berry Syrup
This filling brightens words, aligns views, and encourages teamwork.

You will need:
3 cups blackberries or blueberries, fresh or frozen

1 cup sugar, plus 2 Tablespoons

1 Tablespoon lemon juice, plus 1 Tablespoon

1 cup water

1 cup ricotta

1 teaspoon lemon zest

1 batch crepes (see page 49)

In a medium saucepan, stir together berries, 1 cup sugar, 1 Tablespoon lemon juice, and water. Bring to a boil, then reduce to a simmer and cook for 3 or 4 minutes, stirring continually. Remove from heat and set aside.

In a small bowl, mix together ricotta cheese, remaining sugar, the zest, and the rest of the lemon juice. Mix thoroughly.

To assemble, dollop 2 Tablespoons of the cheese mixture onto a crepe and top with a generous spoon of berry syrup. Fold into quarters and finish with a drizzle of syrup.

Walnut, Pear, and Brie
This filling increases fertility, fosters affection, and cements a friendship. This is my absolute favorite ritzy holiday crepe filling. It is inspired by the addicting and delicious Spencer sandwich made by PBJ's Grilled food cart. It is expensive to make but is always well received by everyone I have ever served it to.

You will need:
1 batch crepes (see page 49)

1 jar walnut butter

1 jar pear butter

1 onion, chopped and caramelized

brie

powdered sugar

Spread each crepe with a thin layer of walnut butter and pear butter. Top with a spoon of onions and a thin slice of brie. Fold into quarters and serve topped with a sprinkle of powdered sugar.

Light and Fluffy Waffles

Waffles aren't just for breakfast. Mix up a batch fueled with an intention and serve as a bread replacement for any sort of sandwich. The light and crispy texture and hint of vanilla flavor make these waffles pleasant to sink your teeth into no matter the filling. This recipe makes about 10 4-inch waffles.

You will need:

2 cups flour

1 Tablespoon baking powder

2 Tablespoons sugar

½ teaspoon salt

1¾ cups milk

1 teaspoon vanilla extract

4 Tablespoons butter, melted

2 eggs, separated

In a large bowl, whisk together the dry ingredients. Mix in milk, vanilla, butter, and egg yolks. In another bowl, beat the egg whites until soft peaks form. Fold the egg whites into the batter. Coat the inside of the waffle iron with nonstick cooking spray and plug in to heat. When the iron is hot (most waffle irons have an indicator light to let you know when the griddle is hot or the waffle is done cooking), pour in a scoop of batter and spread it over the iron. Small irons may only take a ⅓ cup to fill, while larger Belgian waffle irons take up to ¾ cup of batter per waffle. Don't overfill. Cook until steam no longer escapes. For a good chew, the waffle should be stiff and not limp. Cook until the waffle is lightly golden in color. Serve with maple syrup to promote affection. Top with peanut butter to draw prosperity. Serve with banana slices to boost energy or increase sexual stamina.

Multigrain Waffles

These hearty, nutrient-rich waffles will fortify the body and mind for a hectic day. You can also serve them for dinner topped with mayo and sliced tomatoes to unwind and recover. This recipe makes 4 waffles.

You will need:

½ cup corn flour

¼ cup whole wheat flour

¼ cup flaxseed, ground

1 teaspoon baking powder

½ teaspoon baking soda

½ teaspoon salt

1½ cups sour cream

1 egg

1 teaspoon vanilla extract

¼ cup butter, melted

Spray the waffle iron with nonstick cooking spray and preheat. In a small bowl, combine the dry ingredients. In a mixing bowl, mix together sour cream, egg, vanilla, and butter. Slowly whisk the dry ingredients into the wet. Blend until incorporated. Dollop ⅓ cup of batter to fill the griddle (larger Belgian waffle irons take up to ¾ cup of batter per waffle). Don't overfill. Cook until done. Serve with favorite toppings.

Chapter 4
GLUTEN-FREE FLOURS, MEALS, AND GROATS

More and more individuals are avoiding gluten. This diet change has created a market for gluten-free products, and now many specialty flours can be found at most supermarkets. But specialty flours are pricey and have a short shelf life. The higher the oil content, the faster a flour will go rancid. Nut, oat, and whole grain flours are also prone to mold. Buying the whole grains and nuts and grinding them to make your own flour to use as you need it is less expensive and ensures freshness. For example, if left whole, buckwheat groats will last for months, but when ground, they will mold quickly and must be stored in the fridge.

For many nuts, seeds, and groats, you don't need a grain mill, and any spice grinder, food processor, or blender will do the job. I grind flour as I need it, storing the ingredients whole (almonds, buckwheat, oats, and walnuts) to ensure freshness. And of course many groats are wonderful cooked whole in overnight oats, porridge, mush, and pudding.

For better baking results, when substituting a gluten-free flour for wheat flour, pour your batter into the prepared pan and allow it to rest for 30 minutes before putting it in the oven. This allows the ingredients to absorb the moisture and the dough to develop structure, resulting in a better product. Also bake cakes, cookies, and biscuits well past the prescribed baking time to avoid a gooey middle.

Flours

Almond Flour
Abundance, beauty, blessing, communication, health, love, money, and wisdom

The almond tree is one of the earliest domesticated fruit trees. Almonds are a source of healthy fats and are rich in vitamin E and magnesium, both of which support metabolism. Almonds are associated with Thoth, Hermes, Hecate, Zeus, the sun, and Mercury and have a long history as a sacred food. They were used to evoke the energy of deities and add reverence to offertory cakes. Almond energy will boost any working for self-protection.

Almond flour is sold two ways: as plain almond flour, also known as almond meal, and as blanched almond flour. Plain almond flour is made by grinding almonds into a meal. It is darker in color and usually is a coarser grind. Blanched almond flour is made from almonds that have been blanched in boiling water and had their skins removed. It was originally a by-product.

You can make your own almond flour by grinding almonds. It has a zero on the glycemic index and is a high-protein power food. It is easy to use and easy to make, and it tastes great. It is good for cookies, quick breads, and muffins.

Blanched almond flour is lighter and finer, and as a result, it bakes up into lighter, airier cakes and breads. If a recipe calls for blanched almond flour, you will not get the desired results if you use plain almond flour or meal. Use almond flour in recipes to add energy for communication or to fortify connection to spirit. Almond flour will support intentions to improve health, attract riches, or find wisdom.

Amaranth Flour
Energy, health, invisibility, solace, and protection

Amaranth is a small seed like quinoa. It is an ancient grain from Peru, where the seeds are mixed with honey and made into candies as well as ground into flour that was a staple in the diets of pre-Columbian Aztecs. Amaranth flour is a gluten-free flour with a low glycemic index value. It is a wonderful wheat substitute for bakers avoiding sugar and gluten. It is rich in protein, fiber, micronutrients, and antioxidants. It contains more protein than oats and almost twice as much as wheat. Amaranth is packed with manganese, magnesium, and phosphorus, nutrients important for brain function and bone health. It is a good source of iron, which helps your body produce blood. Amaranth also contains lysine, an amino acid not supplied by grains that reduces the symptoms of canker and cold sores and helps improve athletic performance.

Amaranth flour has a sweet, nutty flavor. It is dense and does not allow for good air structure. When baking bread, use amaranth flour in a 1:3 combination with another flour. Add a cup to wheat flour recipes to boost nutrition and add healing energy. Add it to recipes to soothe heartbreak, promote invisibility, or increase protection.

Amaranth is associated with Saturn, Artemis, and immortality. Amaranth flower spires were woven into crowns and given in offering to strengthen bonds with past ancestors. Amaranth holds a comforting energy and can help heal the brokenhearted. Mix up a batch of pancakes but substitute 1 cup of amaranth flour to add a nutty taste and a grounding energy that soothes a broken heart and fosters self-love. Top with butter and maple syrup and serve.

Arrowroot Flour
Defense, love, luck, protection, and psychic awareness

Arrowroot is a starchy tuber used commercially as a thickener and to make arrowroot teething biscuits. Arrowroot is native to the tropics of South America and has a long history of cultivation by native peoples. Arrowroot powder or flour is gluten free but has a high glycemic index value. It is an excellent thickening agent, processed without the use of high heat or harsh chemicals, and can be used as a replacement for cornstarch (use half the amount called for and make a slurry before adding to your recipe). It also binds ingredients together and makes a good egg substitute.

Arrowroot flour is easy on sensitive stomachs. It is incorporated into almond flour recipes for cakes, cookies, and biscuits to lift and lighten and improve the overall texture. Arrowroot is associated with Jupiter. It holds energy to encourage opportunities. Arrowroot's grounding energy can be ingested to end enchantments and open the mind. Simply eat a teething biscuit to ground energy and restore awareness. Add arrowroot flour to recipes to gain calmness or to become centered. Make a slurry by mixing a tablespoon of arrowroot into a cold liquid such as water or milk and whisking until smooth. Add to sauces and heat to thicken and help set a relationship or gel emotions.

Make an empowering Love Me, Love Me Powder by grinding orris root with arrowroot and dried rose petals. Add a pinch of ground sandalwood and dust over your body to boost charm and empower persuasion. When you need to patch a relationship with an angry or jealous person, make an herbal powder by crushing dried bayberry, vetiver, and sassafras with arrowroot flour. Dust the powder over your hands and touch the person to cool emotions. Dust powdered arrowroot over body to shift your destiny. When you face a difficult decision, grind arrowroot with cedar and myrrh and burn it on a charcoal disk to make opportunities more apparent.

Buckwheat Flour
Abundance, health, money, protection, and stability

Buckwheat is considered one of the healthiest of the whole grains. If you are looking for a gluten-free way to bake, buckwheat flour is the ideal alternative. Although it has "wheat" in the name, it is completely wheat and gluten free because buckwheat is not a wheat or even a grain but the seed of a relative of sorrel, knotweed, and rhubarb. The grain-like seeds are high in fiber, manganese, magnesium, copper, and zinc. Buckwheat is a complete protein, which means it contains all nine of the essential amino acids, organic compounds a healthy body requires to function.[42] And buckwheat has a lovely nutty flavor.

Buckwheat groats are ground to make a thirsty flour with a gritty texture. When using buckwheat flour, allow your batter to rest after mixing. This allows the flour to absorb the liquid and vastly improves the texture. When making flour, use raw buckwheat groats. Rinse and air dry them before you process. The flour can be used as a wheat flour substitute cup per cup in any recipe that does not require the dough to rise. Use the flour to make crepes and top with maple syrup to draw love and prosperity. Add buckwheat flour to money-drawing incenses. Form magick circles with the flour for protection. Buckwheat is associated with Mercury and Pluto. Use it in recipes to add energy for health, money, and protection.

Buckwheat isn't just for baking. Toasted buckwheat is known as kasha and is used in cereals. The groats can be simmered like oatmeal to make a warm, delicious porridge. Simply rinse the groats and remove any debris. Add 1 part buckwheat to 2 parts boiling water, turn down the heat, cover, and simmer for about 20 minutes. Or instead of cooking, soak buckwheat in milk overnight. Serve it with a drizzle of honey or maple syrup. Eat it to protect your health. Add to oatmeal for a delicious, chewy porridge brimming with grounding energy to fortify the body and fuel the mind.

....

42. Whole Grains Council, "Buckwheat—December Grain of the Month," accessed March 23, 2021, https://
    wholegrainscouncil.org/whole-grains-101/grain-month-calendar/buckwheat-december-grain-month.

Cassava Flour

See tapioca flour on page 63.

Chickpea Flour

See garbanzo flour on page 60.

Coconut Flour
Beauty, clear thinking, confidence, healing, moon magick, protection, and purification

Coconut flour is a by-product made during coconut milk production from dried coconut meat. It is a dense, thirsty flour with a low glycemic index value. It is a good source of protein and healthy fat. A spoonful will boost the healing energy of any baked good. Add a spoonful of coconut flour to any flour blend to strengthen confidence or help overcome inhibitions. Magickally, coconut energy is associated with the moon and the element water. It will empower recipes for beauty and healing.

Cornmeal and Corn Flour
Abundance, fertility, life, luck, protection, resurrection, and spirituality

Corn was domesticated more than 9,000 years ago in Mexico, but it is a relatively new introduction to Europe.[43] Corn is a symbol of fertility. It represents the circle of life. In *A Curious History of Vegetables*, Dr. Wolf D. Storl writes that Native Americans called corn "our life," "life giver," and "first father," among other names, and that "wherever the corn diva appeared, people's lives changed. Hunters and gathers became sedentary; villages and even cities sprang up; elaborate irrigation systems, stately warehouses, and temples were built—solely for corn."[44] All parts of the plant are used in magick. It is a central theme in harvest rituals, especially Lammas.

Cornmeal is made by grinding dried corn kernels into a fine, medium, or course texture. It is used as a sacred offering by various Native American peoples in the Southwestern United States, often scattered on the wind and sprinkled in blessing.[45] The Pueblo

43. Brigit Katz, "Rethinking the Corny History of Maize," Smithsonian Magazine, December 14, 2018, https://www.smithsonianmag.com/smart-news/rethinking-corny-history-maize-180971038/.

44. Wolf D. Storl, *A Curious History of Vegetables* (Berkeley, CA: North Atlantic Books, 2016), 94.

45. "Prayer Meal," E-Hillerman, University of New Mexico, accessed March 23, 2021, https://ehillerman.unm.edu/node/2865#sthash.nvom6bAt.dpbs.

Indians offered cornmeal to the rising sun. The Navajo used it in sandpainting and hogan blessing ceremonies.[46]

Cornmeal is a biodegradable medium used to draw circles, runes, or sigils. Foods made with cornmeal are eaten on the summer solstice for blessings and prosperity.

Corn flour, which is also sold as *masa harina*, is made with kernels that have been cooked and soaked in limewater. The kernels are dehydrated and ground to produce a fine flour. Corn tortillas and tamales are made with masa harina. It has a slightly sweet and nutty flavor.

Garbanzo Flour
Beauty, fertility, inspiration, luck, prosperity, and protection

Garbanzo beans are ground to make a delicious, sweet flour also known as chickpea and gram flour (not to be confused with graham flour, a type of whole wheat flour named after Sylvester Graham used to make graham crackers). Garbanzo flour holds energy to inspire creativity and communication. Feeling stuck? Add garbanzo flour to recipes to inspire a breakthrough. Garbanzos brim with such positive energy that in traditional Indian weddings, family and friends smear *pithi* paste, made of garbanzo flour, turmeric, and rose water, on the skin of the bride and groom to wish them good luck, writes Mishra Bhatia for HuffPost.[47] For soft, glowing skin, make a beauty mask by mixing 2 teaspoons of garbanzo flour, ¼ teaspoon of turmeric powder, and 1 teaspoon of milk. Apply to clean skin and allow to harden. Rinse well.

Hazelnut Flour
Fertility, finding, healing, luck, knowledge, protection, wisdom, and wishes

Hazelnuts are also called filberts. They are prized for their flavor. If you are a Nutella fan, you will probably go gaga over hazelnut flour. Dry roasted nuts are quick to grind into flour. If using raw hazelnuts, be sure to toast them under the broiler and rub the skins off before you grind. Do not over brown, or the flavor will turn bitter. Add hazelnut flour to recipes to add energy for fertility, good health, healing, knowledge, luck, or protection. Use it to empower dowsing and wish magick.

....

46. Gladys A. Richard, *Navaho Religion: A Study of Symbolism* (Princeton, NJ: Princeton University Press, 1977), 641.

47. Mishri Bhatia, "How to Throw an Authentic Indian Wedding," HuffPost, last modified October 20, 2012, https://www.huffpost.com/entry/indian-wedding_b_1798975.

Magickally, hazelnuts are associated with Mercury and hold energy to encourage inspiration, find knowledge, and grant wishes. Add them to recipes when seeking the truth or desiring to gain information. Make a batch of hazelnut cookies and nibble to gain a silver tongue.

Millet Flour
Bird magick, health, luck, and prosperity

Millet is an ancient cereal grain with a modern history as a birdseed. Though it is often overlooked, this gluten-free grain is a good source of protein, essential amino acids, and dietary fiber. Recently, millet flour has gained popularity as a wheat flour substitute because of its low glycemic index value and lack of gluten. It has a sweet, nutty flavor and pulverizes well, and as a flour it is a great addition by blending 1:3 into any flour blend. Use in recipes to add energy for bird magick, for improved health, and to attract prosperity.

Millet is associated with Jupiter. According to German folklore, on New Year's Day eating millet brings good luck and prosperity throughout the year.[48]

Millet porridge is a creamy, delicious dish with a polenta-like consistency. Measure out ½ cup of millet into a mesh strainer. Rinse well before dumping into a saucepan. Add 1½ cups of water and bring to a boil. Reduce the heat to low, cover, and cook at a very low simmer for 20 to 25 minutes, without stirring, or until the liquid is absorbed and the millet is the consistency of cream of wheat. Remove from heat and serve as a breakfast porridge topped with your favorite toppings or at dinner in place of rice.

Oat Flour
Prosperity, restoration, sustainability, and wealth

Any type of oat (steel, rolled, old fashioned, or quick) can be pulverized into very powdery flour that cooks up nicely in any recipe that does not require rising. Oat flour is gluten free. It has a low glycemic index value and can help stabilize blood glucose levels. Oats are easy on the stomach and have been touted as being good for heart health and lowering cholesterol. But oat flour can be expensive and it goes stale quickly, often before you use the whole bag. To avoid this, buy whole oats and use any blender, food processor, or grain mill to grind your oats into flour. Substitute oat flour for wheat flour 1:1 except when gluten is needed. For

....

48. Cora Linn Daniels and C. M. Stevens, *Encyclopaedia of Superstitions, Folklore, and the Occult Sciences of the World* (Chicago: J. H. Yewdale & Sons, 1903), 1,566.

breads and muffins, you can replace ⅓ of the wheat flour with oat flour without compromising the structure.

Oats are an ancient food and a staple of the Scottish diet, and oatcakes are a traditional food for Beltane celebrations. In the past they were relied upon for their nutritional value and restorative powers. They were given to the sick and prescribed to new mothers to strengthen the body. Magickally, oats have energy to draw abundance. Add oat flour to recipes to draw abundance and prosperity. Bake oat cookies and serve them during meetings to draw opportunity.

Potato Flour
Compassion, protection, stability, stored energy, and wishing

Potatoes are associated with Saturn, Pluto, the moon, and the element earth. They hold a nurturing, grounded energy. Potato flour is ground from whole peeled and trimmed potatoes. It holds in moisture, and when added to yeast bread recipes, it makes a soft, rich loaf. Add the silkiness of potato flour by replacing up to ¼ of the all-purpose, whole wheat, or bread flour in a recipe.

Use potato flour to thicken gluten-free sauces, soups, and gravies. Mix 1 tablespoon of potato flour with 2 tablespoons of water to create a slurry. Whisk or stir the slurry into hot liquid, stirring constantly until the liquid thickens.

Quinoa Flour
Courage, endurance, health, and strength

Quinoa flour has a lovely nutty flavor. It is high in protein and contains all nine of the essential amino acids, which the body needs but cannot produce. It is a gluten-free flour with a low glycemic index value. Its high protein content lends structure to baked goods. Magickally, quinoa holds nurturing energy to bolster determination and fortify endurance. Add to flour blend to improve texture and add energy for vitality and strength.

Rice Flour
Abundance, fertility, rain, prosperity, security, and wealth

Rice feeds more people in the world than any other grain. Rice is a symbol of abundance. The tradition of throwing rice at newly married couples is to impart blessings of abundance and fertility.

Magickally, rice holds energy to protect your home from hunger and want. Store a jar of rice in your pantry to keep your larder full. Rice will not go bad, which makes it the

---

perfect resource, along with honey, dried beans, and powdered milk, to store in case of an emergency. Set a jar near your door to draw prosperity to your home. Share a dinner of rice between friends to renew your bonds.

Rice flour is a main ingredient in many gluten-free products. Add to recipes to boost energy for abundance and growth.

Tapioca Flour
Abundance, courage, health, and protection

Tapioca is a starch from the cassava root. It is a gluten-free starch and flour. Tapioca is an important staple food for over 500 million people. It is high in calcium, dietary fiber, potassium, vitamins B_6 and C, iron and essential fatty acids. It is used as a flour replacement and a thickener for pies, soups, stews, and sauces. Magickally, tapioca holds energy to draw abundance and fortify health.

Xanthan Gum
Banishing, love, lust, preserving, and sweetening

Xanthan gum is created "when sugar is fermented by a type of bacteria called *Xanthomonas campestris*," creating a "goo-like substance, which is made solid by adding an alcohol. It is then dried into the powder," writes Dr. Caroline Pullen.[49] The xanthan gum acts as a binding agent to give baked good structure. It provides the elasticity and stickiness the wheat's gluten would have provided for gluten-free flour mixes. For cakes and cookies, add 1 teaspoon xanthan gum per 1 cup flour; for breads and muffins, add 2 teaspoons xanthan gum per 1 cup flour.

Gluten-Free Mixes and Recipes
All-Purpose Gluten-Free Flour

Use this flour mix to improve health and banish inflammation.

You will need:

2 cups rice flour

1 cup potato starch

---

49. Caroline Pullen, "Xanthan Gum—Is This Food Additive Healthy or Harmful?" Healthline. May 27, 2017. https://www.healthline.com/nutrition/xanthan-gum.

1 cup tapioca flour

2 teaspoons xanthan gum

Mix together and use cup for cup as a wheat flour replacement.

Amaranth Gluten-Free Flour Mix

This gluten-free flour will boost recipes for strength and endurance. Use it in place of wheat flour to improve athletic performance or banish inflammation. Amaranth is known as a tribute to ancestors. Use this mix to bake up food for the dead.

You will need:

⅔ cup amaranth flour

⅔ cup potato starch

½ cup tapioca flour

1 teaspoon xanthan gum

1 Tablespoon baking powder

Whisk so that the flours are blended together. Use as a cup for cup gluten-free flour replacement in any recipe that calls for wheat flour.

Almond Flour Arrowroot Pancakes

The grounding energy in these pancakes can help restore health and end enchantments. Mix up a batch and eat to see your way through circular communications and thwart manipulations. This recipe makes 7 cakes.

You will need:

1½ cups almond flour

1 Tablespoon arrowroot flour

1 teaspoon baking soda

½ teaspoon salt

¾ cup milk

2 Tablespoons butter, melted

2 eggs

1 Tablespoon honey

1 Tablespoon vanilla extract

In a large mixing bowl, sift together the first four ingredients. Mix in the milk, butter, eggs, honey, and vanilla until batter is smooth. Allow the batter to rest for 15 minutes. Scoop ¼ cup of batter into a hot frying pan. Reduce the heat and let cook until air bubbles appear. These cook a little slower than the flour variety. Resist the urge to flip until they are completely cooked through.

Almond and Coconut Flour Pancakes

This recipe mixes the love-inspiring energies of almond and coconut to make hearty pancakes to instill affection and harmony. This recipe makes 4 pancakes.

You will need:

1 cup almond flour

3 Tablespoons coconut flour

3 teaspoons baking soda

¼ teaspoon salt

1 egg, beaten

3 Tablespoons oil or melted butter

1 cup milk

In a medium bowl, mix together dry ingredients. Add the beaten egg, oil, and half the milk. Stir until incorporated, then mix in the remaining milk. Set aside for 15 minutes to allow the flour to absorb the liquid. The batter will be thick. This batter sticks, so for best results use a copper or Teflon-coated pan. Spray the pan and heat at medium. When the pan is hot, drop ¼ cup of batter into the middle of the pan and let cook for 3 minutes. Do not try to flip too soon or the pancake will crumble. Flip and cook the other side for 3 more minutes.

Buckwheat Crepes

Buckwheat is considered one of the healthiest of the whole grains. When added to recipes, it empowers work for abundance, health, protection, and vitality. Buckwheat flour is quick to mold. To allow for a longer shelf life, I buy whole groats and grind them into flour as I need it. As buckwheat is a seed and not a grain, it grinds easily to powder. Store any leftover flour in the refrigerator. This recipe makes about 12 crepes.

You will need:

1¼ cups buckwheat flour

3 eggs

¼ cup butter, melted

½ teaspoon salt

1 cup milk

1 cup water

Place flour in a mixing bowl. Whisk in eggs, butter, and salt. Add liquid and mix until incorporated. Cover and let the batter sit for 30 minutes or more. As the buckwheat absorbs the liquid, the grainy quality of its texture is reduced. Drop ¼ cup of batter into a hot skillet and tilt the pan back and forth so that batter covers the bottom. Cook until golden on the bottom. Flip and cook the other side.

Fill with your choice of filling, sweet or savory. My personal favorite is to fill them with a combination of goat cheese and fig spread and top with a fried over-easy egg.

Buckwheat Pancakes

This recipe makes about 4 pancakes. Buckwheat is loaded with energy for health and stability. Top with maple syrup to encourage abundance or serve with peanut butter to bolster vitality.

You will need:

½ cup buckwheat flour

½ cup spelt or oat flour

1 teaspoon baking powder

1 teaspoon baking soda

¼ teaspoon salt

1¼ cups milk

1 egg

1 Tablespoon honey

1 teaspoon vanilla extract

In a medium bowl, mix together the dry ingredients. Make a well at the center and pour in the milk. Add the egg, honey, and vanilla to the milk and whisk together into the dry ingredients until the two mixtures are just incorporated. Set aside for 10 minutes to allow the flours to absorb the liquids.

Spray and heat the pan. When the pan is hot, pour ¼ cup of batter into the center of the pan. Cook until bubbles form on the top of the pancake and the batter is set, then flip to cook the other side, about 3 minutes per side. Continue with this process until all the batter has been made into pancakes.

Gluten-Free Biscuits

Biscuits are a comfort food. This recipe inspires a positive outlook. Bake up a batch and serve to someone who must avoid wheat to make them feel appreciated. This recipe makes about 8 biscuits.

You will need:

baking sheet

1¾ cups all-purpose gluten-free flour

¼ cup corn flour, potato flour, or arrowroot flour

¾ teaspoon xanthan gum

1 Tablespoon baking powder

½ teaspoon baking soda

½ teaspoon salt

2 teaspoons sugar

8 Tablespoons butter, cold

1 cup buttermilk (or substitute with ¾ cup sour cream mixed with ¼ cup regular milk)

1 Tablespoon butter, melted

Spray a baking sheet with cooking spray and set it aside. In a large bowl, place the flours, xanthan gum, baking powder, baking soda, salt, and sugar, and whisk to combine well. Cut in the cold butter until it resembles small beads. Create a well in the center of the dry ingredients and add the buttermilk. Mix until just combined. Let the batter rest for 30 minutes. Preheat your oven to 425 degrees Fahrenheit. Using a ¼ cup measure, drop the batter onto a baking sheet 1½ inches apart. Press the mounds of dough down gently to flatten the tops and brush lightly with the melted butter. Bake until lightly golden brown or about 15 minutes.

Socca

Go to the South of France and you will find vendors selling cones filled with a coarsely chopped flatbread called *socca*. Bite into a piece and you will discover the crispy edge hides a moist, creamy middle. Though the thin, unleavened garbanzo pancake is also known by the names *farinata, torta di ceci*, and *cecina*, the ingredients are almost always the same: garbanzo flour, water, and olive oil.

You will need:
cast-iron skillet
1 cup garbanzo flour
½ teaspoon salt
1¾ cups water
olive oil

In a bowl, mix together the flour and salt. Add water and 2 Tablespoons of the olive oil and stir until incorporated. Cover and let the batter rest to absorb the liquid for at least 2 hours (or overnight, the longer the better).

When you are ready to cook, preheat the oven to 400 degrees Fahrenheit. Wait until the oven is hot, then drizzle some olive oil into your skillet (about 1 teaspoon) and tilt to coat the bottom. Heat the oil on the stove. When the oil is hot, pour the batter into the center of the skillet and transfer it to the oven. Cook for 20 minutes. Insert a knife to check the middle. It should be moist but not wet. Slice it into wedges, sprinkle with a grind of black pepper, drizzle with olive oil, and serve.

Socca has a subtle sweet and creamy flavor that makes it a good base for both savory and sweet finishes. Try it topped with cheese and olives or drizzled with honey. Make a meal of socca by topping it with over-easy eggs and parmesan cheese.

Sandkaka, Swedish Sand Cake

This rich gluten-free cake is a dense, moist delight brimming with a grounding energy for stability and wealth.

You will need:

9 × 5-inch loaf pan

2 cups potato flour

2 teaspoons baking powder

½ teaspoon salt

1 cup butter, softened

1 cup sugar

1 teaspoon vanilla extract

¼ cup honey

1 Tablespoon lemon juice

3 eggs

Preheat the oven to 350 degrees Fahrenheit. Spray the loaf pan with cooking spray. In a medium bowl, whisk together flour, baking powder, and salt until combined. Set aside.

In a mixing bowl, cream the butter. Scrape down the sides of the bowl then add the sugar and beat to incorporate. Add vanilla, honey, and lemon juice and beat for 3 minutes. Scrape down the sides of the bowl. Add eggs, mixing in one at a time. Stir in potato flour mixture. Pour the batter into the prepared pan and smooth with a spatula. Bake for 40 minutes, until a wooden pick inserted into center comes out clean. Let the cake cool in the pan for 10 minutes, then turn onto a rack to cool.

Groats and Porridge

When I was a child, my father made sure we always had a hot breakfast before school each morning. Often it was in the form of porridge, oatmeal, cream of wheat, or rice. He served it hot, sweetened with a spoon of jam or a drizzle of honey, and topped it with nuts and fruit. There is such comfort in a hot bowl of porridge on a cold winter morning. Its loving, nurturing energy fortifies the body, mind, and soul for the day to come. And while oat, wheat, and rice are still lovely, today amaranth, buckwheat, millet, and quinoa with their sweet grassy flavor and wonderful chewiness add to the varieties of creamy, satisfying porridge.

Overnight Oatmeal

The oatmeal holds an empowering energy to comfort the spirit and bolster good health. Steel-cut oats work great for this recipe. They are chopped oat groats and are the least processed. The more common old-fashioned oats, or rolled oats, are steamed and rolled flat and also work well. Instant oats are precooked and dried and often contain added sugar. They will make a mushy porridge. This recipe makes 2 servings.

You will need:

2 cups milk or milk alternative

1 cup oats

2 Tablespoons chia, flax, or hemp seeds (optional)

1 pinch salt

Measure milk into a bowl and stir in oats, seeds, and salt. Refrigerate overnight. In the morning, add additional liquid to reach desired consistency. Heat or eat cold. Divide it into bowls and top with honey, maple syrup, yogurt, fruit, nuts, nut butter, or seeds. This mixture will keep for several days in the refrigerator.

Oat, Buckwheat, and Quinoa Porridge

This blend is brimming with energy for good health and comfort. This recipe makes 4 servings.

You will need:

1½ cups milk

1½ cups water

¼ teaspoon salt

⅓ cup whole or steel-cut oats

⅓ cup rinsed quinoa

⅓ cup buckwheat groats

In a large saucepan, bring the milk, water, and salt to a simmer. Stir in grains, cover, and reduce heat. Cook until tender, about 20 minutes. Divide into bowls and top with fresh fruit, nuts, and a drizzle of honey or maple syrup.

Granola

This healthy snack will keep you motivated even when things get difficult. Eat alone or serve with milk and berries for a chewy, crunchy, satisfying meal.

You will need:

3 cups oats

1 cup shredded coconut

2 cups nuts, walnuts, pecan, or hazelnuts

1 cup pepitas

⅓ cup coconut oil or butter, melted

¼ cup molasses or honey

⅓ cup maple syrup or brown sugar

1 teaspoon cinnamon

1 teaspoon salt

1 cup dried cranberries, currants, raisins, dates, or figs

Preheat the oven to 250 degrees Fahrenheit. Spray a baking sheet with cooking spray. In a large bowl, combine oats, coconut, nuts, and pepitas. In a small bowl, mix together the oil, molasses, maple syrup, cinnamon, and salt. Stir the liquid mixture into the oat mixture to coat. Spread the granola evenly on the baking sheet and cook for 50 minutes, stirring the mixture every 20 minutes. When finished baking, let it cool for 10 minutes on the baking sheet. Stir in the dried fruit. Do not allow the granola to cool fully on the baking sheet, or it will stick to the sheet.

Chapter 5

BEANS, PEAS, AND LENTILS

Legumes are loaded with protein and fiber. As an ancient food source, they provided food stores to remedy famine. Broad beans, peas, chickpeas, and lentils were Old World foods that have been a part of the human diet since prehistoric times. In the New World common beans (*Phaseolus vulgaris*), or beans that grow in a long green pod, lima beans, and peanuts were staple foods for the indigenous peoples of the Americas. The Three Sisters (a name for the method of planting beans, corn, and pumpkins together in a companion planting that fed the soil and provided a diet of complex carbohydrates, essential fatty acids, and all nine essential amino acids, allowing for less meat consumption) was so important it became part of the mythology of tribes "from the Hopis of the Southwest to the Oneidas of the Midwest and the Iroquois in the Northeast," writes Native American journalist and podcaster Andi Murphy.[50]

---

50. Andi Murphy, "Meet the Three Sisters Who Sustain Native America," PBS, November 16, 2018, https://www.pbs.org/native-america/blogs/native-voices/meet-the-three-sisters-who-sustain-native-america/.

Legumes

Legumes are loaded with protein, fiber, antioxidants, and minerals and have magickal energy to inspire creativity and communication. Dried beans and lentils are inexpensive and provide a lot of nutrition for the cost. When stored in an airtight container and kept in a cool, dry place, out of direct sunlight, they will stay fresh for long periods of time, which makes them a perfect nonperishable pantry staple to stockpile for emergencies.

Black Bean
Healing, love, prosperity, and wisdom

The black bean, or black turtle bean, is a small, shiny bean known scientifically as *Phaseolus vulgaris* or "common bean," as black beans and other beans such as pinto beans, navy beans, and kidney beans all derived from a common bean ancestor native to Peru. Black beans are popular in Latin American, Cajun, and Creole cuisines and are interchangeable in recipes that use pinto beans. Add black beans to recipes to boost healing energy or to increase energy for prosperity. Eat a bowl to open yourself to new ideas.

Black-Eyed Pea
Energy, inspiration, luck, and spirits

A pale-colored legume with a prominent black spot also known as the black-eyed bean, cowpea, and goat pea, the black-eyed pea holds an auspicious energy that has made them a traditional dish served on New Year's Day to bring luck to the coming year. Hoppin' John is a popular Southern black-eyed pea dish rumored to date back to the Civil War. A print recipe first appeared in Sarah Rutledge's 1847 cookbook *The Carolina Housewife*.[51] Black-eyed peas are a traditional food eaten by Sephardic Jews on Rosh Hashanah to usher in blessings.[52] Eat black-eyed peas to increase psychic vision. Add them to soups to add energy for inspiration. Add them to other beans spells to add power. Use black-eyed peas to appease the spirits of the dead. Throw some around the outside of the home to keep a pesky spirit from pestering you.

---

51. Sarah Rutledge, *The Carolina Housewife* (repr., Columbia: University of South Carolina Press, 1979), 83.

52. Devra Ferst, "At Rosh Hashanah, Black-Eyed Peas for Good Fortune," Forward, August 26, 2009, https://forward.com/articles/112887/at-rosh-hashanah-black-eyed-peas-for-good-fortune/.

Cannellini Bean
Communication, inspiration, luck, and prosperity

Cannellini beans are also known as white kidney beans. They are known for their power of persuasion and gift of insight. Serve a bowl to someone who needs help seeing your point of view. Cannellini beans are a Tuscan favorite. They have a subtle nutty flavor. When cooked, they take on a pleasant, almost fluffy texture. Cannellini bean soup is a simple white bean soup and is a staple in classic Italian cooking.

Fava Bean
Energy, inspiration, and luck

A flowering plant in the pea and bean family Fabaceae, the fava bean is native to North Africa and also known as the broad bean, mojo bean, Saint Joseph bean, and wishing bean. Fava beans "have a long history of cultivation in Old World agriculture," writes the Center for Urban Education about Sustainable Agriculture.[53] In Egypt fava beans are a traditional breakfast food eaten with pita bread and a fried egg.[54] In Italy fava beans were associated with the dead, and pots were cooked and left at tombs to feed late relatives' spirits.[55] It was the fava bean that grew into Jack's magickal beanstalk, and it does grow almost overnight into climbing vines. Fava beans are high in protein, fiber, antioxidants, vitamins, minerals, and plant sterols. The young, tender leaves are also nutritious and have a buttery, earthy flavor.

Fava beans hold energy to deter a pesky spirit. If you want to end a haunting, take a handful of beans and toss them one by one over your shoulder as you say, "Spirit, I command you, now depart."

Garbanzo Bean
Beauty, fertility, inspiration, luck, prosperity, and protection

The garbanzo bean (*Cicer arietinum*) is a creamy, delicious bean also known as the chickpea and ceci bean. It was likely domesticated around 7,000 years ago and became a Mediterranean

---

53. Center for Urban Education about Sustainable Agriculture, "Fava Beans," CUESA.org, accessed February 12, 2021, https://cuesa.org/food/fava-beans.

54. Saad Fayed, "Ful Medames (Egyptian Fava Beans)," the Spruce Eats, last modified November 19, 2020, https://www.thespruceeats.com/ful-medames-egyptian-fava-beans-recipe-2355699.

55. Gillian Riley, *The Oxford Companion to Italian Food* (Oxford: Oxford University Press, 2007), 75.

staple.[56] Garbanzos are eaten alone, added to dishes, and even ground into a delicious, sweet flour. They are the main ingredient of hummus and traditional New Year's soups to bring luck to the coming year. Like other beans, garbanzos can be eaten to inspire creative thought. Feeling stuck? Make up a dish of hummus. Sprinkle with paprika and eat to inspire a break-through. Need to open some doors? Add a pinch of sesame seeds and say, "Open sesame!" as you visualize the opportunity opening with each bite.

Great Northern Bean
Communication, inspiration, luck, and prosperity

Great northern beans—or large white beans, as they are often called—refer to a variety of white beans known for having a creamy texture. They are interchangeable in recipes that call for cannellini beans and are often added to soups and casseroles and used to make baked beans and pork and beans. White bean crostini is a popular bean spread eaten on crackers and toast. It is made by mashing cooked white beans with lemon juice, garlic, and cumin. Serve at parties to stimulate communication flow.

Kidney Bean
Energy, healing, love, memory, prosperity, and wisdom

Kidney beans are kidney shaped and are reddish brown in color. They have a slightly sweet flavor and a dense, meaty texture, which makes them a hearty addition to salads, soups, and chilies. They are a good source of proteins, folic acid, calcium carbohydrates, and fiber. Kidney beans are high in vitamin B1, which boosts cognitive functions, and manga-nese, for metabolism and energy. Add them to soups and stews to boost nutrition. Make a kidney bean chili when the weather turns cold to stave off colds and flu.

Lentils
Clear thought, energy, harmony, health, and peace

Lentils are legumes that have been a part of the human diet since late Paleolithic times.[57] Lentils are easy to prepare. They do not require a precook soak like other legumes, so cooking with them is quick and easy. Lentils have a pleasant, earthy flavor. They are very

....

56. Kenneth F. Kiple, *A Movable Feast: Ten Millennia of Food Globalization* (Cambridge, UK: Cambridge Univer-sity Press, 2007), 31.

57. Kiple, *A Movable Feast,* 30.

inexpensive and have a long shelf life. A bag will last a year in the pantry before the flavor begins to degrade. And lentils are loaded with health enhancing energy. Need a boost? Scoop a cup of lentils into your soup and simmer for about 30 minutes to add antioxidants, selenium, and B vitamins. Lentils are loaded with protein, iron, foliate, and fiber.

Magickally, lentils carry a stable, healing energy to nourish, comfort, and boost concentration. They are associated with the moon and the element water, which supports peace and harmony. Lentils vary in size and color. They can be yellow, red, green, brown, or black, and their color can be used to enhance your intention.

Yellow lentils are split, which means their seed coat has been removed and the seed split in half. Split lentils need less time to cook. Yellow lentils have a mild flavor and hold energy for communication, learning, and inspiration. Eat a bowl to boost your immune system or inspire creative thought. Serve to feuding roommates to aid in reconciliation and foster communication.

Red lentils are also split and become soft quickly when cooked. They make great purees. Add to soups to thicken broth and add texture. Red holds energy for vitality, endurance, and action. Cook with onion and garlic and eat to fortify the body before a quest.

Green lentils hold their shape better than the others and will taste better when added to soups and stews with a long cook time. Green holds energy for fertility, good luck, and prosperity.

Brown lentils have a mild earthy flavor. Brown holds energy for groundedness, security, and balance. Eat a bowl to balance your emotions. Use them to empower intentions for harmony or boost energy for financial security.

Black lentils tend to be the most expensive and more nutritious than other types of lentils. They have a firm texture and a stronger earthy flavor. Black holds energy for protection, safety, and banishing. Serve to neutralize anger, stanch aggression, or end gossip.

Lima Bean
Balance, communication, inspiration, health, luck, and prosperity

All beans are called common beans, or *Phaseolus vulgaris*, except for lima beans, which are classified as *Phaseolus lunatus*. Lima beans were named for the capital of Peru, where they have been cultivated for 5,600 years.[58] They come in two sizes: baby limas and large limas. Large limas are also known as butterbeans. The sizes are interchangeable in recipes and

---

58. Kiple, *A Movable Feast*, 115.

both have a creamy, buttery texture. Butterbeans are the largest of the white beans. They brim with earth energy. Eat them to balance and ground. Add them to soups and stews to boost nutrition and healing energy.

Navy Bean
Luck, strength, and will

The navy bean is a small white bean with a mild flavor and a dense texture. Its long shelf life has made it a provisionary staple. It is high in protein and loaded with minerals to boost cognition and memory and protect heart health. Add it to meals to promote healthy circulation. A study published in the *Current Nutrition and Food Science* journal states consumption of navy beans "reduces both the incidence and recurrence of adenomatous polyps or precancerous growths" and that they have "bioactive components that may reduce colorectal cancer risk."[59] Eat them to optimize digestion.

Pinto Bean
Forward motion, inspiration, luck, and protection

The pinto is one of the more popular common beans. In Mexico and the Southwest United States it is a staple. Pinto beans are a source of protein, dietary fiber, and folate. They are good for you. Pinto beans are associated with Mercury and have energy to inspire creativity, facilitate communication, open channels for growth, and initiate forward movement. Eat them to renew your energy. Add to other beans spells to add power. Mix with quinoa and eat to fortify resolve. Like other beans, a handful of pinto beans can be used to appease the spirits of the dead. Drop a handful of beans into your pocket the next time you must go somewhere spooky. If you become frightened, throw a few over your shoulder to distract the negative energy.

Red Bean
Ancestors, energy, happiness, health, and wisdom

Red beans (*Vigna angularis*) are also known as adzuki beans. They are a type of mung bean, sacred in Japan and used to make sweet bean pastes. They are a good source of protein,

59. Erica C. Borresen, Kerry A Gundlach, Melissa Wdowik, Sangeeta Rao, Regina J. Brown, and Elizabeth P. Ryan, "Feasibility of Increased Navy Bean Powder Consumption for Primary and Secondary Colorectal Cancer Prevention," *Current Nutrition and Food Science* 10, no. 2 (May 2014): 112, 118, https://www.ncbi.nlm.nih.gov/pmc/articles/PMC4082309/.

fiber, iron, magnesium, and potassium. Red beans are lower in phytic acid than most other beans, which make them easier to digest. Their sweet, nutty flavor goes well in chili, soups, and casseroles. In Korea, red beans are mixed with rice made into a porridge called *dongji patjuk* that is eaten on the winter solstice to keep evil spirits away. In Japan a rice and red bean dish called *sekihan* is eaten on the Japanese New Year for happiness and served at celebrations.[60]

Split Pea
Ancestors, divination, love, and money

Peas are one of the oldest domesticated crops.[61] They were munched on by hunter-gatherers and later eaten dried as a staple food and carried on ship voyages.[62] Ham and split pea soup is a winter staple in many parts of the world. In Quebec it is a national dish known as *soupe aux pois,* or habitant pea soup, as it is "named after Canada's first settlers, or habitants, from France," writes travel blogger Cindy Baker. "It is often served with bread for dinner on Fridays."[63] In Sweden and Finland pea soup is often eaten with pork and pancakes on Thursdays.[64] In Germany it is called *Erbsensuppe* and can be made with bacon, sausage, or smoked pork and served with a dark rye bread.[65] In the Netherlands it is known as *snert* and is sold at outdoor food stalls along frozen canals and lakes for warmth and comfort.[66] Peas are a type of sweet bean that bring luck in love and finance. Like beans, pea energy aids communication and inspires creativity.

....

60. Namiko Chen, "Sekihan (Japanese Azuki Bean Rice)," *Just One Cookbook* (blog), https://www.justonecook book.com/sekihan-japanese-azuki-beans-rice/.

61. Kenneth F. Kiple and Kriemhild Coneè Ornelas, eds., *The Cambridge World History of Food*, vol. 1 (Cambridge, UK: Cambridge University Press, 2000), 279.

62. Kiple, *A Movable Feast,* 31.

63. Cindy Baker, "Traditional Quebec Foods You Absolutely Have to Try," *Travel Bliss Now* (blog), March 11, 2020, https://www.travelblissnow.com/10-quebec-foods-you-have-to-try/.

64. Catherine Guarnieri, "Mini Twisted History: The Pea Soup Mystery," *Register Citizen,* March 27, 2011, https://www.registercitizen.com/news/article/MINI-TWISTED-HISTORY-The-pea-soup-mystery -12069572.php.

65. Roz Denny, "Erbsensuppe mit Würstchen," German Foods, https://germanfoods.org/recipes/split -pea-and-sausage-soup/.

66. Ena Scheerstra, "Traditional Dutch Pea Soup," Honest Cooking, March 23, 2012, https://honestcooking .com/traditional-dutch-pea-soup/.

Soybean
Awareness, luck, protection, and spirituality

Soybeans were cultivated in ancient China, where they were grown as a staple and deemed one of the "five sacred grains."[67] Today soybeans are the most widely consumed plant in the world. They are eaten as sprouts, tofu, dressings, margarines, vegetable milk, soy meal, and oil.[68] Soybeans are a sacred food in Japan associated with abundance, good luck, and protection. At *Setsubun*, a purification ritual held on the eve of spring, there is a custom called *mamemaki*, or "bean scattering," in which roasted soybeans are thrown out of the home to drive away any lingering evil spirits. Sometimes a person (usually the father of the household) will dress as an *oni* and then the bean will be thrown at him as they yell, "Demons out! Luck in!"[69]

Soybeans are the main ingredient in soy milk, tofu, miso, tempeh, and edamame. They are made into sweet and savory treats, baked, dried, and even covered in chocolate and packaged as snacks. In the United States soybeans are a cheap source of protein used as a main ingredient in many prepared foods. Soy contains good fats and fiber and is a plant-based protein. In the past, soy was held as a superfood. It was the "meat without bones" eaten by Buddhists.[70] Soy is sold as infant formula and prescribed to babies with colic. Recent studies have found that soy contains isoflavones, estrogen-like compounds suspected to impair human development if used as a daily supplement.[71] Until we know more, you should limit your intake of "soy isoflavone supplements and foods made with textured vegetable protein and soy protein isolate, found in many protein powders and nutrition bars," according to Harvard.[72]

....

67. Oxford Reference, s.v. "Five Grains of China," 2013, https://www.oxfordreference.com/view/10.1093/acref/9780192806819.001.0001/acref-9780192806819-e-0925.

68. Kiple and Ornelas, eds., *The Cambridge World History of Food*, vol. 1, 422–26.

69. William Shurtleff and Akiko Aoyagi, *History of Soynuts and Soynut Butter* (Lafayette, CA: Soyinfo Center, 2012), 520.

70. Kiple, *A Movable Feast,* 45.

71. Margaret A. Adgent et al., "A Longitudinal Study of Estrogen-Responsive Tissues and Hormone Concentrations in Infants Fed Soy Formula," *Journal of Clinical Endocrinological Metabolism* 103, no. 5 (May 2018): 1,899–909, https://pubmed.ncbi.nlm.nih.gov/29506126/; Judy C. Bernbaum, et al., "Pilot Studies of Estrogen-Related Physical Findings in Infants." *Environmental Health Perspectives* 116, no. 3 (March 2008): 416–20, https://pubmed.ncbi.nlm.nih.gov/18335112/.

72. Harvard Health Letter, "Confused about Eating Soy?," Harvard Health Publishing, March 2018, https://www.health.harvard.edu/staying-healthy/confused-about-eating-soy.

Bean, Pea, and Lentil Recipes

Homemade Hummus

This recipe combines the inspiring energy of garbanzo beans with the opening power of sesame to make a wholesome flavorful dish chocked-full of positive energy to speed communications, inspire creative thought, and overcome a difficult situation.

You will need:

4 cups cooked garbanzo beans, drained, reserving 1 cup liquid in a separate container

¼ cup fresh lemon juice

¼ cup olive oil, or more to taste

2 Tablespoons tahini

2 cloves garlic, minced, or more to taste

salt to taste

smoked paprika to finish

Combine garbanzo beans, lemon juice, olive oil, tahini, garlic, and salt in a food processor or blender and process until smooth. If the mixture is too thick, add a spoon of garbanzo bean liquid to achieve desired consistency. Add more or less garlic to taste. Drizzle with olive oil and a sprinkle of smoked paprika to finish.

Easy Lentil Soup

Serve a bowl of this grounding, nurturing soup to fortify energy and inspire peace and harmony.

You will need:

3 Tablespoons olive oil

1 onion, chopped

2 cloves garlic, minced

1 carrot, chopped

4 cups chicken or vegetable broth

1 cup lentils, rinsed and sorted

salt and pepper

Heat oil in a large saucepan. Add onions and sauté until caramelized, about 15 minutes. Add garlic and carrots and cook for 3 more minutes. Add broth and lentils and bring to boil. Reduce heat to low, cover, and simmer until lentils are tender, about 35 minutes. Season with salt and pepper and serve.

Make a Pot of Beans

In today's fast-paced, Instant Pot world, beans are often measured out and instantly cooked with little or no preparation. But our grandmothers knew that to make the best beans they need to be washed, sorted, and soaked overnight to make a nourishing dish worthy to serve their family. Soaking beans overnight rehydrates the beans and greatly reduces the cook time. Soaking also ensures that the texture of the beans is at its best. After soaking, always pour off the water and rinse the beans again to ensure they are easier to digest.

I know a lot of you reach for the can. Most of us grew up with the convenience of a well-stocked kitchen or a cabinet loaded with cans of broth and beans and soup at the ready. Back then we trusted the food industry to feed us well. We trusted them to keep our food healthy, clean, and safe. Today's canned food is so mass-produced, it's gross. Don't believe me? Just google "the 10 grossest things people found in their food." Yuck!

And eating canned foods can be dangerous. A 2014 study published in *Hypertension from American Heart Association* shows there are health risks generated by bisphenol A (BPA), a synthetic molecule insoluble in water, which is heavily used to coat food and beverage cans' inner layer, and that "consuming canned beverage and consequent increase of BPA exposure increase blood pressure acutely."[73] Previous studies have also found that BPA can leach into food and drinks and pose a high health risk for infants, children, and people having various conditions such as diabetes, infertility, migraines, obesity, or cancer.

Back to the convenience factor: my number-one canned food of choice is refried beans (which most of us think of as pinto beans, but the truth is you can turn any type of bean into a refried bean). Unfortunately, like oats, glyphosate is being used as a harvest aid on nonorganic dried beans and pea crops. Some samples have registered up to 1,849 ppb of glyphosate because they were sprayed just before the beans went to market.[74] According

73. Sanghyuk Bae and Yun-Chul Hong, "Exposure to Bisphenol A from Drinking Canned Beverage Increases Blood Pressure: Randomized Crossover Trial," *Hypertension* 65, no. 2 (February 2015): 313–19, https://pubmed.ncbi.nlm.nih.gov/25489056/.

74. "Toxic Secret: Pesticides Uncovered in Store Brand Cereal, Beans, Produce," Friends of the Earth, accessed March 23, 2021, https://foe.org/food-testing-results/#pinto-beans-table.

to Dr. Christy Sprague of the Michigan State University Extension, "Preharvest herbicide applications have become more popular as dry bean growers have switched to direct harvesting techniques. Herbicides used prior to harvest, also known as 'harvest aids,' are used to desiccate or dry down 'green' stem and leaf tissue that can hinder dry bean harvest. The main intention of preharvest herbicide applications is to desiccate weeds; however, many growers use these herbicide applications to hurry along or even out the maturing process of dry beans."[75]

Pot of Pinto Beans

Beans are high in protein. They are good for you. They are filling and taste great. Beans hold energy to support and inspire. Serve with chips and salsa to speed communications or get conversations flowing. Eat a bowl to boost energy, inspire creativity, or initiate forward movement.

Homemade beans are not hard to make, just time consuming, as you need to wash, rinse, and then soak your beans for at least 6 hours or overnight. Pour off the soak water and rinse the beans again before adding them to your cooking pot.

You will need:

¼ cup grapeseed oil, butter, or lard

1 onion, chopped

2 cloves garlic, minced

2 cups dried beans, rinsed and soaked overnight

2 teaspoons cumin, ground

1 teaspoon chili powder

salt and pepper to taste

Heat oil in a large pot or a dutch oven. Add onion and sauté until clear. Add garlic and cook 2 more minutes. Add beans and cover with fresh water. Heat until they boil. Then turn down the heat and simmer until the beans are tender. Check at 45 minutes, but depending on the heat of the stove and the pan, this process can take up to 2 hours. Keep

75. Christy Sprague, "Preharvest Herbicide Use in Dry Edible Beans: Caution Needs to Be Taken to Avoid Illegal Residues," Michigan State University Extension, Department of Plant, Soil and Microbial Sciences, August 23, 2012, https://www.canr.msu.edu/news/preharvest_herbicide_use_in_dry_edible_beans _caution_needs_to_be_taken_to_a.

an eye on them and add water if it begins to run out. Do not burn. There are not many things that smell worse than a burnt pot of beans. When the beans are tender, stir in the spices.

Easy Refried Beans

Turn cooked pinto beans into refried beans by reheating them and mashing in a skillet with oil and spices.

You will need:

¼ cup grapeseed oil, butter, or lard

1 onion, chopped

2 cloves garlic, minced

3 cups cooked beans

1 cup bean water (the cooking liquid in the pan if you have it; otherwise add water)

2 teaspoons cumin, ground

1 teaspoon chili powder

salt and pepper to taste

In a cast iron skillet, heat the oil. Add the onion and sauté until clear. Add garlic and cook 2 more minutes. Add the beans, bean water, spices, salt, and pepper. Stir and mash as you stir. Add more liquid as needed.

Taste your beans. You can add flavor by adding lime juice, tamari, or dijon mustard if you desire.

Hearty Pot of Chili

I grew up in a small town in the Southwest where it was tradition for everyone to make a pot of chili as soon as the weather turned cold. When the first frost iced the lawns, chili was offered everywhere. Moms and grandmas put a pot on the stove, and café owners added it to their menus. Although every home had its own twist on the recipe, most were made with kidney beans and ground beef for a hearty, grounding dish to protect health and fortify energy.

You will need:

1 Tablespoon butter

1 onion, diced

4 cloves garlic, minced

1 sweet, serrano, or jalapeño pepper, seeded and chopped

1 pound ground beef

1 Tablespoon chili powder

1½ teaspoons ground cumin

1 teaspoon oregano

1 teaspoon salt

½ teaspoon ground black pepper

2 Tablespoons brown sugar

2 Tablespoons dijon mustard

2 Tablespoons tomato paste

4 cups beef broth

28 ounces diced tomatoes

8 ounces dried kidney or red beans, rinsed and soaked overnight, or 2 cans, drained and rinsed

2 cups water

In a dutch oven or large soup pot, melt butter. Add the onion and cook until clear. Add garlic and pepper and cook 2 more minutes, stirring occasionally. You can use a sweet pepper, serrano, or jalapeño depending upon how much heat you like your chili to have. Add the ground beef. Stir to break it apart. Cook until the beef browns, stirring occasionally. Add the chili powder, cumin, oregano, salt, and pepper. Stir until well combined and cook until fragrant. Add sugar, mustard, and tomato paste and stir to combine.

Add broth, diced tomatoes, and kidney beans. Stir well. Bring the liquid to a low boil. Then reduce to a slow simmer. Cook uncovered for 1 hour, stirring occasionally. Keep your eye on the liquid and add water if needed. Taste and add more chili pepper to raise the heat or more salt if desired. Continue to cook until beans are tender. Scoop into bowls and top with a handful of shredded cheddar cheese, a dollop of sour cream, avocado slices, and chopped green onions, or a spoon of mustard and crumbled saltine crackers.

Chapter 6
Nuts and Seeds

Nuts and seeds are a healthy snack whether eaten by the handful; scattered over salads, cereals, and porridges; or ground into butter and spread on toast. They are loaded with protein, fiber, and vitamin E. Most importantly, nuts contain good fats (monounsaturated fats and omega-3s) for heart health, and according to Harvard Medical School, "Mounting evidence suggests that eating nuts and seeds daily can lower your risk of diabetes and heart disease and may even lengthen your life."[76]

Add nuts and seeds to meals to boost health and enhance vision. They are associated with wholeness of the spirit and fruitfulness of the intuitive mind. Eat a handful to boost energy and increase awareness. Add them to snacks to encourage spiritual enlightenment. Nuts add flavor and crunch to recipes. Use them in recipes for increase and fertility.

Nuts and Seeds

Nuts are easy to store, are easy to carry, and make an easy on-the-go snack. They can be purchased shelled, roasted and salted, or even raw. A handful of nuts can be mixed with toasted oats and dried fruits for a snack food that is sweet, chewy, and satisfying.

....

76. Harvard Women's Health Watch, "Why Nutritionists Are Crazy about Nuts," Harvard Health Publishing, June 2017, https://www.health.harvard.edu/nutrition/why-nutritionists-are-crazy-about-nuts.

Almond
Abundance, beauty, blessing, communication, health, love, money, and wisdom

The almond tree (*Prunus dulcis*) is one of the earliest domesticated fruit trees. There are two varieties: sweet almond, which is the variety we eat, and bitter almond, which contains benzaldehyde and prussic acid and can be lethal unless it is processed or cooked. Bitter almonds are used to manufacture flavoring extracts for foods and liqueurs, such as amaretto, which in Italian means "a little bitter."

Sweet almonds are eaten raw, blanched, and roasted. They are ground and made into the sweet paste marzipan. Today California produces nearly 80 percent of the world's supply.

Almonds are a healthy snack. They are rich in vitamin E and magnesium, both of which support metabolism. Almonds are a source of healthy fats and have a zero glycemic index value. Almond energy will boost any working for self-protection. Almonds are associated with Thoth, Hermes, Hecate, Zeus, the sun, and Mercury and have a long history as a sacred food. Drop an almond in your pocket to open opportunities to you. Place a bowl of almonds on your altar or grind up some and place in an amulet to attract abundance.

Cashew
Employment, energy, heart health, money, and power

Cashews (*Anacardium occidentale*) are the kidney-shaped seeds growing at the end of the fruit of a tropical evergreen tree. They are rich in essential amino acids and are a good source of minerals, and when eaten daily, they will help reduce the risk of coronary heart disease. Cashews are a good source of fat and protein. They are packed with vitamins, minerals and antioxidants like potassium, vitamins E and B_6, and folic acid, which protect heart health. Cashews also contain high levels of lutein and zeaxanthin, which help maintain eye health.

Cashews are associated with the moon, Mars, and the element fire. They have energy to aid quests and are helpful when job hunting. Drop a cashew into your pocket to find that perfect job. Eat a handful before any interview to help your words find favor. Eat a handful before job negotiations or a business meeting to boost performance. Keep a can of cashews in your desk to hold on to employment.

Chestnut
Abundance, fertility, harmony, love, protection, and vision

In Europe and China the chestnut (*Castanea*) is a comfort food roasted and served during the winter holidays. In fact, until the introduction of the potato, the chestnut was a staple providing most of the population's daily carbohydrates. The chestnut is not to be confused with the horse chestnut, a tree in the genus *Aesculus* that produces a nut that looks similar but is mildly poisonous.

Chestnuts are a traditional winter holiday food with energy for fondness and affection. Serve them at holiday gatherings to strengthen relationship bonds and mend quarrels. Serve them to quarreling couples to help them solve their differences. The chestnut is associated with Jupiter and holds energy to increase abundance and virility. Eat to encourage fertility or open opportunities. Serve some at gatherings to banish negativity and promote harmony.

Chia Seed
Endurance, gossip, health, protection, strength, and youth

Chia is a flowering member of the mint family with seeds that turn into a nutritious gel when hydrated. The name *chia* comes from Mayan *chiháan,* which means strength, and these tiny seeds offer a powerhouse of energy and are ideal for vitality and endurance recipes.[77] They are packed with antioxidants, vitamins, minerals, and protein and have been cultivated as a staple by the peoples of Mesoamerica for thousands of years. Today chia seeds are known as one of the superfoods able to supply the body with energy as it combats inflammation and slows the aging process.

Chia seeds can be sprouted and eaten in sandwiches and salads or ground and mixed into a meal called *pinole* that can be baked into cookies, breads, cakes, and biscuits. The whole seeds can be soaked overnight to make a rich, creamy pudding. Top the pudding with fruit to fortify yourself before any sort of workout. Chia seeds boost mental focus and concentration, making them a wonderful breakfast ingredient. Mix into yogurt to improve your health and cognitive abilities. Use them in youth and vitality recipes to boost stamina, energy, and strength. Chia seeds have a reputation for stopping gossip. When the seeds get wet, they gel. Add a spoonful to any liquid and serve it to the one you need to quiet.

....

77. *Merriam-Webster*, s.v. "chia," accessed February 14, 2021, https://www.merriam-webster.com /dictionary/chia.

Always allow the seeds to absorb liquid before you ingest them. Seeds like chia that have the ability to gel can cause health issues if they are not soaked before you eat them. It is important to first let them hydrate, or they might expand in the body and become a choking hazard or a blockage.

Flaxseed
Beauty, grounding, health, money, protection, and psychic abilities

Flax is a food and fiber crop cultivated for thousands of years for the nutrient-rich flaxseed, flax oil, linseed oil, and the textile linen. It is associated with Mercury, Saturn, and the Scandinavian goddess Hulda, who taught humans how to spin. Flax cords are used in knot magick, especially in knot spells to increase luck or money.

Flaxseed is a superfood filled with protein, fiber, omega-3 fatty acids, and alpha-linolenic, an essential fatty acid that reduces inflammation and helps reduce tumor growth and cholesterol deposits. Flaxseed is a rich source of dietary lignans, a class of phytoestrogens "associated with reduced breast cancer risk," concludes a 2013 study in *Cancer Causes & Control*.[78] And daily consumption reduces cholesterol and improves heart health. Add a spoon of ground flaxseed to morning porridge to boost health. Grinding breaks up the seed, making it easier for the body to digest and absorb the full nutritional benefit. Add to breakfast every morning to improve your health and stamina. Mix a spoonful into green drinks, yogurt, or, if you are in a pinch, a glass of water. Add it to recipes to draw prosperity and increase wealth.

Flax holds energy to ground and banish. Place flaxseed and cayenne under the doormat to ward your home of negative energy while ushering in positive. Anoint a yellow candle with flax oil and burn it while meditating to gain wisdom from a spinning/weaving goddess when making decisions regarding fate, destiny, or your life path.

Hazelnut
Fertility, finding, healing, luck, knowledge, protection, wisdom, and wishes

Hazelnuts are nuts of a genus of deciduous trees (*Corylus*) prized for their flavor. Both Nutella and Frangelico liqueur are made from hazelnuts, which are also called filberts.

---

78. Elizabeth C. Lowcock, Michelle Cotterchio, and Beatrice A. Boucher, "Consumption of Flaxseed, a Rich source of Lignans, Is Associated with Reduced Breast Cancer Risk," *Cancer Causes & Control* 24, no. 4 (April 2013), https://pubmed.ncbi.nlm.nih.gov/23354422/.

While Turkey supplies most of Europe, Oregon is the leading producer in the United States, at times supplying up to 99 percent of the United States crop.[79]

Hazelnuts are good for you. They are loaded with monounsaturated fatty acids and magnesium for heart health and are a good source of vitamin E to maintain cell health and fight aging and cognitive decline. Greek physician Dioscorides wrote that it cured chronic coughing if eaten with honey and cured the cold when mixed with black pepper.[80] To the Celts the hazel symbolized wisdom, and those who ate the nuts "gained poetic and prophetic powers," according to the Order of Bards, Ovates & Druids.[81]

Magickally, hazelnuts are associated with Mercury and hold energy to encourage inspiration, find knowledge, and grant wishes. Toast hazelnuts and grind them into flour to give recipes a boost of positive energy. Place a dish of hazelnuts near a doorway to draw luck and invite the presence of faery folk. Tuck a hazelnut into your pocket to improve fertility. Frost the center of a chocolate birthday cake with Nutella, and top the cake with chocolate ganache for an extra special cake that will bring happiness to the coming year.

Hemp Seed
Healing, longevity, meditation, and vision

Hemp is a fast-growing annual valued as a source of fiber, food, oil, mood enhancer, and medicine. Hemp is one of the earliest known cultivated plants with a history going back thousands of years. It is hardy and inexpensive to grow, and bees love hemp pollen. Hemp fiber is a strong natural plant fiber used to make rope, twine, textiles, canvas, and paper. If we embraced hemp production, we could stop deforestation. A study published in *Nature* estimated "that over 15 billion trees are cut down each year."[82] Hemp grows fast and can replace forest products in the production of paper and building materials. A 1916 Department of Agriculture report found that an acre of industrial hemp produced four times as

79. "Hazelnuts: The Potential of Expanded Commercial Production," Arbor Day Foundation, https://www.arborday.org/programs/hazelnuts/consortium/production.cfm.

80. Pedanius Dioscorides, *De Materia Medica*, trans. Tess Anne Osbaldeston (Johannesburg: Ibidis Press, 2000), 177.

81. Susan Gregg, *The Complete Encyclopedia of Magical Plants* (Beverly, MA: Fair Winds Press, 2008), 130; Mara Freeman, "Hazel," the Order of the Bards, Ovates & Druids, accessed March 23, 2021, https://druidry.org/resources/tree-lore-hazel.

82. Rachel Ehrenberg, "Global Count Reaches 3 Trillion Trees," *Nature*, September 5, 2015, https://www.nature.com/news/global-count-reaches-3-trillion-trees-1.18287.

much dry fiber as an acre of trees.[83] And according to American Golden Biotech, hemp can now be used "to produce particleboards, as well as drywall, insulation, furniture, and cabinets. In fact, it's now possible to build a house using hemp without causing too much pollution and without the need to cut a single tree."[84]

Hemp seeds are a good source of fiber, iron, and magnesium. They provide plant-based protein with all the essential amino acids the body needs to maintain good health. Mix a spoonful into green drinks, yogurt, or water. Take every morning to improve your health.

Hemp is associated with Saturn, Neptune, and Pisces and holds energy for visionary work. It is often burned at midsummer rituals. Hemp twine is long lasting and water resistant. Use it in knot spells and cord magick. String an amulet with hemp twine to increase power. Hemp oil will magnify any working. Anoint your third eye with hemp oil to stimulate psychic sight. Add a few drops to a dream pillow to enhance dream recall.

Macadamia Nut
Beauty, energy, health, love, prosperity, and youth

Macadamia nuts have a high fat content, second only to pecans. They are high in manganese, promote bone and collagen development, and accelerate wound healing. Macadamias are a good source of vitamin B_1, or thiamin, which is important for muscle contraction and nerve-signaling conduction. They are also rich in omega-3 fatty acids to enhance vision and brain function. Eat a handful of macadamias while looking in the mirror to boost attraction magicks. Add them to dishes to energize recipes to draw love and prosperity. Serve a dish of macadamias with tea to elicit kindness or heal an injured spirit. Cover with chocolate and serve to encourage love.

Pecan
Abundance, employment, inspiration, health, money, and prosperity

The pecan is the nut of a species of hickory native to the South-Central United States. Pecans are good for you. They contain antioxidants to help you stay healthy and have a

83. Lyster H. Dewey, and Jason L. Merrill, "Hemp Hurds as Paper-Making Material," bulletin no. 404 (United States Department of Agriculture, October 14, 1916), 24, http://www.lysterdewey.com/usda-bulletin-404-hemp-hurds-papermaking-material/.

84. "Can Hemp Be a Replacement for the Troubled Timber Industry?" American Golden Biotech, April 11, 2019, https://www.americangoldenbiotech.com/can-hemp-be-a-replacement-for-the-troubled-timber-industry/.

concentrated source of plant sterols that naturally lower cholesterol. Eat a handful to stimulate the immune system and avoid illness. Not only are pecans loaded with vitamins and minerals, but they also hold positive energy to cheer and inspire, making them an ideal work snack.

Magickally, pecans are associated with strength, abundance, the element air, Jupiter, and Mercury. Use to empower prosperity magick. Add to money-drawing and employment-gaining recipes. Eat or carry a pecan to find a desired job. Snack on pecans at work to help you stay positive about your current employment. Eat before any meeting to help your words find favor.

Peanut
Energy, prosperity, and sustenance

The peanut is also known as the goober. It grows underground and is actually a legume related to beans and lentils. The peanut plant originated in South America. It bears a yellow flower that once fertilized, pegs, or moves underground by slowly bending down until it penetrates the soil several inches. Peanuts are associated with Jupiter and wealth. To the Incas peanuts were preferred offerings, often entombed with the dead to sustain them after death. Peanuts are a popular snack. They are loaded with protein and good fats. Add them to trail mixes to boost energy for endurance. Serve a bowl of peanuts with beer to energize a gathering with a positive, feel-good vibe. Snack on peanuts to boost productivity.

Pine Nut
Abundance, fertility, hospitality, regeneration, and spiritual awakening

Pine nuts, also known as piñons, are the seeds of the pine cone. Since classical times, the pine cone has symbolized fertility, regeneration, and enlightenment. Pine nuts hold sociable qualities. They are known for their ability to inspire hospitality and generosity. Sprinkle over goat cheese and serve to guests to make them feel welcome. Toast pine nuts to enhance their nutty flavor. Sprinkle them over food to boost energy for fertility, or grind them and dust over hands to boost charm. Smile and touch anyone you want to impress. Drop a pine nut into your pocket to carry as a fertility charm or use it in any sort of dragon magick.

Pistachio
Antidote, energy, health, longevity, love, and sight

The pistachio is the nut of a small tree in the cashew family. It has been consumed as food for thousands of years. The pistachio is one of two nuts mentioned in the Bible (the other is the almond).[85] Pistachios symbolize wellness and longevity. They are a source of natural energy associated with self-heating and spontaneous combustion.[86] The small nuts are chock-full of energy and nutrition.

Magickally, pistachios are associated with Mercury and the element air and hold an antidotal energy to break spells and end enchantments. Keep a packet of pistachios in your desk drawer to remedy gaslighting and foil a manipulator. Eat before a meeting to keep your wits sharp and your thoughts from becoming distracted. Grind into powder and dust over hands to ward yourself from falling under someone's influence. Eat before a meeting to improve discernment so that you can see the lies for what they are and not lose your way in a circular discussion.

Pistachios are also a food of love associated with Venus and can be used to encourage affection and nurture relationships. Sprinkle chopped nuts over salads and desserts and serve to the one you love. Eat before meditation to help become grounded and connect with spirit. Eat before divination to gain clear sight.

Popcorn
Manifest, rest, and wishes

Popcorn is a popular snack. It is cheap, is easy and quick to prepare, and can be healthy if it's not coated in butter, salt, and sugar. Popcorn is a whole grain. It is high in fiber and low in calories. It contains the amino acid tryptophan, which makes it a sleep aid if eaten before bed.

Magickally, popcorn is associated with wish magick. It holds corn's energy to manifest. Make a pot of popcorn and as the kernels pop, shout wishes into the air for the energy of the corn to manifest. Buy a bag of organic popcorn. Many popular brands of popcorn

---

85. Genesis 43:11 (New American Standard).

86. Transport Information Service, "Pistachio Nuts," German Insurance Association, https://www.tis-gdv.de /tis_e/ware/nuesse/pistazie/pistazie-htm/.

use kernels that have been drenched in herbicides and pesticides that are killing the bees.[87] Measure out the popcorn kernels. Take a deep pan with a lid and heat a spoonful of oil. Grapeseed oil with its neutral flavor works perfectly here. If you are feeling adventurous, try avocado oil with its rich flavor and high smoke point or the slightly sweet coconut oil. Drop in two test kernels and heat over medium heat. When the test kernels pop, dump in the rest of the kernels, keeping in mind that each kernel is about to expand forty times its size. Cover and give the pan a shake every so often as you listen for it to stop popping. When the popping has almost stopped, remove from heat. Follow this guide for yields:

- 2 Tablespoons kernels will make 3½ cups popcorn
- ¼ cup will make 7 cups popped popcorn
- ⅓ cup will fill a 2-quart saucepan

Now it's time to finish your popcorn. While butter and salt are the standard, for a healthier, no-cholesterol option, drizzle with olive oil. Spice it up with a sprinkle of garlic salt or a sprinkle parmesan cheese. Olive oil and a sprinkle of cayenne pepper will heat things up. Or you can sweeten it with a drizzle of honey and sprinkling of cinnamon.

Not any old corn kernel will pop. It takes a special breed of flint corn with a hard exoskeleton so that it will burst as the steam expands. But popcorn is not the only grain that pops. Amaranth, millet, quinoa, and sorghum grain will also puff up when heated as the pressure from expanding steam breaks open the seed coat.

Pumpkin Seeds and Pepitas
Banishing, divination, health, prosperity, and revealing the unseen

Pumpkin seeds are a good source of healthy fats, vitamins, and minerals. They are high in vitamins K, B_2 (riboflavin), and B_9 (folate), which promote proper cell division. They are loaded with minerals and are a good source of phosphorus, manganese, magnesium, iron, zinc, and copper. Studies have shown that a daily dose improves heart health and helps treat symptoms of an overactive bladder. Eat a handful to reduce inflammation and boost

------

87. Matteo Marzaro, "Corn Seed Coated with Neonicotinoids: Environmental Contamination and Bee Losses in Spring," doctoral thesis, University of Padua, 2013, http://paduaresearch.cab.unipd.it/5398/1 /marzaro_matteo_tesi.pdf.

health. Pumpkin seeds are a natural source of tryptophan, an amino acid that aids sleep. Eat a handful before bedtime to fall asleep more easily.

Pepitas are seeds from varieties of pumpkins that do not have hulls. They can be substituted in any recipe that calls for pumpkin seeds, but as pumpkin seeds have hulls, they cannot be substituted in recipes that call specifically for pepitas.

Both pumpkin seeds and pepitas are associated with autumn festivals, Halloween, Samhain, and Thanksgiving. They hold the power to banish habits, unwanted spirits, or abusive people from your life. They are rich in cucurbitin, an amino acid that helps kill internal parasites. Eat raw pumpkin seeds to banish parasites. Add to granola and trail mix to banish negativity and boost a positive outlook.

Sunflower Seed
Abundance, beauty, beginnings, cheer, fertility, luck, protection, and success

Sunflowers hold a positive, joyous energy to boost fertility and encourage good luck. They are associated with the sun, Litha, the summer solstice, and faery magick. Eat sunflower seeds to reverse aging and increase beauty. Add them to granolas or heap over yogurt to boost positive energy and encourage cheer.

Walnut
Communication, fertility, healing, love, mental powers, protection, and wishes

A tree of the genus *Juglans* that produces an edible nut that was a prehistoric food source important to early humans. The tree grew wild in central Asia but quickly spread to western China, the Caucasus, Persia, and Europe. For more than two millennia medical practitioners extolled the virtues of walnuts, citing that they cured everything from the plague to baldness. The Romans thought the nuts resembled testicles, which later inspired the botanical name *Juglans regia*, or "Jupiter's royal nut," and the nut became a symbol of fertility.[88] They were included in marriage ceremonies. Pliny described a wedding custom of walnuts "scattered by the groom among the young people while they sang 'obscene songs.'"[89]

....

88. Allison Keene, "Dietribes: Walnuts," Mental Floss, December 28, 2011, https://www.mentalfloss.com/article/29595/dietribes-walnuts.

89. Allison Keene, "Dietribes: Walnuts," Mental Floss, December 28, 2011, https://www.mentalfloss.com/article/29595/dietribes-walnuts.

Walnuts are a nutrient-dense source of plant-based protein and fats. They are high in antioxidants to bolster your health and rich in omega-3 fatty acids, which makes them a brain food. Eat a handful of walnuts before any test to increase mental abilities. When faced with a difficult decision, try using a walnut as a focus during meditation to facilitate communication and receive a quick reply. Eating a handful of walnuts also greatly increases the level of melatonin, the sleep regulating hormone, in the body.

Magickally, the walnut is associated with Diana, Juno, Saturn, the sun, and the element fire. It holds energy to increase knowledge, fertility, and affection. In Hoodoo the nuts are used to break the power of the past and prevent things from coming to fruition.

Chapter 7

OILS AND VINEGARS

Today there is a plethora of culinary oils available to the cook. Exotic oils like avocado, hazelnut, macadamia, and walnut can now be found at most grocery markets, but be warned: not all oils are created equal. There are good oils and bad oils and there are blends, like "vegetable" oil, which is made from whatever oil the manufacturer chooses. "Vegetable oil is guaranteed to be highly processed. It's called 'vegetable' so that the manufacturers can substitute whatever commodity oil they want—soy, corn, cottonseed, canola—without having to print a new label," explains cookbook author Lisa Howard, interviewed by *Time*. Some oils, like corn, cottonseed, and soy oil, "have been pushed past their heat tolerance and have become rancid in the processing."[90] Others, like palm oil, are destroying ecosystems and degrading the land for production.[91] In *Pandora's Lunchbox*, Melanie Warner writes, "The demand has caused widespread deforestation" in both Malaysia and Indonesia, which is threatening the orangutan with extinction.[92] Have care when choosing your oils.

....

90. Alexandra Sifferlin, "The 10 Best and Worst Oils for Your Health," *Time*, July 23, 2018, https://time.com /5342337/best-worst-cooking-oils-for-your-health/.

91. Melanie Warner, *Pandora's Lunchbox: How Processed Food Took Over the American Meal* (New York: Scribner, 2013), 138.

92. Warner, *Pandora's Lunchbox*, 138.

Some oils have a very low smoke point, which makes them dangerous to heat.[93] Some oils have a short shelf life and need to be stored in a cool, dark place or in the refrigerator after opening to avoid them turning rancid. Rancid oils are dangerous to your health. They quickly create cancer-causing, cell-damaging free radicals. If you come across an oil with an unpleasant odor, throw it out. Eating rancid oil can cause long-term cell damage and potentially lead to the development of chronic diseases.[94]

Culinary Oils

Apricot Kernel Oil
Attraction, beauty, emotional issues, and love

Apricot kernel oil is a delicate, expensive oil pressed from the pit of the apricot. It is yellow in color and has a lovely aromatic scent, a rich and nutty almond-like flavor, and a short six-month shelf life. Use apricot kernel oil in salad dressings and dessert recipes or as a substitute for bitter almonds. It is an excellent source of essential fatty acids and antioxidants. Apricot kernel oil is associated with Venus and the element water. Its rejuvenating properties make it a wonderful oil to moisturize skin and hair. Anoint candles with apricot kernel oil to empower love and attraction magick.

There are all sorts of apricot oils on the market, most for soap and candle making or intended as massage oil. When purchasing one for cooking, make sure you are buying a culinary-grade oil.

Avocado Oil
Aphrodisiacs, beauty, clear sight, fertility, health, love, and youth

Avocado oil is a lovely oil. It has a creamy, lightly grassy flavor. It is loaded with healthy fats that reduce the risk of heart attack and stroke, improve arthritis, and reduce inflammation. Its light flavor makes it a lovely oil for dressings and mayonnaise. It is less prone to oxidation than most other oils, and because of its high smoke point (520 degrees Fahrenheit),

---

93. Anita Bancroft, "Cooking with Fats and Oils: Can They Withstand the Heat?" Kendall Reagan Nutrition Center, Colorado State University, April 2019, https://www.chhs.colostate.edu/krnc/monthly-blog/cooking-with-fats-and-oils/.

94. Rekhadevi Perumalla Venkata and Rajagopal Subramanyam, "Evaluation of the Deleterious Health Effects of Consumption of Repeatedly Heated Vegetable Oil," *Toxicology Reports* 3 (2016): 636–43, https://www.ncbi.nlm.nih.gov/pmc/articles/PMC5616019/.

avocado oil is a good cooking oil. Use as a stir-fry oil or as a marinade for meats and vegetables. Use for grilling, roasting, and baking. Use for love-drawing recipes and to enhance beauty. Avocado oil is associated with Venus and the element water. Mix with vanilla or rose essential oil to make an attraction oil to wear as perfume or use to anoint candles in love spells.

Butter
Beauty, healing, love, success, and wealth

While butter is found in the fridge and not the pantry, it does provide a rich oil with a creamy flavor to enrich the taste of soups, sautés, baked goods, and sauces. Butter has a smoke point of 350 degrees Fahrenheit. It is made from mother's milk, a mystical gift representing pure goddess energy. Butter is associated with Imbolc, the moon, Hathor, Venus, Mercury, and maternal love.

Coconut Oil
Beauty, clear thinking, moon magick, healing, protection, purification, and transformations

Coconut oil is loaded with compounds to nourish hair and skin cells and give beauty a glowing boost. When eaten, it increases HDL (the good cholesterol), boosts thyroid function, and improves cognitive ability. Coconut oil contains medium chain triglycerides (MCT) like human breast milk. Medium chain triglycerides are easily metabolized by the liver to produce ketone bodies that fuel the brain and improve brain function.

Coconut oil is known for its sweet flavor and long shelf life. It has a smoke point of 350 degrees Fahrenheit, which means it is not suitable for high-temperature cooking but can be used in many recipes for baking cakes, cookies, and muffins. It is associated with the moon and the element water. Its energy strengthens confidence and inner resolve. Use coconut oil to bake or sauté. It adds a nice sweetness. Use as a base for beauty and healing oil blends. Rub into skin or the bottoms of your feet to renew vigor.

Corn Oil
None

While corn is a symbol of abundance and fertility, corn oil is so highly refined that its good qualities have been processed to death. The oil is not considered a healthy fat because it is high in omega-6, which makes it highly inflammatory. It is bad for your arteries and damaging to your heart. Corn oil is not heat stable. I avoid corn oil.

Flaxseed Oil
Beauty, grounding, health, money, protection, and psychic abilities

Flaxseed is a nutritional powerhouse, high in lignans, chemical compounds with high anti-carcinogen properties that studies have shown help reduce both breast and prostate cancers.[95] Unfortunately, flaxseed oil is not a stable oil and can quickly turn rancid. Heating flaxseed oil is not recommended. It has a low smoke point (225 degrees Fahrenheit), so it should only be used as a finishing oil. Store the opened bottle in the refrigerator to avoid rancidity. Anoint a yellow candle with flaxseed oil and burn it while meditating to gain wisdom from a spinning/weaving goddess when making decisions regarding fate, destiny, or your life path.

Grapeseed Oil
Abundance, dreams, fertility, garden magick, mental powers, and money

Have care when buying grapeseed oil. Many grapeseed oils are a by-product of winemaking, pressed from the seeds of wine grapes and extracted using various chemicals, including the toxic solvent hexane. Choose a cold-pressed or expeller-pressed oil. If your oil doesn't state how it is processed, then assume that it was extracted with hexane.

A good grapeseed oil contains energies to complement a host of intentions. It holds the magickal properties of fertility and prosperity. It is associated with the moon and the element water. Grapeseed oil has a high smoke point (420 degrees Fahrenheit) and a neutral taste, which makes it a good oil for baking, frying, sautéing, or even making popcorn.

Hazelnut Oil
Fertility, finding, healing, luck, knowledge, protection, wisdom, and wishes

Hazelnuts, which are also called filberts, are nuts from hazel trees. Magickally, the hazel is associated with Mercury and holds energy to encourage inspiration, find knowledge, and grant wishes. Hazelnut oil has a 430 degrees Fahrenheit smoke point. It adds a rich flavor to sauces, cakes, and cookies. Drizzle it over cheese, vegetables, and fruit dishes. Use as a

---

95. Jaehee Lee and Kyongshin Cho, "Flaxseed Sprouts Induce Apoptosis and Inhibit Growth in MCF-7 and MDA-MB-231 Human Breast Cancer Cells," *In Vitro Cellular & Developmental Biology—Animal* 48 (2012): 244–50, https://link.springer.com/article/10.1007%2Fs11626-012-9492-1; Xu Lin, Jeffrey R. Gingrich, Wenjun Bao, Jie Li, Zishan A. Haroon, and Wendy Demark-Wahnefried, "Effect of Flaxseed Supplementation on Prostatic Carcinoma in Transgenic Mice," abstract, *Urology* 60, no. 2 (November 2002): P919–24, https://www.goldjournal.net/article/S0090-4295(02)01863-0/fulltext.

finishing oil for salads and pastas. It has a potent hazelnut flavor and is often mixed with other oils.

Hazelnut is a delicate oil. Refrigerate after opening. It will keep for up to eight months in the fridge. Add to recipes to add energy for wisdom or fertility. Use to draw luck and invite the presence of faery folk. Anoint candles with hazelnut oil to empower wish magick.

Hemp Seed Oil
Healing, love, meditation, and psychic abilities

Hemp seed is a superfood offering a source of protein and all the essential amino acids the body needs to maintain good health. Hemp seed oil is a delicate oil with a low smoke point (300 degrees Fahrenheit) and a three-month shelf life. It is not suitable for heating but is ideal for salad dressings, dips, pesto, and homemade mayonnaise. Use it as a finishing oil. Drizzle over hummus, tabbouleh, or salads. Blend it into sauces and vinaigrettes. Use as a dipping oil for bread and toast. Store it in the fridge.

Hemp seed oil has a green color and a strong flavor. It is associated with the moon, Saturn, Neptune, Pisces, and the element water. It holds energy for visionary work. Hemp seed oil will magnify any working. Anoint your third eye with hemp oil to stimulate psychic sight. Add a few drops to a dream pillow to enhance dream recall. Anoint candles with hemp seed oil to deepen meditation.

Macadamia Oil
Beauty, energy, health, love, prosperity, and youth

Macadamia oil is a stable oil loaded with antioxidants. An open bottle will stay fresh for up to two years without refrigeration. Macadamia nuts have a high fat content, second only to pecans. They are high in manganese to promote bone and collagen development and accelerate wound healing. Macadamias are a good source of vitamin B_1, or thiamin, which is important for muscle contraction and nerve-signaling conduction. They are rich in omega-3 fatty acids, which help enhance vision and brain function. Macadamia oil is high in tocotrienols that help lower cholesterol. It makes a lovely massage oil because it is quickly absorbed by the skin. Macadamia oil is a beauty oil. It contains phytosterols that quickly help reduce redness and itchiness, the antioxidant squalene that speeds regeneration and heals chapped and cracked skin, and palmitoleic, an antiaging acid that boosts the synthesis of elastin and collagen, proteins that keep your skin young and reduce wrinkles.

Macadamia oil has a smooth, buttery flavor. You can use it as a substitute for butter when baking. It has a smoke point of 390 degrees Fahrenheit, which makes it wonderful for baking and roasting. Macadamia oil is a delicious finishing oil and a good base for salad dressings. Use it in beauty and attraction recipes or as a base for beauty oil blends. Anoint candles with macadamia oil to deepen meditation or empower prosperity magick.

Olive Oil
Beauty, fertility, healing, love, lust, peace, potency, prosperity, protection, and youth

Olive oil is a thick, luxurious oil with a somewhat heavy scent. It is a standard culinary oil in kitchens across the world. When tightly sealed and stored in a cool, dark place, it can stay fresh for up to two years. Olive oil has a smoke point of 400 degrees Fahrenheit. Roasting a vegetable in olive oil brings out its very best flavor. Wash, chop, and put the vegetable in a bowl. Drizzle it with olive oil and stir until it is coated. Then sprinkle it with salt and pepper, spoon onto a baking sheet, and roast in the oven until caramelized.

Olive oil is a wonderful oil for baking. It can be used as a substitute for butter in just about every recipe except when the fat in the recipe needs to remain in solid form (for example, some biscuit, cookie, and frosting recipes). Use olive oil in recipes for cakes and muffins to add a rich moistness and a unique floral flavor. Substitute olive oil in recipes that call for butter to cut the cholesterol and saturated fat and add antioxidants.

Olive oil is the base of most salad dressings. It is one of the healthiest finishing oils. Drizzle olive oil over toast or serve it as a dipping sauce with bread to offer a healthier option than butter.

A good olive oil contains energies to complement a host of intentions. Extra-virgin olive oil comes from the first pressing and is brimming with energy for beauty, love, harmony, and prosperity. Anoint candles with olive oil and burn to promote positive energy flow. Roll anointed candles in crushed coriander and use in love spells. The olive is associated with the sun and the element fire. It is one of the original blessing oils used to anoint the head, hair, and feet.

Peanut Oil
Energy, prosperity, and sustenance

Peanut oil is a popular oil for frying, sautéing, and adding flavor. It has a high smoke point (440 degrees Fahrenheit), which makes it good for high-heat recipes. Its nutty flavor complements many Asian recipes. Most peanut oils on the market have been refined. Look for virgin or cold-pressed peanut oil, which retains much of its natural flavors and aromas and magickal energy. Peanut oil is associated with Jupiter and wealth. Use for grilling, searing, panfrying, sautéing, roasting, and salad dressings. Anoint candles with peanut oil to empower prosperity spells.

Sesame Oil
Beauty, health, luck, opportunity, riches, and wealth

Sesame oil, also known as gingelly oil and til oil, is derived from sesame seeds. It is available as light sesame oil and dark sesame oil or roasted. The dark has a stronger flavor. Sesame oil has a high smoke point, so it is good for high-heat recipes (410 degrees Fahrenheit).

Sesame oil contains sesamol and sesaminol, two antioxidants that reduce cell damage caused by free radicals. It contains healing energy and anti-inflammatory properties to speed the healing of wounds and burns. Sesame seed oil is good for you. It helps lower blood pressure and reduces inflammation.

Sesame seeds are associated with Ganesha, the sun, and the element fire. Sesame oil has energy to attract money, lust, and love. But sesame energy is known for its legendary powers to open opportunities and discover hidden treasures, hence the term "Open sesame!"

Sunflower Oil
Abundance, beauty, beginnings, cheer, fertility, luck, protection, and success

Sunflower oil is made from the pressed seeds of sunflowers. It is high in vitamin E to protect cells and boost immune system health. It does contain a fair amount of omega-6 fatty acids, so it should be eaten in moderation. Sunflower oil has a high smoke point (440 degrees Fahrenheit) and a mild flavor, which makes it good for cooking. Use it for baking, grilling, frying, sautéing, and roasting. It is associated with the sun and the element fire. Sunflower oil makes nice vinaigrettes and lovely mayonnaise. Anoint candles with sunflower oil to honor the sun. Sunflower oil does turn rancid more quickly than other oils, but when stored in the refrigerator, it will keep for six months.

Walnut Oil
Communication, fertility, healing, love, mental powers, protection, and wishes

Walnut oil is a delightful cooking oil, but it has a short shelf life. After opening, it will only keep for up to three months if refrigerated. Walnut oil is rich in omega-3 fatty acids, which means it is a brain food. Use walnut oil to increase mental abilities.

Walnut oil has a smoke point of 320 degrees Fahrenheit. It is expensive and big on flavor. It is usually drizzled over dishes and added to salad dressings to instill a rich, nutty flavor.

Magickally, walnut is associated with Diana, Juno, Saturn, the sun, and the element fire. It holds energy to increase fertility and foster affections, making it a good addition to recipes for abundance, beauty, or love. Anoint candles with walnut oil to foster spiritual growth.

Oil Blends to Power Up Your Rituals

Not all oil blends are for consumption. Some are created specially to anoint candles, burn in a diffuser, or wear on the skin to empower magick spells and rituals. Scent is a commanding trigger with the power to set emotions reeling or activate a mindset. Catching the scent of a personal oil blend can be a cue to move your mind into a quiet state. In spellcraft, oil blends are often used to dress candles to heighten the other energies present and bind them to an intention.

Meditation Oil

This oil blend can be used in a diffuser or worn on the pulse points to signal your mind to switch into quiet mode.

You will need:

1 teaspoon sweet almond oil

3 drops patchouli essential oil

3 drops cinnamon essential oil

In a small bowl add sweet almond oil. Add patchouli oil and cinnamon oil. Dip your finger in and mix. Touch your oil-coated finger to your pulse points.

Open Sesame Oil Blend

This magickal blend opens and activates energy flow.

You will need:

small decorative bottle with a tight-fitting lid

2 Tablespoons sesame seed oil

9 drops bergamot essential oil

3 drops nutmeg essential oil

Add the sesame seed oil into a small bottle. Add the bergamot essential oil and nutmeg essential oil. Swirl to mix. Use this oil blend to remove obstacles and draw riches to your home. As you apply the oil say, "Open sesame! The gates open and my life floods with opportunities."

Attraction Oil

You will need:

1 cup rose petals

sweet almond oil

1 Tablespoon ground coriander

Stuff a small canning jar half full with the rose petals. Cover with sweet almond oil and add the coriander. Seal jar and shake to mix. Place on a dimly lit shelf. Allow the oil to steep for 4 to 6 weeks. Be sure to check on it every few days and give it a gentle shake as you reinforce your intention. Strain out the herbal matter. The rose petals will rot and ruin your oil if not removed. Wear the oil as perfume to become irresistible. Add it to bath salts to boost attraction power. Use it to anoint candles in attraction spells to empower working.

Oil to Sharpen Sight

Juniper and clove come together to sharpen awareness and open the mind. Wear this oil during meditation to sharpen focus and concentration. Wear it while outside to increase awareness of faery folk and nature spirits. The gentle healing energy of this oil can be massaged into skin to remedy the aches and pains of both the body and the mind.

You will need:

small jar with a lid

1 teaspoon of juniper berries

1 teaspoon of whole cloves

olive oil

Place juniper berries and cloves into the jar and cover with oil. Seal and place on a dimly lit shelf. Allow the oil to steep for 2 weeks. Be sure to check on it every few days and give it a gentle shake as you reinforce your intention. Strain the oil and discard the berries. Store the oil in a clean jar. Rub the oil into skin or wear it on pulse points to sharpen sight. Add a spoonful to your bathwater to let go of troubling thoughts and aid relaxation.

Bring Me Luck Oil

This oil is a good staple to empower your magicks with positive energy to draw luck and good fortune.

You will need:
small canning jar with a tight-fitting lid

1 teaspoon allspice, whole or ground

1 teaspoon cloves, whole or ground

2 cinnamon sticks

1 whole nutmeg or ½ teaspoon ground

3 star anise pods

olive oil

Take your jar and add the allspice and cloves. Break the cinnamon sticks into sections and add to the jar. Drop in the nutmeg and the star anise pods. Cover with olive oil. Seal the jar and shake to mix. Place on a dimly lit shelf. Allow the oil to steep for 4 to 6 weeks. Be sure to check on it every few days and give it a gentle shake as you reinforce your intention. Strain out herbal bits and use the oil to empower luck and money magicks.

Cooking Vinegars

The art of cooking is all about chemistry. Not only do we change an ingredient with heat or cold or with brute force by stirring, smashing, or kneading, but we also look at how one ingredient complements or reacts with another, such as the chemical reactions of acids and bases working together to enhance and balance flavor.

Vinegar is one of the important acids added to balance the salty-sweet of a dish and improve the way it tastes. A dose of good vinegar can turn a bland dish into a tasty one. While basic white vinegar may be good for pickling, it would not add the complexity that a medium-bodied, delicately sweet sherry vinegar would bring to a sauce or the flavor a rice vinegar lends to a stir-fry.

There are many kinds of vinegar, each with its own unique flavor. Here are a few of the more common varieties:

Apple Cider Vinegar
Beauty, brightness, fertility, healing, invigorate, love, and youth

Apple cider vinegar is valued as a beneficial source of probiotics, enzymes, and vitamins that lift health as well as spirits, and it is known to elicit fond affections. It is often taken as a tonic to boost health, detox the body, and dissolve kidney stones. Apple cider vinegar has a tart fruity flavor that complements fruits, salads, coleslaws, and sauces. Just like the apple, this vinegar holds properties for youth and beauty. Add it to a hair rinse water to improve luster. Dilute it with water and use it as a face rinse to improve skin tone. Dab it on skin to lighten dark spots. Pour 1 cup of apple cider vinegar into a warm bath and soak to soothe sunburn. Add it to recipes to brighten energy and flavor.

Balsamic Vinegar
Abundance, beauty, celebration, fertility, and vigor

Balsamic vinegar is a sweet, syrupy vinegar made from grapes that have been fermented in oak barrels. The longer it is aged the better the flavor and the more expensive it is. Expensive varieties are often used as a finishing vinegar, drizzled over foods to balance flavor while cheaper balsamic vinegars are whisked with olive oil and used as dressings and marinades or reduced to a thicker sauce to top meats and vegetable dishes.

Make a balsamic glaze by reducing 1 cup of balsamic vinegar in a small pan over medium heat until it begins to simmer. Turn down the heat and reduce for 7 to 8 minutes. The glaze should thicken to a honey-like consistency. Drizzle it over fruits and vegetables to heighten flavor. Add a sprinkle of brown sugar as the glaze cools to intensify sweetness. Balsamic vinegar carries the uplifting celebratory energy of the grape. Serve a reduction with melon to boost cheer. Drizzle it over bruschetta and serve at a party to enrich the celebration.

Champagne Vinegar
Abundance, beauty, celebration, fertility, and success

Most champagne vinegar is made from chardonnay and pinot noir grapes. It is valued for its light floral flavor and is used to make vinaigrettes and sauces. Like other wine and cider vinegars, it is produced by the introduction of a "vinegar mother" that grows as it converts the sugar into alcohol. Champagne vinegar holds a festive, nurturing energy that brightens dressings and sauces. Blend champagne vinegar with olive oil and use it to dress a salad to draw abundance and boost spirits. Make a dressing with a mixture of champagne vinegar, olive oil, a squeeze of lemon juice, and a spoon of mustard and honey. Use it to dress salads to brighten energy and boost conversation. Infuse champagne vinegar with rosemary, thyme, and peppercorns to boost energy for success.

Malt Vinegar
Health, love, money, and protection

Malt vinegar has a pleasant caramel-yeasty flavor. It is made from malted barley and holds a healing, prosperous energy. In England and Canada, malt vinegar is a prized condiment served with fries and to top fish and chips. Magickally, its bright energy can change negative feelings into positive ones. Serve it to cancel out any negativity that originated from an outside source.

Rice Vinegar
Abundance, detoxifying, fertility, health, and security

Rice vinegar is made from fermented rice. It has a delicate, sweet flavor and is used in Japanese and Chinese cuisines, among others. It is loaded with beneficial compounds to boost immunity and detoxify the body. Magickally, it holds a prosperous energy to protect your home from hunger and want. Rice vinegar is used in Asian dishes, dipping sauces, and marinades.

White Vinegar
Cleansing, disinfecting, and purity

White vinegar is made from alcohol distilled from grain. It has a strong clean flavor. It is used to pickle vegetables and tame sweet sauces like barbecue and ketchups. But most notably, white vinegar is a cleaning agent mixed with water to disinfect countertops and clean windows without streaking. Add a sprig of rosemary and ½ cup of white vinegar to a spray bottle, top with water, and use to cleanse a room of negative energy.

Wine Vinegar
Abundance, beauty, celebration, and fertility

Wine vinegar comes red and white. It is made by oxidizing wine. Wine vinegar contains trace minerals, acetic acid, and probiotics. It is the favored vinegar in many French and Italian recipes and is used to make marinades and dressings.

Red wine vinegar has a stronger flavor and goes with hearty foods, like roots and roasted vegetables. White wine vinegar has a lighter, tangy flavor. It is used to make béarnaise and hollandaise sauces, to make vinaigrettes, and to complement chicken and fish dishes.

Chapter 8
SUGARS AND SWEETS

Who doesn't enjoy a sweet treat? Sweets are luxurious. Sweets are eaten to satisfy urges, comfort the frazzled, and woo a lover. A sweet bit is eaten for a quick energy boost, an instant mood lift, or a moment of pampering. All over the world bakers dedicate hours to making cakes, pies, muffins, cookies, or sweet breads to enliven festivities. Fancy desserts are made and served to honor guests and reward loved ones. They are served to woo, compel, and sweeten. A little sweet is nice. A little sweet is elevating. But too much can lead to addiction, and unfortunately modern food has come to a point where sugar is hiding in just about everything. Many of the foods we consider healthy or "good for the diet" are loaded with it. Many yogurts, especially the low-fat varieties, are loaded with sugar. Manufacturers add sugar to make a low-fat product that tastes just as good as the full-fat choice. There is sugar in pasta sauce and salad dressing. It is in flavored oatmeal and breakfast cereals. You can even find added sugar in dried fruit and peanut butter.

According to research by Euromonitor, "In the United States, the average person consumes more than 126 grams of sugar per day ... twice the average sugar intake of all 54 countries" in the study and "twice what the World Health Organization recommends for daily intake."[96] Consuming too much sugar causes more than just dental decay. Eating too much sugar "raises the risk of several dangerous health problems, including obesity, type 2 diabetes, and increased pressure on the heart and blood vessels," writes Joseph Nordqvist for *Medical News Today*.[97]

Sugar is addicting. Most of us crave a sweet bit from time to time. But there are alternatives—some healthier than others—that are easy to substitute when you find yourself in need of a sweet fix.

Sweeteners

Agave
Banishing, binding, healing, and nurturing

Agave nectar is a natural sweetener made from several species of agave, including *Agave salmiana* and *Agave tequilana*, a desert plant harvested to make tequila one of Mexico's best-known exports. The agave was an important food source for early Native Americans. It has been cultivated for over 9,000 years and used to make an ancient drink. The sword-like leaves contain an aloe like gel that accelerates the healing of wounds and burns due to its antioxidant and antibacterial properties. Fiber from the leaves was used for roof thatching, clothing, and ropes. The Aztecs used it to make a pulp for paper.

Agave sap, known as *miel de agave,* was revered for its therapeutic properties and was used as a sweetener, a medicine, and as a fermented drink enjoyed for centuries. Then came industrialization and the mass production of agave sweetener, reducing the nourishing sweetness to a highly refined syrup made by treating agave sugars with heat and enzymes. If you wish to use agave nectar, read the labels and choose the raw version. The refining process is much slower using lower heat, so the sap can retain more of its natural properties. With its low glycemic index value, use agave as a sugar replacement to boost nourishing qualities.

96. Roberto A. Ferdman, "Where People around the World Eat the Most Sugar and Fat," *Washington Post*, February 5, 2015, https://www.washingtonpost.com/news/wonk/wp/2015/02/05/where-people-around-the-world-eat-the-most-sugar-and-fat/.

97. Joseph Nordqvist, "How Much Sugar Is in Your Food and Drink?," *Medical News Today*, February 14, 2018, https://www.medicalnewstoday.com/articles/262978.

Coconut Sugar and Nectar
Beauty, clear thinking, moon magick, healing, protection, and purification

Both coconut sugar and nectar come from the coconut palm. It is less refined than cane sugar and contains magnesium, potassium, zinc, and iron. Coconut sugar has a lower glycemic index value than cane sugar, which means that after ingestion, we experience a less dramatic spike in blood sugar and less of a sugar crash. It adds a pleasant molasses-like flavor to baked goods. Magickally, coconut energy is associated with the moon and the element water. Its energy strengthens confidence and inner resolve. Sprinkle coconut sugar over porridge to help overcome inhibitions. Add to recipes to amplify energy for beauty and healing.

Dates
Abundance, fertility, potency, spirituality, and wishes

Dates are the sugary fruit of the date palm, a food that has been consumed for thousands of years. Dates have been considered sacred since the dawn of time, as they were thought to store a heavenly flame, an energy that would aid one in the progress of one's life path and support expansion and growth. Dates were used as offerings to the gods in Babylon and Greece. Date syrup was holy to the Hebrews. The fruits were also used by ancient Persians to celebrate the death and resurrection of Zoroaster, a Christ figure who dates back to 500 BCE.

Dates are incredibly sweet. Medjool dates are the sweetest and are a healthy alternative to cane sugar. Add them to baked goods to increase abundance. Mix them into smoothies for a sweet, refreshing drink that will lift both your mood and your energy.

Dates boost spirituality. Serve dates to guests to improve friendship. Mix figs, dates, and walnuts and serve to instill positive energy. Eat a date as you dream to grant power to your wishes. If you have a blender, you can make a decadent date shake by blending 1 cup of milk with 1 cup of ice and 9 pitted Medjool dates. Whiz until smooth and serve to sweeten and renew affections, or serve to yourself to nourish and foster self-love.

Honey
Abundance, attraction, compulsion, happiness, health, love, prosperity, solar magick, and truth

Honey is created from the nectar of many plants, and it holds powerful energies. It is one of the oldest foods created by bees, once held to be messengers of the gods. This sweet, delicious treat is created by bees visiting flower after flower and extracting the nectar using their long, tube-shaped tongue. They store the nectar in their second stomach, where it mixes with enzymes and partially digests. Upon reaching the hive, the bee regurgitates into the mouth of another bee, who then deposits the substance in beeswax made from the liquid secretions from its abdomen. The bee then dries the honey with air from its buzzing wings.

Hindu texts describe honey as one of the five sacred elixirs of immortality. It is said that if you eat a spoonful of local honey a day when you move to a new area, it will protect you against developing allergies. Honey has antibacterial and antifungal properties, which makes it a wonderful wound salve. Honey does not need to be processed. It does not rot. In antiquity it was held as a miracle food associated with purity and truth. It can be fed to someone to compel them to speak the truth.

Honey is one of the most counterfeited food items in the United States. Don't believe me? Just google "honey food fraud," and you will be amazed by the greed. Most of the counterfeit stuff comes from China and Taiwan. They ship it to India, Malaysia, Indonesia, Russia, South Korea, Mongolia, Thailand, Taiwan, and the Philippines, where it is relabeled and sent on to the United States. The honey is filtered to remove the pollen and diluted with rice sugar, molasses, and even corn syrup. Yuck! Be vigilant when choosing a honey. Read the label and buy from reputable sources, or you might end up with an impostor.

Honey is sacred to Aphrodite, the goddess of love and beauty. It is said that Cleopatra's secret for her radiant skin was that she soaked in a milk and honey bath. To replicate her beauty bath, add 1 to 2 cups organic whole milk and ½ cup honey to warm bathwater and soak.

Honey is also brimming with energy for prosperity. To bring quick money, burn a green candle that has been anointed with sweet orange essential oil, a drizzle of honey, and sprinkle of ground cinnamon.

Honey is a favored offering often left for nature spirits, elementals, and the dead. Offer a dish of milk and honey to elicit the favor of a deity or a nature spirit. Leave out a dish of milk and honey on your hearth to garner favor of a household spirit.

Honey is also a food of prosperity. Place three silver coins in a dish and drizzle them with honey to attract wealth. It holds energy to comfort the sick or lift someone's spirits. Just add fresh rose petals and honey to a cup of hot tea and sip. For the kitchen witch, honey is a healthy, smart way to tap into energy and add sweetness. Need to sweeten a relationship? Invite your target to tea. Sweeten it with honey and make the visit a positive experience. Smile; be pleasant. Their opinion of you will turn positive.

The magickal honey jar is an old sweetening spells made to gain favor or sweeten someone's opinion of you. Write down your petition. Take a canning jar and drop in the paper with your petition, something of yours, and something of the person you wish to create a link to. Whisper your intention as you pour honey over the objects until they are completely covered. Screw on the lid and place the jar where it will catch your eye. Focus your intention on it whenever it catches your attention.

Maple Syrup
Divination, longevity, love, luck, and wealth

I don't use very much sugar. My body does not like it. It triggers inflammation in my shoulders, knees, and hips. Since I prefer to be agile and pain free, I avoid sugar as much as possible. However, I do like sweets, and maple syrup is my go-to sugar replacement. Maple syrup carries the energy of the maple tree. It is associated with Jupiter, good health, long life, and abundance. It is added to food to draw good health, love, and wealth. I also add it to any recipes I want to make sweet.

Maple syrup comes from the sugar maple, a tree associated with the moon, Jupiter, and the element water. It holds energy to manifest abundance, happiness, good health, and long life. Maple syrup is made by boiling sap. It is boiled down into a delicious syrup in the fall as the leaves shift into brilliant shades of yellow and red. The syrup is a healthy sweetener and can be used as a sugar replacement. A splash of maple syrup adds positive energy to draw happiness, good health, love, and wealth to food spells. Cook up some pancakes and top them with the loving energies of butter, maple syrup, and fresh raspberries. Serve them to the one you love to sweeten affections. Use maple syrup as a sugar alternative to add positive and supportive energy to recipes to heal and help one adapt in times of change.

Molasses
Banishing, love, lust, preserving, and sweetening

Molasses is a thick, dark syrup with a sweet, smoky caramel flavor. It is used for sweetening and flavoring foods. Molasses is made in the steps of refining sugarcane. Processing sugar is done in three boils. Light molasses is the syrup left over after the first boiling cycle of sugarcane juice. It contains the most sugar. It is the lightest in color and mildest in flavor.

Dark molasses, or B-grade molasses, comes from the second boiling. This is the molasses most bakers use. When a recipe calls for molasses, this is the grade they are calling for. It is a darker, thicker syrup with a stronger, less sweet flavor. It is molasses that gives gingerbread and ginger cookies their distinct color and flavor.

Blackstrap molasses, or C-grade molasses, is the residue remaining after the third and final boil. It has the strongest flavor, and because three rounds of sugar crystals have been removed, it has less sugar and nutrients. Drizzle it over oatmeal for a quick energy boost. Mix a spoonful into a glass of water and drink to remedy fatigue. Magickally, molasses has energy to sweeten and compel. Add blackstrap molasses to savory dishes like baked beans and pulled pork and serve to encourage someone to see your side of things.

Sugarcane
Banishing, love, lust, preserving, and sweetening

Most people think of white sugarcane sugar when they think of sugar. It is a sweetener and baking staple. You can find a bag of sugar in almost every home. But sugar production has changed. Nearly a decade ago all United States sugar beet producers started growing crops that were genetically modified to resist the herbicide glyphosate, also known as Roundup. I want my sweets sweet, not poisoned, not chemically altered. I want the energy pure and earthy, not contaminated and toxic. And Roundup is toxic. It can cause cancer. Studies have shown that glyphosate disrupts the endocrine system and the balance of gut bacteria.[98] It may damage DNA and may cause hormonal disorders.[99]

Today you must read the labels on the food you are buying, even your sugar bag. If it doesn't say "cane sugar," you can bet that it is not. Sugarcane sugar carries energy to woo and compel. It is used to sweeten someone's attitude or feelings toward you.

---

98. Anthony Samsel and Stephanie Seneff, "Glyphosate, Pathways to Modern Diseases II: Celiac Sprue and Gluten Intolerance," *Interdisciplinary Toxicology* 6, no. 4 (December 2013): 159–84, https://www.ncbi.nlm.nih.gov/pmc/articles/PMC3945755/.

99. Marta Kwiatkowska, Edyta Reszka, Katarzyna Wozniak, Ewa Jabłonska, Jaromir Michałowicz, and Bozena Bukowska, "DNA Damage and Methylation Induced by Glyphosate in Human Peripheral Blood Mononuclear Cells (In Vitro Study)," *Food and Chemical Toxicology* 105 (July 2017): 93–98, https://pubmed.ncbi.nlm.nih.gov/28351773/; Marta Kwiatkowska, Jarosiewicz Pawel, and Bozena Bukowska, "Glyphosate and Its Formulations—Toxicity, Occupational and Environmental Exposure," *Medycyna Pracy* 65, no. 5 (2013): 717–29, https://pubmed.ncbi.nlm.nih.gov/24502134/.

Stevia
Friendship, healing, nurturing, and uplifting

Stevia comes from the leaves of an herb native to South America also known as sweetleaf and sugarleaf. It has been used for centuries as a sweetener and as a contraceptive. The leaf has a sweet flavor with a slightly bitter aftertaste, and though new to the West, stevia has been used for decades in many countries as an alternative to sugar. It contains chemicals that taste sweet but, unlike sugar, does not metabolize when ingested and does not cause a change in blood sugar. Thus, it has become a guilt-free sweetener. Stevia is an easy-to-grow plant, and adding it to the herb garden makes it easy to incorporate into your diet.

Unfortunately, like most good things, it was noticed, has become corrupted by Big Food, and is now being marketed under the names Truvia, PureVia, and Stevia in the Raw, none of which are natural. In fact, Truvia, for example, goes through a patented 42-step processing method and does not contain stevia but rebaudioside A, a sweet compound isolated from the stevia plant, and erythritol, a sweetener fermented from corn.[100] In 2015 Cargill settled a class-action suit for deceptive marketing practices, paying out 6.1 million dollars to customers who purchased their product from early 2008 until July 2014, believing the product to be a "natural sweetener" as described on the label, only to find out that Truvia was in fact just another artificial sweetener.[101]

Real stevia is in the form of leaves of the stevia plant. Use it in place of sugar to improve health and instill a sense of well-being. Add a handful of leaves to a pitcher of iced tea to promote happiness and sweeten relationships. Stevia has energy to gently compel. Serve at a meeting when you wish to get your ideas across. Stevia holds energy to sweetly encourage your idea while casting the opposing side in a less favorable light. Float a sprig of stevia in a glass and give to someone to sweetly persuade them or influence their opinion. Sprinkle dried stevia over the food to gain influence.

....

100. Mingu Yang, Jun Hua, and Ling Qin, "High-Purity Rebaudioside A and Method of Extracting Same," Google Patents, December 4, 2011, https://patents.google.com/patent/US7923541B2/en; Joe Leech, "Truvia: Good or Bad?," Healthline, November 19, 2018, https://www.healthline.com/nutrition/truvia-good-or-bad#what-it-is; Annette McDermott, "Everything You Need to Know about Stevia," Healthline, last modified December 3, 2018, https://www.healthline.com/health/food-nutrition/stevia-side-effects.

101. Larry Bodine, "$6.1 Million Settlement Reached in Truvia Natural Sweetener Class Action," National Trial Lawyers, January 7, 2015, https://thenationaltriallawyers.org/2015/01/truvia/.

The Delight of Chocolate

Carob
Affection, beauty, health, luck, and protection

The carob tree, also known as the locust bean, produces a sweet-tasting bean pod that is used as a substitute for chocolate. It was eaten by ancient Greek, Roman, and Egyptians four thousand years ago.[102] Unlike chocolate, carob is fat and caffeine free. It does not contain tyramine, a migraine-triggering compound found in chocolate. Carob is a good source of vitamins A and B_2, which are good for skin and eye health.

Carob is associated with Jupiter and Saturn. Its energy can be used to sweeten a relationship, guard against loneliness, help maintain good health, and protect against evil forces. Carob beans may be carried or worn for protection. A carob bean tucked in the pocket will aid a traveler's passage and increase a gambler's luck.

Cacao
Gratitude, happiness, health, longevity, love, luxury, and riches

Cocoa is made from the seeds of the cacao tree. The raw cacao bean is a concentrated source of antioxidants. It has more antioxidants than red wine and green tea, which makes it one of the most healing longevity foods. To the people of Central America, the cacao tree was a gift from the god Quetzalcoatl, as it contains compounds that induce a sense of well-being.

Cacao nibs are cacao beans that have been roasted and husked before being broken into smaller pieces to make an amazing joyful food loaded with the psychoactive feel-good chemical anandamide and the love chemical phenylethylamine, which releases dopamine in the pleasure centers of the brain. Cacao also contains tryptophan, an amino acid that converts into serotonin, a neurotransmitter known to promote a sense of well-being and relaxation. And it's good for your brain, as it contains the compound resveratrol, which has been found to slow cognitive decline.[103] Sprinkle cacao nibs over your cereal or add to smoothies to add nutrition and elevate your spirit. Mix a spoonful into green drinks, top

---

102. Nancy J. Hajeski, *National Geographic Complete Guide to Herbs and Spices* (Washington, DC: National Geographic, 2016), 203.

103. Arrigo F. G. Cicero, Massimiliano Ruscica, and Maciej Banach, "Resveratrol and Cognitive Decline: A Clinician Perspective," *Archives of Medical Science* 15, no. 4 (July 2019): 936–43, https://www.ncbi.nlm.nih.gov/pmc/articles/PMC6657254/.

yogurt with them, or sprinkle them over oatmeal. Add a spoonful to a glass of water and drink for an instant energy boost.

Cacao is processed and mixed with sugar to make chocolate, the popular candy eaten to induce happiness and feelings of love. Give a box of chocolates to show affection or admiration. Dark chocolate is associated with passion and romance. Milk chocolate is associated with nurturing and friendship.

While humans may consider chocolate to be a divine gift that evokes euphoria, it is toxic to many animals, which makes it inappropriate to be left outside.

Stuff of the Sweet Life

When life is sweet, it is joyous and worry-free and filled with the things and the people we love. When we think of "the sweet life," we think of things that are rich and delicious. We remember vacations and celebrations and time spent well with someone special.

Celebration Cake

This recipe is for the best chocolate cake I have ever baked. It is a tall old-fashioned cake that is moist and delicious. It uses a good semisweet chocolate. I bake it for birthdays and holidays and top it with chocolate ganache for a decadent treat that inspires happiness, friendship, and wishes granted.

You will need:

2 9-inch cake pans

1½ cups fresh hot coffee

3 ounces good dark chocolate, finely chopped (I use the 85% Valrhona bar)

3 cups sugar

2½ cups flour

1½ cups unsweetened cocoa powder

2 teaspoons baking soda

¾ teaspoon baking powder

1 teaspoon salt

3 eggs

¾ cup olive oil

1 cup sour cream

½ cup milk

1 teaspoon vanilla extract

pack of birthday candles

Preheat the oven to 325 degrees Fahrenheit. Spray the pans with cooking spray and dust with flour. In a small bowl, pour hot coffee over chopped chocolate to melt. Stir until smooth. In a large bowl, sift together sugar, flour, cocoa, baking soda, baking powder, and salt. In a mixing bowl, beat eggs until thick. Slowly add oil, sour cream, milk, vanilla, and melted chocolate mixture to the eggs. Beat until combined. Add sugar mixture and beat until combined. Divide between the pans and bake for 50 minutes or until a cake tester comes out clean. Cool cakes in their pans for 10 minutes, then run a knife around the edge and turn them out onto a rack to cool.

Assemble the cake by filling and frosting with chocolate ganache.

Chocolate Ganache Frosting

This sweet, chocolaty frosting is loaded with positive, feel-good energy for happiness and pleasure. Spread over cake to inspire affection. Spoon on top of cupcakes to make someone feel special.

You will need:

1 cup heavy cream

12 ounces good semisweet chocolate chips

1 teaspoon vanilla extract

In a small saucepan heat cream until it just begins to simmer. Do not allow it to boil. Remove from heat and stir in chocolate. Add vanilla and stir until the mixture is smooth and shiny. Allow it to cool for 10 or 15 minutes.

Frost a cake and top with candles for a birthday blessing. Light the candles and say,

A cake baked,
bright candles lit,
to grant birthday blessings,
blown with a wish for happiness, luck, and all of life's blessings.

By air and fire, water and earth,
bright blessings to you on the day of your birth.

Prompt the person celebrating to blow out the candles. Cut the cake and eat it together.

Lemon Blueberry Ricotta Cake

This is my go-to recipe to boost mood and put a smile on someone's face. Lemon brightens the uplifting energy of blueberry and the nourishing energy of ricotta for a moist, delicious cake brimming with positive feel-good energy.

You will need:

deep tube pan

1½ cups sugar

½ cup olive oil

5 eggs

1¼ cups ricotta cheese

1 Tablespoon lemon zest

3 Tablespoons lemon juice

2 teaspoons vanilla extract

2½ cups flour

1 teaspoon salt

1 Tablespoon baking powder

4 cups blueberries, fresh or frozen

Preheat the oven to 350 degrees Fahrenheit. Spray a deep tube pan with nonstick cooking spray. In a large mixing bowl, beat together sugar and oil until smooth. Break eggs into a separate bowl and beat in one at a time while the mixer is running. Mix in ricotta, lemon zest, juice, and vanilla until combined.

In a separate bowl, whisk together flour, salt, and baking powder. Add flour mixture to the sugar-egg mixture and stir until combined. Gently fold blueberries into the batter. Spoon batter into the tube pan and bake 60 to 70 minutes or until the cake is golden brown and a skewer inserted into the middle comes out clean. Let cool in the pan for 10 minutes. Then turn out onto a serving plate and frost with a glaze.

Lemon Glaze

This easy glaze holds a bright energy to sweeten and cheer. Pour over the top of pound cakes to moisten and make them more decadent.

You will need:

1 Tablespoon lemon juice

1 Tablespoon milk

1½ cups powdered sugar

In a mixing bowl, mix together lemon juice, milk, and powdered sugar. Spoon the glaze over the top of the warm cake.

Gluten-Free Chocolate Spice Cookies

These chocolaty cookies hold just a hint of spice to encourage happiness and love.

You will need:

1 cup almond flour

1 cup hazelnut flour

1 cup powdered sugar

6 ounces good chocolate, chopped into small bits

3 Tablespoons unsweetened cocoa

1 teaspoon cinnamon

1 teaspoon salt

2 egg whites

1 teaspoon vanilla extract

Mix together the flours or grind together almonds and hazelnuts to make flour. Add powdered sugar, chocolate, cocoa, cinnamon, and salt and grind together until finely ground. Add egg whites and vanilla and process until a sticky dough forms. Dump the dough onto parchment paper and roll into a log about 3 inches wide. Then place the roll in refrigerator for 10 minutes.

Preheat the oven to 325 degrees Fahrenheit. Slice dough into ¼-inch rounds and place them on a greased cookie sheet. Bake for 15 minutes. Let the cookies cool on the sheets for 10 minutes before removing.

Walnut and Raspberry Cookies

This crumbly melt-in-your-mouth cookie combines the energy of raspberries, walnuts, and cornmeal to bake up a tasty treat loaded with earth energy, happiness, and love. My family raves over these gems, and it is the treat they most often request. This recipe is a bit time intensive, as the crumb uses walnut meal made by toasting 1 cup of walnut halves and then cooling and grinding the toasted nuts into a meal that is cut with cold butter. The butter must remain cold to achieve the best texture.

To begin, make the walnut meal: Place 1 cup of walnuts in a single layer on a baking sheet. Toast under the broiler until brown. Do not burn. They will become bitter and change the taste of the crumb. When the walnuts have cooled, grind them into a coarse flour.

You will need:

½ cup walnut meal

2 cups flour

1 Tablespoon baking powder

2 Tablespoons cornmeal

¾ teaspoon salt

3 Tablespoons sugar

1 cup cold butter

⅓ cup milk

good raspberry jam for the center (plum, strawberry, and apricot are good too)

In a large bowl, combine the dry ingredients. Cut in cold butter. As you cut in the butter, use the energy of your work to program an intention into the dough. When the butter has been cut through the dough, mix by pushing your palm through the crumbs. Work the dough until the butter is distributed throughout in small pea-size beads. If the dough becomes sticky, return the bowl to the refrigerator until the butter is firm. Add the milk. Mix delicately by pushing your palm through the dough and turning the crumb a couple of times. Do not over mix. At this stage too much handling will ruin the texture. Dump the dough onto a piece of parchment paper. Press into a log that is about 3 inches wide, and refrigerate at least 2 hours or overnight. These cookies are best the day they are baked, so bake only the portion you are going to serve. Tightly wrap the dough in plastic wrap and store in the refrigerator, and it will remain fresh-tasting for up to 1 week.

Heat the oven to 375 degrees Fahrenheit. Slice the dough into ½-inch thick rounds and place on a baking sheet, well-spaced. Set aside so the dough can start to come to room temperature. You do not want the butter to melt, only to become pliable enough for the dough to indent without cracking. When the dough will yield, press a spoon into the center of each cookie to create a depression to hold a pool of jam. Fill the depression with a bit of good jam. Bake for 25 minutes or until browned. Carefully remove the cookies from the baking sheet and allow them to cool before serving.

Fresh Jam

If you are lucky to live in an area with a berry-picking season, you can adapt this recipe to the berries of your region.

You will need:
5 cups fresh raspberries or blackberries

2 cups sugar

1 teaspoon lemon juice

1 cup water

Put all ingredients into a saucepan. Cover and heat on low flame for 10 minutes or until the berries fall apart. Remove the cover and simmer until jam thickens, stirring often. As you stir, talk to the jam to program it with the energy you are creating. Raspberries and blackberries both have energy for healing, love, and protection. They are often used in food magick to warm romantic love in a relationship. Depending upon the berry, this process can take up to 20 minutes. Watch it closely. There is no saving it once the sugar burns. Cool. Use as needed, discarding the unused portion after 1 week.

The Art of Pie

Today when we think of pie, the first thought is usually of a sweet fruit-filled dessert, but early pies were made of meat. "The first pie recipe was published by the Romans and was for a rye-crusted goat cheese and honey pie," shares the American Pie Council, which consequently still sounds delicious.[104] I love pie. I love sweet pies and savory pies, big pies and hand pies. They are all delightful and they all begin with a good crust.

Basic Pie Crust

This recipe makes 1 crust.

You will need:

1½ cups flour

2 teaspoons cornstarch

2 Tablespoons sugar

½ teaspoon salt

½ cup cold butter

3 Tablespoons shortening

up to ⅓ cup water, cold

In a large mixing bowl, combine flour, cornstarch, sugar, and salt. Cut in the butter and shortening until the mixture resembles coarse meal, with some pea-size clumps. Mix in water, one spoon at a time, until the dough holds together. Cover a work surface with a sheet of parchment paper and turn the dough out on it. Press into a disk and roll out. Chill the dough for 1 hour. Transfer to a pie pan and finish the edges.

---

104. "History of Pie," American Pie Council, accessed March 23, 2021, http://www.piecouncil.org/Events /NationalPieDay/HistoryOfPies.

Gluten-Free Pie Crust

You will need:

⅓ cup amaranth or sorghum flour

⅓ cup millet flour

⅓ cup arrowroot flour, tapioca flour, or cornstarch

¼ cup rice flour

¾ teaspoon xanthan gum

½ teaspoon salt

½ cup cold butter

2 Tablespoons shortening

1½ teaspoons apple cider vinegar

up to ⅓ cup cold water

In a large mixing bowl, whisk together the flours, xanthan gum, and salt. Cut in the cold butter and shortening until the mixture resembles coarse crumbs. Add the apple cider vinegar and water, and mix until the mixture comes together to form a dough. Cover a work surface with parchment paper. Place the dough on the parchment paper and press into a disk. Sprinkle the disk with flour, and roll the dough into an 11-to-12-inch circle.

Hand Pie Pastry

Makes 6 hand pies.

You will need:

2 cups flour

1 teaspoon salt

7 Tablespoons cold butter

1 egg, plus 1 beaten egg for egg wash

1 to 2 Tablespoons cold water

2 teaspoons vinegar

filling of choice

Sift together the flour and salt. Cut in the cold butter until the dough resembles coarse crumbs and the butter is distributed throughout in pea-size beads. Whisk together 1 egg, water, and vinegar. Make a well in the dry ingredients and add the liquid. Stir with a fork until the dough becomes shaggy. Dump the dough onto a flour-dusted work surface and knead until it forms a smooth ball. If the dough is too dry, sprinkle with water and work until it holds together without cracking. Cover with plastic wrap and chill for 2 hours or more.

Preheat the oven to 375 degrees Fahrenheit. Divide chilled dough into 6 balls. Roll out each one into a 6-inch oval. Fill with filling and fold one side over the other. Crimp the edge with a fork. Poke once with a fork to vent. Brush the top with egg wash and bake for 40 minutes or until the edges are golden brown.

Can She Bake a Cherry Pie?

It is said that the way to a man's heart is through his belly, and it is an old custom to serve up a freshly baked cherry pie to win a man's affections. Cherries represent fertility and youthfulness. In the Pacific Northwest cherry trees produce an abundance of cherries from early June to July. This recipe uses fresh cherries, so you do not need to cook the mixture as you would with canned cherries to cook down the juices.

You will need:

1½ cups sugar

4 Tablespoons cornstarch

2 Tablespoons lemon juice

5 cups fresh cherries, pits removed

2 pie crusts

cinnamon

1½ Tablespoons butter

Preheat the oven to 400 degrees Fahrenheit. In a mixing bowl, mix together the sugar and cornstarch. Add lemon juice and fresh cherries and stir to coat. Make sure the cherries have been pitted. No need to break a tooth! Set aside.

Line your baking dish with pie crust. Spoon the cherry mixture in. Sprinkle with cinnamon and dot with butter. Cover with a top crust. Flute the edges. With a sharp knife, cut vents in the top crust. Place the pie on a foil-lined cookie sheet and bake for 50 minutes until golden brown. Let cool before serving.

Blackberry Pie

My neighbor has a monster blackberry bramble. It is a blessing and a curse, as it creeps over my wall and up into my trees. While I fight it every summer, pulling out new shoots and trimming back its briars, the berries are large and tart and so plentiful that every weekend this summer I was able to gather a large bowl of berries and bake decadent treats the whole family loved. Blackberry pie has energy to sweeten relationships, promote happiness, and turn resentment into acceptance.

This recipe makes 1 pie.

You will need:

2 pie crusts

1 cup sugar (or a little more depending on how sweet your berries are)

1 teaspoon lemon juice

1 teaspoon lemon zest

½ teaspoon ground cinnamon

¼ teaspoon almond extract

4 Tablespoons quick-cooking instant tapioca

5 cups blackberries, rinsed, picked clean, and patted dry

Line your baking dish with pie crust. Mix together sugar, lemon juice, lemon zest, cinnamon, almond extract, and quick-cooking instant tapioca in a large bowl. Gently fold in the berries until they are all well coated with the mix. Let sit for 30 minutes.

Preheat the oven to 425 degrees Fahrenheit. Pour the berry mixture into the crust and top with the second crust. You may use a lattice or cover whole. If you are covering, take a fork and vent by pricking the crust in several places. Bake for 15 minutes. Reduce the temperature of the oven to 375 degrees and bake 25 minutes more or until the filling is bubbly and the crust is golden brown. Do not serve until the pie has cooled, as this will allow the filling to thicken.

Blueberry Pie

This is my husband's favorite. Whether the berries are fresh or frozen, this sweet pie is brimming with energy for happiness, prosperity, and luck. If using frozen berries, only thaw the berries to the point you can measure and coat them. You may need to increase the baking time by 10 to 15 minutes. Bake until the center of the top crust turns golden brown.

You will need:

2 pie crusts

1 cup sugar

3 Tablespoons cornstarch

3 Tablespoons tapioca pearls or tapioca flour

½ teaspoon salt

5 cups blueberries, fresh or frozen

1 Tablespoon lemon juice

sprinkling of sanding sugar

1 Tablespoon butter, to dot

Preheat the oven to 400 degrees Fahrenheit. Line your baking dish with pie crust. In a large bowl, whisk together sugar, cornstarch, tapioca, and salt. Add blueberries and stir to coat. Set the berry mixture aside for 30 minutes and then add lemon juice. Pour the mixture into the crust. Cover with the top crust, flute the edges, and vent. Sand with sugar and dot with butter, then bake for 25 minutes. Turn the oven temperature down to 325 degrees Fahrenheit and bake 30 minutes more or until the filling is bubbly and the crust is golden brown. Do not serve until the pie has cooled, as this will allow the filling to thicken.

A Healthier Pumpkin Pie

Not only does this low-sugar recipe taste amazing, but it melds the magickal energies of pumpkin with the energy of hazelnuts (healing and luck), maple syrup (love, luck, and wealth), and the spices: ginger, cinnamon, nutmeg, and cloves (love, luck, and prosperity) to create a pie brimming with healthy, positive magickal energy.

You will need to toast and grind 2½ cups of hazelnuts to make the crust. Spread the hazelnuts in a single layer on a baking sheet. Bake at 325 degrees Fahrenheit for 7 minutes or until they brown and split. Check at the 4-minute mark and stir. Remove and cool enough to handle comfortably. Then gently rub the skins off. Allow them to cool completely and then grind them in a food processor into a meal.

For the crust, you will need:
1½ cups hazelnut meal

¾ cup flour

¾ teaspoon salt

2 Tablespoons sugar

½ cup cold butter, cut into slices

2 Tablespoons cold water

Preheat the oven to 350 degrees Fahrenheit. In a mixing bowl, whisk together hazelnut meal, flour, salt, and sugar. Cut in the butter until it is incorporated in pea-size pieces. Add a sprinkling of water and press until the dough comes together. Roll out the dough or press it to fill the pie dish and flute the edges. Bake for 8 to 10 minutes until the bottom is set.

For the filling, you will need:
3 eggs

½ cup maple syrup

2 cups baked pumpkin (see page 136)

¾ cup heavy cream

1 teaspoon ground cinnamon

½ teaspoon ground ginger

¼ teaspoon ground nutmeg

¼ teaspoon ground cloves

1 teaspoon salt

zest of 1 lemon

Preheat the oven to 350 degrees Fahrenheit. In a mixing bowl, cream together eggs and syrup. Add pumpkin. Mix until smooth. Add the rest of the ingredients and mix. Pour into the prepared crust and bake for 50 minutes or until the pie is set. Cool and refrigerate. This custard-like pumpkin pie is best served cold.

Summer Peach Pie

Sweet and fragrant, the bright summer flavor of peaches is hard to beat. This pie is loaded with energy for love and happiness.

You will need:

1 cup sugar

¼ cup cornstarch

1 cup water

1 Tablespoon lemon juice

1 teaspoon vanilla extract

½ teaspoon cinnamon

½ teaspoon salt

5 cups peaches, peeled, pitted, and cut into slices

2 pie crusts

1 Tablespoon of butter

Preheat the oven to 400 degrees Fahrenheit. In a large saucepan, whisk together sugar and cornstarch. Add water and lemon juice and cook on medium heat, stirring constantly, until the mixture becomes thick (about 5 to 8 minutes). Remove the pan from heat and add vanilla extract, cinnamon, salt, and peach slices. Stir to mix. Pour into the pie crust. Top with the second crust and dot with butter. Bake the pie for 10 minutes, then reduce oven temperature to 350 degrees and bake for 30 more minutes, until the crust is brown and the juice begins to bubble through the vents. Serve warm or cold.

Easy Sweet Quick Breads

Quick breads are recipes that don't use yeast as a leavening agent, so they do not require any rise time. Quick breads come together quickly. Some are known as "dump" recipes because the ingredients can be added together in one mixing bowl and then mixed with good results.

Banana Bread Recipe

This quick bread brims with fertile, uplifting energy to inspire love and abundance. This recipe makes 1 loaf.

You will need:

9 × 5-inch loaf pan

3 or 4 ripe bananas

1 teaspoon baking soda

⅓ cup butter, melted

1 cup sugar

1 egg, beaten

1 teaspoon vanilla extract

1½ cups flour

½ teaspoon salt

Preheat the oven to 350 degrees Fahrenheit. Spray a loaf pan with cooking spray and set aside. In a large mixing bowl, mash bananas, baking soda, and butter. Mix in the sugar, egg, and vanilla. Add the flour and salt and mix until smooth. Pour the mixture into a loaf pan and bake for 1 hour or until a skewer inserted into the center comes out clean. Eat a slice for quick energy or serve with tea to a friend to sweeten relationships.

Chocolate Zucchini Loaf

This delicious, sweet loaf holds energy to expand awareness and enhance psychic vision. Serve it to align viewpoints or open your mind to someone else's perspective. This recipe makes 1 loaf.

You will need:

9 × 5-inch loaf pan

1½ cups all-purpose flour

¼ cup unsweetened cocoa

1 teaspoon baking soda

½ teaspoon salt

½ teaspoon cinnamon

1 cup sugar

½ cup olive oil or melted unsalted butter

1 egg

2 cups grated zucchini

½ cup strong coffee

1 teaspoon vanilla extract

1 cup chocolate chips

Preheat the oven to 350 degrees Fahrenheit. Spray a loaf pan with cooking spray and set aside. In large bowl, whisk together flour, cocoa, baking soda, salt, and cinnamon. In a mixing bowl, combine sugar, oil, and eggs. Beat until smooth. Add zucchini, coffee, and vanilla and mix until combined. Stir in the flour mixture until combined. Add chocolate chips and stir until combined. Spoon the mixture into a greased loaf pan. Bake at 350 for 50 minutes or until a skewer inserted into the center comes out clean.

Easy Pumpkin Bread

Pumpkin holds energy for abundance, banishing, divination, health, prosperity, and revealing the unseen. Add in the magickal energies of cinnamon, nutmeg, allspice, and walnuts, and you have a sweet treat brimming with energy to banish the negative and boost a positive outlook. Serve to instill happiness or gain clarity of vision. This recipe makes 1 loaf.

You will need:

9 × 5-inch loaf pan

1 cup sugar

2 eggs

½ cup olive oil

1 cup cooked pumpkin (see page 136)

1½ cups flour

¼ teaspoon of salt

1 teaspoon baking powder

½ teaspoon ground cinnamon

¼ teaspoon ground nutmeg

⅛ teaspoon ground allspice

½ cup chopped pecans or walnuts

Preheat the oven to 350 degrees Fahrenheit. Spray a loaf pan with cooking spray and set aside. In a mixing bowl, combine sugar, eggs, and oil. Mix until combined. Add pumpkin puree and beat until smooth. In a small bowl, whisk together flour and spices. Stir the flour mixture into the pumpkin mixture until combined. Stir in pecans and spoon the mixture into a loaf pan. Bake for 1 hour or until a skewer inserted into the center comes out clean.

How to Bake a Pumpkin

Baking a pumpkin is the same as baking any of the large squashes. When you buy a pie pumpkin, keep in mind that a 3-pound pumpkin will give you about 2 cups of fresh pumpkin flesh. Begin by washing your pumpkin and cutting the stem off. Next, cut it in half. Scoop out the seeds and set them aside. You will want to save some for planting next summer. Scrape away the stringy pulp.

Preheat your oven to 400 degrees Fahrenheit.

For Sweet Recipes

Set the pumpkin halves cut-side down in a large baking dish. Pour in ¼ inch of water and bake until tender. This will vary by the size of your pumpkin. If it is small, it might only take 30 minutes; if it is giant, it could take up to 1 hour. When your fork slides easily into the flesh, it is ready. Let it cool until you can touch it without burning your fingers, and then peel off the skin. Allow it to cool and drain off the liquid. Use it in your favorite pumpkin recipes.

For Savory Recipes

Drizzle the cut side of the pumpkin with olive oil and season with salt and pepper. Place the pumpkin halves cut-side up in a baking dish and roast until tender, about 35 to 45 minutes.

Chapter 9
VEGETABLES

Everyone knows that vegetables and fruit are important parts of a healthy diet. From a young age we are told to "eat our vegetables." Not only are they loaded with nutrients, but many also offer protection against various diseases. According to the Harvard School of Public Health, a diet that includes vegetables can "lower blood pressure, reduce the risk of heart disease and stroke, prevent some types of cancer, lower risk of eye and digestive problems, and have a positive effect upon blood sugar."[105]

Numerous studies have concluded that eating eight ounces of vegetables per day may increase your lifespan.[106] Vegetables are good for you and, if they are fixed right, can taste delicious. Every vegetable also holds its own unique brand of magickal energy that can be aligned with a magickal intent.

Lettuces, Greens, and Sprouts

Leafy vegetables are grown and eaten in cultures across the world. They are usually defined as leaves and stems that are eaten raw or cooked, from cabbage to kale, and even

105. The Nutrition Source, "Vegetables and Fruit," Harvard School of Public Health, accessed February 19, 2021, https://www.hsph.harvard.edu/nutritionsource/what-should-you-eat/vegetables-and-fruits/.

106. Alina Petre, "How Many Servings of Vegetables Should You Eat per Day?," Healthline, November 26, 2017, https://www.healthline.com/nutrition/servings-of-vegetables-per-day.

include dandelion greens. Mothers the world over encouraged their children, "Eat your greens. They are good for you." And they are! Greens are loaded with nutrients. They are packed with vitamins and minerals and are a good source of folate and fiber. Eating greens aids digestion and detoxifies the liver. The beta-carotene in greens promotes skin health, while the phytonutrients protect eye health. Adding a daily helping of leafy green vegetables to your diet can protect against age-related cognitive decline.[107]

Eat greens that are in season. Dandelion greens are best in spring and summer; swiss chard and beet greens in spring through fall; and collard, kale, mustard, and turnip greens in October through early spring.

Alfalfa Sprouts
Abundance, ground, luck, money, and stability

Alfalfa, also known as lucerne, is a perennial flowering plant in the pea family cultivated worldwide for livestock fodder. Alfalfa sprouts are nutritious microgreens with energy for focus and concentration. Add them to your diet to gain insight into difficult situations. Top sandwiches with a handful of sprouts to ramp up nutritional value and empower cognitive abilities.

Alfalfa is an antipoverty herb associated with Jupiter, Venus, and the element earth. Use the seeds in quick-money spells. Add them to luck spells to boost the working. Keep a small jar of alfalfa seeds in your kitchen to protect your home from hunger.

Beet Greens
Aphrodisiac, beauty, clear sight, earth energy, healing, love, and youth

Beet greens are the broad leaves of the garden vegetable known for its large, sweet taproot. In most kitchens, they are usually discarded even though they are chock-full of nutrients. Beet greens are a good source of calcium, vitamins A and K, riboflavin, potassium, and fiber. They also contain the antioxidants beta-carotene and lutein for healthy eyesight. Beet greens have a sweet, mild flavor similar to spinach and kale. They can be sautéed and

....

107. Martha Clare Morris, Yamin Wang, Lisa L. Barnes, David A. Bennett, Bess Dawson-Hughes, and Sarah L. Booth, "Nutrients and Bioactives in Green Leafy Vegetables and Cognitive Decline," *Neurology* 90, no. 3 (January 2018): 214–22, https://www.ncbi.nlm.nih.gov/pmc/articles/PMC5772164/; Jae H Kang, Alberto Acherio, and Francine Grodstein, "Fruit and Vegetable Consumption and Cognitive Decline in Aging Women," *Annals of Neurology* 57, no. 5 (May 2005): 713–20, https://pubmed.ncbi.nlm.nih.gov/15852398/.

eaten as a side dish or added to salads and soups. The leafy greens have a higher nutritional value than the root and hold energy to heal past hurts and ease old wounds. Add young leaves to a salad to patch up a relationship. They are packed with antioxidants and have more iron than spinach. All greens are associated with money and growth, but these ultra-healthy greens can be cooked up and added to recipes to improve decision-making and gaining clear sight.

Bok Choy
Beauty, health, prosperity, and vitality

Bok choy is also known as pak choi. It is a Chinese cabbage loaded with nutrients. Bok choy contains phosphorus, zinc, sodium, copper, manganese, selenium, niacin, folate, choline, beta-carotene, and vitamin K. Its powerful antioxidants help protect cells against damage by free radicals. Bok choy is one of the miracle anti-inflammatory foods. Its beta-carotene and folate helps to repair cell damage. Add young leaves to any salad to boost nutritional value. Chop and add to soups and stir-fries to fortify health and wellness. Bok choy is good for your skin. Make a beauty mask by blending bok choy with yogurt and honey until smooth. Apply to the face and relax for at least 15 minutes. Rinse.

Bok choy holds a soothing, restorative energy to heal and nourish. Eat young leaves raw to boost vitality. Steam and eat bok choy to stave off a cold. Pour boiling water over the leaves and use them as a poultice to soothe irritated skin.

Cabbage
Beauty, health, luck, and protection

Cabbage contains glucosinolates, which stimulate the production of detoxifying enzymes that remove carcinogens. It is an excellent source of vitamin K, vitamin C, and fiber. Chop cabbage and add it to salads or soups to add healing energy. Cabbage is associated with the moon and the element water and holds energy to stimulate intuition. Eat it before bed to help fix your sleep cycle or gain protection from nightmares. Use green cabbage in money-drawing food magicks. Tuck a cabbage leaf under your hat to break a spell of bad luck. Tuck a cabbage leaf into your left pocket before facing a tricky situation.

Collard Greens
Abundance, beauty, good luck, health, nurturing, and protection

Collard greens are chock-full of antioxidants. They are a good source of vitamins A, B_1, B_3 (niacin), B_5, B_9 (folate), C, E, and K. They are high in dietary fiber and calcium and are a good source of copper, magnesium, phosphorus, and potassium to protect health, guard against cancer, and nourish and repair your body at a cellular level. Add them to your diet to bolster health and gain glowing skin and shining hair. Southern lore holds that eating collard greens on New Year's Day will ensure prosperity in the coming year. To prepare them, cut away the tough stem with kitchen shears or a small sharp knife so that the leaves are cut in half lengthwise.

Cress
Remembrance, sex, and transitions

A small-leafed annual also known as garden cress, pepper grass, pepperweed, pepperwort, window cress, and windowsill cress, cress (*Lepidium sativum*) is an ancient food eaten by the Greeks.[108] It is one of the Old Testament "bitter herbs" eaten during the seder.[109] Cress is now a popular microgreen. The sprouts are harvested and eaten just a week after germination. They have a refreshing peppery flavor and a high nutritional content, making them a healthy addition to sandwiches and salads.

Magickally, cress is an herb of borders and crossroads associated with Hecate, Saturn, and Taurus. Top toasted slices of organic whole grain bread with a scoop of egg salad and a handful of cress for a treat brimming with liminal energy. Serve it to open doors to new possibilities. Use cress seeds in sprouting spells to fill your kitchen with opportunity.

Dandelion Greens
Beauty, divination, health, luck, prophetic dreams, spirit magick, and wish magick

Dandelion (*Taraxacum officinale*) is a flowering herbaceous perennial known as the wishing flower or blow balls, as its yellow flower matures into a fluffy seed ball that, when blown, floats upon the wind. Before lawns, gardeners cultivated dandelions, prizing them as food, medicine, and magickal plants. American colonists carried the flowers with them,

---

108. John M. Wilkins and Shaun Hill, *Food in the Ancient World* (Malden, MA: Blackwell, 2006), 18.
109. Exodus 12:8 and Numbers 9:11.

and as garden escapees, dandelions have come to naturalize in many countries.[110] Though today the dandelion is widely considered a weed, many gardeners are coming to recognize its value. It is making a resurgence as a culinary and medicinal herb and is valued for its importance to the many pollinators who depend upon it as a food and pollen source.

Dandelion leaves are nutritious greens and can be eaten raw, sautéed, or steamed. Add young leaves to salads to enhance psychic sight. Add to sautés to add positive energy for empowerment. Magickally, dandelions are associated with Jupiter, Sagittarius, and Hecate and are symbols of hope, summer, and childhood.

Endive
Confidence, libido, loneliness, love, and opportunities

Endive is a bitter salad green that can be eaten to rouse passions and to soothe a bitter stomach. Raw endive leaves are loaded with vitamins K, A, and B_9 (folate). They are also a source of kaempferol, an antioxidant known to reduce inflammation and inhibit the growth of cancer cells. Make a green drink by whizzing the leaves with coconut water. Sip it to open the mind and become aware of opportunities or open to possibilities. Add the crisp, slightly bitter leaves to your salads to boost health and lift mood. Endive has an uplifting energy to help the mind release the past and look ahead with hope. Pour boiling water over a cup of chopped endive leaves and infuse for 10 minutes. Strain and add the liquid to bathwater to ease the pain of a broken heart. Or sip it as tea to soothe headaches and banish troubled feelings. Stuff a jar with endive and cover with olive oil. Seal tightly and allow it to macerate for 2 weeks. Strain out the herb and use oil as massage oil to boost confidence and remedy loneliness.

Fenugreek
Beauty, increase, and money

Fenugreek is used as an herb, a spice, and a vegetable called *methi* popular in Indian cuisine. The fresh clover-like leaves are used in salads and eaten as microgreens. They are added to sauces, stews, and curries. Fenugreek is an herb of increase. Women in the Middle East, North Africa, and India have used the seeds and leaves of fenugreek since ancient times

110. Brigitte Mars, *Dandelion Medicine: Remedies and Recipes to Detoxify, Nourish, and Stimulate* (Pownal, VT: Storey Publishing, 1999), 26.

to stimulate and increase milk flow.[111] Fenugreek is associated with Mercury and Apollo. It has energy to increase charisma. Add a fenugreek infusion to bathwater and soak to empower a sparkling personality. Fill a jar with fenugreek leaves and cover with olive oil. Seal tightly and allow the oil to macerate for 2 weeks. Strain out the herb. Massage the oil into skin or use in hair to increase health and beauty.

Kale
Clean thinking, energy, expansion, happiness, health, and mood

Kale is a nutrient-dense green leafy vegetable that is a member of species *Brassica oleracea* and is also called leaf cabbage. Recipes that mention kale, along with cabbage and turnips, were recorded in the oldest medieval Italian manuscripts dating back to the 1400s.[112] Kale is packed with vitamins, minerals, fiber, and protein. It is a source of easily digested calcium. It is loaded with phytonutrients, powerful inflammatory molecules that improve liver function and protect brain cells. Add kale to a smoothie to cleanse, revitalize, and alkalize your body's chemistry. Drink whenever you need a mental reset. Eat young raw kale leaves to gain strength and courage. Add leaves to salads with beets and feta to improve clear sight. Make a smoothie with 1 cup of fresh kale, 1 cup of coconut water, and a handful of ice to drink before any meeting for a quick wit and focused mind. All greens are associated with money and growth, and kale is no exception. Add it to expansion and wealth recipes to boost energy.

Lettuce
Luck, money, peace, restoration, and wealth

Lettuce is a common name to cultivars in the daisy family first cultivated by the ancient Egyptians for its edible leaves.[113] Lettuce is a diuretic, as it stimulates the kidneys. It is a rich source of antioxidants that slow the aging process. The milky juice contains a mild sedative called lacturcarium that induces calmness and sleep. Eat before bed to treat anxiety and insomnia or aid in dreamwork. Lettuce possesses anti-inflammatory properties

---

111. Roger Phillips and Nicky Foy, *The Random House Book of Herbs* (New York: Random House, 1990), 17.

112. Ariane Helou, trans., "An Anonymous Tuscan Cookery Book," *Ariane Nada Hedou* (blog), June 26, 2013, https://arianehelou.com/2013/06/26/an-anonymous-tuscan-cookery-book/. The *Anonimo Toscano* is a fourteenth-century manuscript written by an anonymous Tuscan. It contains 183 recipes from the Middle Ages. It was first published in Bologna in 1863 and is now kept in the Bologna University Library.

113. Joan P. Alcock, *Food in the Ancient World* (Westport, CT: Greenwood Press, 2006), 55.

that help with controlling inflammation. It is associated with Jupiter, the element water, and the moon. Lettuce has energy for health, peace, and prosperity. Combine with watercress for a healthy serving of protection.

Mustard Greens
Courage, faith, fertility, and protection

The mustard family is a huge family, some of whose members are grown for their nutrient-rich greens and spicy-flavored seeds, which are ground to produce the popular condiment mustard. The ancient Greeks believed mustard was given to mankind by Asclepius, the god of healing, and a plaster of mustard paste has been used down through the ages to relieve chest congestion, muscle cramps, digestive problems, and toothaches.[114] Mustard also has properties for fertility and protection. Before working with a dark energy, disguise yourself with a string of mustard leaves to wear on your head. Or staple mustard leaves to a plain Halloween mask to conceal your identity.

Add mustard greens to meals to promote courage and valor. Rinse them well and cut out the tough stem by tearing or running a knife down the length to strip the leaf part away before preparing.

Spinach
Clear sight, health, longevity, money, strength, and vitality

An edible flowering plant in the Amaranthaceae family, spinach is native to Asia. Spinach is loaded with nutrients, and when included in one's diet, it improves health and vitality and sharpens the ability to think clearly. Spinach is loaded with vitamin K, vitamin B_9, lutein, and beta-carotene, which helps slow cognitive decline. Add spinach to your diet to protect your brain from Alzheimer's disease, increase health, and boost physical strength. Magickally, spinach is associated with Jupiter and Mars, and like other greens, spinach has properties for money and growth. As with kale, you can make a smoothie with 1 cup of fresh spinach, 1 cup of coconut water, and a handful of ice. Drink before any meeting in which you need to think on your feet or go head-to-head with someone. Eat spinach to gain strength and courage or clear sight.

....
114. Claudia Karabaic Sargent, *A Gift of Herbs* (New York: Viking Studio Books, 1991), n.p.

Swiss Chard
Antiaging, beauty, health, and vitality

Chard is also known as silver beet. The young leaves are eaten for salads, while mature leaves are steamed or sautéed. They are loaded with vitamin K: one cup contains three times your daily requirement. Chard is also packed with vitamins A, C, and E. It is high in fiber and contains riboflavin and B_6. It is a good source of manganese, magnesium, potassium, and iron. Eat chard to protect your health. Add to meals to prevent premature aging, anemia, and sickness. Chard is also high in beta-carotene, which helps protect the skin. It fortifies eye health, helps reduce blood pressure, and helps prevent heart disease and cancer. Eating chard also reduces inflammation and can hasten recovery after a rigorous physical workout. Eat it to enhance athletic performance.

Turnip Greens
Banishing, ending relationships, money, protection, and warding

Turnips are members of the mustard family. Turnips were cultivated by the Celts and Germans.[115] They were a staple food across Europe, as they store for months and survive freezing winters. Turnip greens are a good source of vitamins K, A, and C, manganese, and fiber. They are associated with money and growth and both Lughnasadh/Lammas and Samhain. Incorporate them into spells for banishing negative energy and warding your home. To deter unwanted advances, serve turnips to the one you are trying to evade. To prepare turnip greens, cut out the tough stem by tearing or running a knife down the length to strip the leaf part away.

Watercress
Aphrodisiac, cleansing, fertility, healing, protection, strength, and wisdom

Watercress (*Nasturtium officinale*) is a fast-growing semiaquatic member of the mustard family with edible leaves. Although it shares the genus *Nasturtium*, watercress is different from the garden flower nasturtium, which was named after it because it has a similar peppery flavor. Watercress is a living food, eaten since antiquity. To the Greeks it was an herb to treat blood disorders, while some Romans ate watercress to "help them make 'bold

---

115. Christopher Cumo, *Foods That Changed History* (Santa Barbara, CA: ABC-Clio, 2015), 400.

decisions.'"[116] In England watercress is popular in soups and tea sandwiches. It is packed with nutrients to boost health and aid brain function. The old phrase "he never ate his watercress" refers to someone who lacks intelligence.

Watercress has a pleasant crunch and a lightly pungent and peppery flavor. It is loaded with vitamins, minerals, and antioxidants and even has anticancer properties. A serving of watercress boosts health as it detoxifies environmental toxicants and carcinogens.

There is an old saying that professes, "Watercress should not be gathered when there is no *R* in the month." And as we know with old sayings, the warning is usually about mold growth or algae bloom.

Watercress seeds work well in sprouting spells to promote healing and inspire new opportunities. The sprouts brim with a primeval life force that can be used to fuel any intention you choose to set. Eat the sprouts to boost health and vigor and to strengthen cognitive abilities.

Raw Lettuce, Greens, and Sprouts Recipes

Mom's Italian Chopped Garden Salad

Dinner at our house was not complete without a side of Mom's salad. Every summer evening, no matter what she was serving, she'd get out her giant teak salad bowl and proceed to fill it with a concoction. While it always started with a chopped onion and romaine, Mom would add other vegetables, gifts from Dad's garden, as they came available. Sometimes she would chop up a large sweet red pepper or add a sliced cucumber, or some evenings it would be a shredded carrot, but I always liked it best when it was topped with a chopped avocado and garden sweet tomatoes. Occasionally she would make it fancy by tossing in a handful of pitted olives or a crumble of feta cheese, but always it was made with love and finished with a simple balsamic vinegar and olive oil vinaigrette that my brothers would always polish off, using torn pieces of bread to wipe the last bits out of the bowl.

This salad is brimming with refreshing mother-love energy to nurture and comfort.

For the salad, you will need:

1 cup onion, chopped (I favor red, but use your favorite.)

1 large head romaine lettuce, washed, dried, and chopped

....

116. "Watercress History & Facts," B&W Quality Growers, accessed February 22, 2021, https://bwquality growers.com/watercress/history-and-facts/.

1 large sweet garden tomato, chopped, or a handful of grape tomatoes, halved

1 avocado, halved, peeled, pitted, and cut into chunks

While this is a simple salad, you can personalize it by adding other veggies.

For the vinaigrette, you will need:

 good virgin olive oil

 good balsamic vinegar

 salt and pepper to taste

Mix together to taste, pour over the salad, and toss.

Endive, Avocado, and Grapefruit Salad

This salad boasts a bright, refreshing energy to energize gatherings and nurture relationships.

For the salad, you will need:

 2 avocados, peeled, pitted, and cut into slices

 4 medium endives, trimmed, leaves separated

 1 red grapefruit, peeled and segmented

 2 tangerines, peeled and segmented

 ½ cup walnut pieces

For the vinaigrette, you will need:

 1 teaspoon honey

 2 Tablespoons tangerine juice

 1 Tablespoon apple cider vinegar

 ¼ cup olive oil

 1 shallot, chopped

 salt and pepper to taste

Arrange the avocado slices, endive leaves, and citrus segments on a large platter. In a small bowl, whisk together honey, tangerine juice, and vinegar. As you whisk, slowly add in the oil, whisking until emulsified. Add the shallot, and let the vinaigrette sit for at least 10 minutes. Spoon the vinaigrette over the salad and top with walnuts. Season with salt and pepper to taste.

Cucumber, Watercress, and Alfalfa Sprout Tea Sandwich

Whip up a plate of these refreshing tea sandwiches to restore energy, promote healing, and inspire new opportunities. Both cucumbers and watercress hold a restorative, healing energy to lift the spirit, body, and mind.

You will need:

1 cucumber, peeled and very thinly sliced

½ cup butter, room temperature

½ cup watercress leaves, coarsely chopped

16 slices good white bread

salt

alfalfa sprouts

Place cucumber slices between layers of paper towels to remove excess moisture. In a small bowl, combine butter and watercress. Spread butter on one side of each slice of bread. Lay cucumber slices onto the buttered side of 8 slices of bread. Sprinkle with salt. Cover each with alfalfa sprouts. Top with the remaining slices of bread, buttered side down.

You may choose to carefully cut the sandwiches in half diagonally and then cut in half again. This recipe will yield 8 whole sandwiches, 16 halves, or 32 fourths. You may wish to trim off the bread crust.

For a lighter, brighter-tasting alternative, mix mayonnaise with lemon juice and use as spread instead of butter.

Cook Your Greens

Greens are very versatile. If you are cooking up delicate greens like spinach, all you need is to briefly wilt them in olive oil to make them palatable. Cabbages and bok choy do well in high-heat stir-fries that brown the tender leaves while leaving a bit of crunch in the stalk. Bitter greens like collard or mustard greens need a slow braise in bacon fat to mellow the bitterness. Some recipes call for mustard greens, collard greens, and turnip greens all together in one pot, and I've found this tastes good too.

Avoid grit in your greens by always rinsing them thoroughly, then dunking them in a large bowl of cold water. Change the water and repeat until there is no sandy residue on the bottom of the bowl.

Wilted Spinach with Hot Pepper Flakes

This recipe is loaded with feel-good energy to motivate, inspire, or get something moving.

You will need:

olive oil

2 cloves garlic, minced

red pepper flakes

3 cups spinach

salt and pepper

1 lemon, cut into wedges

In a large skillet, heat the olive oil. Add garlic and red pepper flakes and cook until fragrant, about 1 minute. Add spinach and stir to coat. Cook until greens begin to wilt. Season with salt and pepper. Serve hot with a squeeze of lemon.

Italian Cooked Cabbage and Toasted Cheese

This dish is known as *crostone* in Italy. It is often served in the fall and winter when lettuce and tomatoes are out of season. The cabbage brings energy for good health and luck while the nurturing rich energy of cheese adds energy for success and vitality, making this an energizing, healthy way to improve your diet during the colder months.

You will need:

olive oil

1 onion, chopped

½ pound red or purple cabbage, thinly sliced

3 cloves garlic, minced

1 Tablespoon red wine vinegar or apple cider vinegar

salt and pepper

8 slices bread

8 slices semisoft melting cheese like fontina, gruyère, provolone, gouda, or emmental

Add 1 Tablespoon of olive oil to a sauté pan and heat over medium heat. Add the onion and cook until clear. Drizzle olive oil over the cabbage and toss to coat. Add to the pan with the onion and cook for 5 minutes. Stir in garlic and vinegar and season to taste with salt and pepper. Cover pan and cook for 5 more minutes. When the cabbage is tender, remove from heat. Toast the bread and arrange the slices in a single layer on a baking sheet. Preheat the broiler. Top each slice of bread with a mound of cabbage and a slice of cheese. Put the baking sheet under the broiler until the cheese bubbles. Watch closely so the bread does not burn. Serve immediately.

Roasted Chard, Collards Greens, or Kale

Just as roasting brings out the deliciousness of most veggies, so it does with sturdy greens. Even the purest haters will change their mind after trying this dish. Serve it as a healthy snack to fortify health. Serve as a side to encourage prosperity.

You will need:
4 cups sturdy cooking greens: kale, chard, mustard, beet, collard, or turnip

olive oil

salt and pepper

Preheat the oven to 400 degrees Fahrenheit. Slide a baking sheet in to heat before you wash your greens. Wash your greens well, then remove the stem by running a knife down the edge of the thick portion to separate the leafy part. Discard the stem parts. Place the greens in a large bowl and sprinkle liberally with olive oil, stirring to coat. Season with salt and pepper. Carefully remove the hot baking sheet and arrange the greens over it. It will sizzle as the wet greens hit the hot surface. Return the baking sheet to the oven and roast for 10 minutes, flipping the greens halfway through cooking. When the greens are covered in brown spots, they are ready. They should be crispy but not burnt.

Green Drink

If you have trouble eating enough greens, you can drink them! In the summer a cold glass of spinach or kale gives your energy a zing. Drink it to punch up your health and vigor.

You will need:
1 cup coconut water

1 handful ice

1 handful greens

Any kind of green is good here, whether it's spinach, kale, or micro greens. Put the ingredients into a blender and whizz until drinkable. To make it sweet, blend in a banana, a handful of blueberries, or a couple of dates. To power up a detox, add cilantro and cucumber. Drink to empower. Green drinks are loaded with energy for vitality and success and will make your energy positively sparkle.

Green Sauce

This creamy sauce brims with energy to activate creative thought and prosperity.

You will need:

1 cup watercress

½ cup flat-leaf parsley

2 cloves garlic, chopped

1 Tablespoon apple cider vinegar or the juice of 1 lemon

½ cup plain yogurt, sour cream, or crème fraîche

salt and pepper to taste

dash of Worchestershire sauce, cayenne pepper, or favorite hot sauce
   (optional)

Add all greens, garlic, and vinegar or lemon juice to blender or food processor. Blend well and add yogurt to desired flavor and consistency, about ½ cup. Add salt, pepper, and optional seasoning to taste. Serve over eggs or fish.

Show Me the Money Green Mayonnaise

This rich mayonnaise is lovely over both potatoes and tomatoes. You can also use it as a dip or dressing to add fat and flavor to fish and chicken dishes. While arugula is the traditional green for green mayo, watercress and young dandelion greens also bring positive green energy to inspire new opportunities for prosperity and wealth.

You will need:

1 cup green leaves, stems removed

1 clove garlic

1 egg yolk

½ cup olive oil

2 Tablespoons lemon juice

salt and pepper

In a blender, combine greens with garlic, egg yolk, 1 teaspoon of olive oil, lemon juice, and salt and pepper. Whiz until incorporated. With the blender running, slowly add more oil and whiz to thicken. Refrigerate until ready to serve.

Jazz up this recipe with a handful of fresh herbs. Some I've used are basil, chives, dill, mint, oregano, parsley, and tarragon.

Sprouting Intentions Spell

Use the life force of the seed to sprout your deepest desires. This spell can be applied to any intention you wish to grow. Sprouts can be grown inside all year long. They can be cultivated in decorative jars, and once they've sprouted, add them to sandwiches and salads for an added energy boost to your meals.

This spell requires daily monitoring, so only begin when you have the time to spend a few moments with it each day for six consecutive days. Do not work this spell if you cannot afford the time. There is a danger of growing mold and bacteria if the seeds are not rinsed daily. Keep the process clean to reduce the chance of growing *E. coli*. Proceed with caution.

Choose your seeds, match them to your intention, and rinse them well. Some good choices for this spell include the following:

- Alfalfa (*Medicago sativa*), to increase fertility, harmony, or prosperity
- Cress (*Lepidium sativum*), to aid transitions and for remembrance
- Daikon Radish (*Raphanus sativus* var. *longipinnatus*), to increase joy, to promote health, and protect home
- Fenugreek (*Trigonella foenum-graecum*), to increase beauty or wealth
- Watercress (*Nasturtium officinale*), to promote healing, inspire new opportunities, and to strengthen the mind

You will need:

seeds of your choice

jar

piece of plastic needlework canvas or a thin piece of cheesecloth to top the jar

canning band (lid ring) if using canvas, or a rubber band if using cheesecloth,
  to hold it securely in place

masking tape or jar label

any symbol or image to tape to the jar to encourage your intention

Place the rinsed seeds in a large bowl and cover with water in a ratio of 1 part seeds to 3 parts water. Soak small seeds for 2 to 6 hours and large seeds like peas, lentils, and grains for 6 to 12 hours. Each seed contains a dormant plant. The soaking process wakes it so that it begins to grow. This life force is a primeval power, brimming with potential to fuel any intention we set.

Next, set up your jars so that you can keep the seeds rinsed. The goal is to create lids that secure the seeds in the jar while allowing the water to drain out. A daily rinse is necessary to inhibit bacterial growth. You can use cheesecloth and rubber bands or plastic needlework canvas cut to fit inside the lid rings for jar toppers. Plastic needlework canvas is cheap, it can be cut to fit any size lid, and it makes rinsing quick and easy. If you decided to use needlework canvas, choose the right gauge for your seed size and color for your intention. Take a marker and trace the lid. Cut the canvas out. Set the canvas in your canning band.

Fill the jar with seeds and water and put the lid on the jar. Turn the jar upside down to make sure the seeds stay in while the water drains out. Affix a label on the jar. Include any word, symbol, or image you want to influence your working. Intentions to strengthen a relationship, draw love or wealth, or increase health or beauty will be empowered.

When your jars are assembled, you will need to rinse your seeds again with clean water. Drain out the excess water and place in indirect sunlight. Make sure that you rinse and drain your jar 2 or 3 times each day with fresh cold water. Turn the jar upside down and gently shake so the excess water drains out as you say,

Welcome, tiny seeds, holders of life.
By the power of water and energy of the sun,
the embryo within wakes, a new life begun,
aligning energy to flow with intentions true,
fueling the work with blessings imbued.
(Speak your intention.)

Place the jar on a shelf. Monitor closely. The seeds should begin to sprout in 3 to 6 days. When the seeds have sprouted completely, remove them from the jar and rinse. Store the sprouts in the refrigerator to use in salads and sandwiches. You have just created a superfood brimming with life energy. When you eat it, remember your intention.

More Cruciferous Vegetables

Vegetables of the family Brassicaceae (also called Cruciferae) include arugula, bok choy, broccoli, brussels sprouts, cabbage, collard greens, kale, kohlrabi, and turnips and are also called cruciferous vegetables. The botanical name Cruciferae is New Latin for "cross-bearing," as the shape of the flower petals is thought to resemble a cross. These vegetables are loaded with energy for good health and protection and are rich in vitamins and minerals such as folate and vitamins C, E, and K. They contain sulforaphane, a sulfur-rich compound that helps fortify heart health and improve digestion, and glucosinolates, which have antibacterial and antiviral effects, protect cells from DNA damage, and help fight cancer.

Broccoli
Health, prosperity, protection, power, and vitality

Broccoli is a member of the cabbage family. The stalk and large flowering head are eaten as a vegetable. Broccoli is good for you. It is a superfood when it comes to fighting cancer. It contains sulforaphane, a substance that boosts the functions of human proteins that inhibit cancer cell growth.[117] Sulforaphane also reduces damage to arteries. Raw broccoli has ten times more sulforaphane than cooked broccoli. Broccoli is also a good source of the blood pressure–regulating minerals magnesium, calcium, and potassium. Broccoli holds energy to promote good health and vitality. Add it to recipes to guard against illness. Add raw broccoli to your diet to reduce inflammation, manage high blood pressure, and prevent heart attacks and strokes. Eat it with hummus to fortify heart health. Steam cauliflower and broccoli and top with a horseradish sauce to double the protective energy. Peel the stalk and add it to soups and stir-fries for a delicious, creamy addition.

....

117. Reza Bayat Mokhtari, Narges Baluch, Tina S. Homayouni, Evgeniya Morgatskaya, Sushil Kumar, Parandis Kazemi, and Herman Yeger, "The Role of Sulforaphane in Cancer Chemoprevention and Health Benefits: A Mini-Review," *Journal of Cell Communication and Signaling* 12, no. 1 (March 2018): 91–101, https://www.ncbi.nlm.nih.gov/pmc/articles/PMC5842175/.

Broccoli sprouts are power packed and at three days old contain twenty times more of the antioxidant glucoraphanin, the compound that converts to sulforaphane, than mature broccoli.[118] A recent study found that when broccoli is included in a daily diet, it improves social interaction, awareness, and communication of patients with autism spectrum disorder.[119] Broccoli is associated with Jupiter, the moon, and the element water.

Brussels Sprouts
Endurance, stability, protection, and water

Brussels sprouts are vegetables resembling small cabbages that grow along a stalk. They are good for you. They contain vitamins that grant energy for good health, and, if fixed correctly, brussels sprouts are delicious. Drizzle with olive oil and roast until tender for a treat with energy to awaken awareness of the magick afoot. Serve to family members to encourage good health and harmony. Or roast with carrots and potatoes and smash to make a delicious and hearty dish called bubble and squeak (see page 155) that can enhance your health, endurance, and tenacity. Brussels sprouts are a source of glucosinolates that help fight cancer, and the indole-3-carbinol that comes from the breakdown of those glucosinoltes is a chemical that boosts DNA repair. They are a member of the cabbage family and, like the cabbage, hold the power of protection. Brussels sprouts are associated with the moon and the element water.

Cauliflower
Health, nurturing, and protection

Cauliflower is an autumn food brimming with a protective, nurturing feminine energy that guards against illness when eaten. Cauliflower is loaded with vitamins and antioxidants to nourish and repair your body at a cellular level. It has anti-inflammatory properties and

....
118. Ming Tian, Xiaoyun Xu, Hao Hu, Yu Liu, and Siyi Pan, "Optimization of Enzymatic Production of Sulforaphane in Broccoli Sprouts and Their Total Antioxidant Activity at Different Growth and Storage Days," *Journal of Food Science and Technology* 54, no. 1 (January 2017): 209–18, https://www.ncbi.nlm.nih.gov/pmc/articles/PMC5305717/.

119. Rhoda Lynch, "Sulforaphane from Broccoli Reduces Symptoms of Autism: A Follow-Up Case Series from a Randomized Double-Blind Study," *Global Advances in Health and Medicine* 6 (October 2017), n.p., https://journals.sagepub.com/doi/full/10.1177/2164957X17735826; Gail Sullivan, "Study: Chemical in broccoli shows promise as autism treatment," *Washington Post,* October 15, 2014, https://www.washingtonpost.com/news/morning-mix/wp/2014/10/15/study-chemical-in-broccoli-shows-promise-as-autism-treatment/.

contains glucosinolates and thiocyanates, which increase the liver's ability to neutralize toxins. It is low in calories, high in fiber, and rich in indole-3-carbinol, a compound that comes from the breakdown of the glucosinolates, which may have cancer-fighting properties. Steam and eat it to protect your health. Steam cauliflower with potatoes and mash. Season with dill, mustard seeds, or rosemary for a protective dish that will fortify your family during the cold and flu season. Even the leaves are edible and can be roasted with olive oil to make a delicious, nutritious dish brimming with positive energy. Cauliflower is associated with the moon and water.

Kohlrabi
Beauty, health, protection, and sight

Kohlrabi is a bulbous vegetable also called a German turnip. It is popular in Eastern Europe, where it is often eaten whole like an apple. Like other brassicas, kohlrabi contains phytochemicals that help reduce inflammation and lower the risk of heart disease and cancer.[120] Kohlrabi is a good source of vitamins C, B_6, and fiber to boost immune health and aid cell repair from free radical damage.[121] Kohlrabi has a sweet but peppery, cabbage- or radish-like flavor. Peel and cut it into crunchy strips and eat raw. Or drizzle with olive oil and roast until tender. Boil and mash kohlrabi and mix it in with potatoes to spice up the flavor.

Kohlrabi greens are cooked and eaten like turnip greens. Pick young leaves and add them to sandwiches and salads to boost healing energy. Kohlrabi also holds energy to ward and will ward a space of unwanted presences. Take a large kohlrabi bulb and carve a face on it. Add it to fall decorations to add protection to your home. Grow it in the garden to ward the space of mischievous energies.

Bubble and Squeak

Bubble and squeak is Brit-speak for leftovers. Apparently it's a common thing over there to dump all your leftovers together and make a "mashup." Don't let the idea put you off. My family learned to love brussels sprouts with this hearty and satisfying meatless meal. The buttery potatoes mellow the flavor of the brussels sprouts, and the leftovers serve up

120. Katey Davidson, "What Is Kohlrabi? Nutrition, Benefits, and Uses," Healthline, August 15, 2019, https://www.healthline.com/nutrition/kohlrabi.

121. Katey Davidson, "What Is Kohlrabi? Nutrition, Benefits, and Uses," Healthline, August 15, 2019, https://www.healthline.com/nutrition/kohlrabi.

even better the next day. Serve it to boost magickal energies for endurance, stability, and protection.

You will need:

1 pound brussels sprouts, washed and halved lengthwise

1 pound carrots, peeled and coarsely chopped

1 onion, coarsely chopped

olive oil

4 cups peeled and cubed potatoes

butter

salt and pepper to taste

Preheat your oven to 400 degrees Fahrenheit. In a roasting pan, add the brussels sprouts, carrots, and onion pieces and toss with olive oil until coated. Roast until dark and caramelized, about 50 minutes.

As the vegetables roast, boil the potatoes until they are tender. Drain off the water, mash the potatoes with butter, and season with salt and pepper to taste.

Mix the vegetables with the potatoes and serve. If you end up with leftovers, you can pat the cold mixture into disks and pan-fry until brown and crispy. Both ways are delicious.

The Alliums

The onion, shallot, leek, garlic, and scallion are all members of the *Allium* genus, and all contain sulfur compounds that give them their characteristic taste, smell, and eye-irritating qualities as well as their many health benefits. Each contains an embryo plant inside waiting to come to life, and each holds magickal properties for healing, protection, and strength.

Chives
Health and protection

Chives are the smallest of the edible onions. They are packed with goodness, so sprinkle a teaspoon on your baked potato. Chives are loaded with potassium, calcium, beta-carotene, folic acid, and vitamin K. Eat them to protect your health. Plant them around your home for protection. Tie them in bunches and hang them to ward off negative energy. Chives can be used in knot magick. Take a bunch of chives and braid them together as you visualize the problem being tied up with the chives. Tie the braid into a knot and bury where it will not be disturbed.

Garlic
Evil eye, fertility, health, protection, purification, strength, and warding

Garlic has been used for thousands of years for food, seasoning, medicine, and magick. Its name in Sanskrit means "slayer of monsters."[122] Through the ages people have carried garlic to ward against all sorts of evils.[123] Heads of garlic were strung and worn to repel vampires, and even the smaller blood suckers—mosquitoes and ticks—will avoid you when you wear it. Hang a braid of garlic to guard against evil and deter thieves.

Garlic is associated with Mars and the element fire. It is loaded with warrior energy for protection. Add it to soups and sauces to protect health and ward your body of negative energy. Eat a clove of garlic to preserve your personal space. When you have to go up against someone, carry a clove with you to shield yourself from their negative energy and keep it from following you. Wear garlic or rub it on your skin to stay hex free. Before meeting a rival or going to a haunted place, take 3 cloves of garlic and grind them into a paste. Rub the paste on the soles of your shoes to keep the negative energy from following you home. Rub it on the front step of your home to keep a troublemaker away. Stuff the mouth of a poppet with a clove of garlic and then sew the mouth shut to stop gossip. If your luck turns bad, your health fails, or you suspect you may have been cursed by the evil eye, make a garlic infusion with 9 cloves of garlic, boiled for 9 minutes in spring water. Strain, add to bathwater, and soak.

Garlic is highly nutritious. It contains allicin, a compound with the power to combat sickness, including the common cold. Garlic lowers the risk of heart disease by lowering high blood pressure and high cholesterol. And new studies are showing that the antioxidants contained in garlic help prevent Alzheimer's disease and dementia by repressing free radicals that contribute to the aging process.[124] When you find yourself in the midst of

....

122. Health Research Staff, *Garlic* (Pomeroy, WI: Health Research Books, 1983), 20.

123. Health Research Staff, *Garlic*, 20.

124. Carmia Borek, "Garlic Reduces Dementia and Heart-Disease Risk," *Journal of Nutrition* 136, no. 3, supplement (March 2006): 810s–12s, https://pubmed.ncbi.nlm.nih.gov/16484570/; B. C. Mathew and R. S. Biju, "Neuroprotective Effects of Garlic," *Libyan Journal of Medicine* 3, no. 1 (March 2008): 23–33, https://www.ncbi.nlm.nih.gov/pmc/articles/PMC3074326/.

cold and flu season, combine crushed garlic with ginger, onions, and broth for a powerful soup to bolster your immune system.

Garlic cloves add a spicy, pungent flavor that mellows as it cooks. It is peeled and minced and added to recipes to give depth to the flavor. Sometimes whole garlic cloves are roasted until caramelized. They are used as garnish or mashed and added to sauces and dressings. Add a squeeze of lemon and a spoon of roasted garlic to mayonnaise for a creamy, rich aioli to use as dip or spread to jazz up chicken, vegetables, or even a sandwich. When you come upon a clove too small to use, tuck it pointed-side up into a pot of soil. Each clove contains an embryo plant waiting to wake.

The clove is not the only edible part of the garlic plant. Garlic shoots, or scapes, can be clipped in the spring and early summer to add a delicate garlicky flavor to savory dishes. And when you cook with garlic, don't toss out the paper skins. Put them aside to burn in rituals for exorcism, repulsion of energy suckers, and purification of spaces and objects. Crumble garlic skins with bay leaves and burn to rid yourself or your house of negativity.

Green Onion
Clear thinking, healing, and protection

The green onion is also known as the scallion. Green onions have a milder taste than most onions. They are a good source of vitamin A for healthy eyesight and to treat colds. They contain a high level of vitamin K, which helps decrease the effects of Alzheimer's disease. Shred green onions and use to top soups, chilies, and noodle bowls. Add a green onion to a bowl of ramen to increase flavor and healing energy. Chop a green onion and serve it with chopped tomato to dress up bean dishes or Mexican foods. Add chopped green onion and a dollop of sour cream to a baked potato and serve for a simple, hot, nourishing meal with nurturing energy to comfort and protect.

Leek
Exorcism, health, love, luck, and protection

The leek is an elegant onion with a mild flavor and a tender texture. Leeks add a wonderful flavor to potato soups. They contain healing properties and, when added to recipes, protect the physical body from illness. Leeks lower blood sugar levels in your body. Boiled leeks offer a flavorful, easy way to boost health and fight dangerous free radicals in your body. Take 1 pound of washed leeks. Chop off the green stalks and discard. Take the white and light green part of the leek and remove the root end. Cut each stalk in half lengthwise.

Rinse well. Soil is often trapped between the layers. Place the leek pieces in a pot and cover with water. Bring to a boil and simmer uncovered for 20 minutes. Pour off liquid to sip as cleansing soup. Drizzle the cooked leek pieces with olive oil and lemon juice and serve as a side vegetable to protect against sickness. Or puree and serve under grilled sausages or fish for a hearty meal brimming with protective energy. Eat leeks in moderation. They are high in fiber and can cause stomachaches.

Magickally, leeks are associated with Mars and the element fire. They hold energy to draw good luck and boost positive energy, and like other alliums, leeks contain bold protective powers. When you are preparing leeks, chop off the root end and tuck it into a pot of soil. Like celery and green onions, the root can regrow a whole new plant. Set the pot near the entrance of your home to discourage negativity and thwart psychic attacks. Hang items decorated in leek motifs to stand guard and protect.

Onion
Banishing, healing, lust, money, oaths, prophetic dreams, and protection

A strong-tasting bulb rich in a variety of organic sulfur compounds, onion has been used as a food source since ancient times. In Egypt onions represented eternity and were a favored funeral offering second only to bread.[125] Onions are loaded with flavorful volatile oils, and sautéing one in butter is the first step in many modern recipes.

Onions hold energy for protection. They are used in recipes to banish harmful energies and ward against hexes and hauntings. Plant in the garden to protect the home. When harvesting, leave the tops and braid them for a talisman to hang in your kitchen. Cut an onion into quarters and place at the four corners of a room to break a hex or absorb negative emotions after a confrontation. Set an onion out in a room to absorb the negative energy of a previous occupant. Or burn onion skins to drive out what you want to banish. Mix with garlic skins to deflect malevolent words and jealous eyes. Make an onion talisman to ward your home with a small white onion and nine black-headed pins. Stick the pins in the onion and place in a window to stand guard against evil trying to enter.

Onions come in different varieties, each with its own flavor of protection:

- White onions clear away obstacles. When preparing them, come to center and peel away the layers as you visualize the obstacle growing smaller.
- Yellow onions can be served to end quarrels and heal a rift between friends.

....

125. Kiple, *A Movable Feast,* 32.

- Red onions add fiery energy for lust and action.
- Purple onions can instill popularity and power.

Shallot
Health, protection, and purification

The shallot is a small onion, a member of the *Allium* genus. Though shallots have a milder flavor than other members of the onion family, they contain more flavonoids and phenols, which make them flavorful and nutritious. The energy of the shallot is both cleansing and protective. When you find yourself stuck in a rut or caught in a loop of misfortune, add an infusion made from shallots to your bathwater and soak in it to change your luck.

The shallot has a paper skin that can be burned to remove negativity from your home. Mix with other allium skins to break a curse or remedy the evil eye.

The Hearty Roots

Roots and tubers are believed to be the first regularly gathered vegetables as they were protected from the elements and could be stored for long periods. Carrots and turnips have been cultivated for more than 5,000 years.[126] Parsnips too have a long history. They have been found on archaeological sites that dated back to the Iron Age.[127] It was the cooked starches in these foods that are now being attributed as the factor that "triggered and sustained the growth of the human brain."[128] Our big brains need carbs, and it was the starch in the ancestral diets that supplied the glucose needed.

Beet
Aphrodisiac, beauty, clear sight, earth energy, healing, love, and youth

A vegetable plant with broad leaves and a large taproot, the beet is also known as garden beet, table beet, and beetroot. Beets are delicious and easy to prepare. Simply wash and trim the root and place it in a baking dish. Cover with foil and roast at 400 degrees Fahr-

---

126. John Stolarczyk and Jules Janick, "Carrot: History and Iconography," *Chronica Horticulturae* 51, no. 2 (2011): 1–2, http://www.carrotmuseum.co.uk/finaljournal.pdf; Cumo, *Foods That Changed History*, 400.

127. Alcock, *Food in the Ancient World*, 52.

128. Karen Hardy, "Starchy Cards, Not Paleo Diet, Advanced the Human Race," University of Sydney News, August 10, 2015, https://www.sydney.edu.au/news-opinion/news/2015/08/10/starchy-carbs--not-a-paleo-diet--advanced-the-human-race.html.

enheit until tender. This could take between 50 and 90 minutes depending upon the size of the roots. Remove the skin and serve hot or cold. And don't throw out the greens. The leafy greens have a higher nutritional value than the root and hold energy to heal past hurts and ease old wounds. Add young leaves to a salad to patch up a relationship. They are packed with antioxidants and have more iron than spinach. All greens are associated with money and growth, but these ultra-healthy greens can be cooked up and added to food magick to improve decision-making and aid clear sight.

The ancient Greeks and Romans believed eating beets "builds up the blood," explains organic gardener Wolf Storl in *A Curious History of Vegetables*.[129] Beets hold energy to prolong life and maintain health and beauty. They have a lovely earthy flavor and are imbued with earth energy, and when consumed, they can aid in grounding and balancing emotions. Beets are also a food of love. The deep red root is associated with Aphrodite. The root, as with all roots, can be used as a poppet to ground a relationship or bind a lover. Red ink made from beetroot juice will boost love magicks.

Carrot
Beauty, clear sight, fertility, protection, strength, and youth

Carrots have been a favorite garden root vegetable down through the ages. Both the Greeks and the Romans cultivated carrots, although they weren't orange but off-white or purple. It wasn't until the 1500s that orange carrots were developed.[130] Carrots are rich in beta-carotene, an antioxidant that fights free radicals, repairs skin tissue, protects against sun damage, eliminates wrinkles, protects eye health, and slows aging. A daily snack of raw carrots will remedy night blindness and restore hair and nail health. For a supertonic loaded with magickal health benefits, juice equal amounts of carrots, apples, and beets. Drink immediately to imbue beauty energy, boost health, and restore vigor.

Carrots are associated with Mars and masculine energy. Add them to meals to strengthen male virility or boost a woman's energies for confidence, leadership, and strength. Serve a dish of carrots to balance emotions and stimulate the mind. Eat them raw to open communication channels, boost awareness, or stimulate fertility. Carrot seeds aid in vision quests and clear-seeing exercises.

....

129. Storl, *A Curious History of Vegetables*, 233–34.

130. "Carrots History: The Early Years," World Carrot Museum, accessed March 24, 2021, http://www.carrot museum.co.uk/history1.html.

Celeriac
Beauty, cheerfulness, lust, mental powers, prosperity, and rest

Celeriac, also known as celery root, is a variety of celery with a bulbous root. It was used in Egypt, Greece, and Italy and is suspected to be the plant *selinon* mentioned in Homer's *Odyssey*.[131] It is high in fiber and low in fat and calories. It is a good source of vitamins B_6, C and K, manganese, phosphorus, and potassium. A 2018 study speculates that eating celeriac, used in traditional Chinese medicine to reduce tension in the walls of blood vessels, is helpful in combating Parkinson's disease in mice.[132] Celeriac is peeled and cooked to produce a creamy, delicious dish with energy to boost awareness and draw opportunities.

Jicama
Beauty and health

Jicama is a round and bulbous root vegetable native to Mexico and Central and South America. It is eaten both raw and cooked. It is a good source of vitamin C to reduce inflammation and boost the immune system. Jicama is high in fiber and low in calories, making it a lovely fat-flushing snack. Jicama is loaded with earth energy to ground and balance. Eat it raw like an apple or slice it and use in place of chips or crackers. Dip it in a healthy dip for a satisfying grounding snack. Peel and chop it and add it to stir-fries for a crunchy, energetic boost. Cut it into matchsticks and toss with shredded apples, carrots, mayo, and vinegar for a bright slaw loaded with energy to protect health and encourage clear thinking.

Parsnip
Creation, earth, health, male, and sex magick

The parsnip was a wild root that grew across most of Europe. It was popular with Celtic and German tribes who grew fields of the root. Though they look like a white carrot, their slightly sweet, earthy-woodsy flavor is unique. History tells that Roman Emperor Tiberius

131. Jack Staub, *75 Exciting Vegetables for Your Garden* (Layton, UT: Gibbs Smith, 2005), 54.

132. Pennapa Chonpathompikunlert, Phetcharat Boonruamkaew, Wanida Sukketsiri, Pilaiwanwadee Hutamekalin, and Morakot Sroyraya, "The Antioxidant and Neurochemical Activity of *Apium graveolens* L. and Its Ameliorative Effect on MPTP-Induced Parkinson-like Symptoms in Mice," *BMC Complementary Medicine and Alternative Medicines* 18, no. 1 (March, 2018): 103, https://www.ncbi.nlm.nih.gov/pmc/articles/PMC5859653/.

liked them so much he had them imported.[133] While most of the world ate parsnips, the Irish made a beer out of them.[134] Though they look like a white carrot, they have a unique flavor that is part earthy, part woodsy, and slightly sweet. These delicious roots are most often roasted, mashed into potatoes, or made into chips. The parsnip was treasured as one of the earliest fresh harvests of the year. For unlike the carrot, the parsnip can be left in the ground all winter. In fact, the chill of frosts improves its sweetness and flavor. Dig it up just before use, when the ground is not frozen.

Potato
Compassion, protection, stored energy, and wishing

The potato is a tuberous root of a perennial in the nightshade family. Though many think of the Irish when they think of the potato, it was first cultivated in South America, where it was a staple food, about eight thousand years ago.[135] The Incas believed that the potato was one of the Earth Mother's daughters. They named her Axomamma (also Acsumamma and Ajomamma) and held potatoes as "emblems of female powers of creation."[136] Spanish explorers introduced potatoes to Europe in the second half of the sixteenth century. By 1600, they'd slowly spread from Spain to France and Italy but were treated with suspicion due to being members of the nightshade family. But as Europe's population continued to rise, the monarchs began to see the potential of the potato as a protection against famine should a grain crop fail. The working class was slow to warm to it. It took propaganda in the form of pamphlets and recipe booklets and even a bit of reverse psychology to get the European diet to embrace it.[137]

Potatoes are associated with Saturn, Pluto, the moon, and the element earth. They hold a nurturing, grounded energy. Make up a meal to ground and comfort by serving a baked potato with butter and sour cream. Add chives, rosemary, parsley, or dill to add protection.

....

133. Storl, *A Curious History of Vegetables*, 188–89.

134. Storl, *A Curious History of Vegetables*, 186.

135. National Research Council, *Lost Crops of the Incas: Little-Known Plants of the Andes with Promise for Worldwide Cultivation* (Washington, DC: National Academy Press, 1989), 93.

136. Rebecca Earle, *Potato* (London: Bloomsbury Academic, 2019), 14; Irene Silverblatt, *Moon, Sun, and Witches* (Princeton, NJ: Princeton University Press, 1987), 27.

137. Michel Pitrat and Claude Foury, *Histoires de légumes* (Paris: Institut National de la Recherche Agronomique, 2003), 167.

Steam cauliflower with potatoes and mash to make a protective dish that will help your family avoid sickness. A potato can be used as a poppet.

Radish
Health, joy, and protection

An edible root of the Brassicaceae family native to Asia, the radish was domesticated in Europe in pre-Roman times and now is grown throughout the world as a popular vegetable eaten raw, pickled, and cooked.[138] In the past it was a winter diet of shredded radish and beer that sustained much of Europe's country population and prevented scurvy.[139]

The radish holds robust male energy for protection and, when eaten, can protect against the evil eye. Radishes have a short germination time, making them one of the first garden vegetables to sprout. Radish sprouts are a spicy-flavored microgreen loaded with enzymes, antioxidants, protein, minerals, and vitamins. Add a handful to any sandwich to add a spicy crunch, boost nutrition, and protect health. Perform a sprouting spell with radish seeds to encourage positive energy to grow in your life. Plant radishes in kitchen window pots to promote happiness and cheer. Add them to foods to increase good humor and protect health. A tea made from an infusion of grated radish promotes digestive health. Radish greens are chock-full of vitamins and antioxidants. Eat them raw or steamed to boost health and increase vitality.

Rutabaga
Earth, health, luck, male, prosperity, and protection

Most of the world calls this vegetable a "swede," but in North America this root is known as the rutabaga. Rutabagas have a unique delicate sweetness and a slight peppery flavor that is milder than turnips. Rutabagas are members of the mustard family. They are high in fiber and are a good source of potassium, beta-carotene, and calcium. Like most root vegetables, rutabagas carry earth energy. Eat them to stay grounded. When the weather turns cold, roast a bunch of roots. Take ½ pound each of carrots, parsnips, rutabagas, and turnips. Wash, peel, and cut into 1-inch wedges. In a large mixing bowl, crush 3 cloves of garlic. Add the chopped roots and drizzle generously with olive oil. Stir to coat and season

---

138. Staub, *75 Exciting Vegetables for Your Garden*, 174.

139. Storl, *A Curious History of Vegetables*, 225.

with salt and pepper. Cover with foil and roast on a baking sheet at 400 degrees Fahrenheit until roots are tender, about 1 hour. Serve to bolster health and foster bonding.

Sweet Potato
Ancestor veneration, beauty, comfort, health, and love

Sweet potatoes are the edible tuberous roots of an herbaceous perennial vine. While they are often grouped with their distant relative the potato (*Solanum tuberosum*), the sweet potato is actually in the *Ipomoea* genus along with the moon flower and the morning glory.

Sweet potatoes are good for you. They are high in fiber, minerals, and vitamins, including beta-carotene, a potent antioxidant that fights free radicals as it protects cell health. Sweet potatoes are associated with Venus, love, and the earth. Magickally, sweet potatoes enhance the abilities to give and to receive love. Eating them will help balance and center energy and bring comfort to the brokenhearted. Serve them to the one you desire, to encourage love and protect health. Sprinkle them with ginger to turn your encounter lusty. A sweet potato can be used as a poppet or carved as an effigy to use in love magicks.

Turnip
Banishing, ending relationships, money, protection, and warding

Turnips are members of the mustard family. They were a staple food across Europe as they store for months and survive freezing winters. They have a mild, slightly peppery flavor, and when pulled from the garden and eaten raw, they taste similar to a radish. Peel, cube, and toss with olive oil and roast in the oven for a healthy dish similar to roasted potatoes.

Turnips are good for you. They are a good source of fiber and are loaded with antioxidants and minerals. They contain vitamins A, B_1, B_2, B_3, B_5, B_6, B_9 (folate), C, E, and K, as well as calcium, manganese, magnesium, potassium, iron, and copper. And turnips contain glucosinolates and phytochemicals, compounds that may lower your risk of developing cancer and boost liver function.

Magickally, turnips carry grounding protective earth energy. They were the original jack-o'-lanterns used to ward off unwanted presences and are associated with both Lammas and Samhain. Incorporate them into recipes to banish negative energy and ward your home. Turnips hold energy to deter attention. Serve them to someone you are trying to evade to avert their advances. Turnip greens are a good source of vitamins K, A, and C, manganese, and fiber. They are associated with money and growth.

Root Vegetable Recipes

Roasted Root Vegetables

This is a warm, hearty dish brimming with earth energy for balance, good health, and comfort.

You will need:

3 carrots

1 sweet potato

1 kohlrabi

2 parsnips

1 turnip or rutabaga

1 beet

3 cloves garlic, minced

rosemary

salt and pepper

olive oil

Preheat the oven to 400 degrees Fahrenheit. Clean and peel the vegetables and chop them into ½-inch chunks. Place them in a bowl. Add garlic, rosemary, salt, pepper, and a generous drizzle of olive oil. Toss until coated. Spread them over a baking sheet and roast until tender, 30 to 40 minutes.

Mashed Parsnips and Potatoes with Roasted Leeks

Root vegetables mash nicely by themselves or in combination with other root vegetables. Try them instead of the usual mashed potatoes. Parsnips hold male, earth energy for creation, health, and sex magick. Leeks are elegant onions with a mild flavor and a tender texture. They add healing properties and will protect the physical body from illness when added to food. Nutmeg energy draws love, luck, and money while granting clarity of vision.

You will need:

1½ pounds parsnips, peeled and cut into 1-inch chunks

½ pound potatoes, peeled and cut into 1-inch chunks

1 Tablespoon butter, plus more at room temperature for mashing

2 small leeks, white part only, chopped

¼ cup milk, warmed

¼ teaspoon nutmeg

salt and pepper

Put parsnips and potatoes in large saucepan and cover with water. Bring to a boil and boil gently, about 12 minutes or until tender. In another pan, melt 1 Tablespoon butter, add leeks, and sauté over low heat until leek pieces are nicely browned. Drain parsnips and potatoes and return them to the pan. Cook over low heat, mashing as you slowly add milk and butter to reach desired consistency. Fold in the leeks and season with nutmeg, salt, and pepper.

Roasted Golden Beets with Goat Cheese

Beets are imbued with earth energy, which give both the root and leaves an earthy flavor that, when consumed, can aid in grounding and balancing emotions. Beets are also a food of love associated with Aphrodite. Add the nurturing energy of goat cheese, with its properties for drawing love, wealth, and riches; a sprinkling of hazelnuts, for the eater to be able to see what is right before their eyes; and a drizzle of honey to sweeten—and you get a grounding treat with the power to woo and entice. (This only works if the person you are serving it to likes beets!)

You will need:

1 beet per serving

1 or 2 ounces goat cheese per serving

drizzle of honey

1 Tablespoon chopped hazelnuts or pistachios per serving

Trim, wash, and set the beats in a roasting dish with ¼ cup water. Cover with foil and roast at 400 degrees Fahrenheit until tender, about 1 hour. Remove the beets from the dish and allow them to cool until cool enough to handle. Peel off the skin and slice. Serve with goat cheese. Drizzle with honey and top with chopped hazelnuts.

Sweet Potato Love Me Spell

Sweet potatoes hold energy to enhance the ability to give and receive love, while honey sweetens and cinnamon warms.

You will need:

3 medium-size sweet potatoes, peeled and chopped into 1-inch pieces (about 4 cups)

olive oil

honey

cinnamon

salt and pepper

Preheat the oven to 375 degrees Fahrenheit. Put the sweet potato pieces into a bowl and drizzle with olive oil. Stir, turning several times to coat. Arrange the pieces in a single layer on a baking sheet. Drizzle with honey and sprinkle with cinnamon. Bake for 30 minutes or until the sweet potatoes are tender and browned. Add a dash of salt and pepper to season and serve.

Mashed Potato Cakes

When I was a child, my grandmother used to make potato cakes out of leftover mashed potatoes. She never used a written recipe, and when I tried to recreate it as an adult, I failed. The cakes never turned out well, often sticking to the pan in a gloppy mess. Some forty years later, I found this recipe and learned the secret of a good potato cake lies in the quality of not only the mashed potato but also the pan. These cakes hold a grounding energy to nurture and comfort.

You will need:

nonstick pan

2 eggs, beaten

¼ cup blanched almond flour or 2 Tablespoons flour

¼ cup finely chopped yellow, white, or green onion

1 teaspoon rosemary

1 teaspoon coarse salt

½ teaspoon black pepper

2 cups cooled mashed russet, red, or yellow potatoes

Break 2 eggs into a medium-size bowl and beat until yolk and white are incorporated. Add almond flour, chopped onion, rosemary, salt, and pepper and mix together. Add mashed potato and stir until combined.

Heat 1 teaspoon of oil in a nonstick pan. Then drop in ¼ cup of batter. Let the cake cook until the first side has cooked firmly. Do not rush or the cake will glob apart. When first side has cooked almost through, flip it over and gently press it with a spatula to flatten. Cook until you can see that the edges of the bottom are crisp and golden brown, 3 to 5 minutes. Flip again and give the first side another minute or two now that it is flat. When your cake is brown and crispy, remove it from the pan and drop in another scoop of batter. Serve immediately or transfer to a baking sheet and place in the oven to keep warm while you fry the rest of the batch.

Quinoa and Potato au Gratin

Bring together the mother energies of quinoa and potato and you get a dish brimming with grounding, nurturing energy to fortify and comfort.

You will need:

2 Tablespoons butter

1 medium onion peeled and chopped

8 small red potatoes, steamed until tender

1 8-ounce can tomato sauce

1 4-ounce can mild green chilies

2 Tablespoons fresh minced cilantro

1 cup quinoa, rinsed and cooked

1 cup evaporated milk

8 ounces cheddar or pepper jack cheese

salt and pepper to taste

In a skillet, melt the butter and sauté the onion until caramelized. Slice the cooked potatoes and add to the pan. Stir in tomato sauce, chilies, and cilantro and simmer for several minutes. In a separate bowl, stir together the quinoa and milk. Add the skillet contents into quinoa mixture and stir in half the cheese. Season to taste with salt and pepper, then transfer the mixture to a baking dish. Top with remaining cheese. Bake at 350 degrees Fahrenheit for 20 minutes.

Jicama and Cabbage Slaw

Munch this salad to boost energy and attraction.

You will need:

1 cup mayonnaise

1 Tablespoon dijon mustard

3 Tablespoons vinegar

juice of 1 orange

juice and zest of 1 lime

3 Tablespoons honey

2 cups shredded cabbage

1 cup grated jicama

1 small carrot, shredded

4 scallions, chopped

¼ cup cilantro

salt and pepper to taste

In a large salad bowl, whisk together mayonnaise, mustard, vinegar, orange juice, lime juice and zest, and honey. Add the cabbage, jicama, carrot, scallion, cilantro and toss to coat. Season with salt and pepper to taste.

Other Vegetables

Artichoke

Attraction, love, personal growth, and protection

The artichoke is a member of the daisy family. It is associated with Venus, Scorpio, and Zeus, who is said to have created it from a lovely young girl named Cynara, who caught his eye. He seduced her and made her a goddess and carried her off to Mount Olympus. At first, Cynara was happy with the arrangement, but after a while she began to miss her mother. She snuck back to the world of mortals for a visit but was caught upon her return, and Zeus was so angry he hurled her back to Earth, transforming her into the spiky plant we know as the artichoke.[140]

The artichoke is one of the oldest-known cultivated vegetables. "The Romans ate them pickled in honey and vinegar, and seasoned with cumin," writes Rebecca Rupp for *National Geographic*.[141] The budding flowers are cut before they bloom and are steamed. Then the heart of the flower and the small tender leaves are eaten to enhance personal growth. Artichoke hearts are drizzled with olive oil and balsamic vinegar and eaten to heat passions and encourage love. In spellwork pinches of dried leaf are added to attraction baths to increase sexual desire and stuffed into mojo bags to increase ability to charm.

Asparagus
Desire, health, love, and virility

This tasty vegetable is native to the Mediterranean. Asparagus is a great source of vitamin A, C, B_6, thiamin, folic acid, and potassium. The tender shoots were popular with both the Romans and the Greeks, who equated the phallic shape of the emergent asparagus shoots to having aphrodisiac properties and attributed it to Aphrodite, writes organic gardener Wolf Storl.[142] At wedding ceremonies, Boeotians decorated with wreaths made of wild asparagus.[143] Nicholas Culpeper, an English herbalist from the seventeenth century, wrote that asparagus "stirreth up bodily lust in man or woman."[144] It was also a traditional food served to bridegrooms at their wedding dinners in nineteenth-century France.[145]

Asparagus is a good source of protein, fiber, folate, and vitamins A, C, and K, antioxidants that improve the body's ability to neutralize cell-damaging free radicals, slow the aging process, and reduce inflammation. Steam and serve with a butter or roast with lemon and olive oil for a delicious and healthy side.

....

140. John Warren, *The Nature of Crops: How We Came to Eat the Plants We Do* (Wallingford, UK: CAB International, 2015), 153.

141. Rebecca Rupp, "The History of Artichokes," *National Geographic*, November 12, 2014, https://www.nationalgeographic.com/culture/food/the-plate/2014/11/12/artichokes/.

142. Storl, *A Curious History of Vegetables,* 25.

143. Lydia Maria Child, *The History of the Condition of Women, in Various Ages and Nations*, vol. 2 (London: J. Allen & Company, 1835), 13.

144. Nicholas Culpeper, *The Complete Herbal* (Manchester, UK: J. Gleave and Son, 1826), 4.

145. Rebecca Rupp, "This Veggie Was the 19th-Century Version of Viagra," *National Geographic,* May 13, 2014, https://www.nationalgeographic.com/culture/article/asparagus-vegetable-version-viagra.

Asparagus is an early spring vegetable. In most hardiness zones, plant it once and it will return each year to furnish you with new shoots. Asparagus is associated with vitality, Ostara, Zeus, Jupiter, and Mars.

Avocado
Beauty, clear sight, fertility, health, love, vision, and youth

The avocado is a fruit native to the Americas and is a healthy source of fat that helps the body reduce cholesterol and may decrease the risk of heart disease. Avocados contain twenty different vitamins and minerals, including an incredible amount of potassium, which lowers blood pressure, and lutein and zeaxanthin, both important for eye health. The Aztecs called the fruit *ahuacuatl*, or testicle, and held that it was an aphrodisiac loaded with energy for fertility.[146] The avocado is one of the foods of love associated with Venus and the element water. Avocados are high in folic acid, a nutrient important for cell health. Eat the fruit to reverse aging. Split an avocado in half and eat with a spoon. After each bite, say,

Fruit of Venus, bless me with your power. With each bite, I am empowered.

Save the pit and grow it in a kitchen window to draw love and happiness into the home.

Butternut Squash
Beauty, deepening relationships, influence, health, and prosperity

The butternut squash is a winter squash that is one the numerous gourds of the genus *Cucurbita*. It has a sweet taste similar to pumpkin. Not only is it flavorful, but a serving will boost the immune system. Butternut is loaded with dietary fiber, vitamin C, vitamin A, and beta-carotene to support eye health and fight macular degeneration. It is a powerful antioxidant that protects cells against cancer and aging. Make a comforting butternut soup to boost the immune system, support cellular health, and maintain youthful, glowing skin. Plant butternut in your garden. It is easy to grow and has a long storage life.

Magickally, butternut squash holds healing energy to foster bonds, aid clear sight, and draw prosperity. Add it to meals to aid relationships. Its warming energy can be used to deepen feelings and influence others to see your view of things.

....

146. Christopher Cumo, ed., *The Encyclopedia of Cultivated Plants* (Santa Barbara, CA: ABC-CLIO, 2013), 58.

Celery
Beauty, cheerfulness, lust, mental powers, prosperity, and rest

Modern celery was cultivated from a small wild celery called smallage. The stock of the celery plant and root are eaten as a vegetable. The seeds are used as a spice. Celery has a stable, refreshing energy. It has been paired with onion as the basis for soups, stews, and casseroles down through the ages. It contains the compounds apigenin and luteolin that help destroy free radicals and may fight cancer. A mixture of celery juice and honey has been used in China as an age-old remedy to lower blood pressure and cholesterol. Add it to dishes to strengthen and restore. Eating celery increases libido and passion. Serve it with cheese to encourage a shy lover.

Corn
Abundance, fertility, life, luck, protection, resurrection, and spirituality

Fresh sweet corn is a deliciously sweet and starchy vegetable, a summer favorite often boiled or barbecued, and organic corn is brimming with energy and nutrients. It is high in vitamin C to protect cells from damage and may ward off diseases like cancer and heart disease. Corn contains vitamins B, E, and K, along with minerals such as magnesium and potassium. It is a good source of lutein and zeaxanthin, two phytochemicals that promote healthy eyesight, and it is high in insoluble fiber to aid digestion.

Corn is a symbol of fertility, depicting the circle of life. All parts of the plant are used in magick. It is a central theme in harvest rituals, especially at Lammas. Corn dolls are made from cornhusks as a fertility amulet and to symbolize the bounty of the season.

Corn pollen is used in rainmaking ceremonies and cornsilk holds energy to ground and balance. Dried corn silk makes a tasty tea and is taken to help treat urinary tract infections. Drink it to stay centered and connect with the earth. A traveler can braid corn silk into a bracelet and wear it to avoid getting lost. Add corn silk to love spells to attract the person you desire. Cornstalks have the energy to draw prosperity and grant blessings. Add them to harvest decorations. Bunch them together and hang over a mirror to bring good luck to the household.

Cucumber
Beauty, fertility, healing, and refreshing

A member of the gourd family grown as a vegetable crop, the cucumber is usually eaten fresh or pickled in vinegar. Cucumbers are rich in vitamins and minerals that nourish the skin. They contain phytochemicals that tighten and reduce wrinkles and cellulite. Rub a slice over problem areas. Cucumbers have a cooling energy to restore and refresh. Place a slice over each eye and rest to reduce eye fatigue. Press peel to forehead to relieve head-ache pain. Cucumbers are associated with the moon and the element water. They have a cool healing energy that lifts the spirit. Blend a cucumber with a handful of ice and 1 cup of coconut water to make a refreshing drink to inspire creativity and refresh thought.

Eggplant
Health, prosperity, and youth

A common fall vegetable also known as aubergine, melongene, garden egg, and guinea squash, the eggplant is a nightshade native to India. It is loaded with vitamins and antioxi-dants including chlorogenic acid and nasunin, free-radical fighters that protect cells from damage and guard against age-related diseases. A 2000 study published in the journal *Toxi-cology* found that the nasunin in eggplant skins helps fight perioxidation of lipids, which may help prevent cancer, in rats.[147] The leaves of the eggplant are toxic when eaten but can be made into a beneficial poultice to treat abscesses, burns, and cold sores. The eggplant is associated with Jupiter and the earth. Add it to your garden to attract positive energy. Eat it to promote health and youth. Cook and serve eggplant to attract health and prosperity. Add its dried flowers to prosperity charms to boost working.

Green Bean
Abundance, fertility, luck, and money

The green bean is a slender stringless green bean with an edible pod and is also known as common bean, the French bean, and *haricot vert*. Green beans are good for you. They are a good source of vitamin A, B_6, B_9 (folic acid), C, and K and the minerals calcium, copper, manganese, potassium, and silicon. They contain twice the iron of spinach. Green beans

---

147. Y. Noda, T. Kneyuki, K. Igarashi, A. Mori, and L. Packer. "Antioxidant Activity of Nasunin, an Anthocy-anin in Eggplant Peels," *Toxicology* 148, no. 2–3 (August 2000): 119–23, https://pubmed.ncbi.nlm.nih.gov/10962130/.

are easy and quick to grow. They are associated with Venus, Mercury, Jupiter, and the moon. They are considered a sacred food in Africa. Shinto lore tells they are one of the foods that sprang from the body of the benevolent goddess Ukemochi to feed the people.[148] Add green beans to your garden to draw prosperity to the home. Green beans hold life energy. Add them to meals to improve health. Serve them to friends and family to attract abundance. Eat them to find new opportunities in old ways of doing things.

Okra
Invisibility, love, protection, shielding, and uncrossing

Okra is a flowering plant in the mallow family valued for its edible green seed pod. It is also known as lady fingers, bamia pod, and in Spanish *quimbombó*. Okra is a native of Africa and the Middle East and is an integral ingredient in many African and Arabic recipes. It traveled to the New World, now is grown in gardens across the South, and is commonly associated with southern, Creole, and Cajun cooking. It is an original ingredient in gumbo. Magickally, okra holds energy for protection and invisibility. It is used as an aphrodisiac and to slip out of bad situations. Slide negative thinking out of your mind by frying up a batch of breaded okra. Select a piece and eat it slowly as you say, "Out of sight, out of mind."

Okra has a grassy flavor and a chewy-slimy texture that you either love or hate. It is delicious breaded and fried but is often steamed, sautéed, baked, grilled, pickled, and boiled. Sauté it with garlic or toss it with olive oil and grill for a delicious side dish. Add grilled okra to a grilled vegetable platter and serve to partygoers to keep negative words off everyone's lips.

Pepper
Creativity, energy, hex removal, love, and passion

Capsicum annuum is a species of domesticated American shrub of the nightshade family that produce a fruit known as a pepper. The pepper comes in a wide variety of shapes and sizes, but whether hot or sweet, all varieties from the sweet bell to the spicy ancho, jalapeño, chilaca, serrano, *chile de árbol*, New Mexico chili, and the hot cayenne, all fall the under the same botanical name. Peppers are native to the New World. They are good for you. Peppers are high in vitamin C and carotenoids to boost immune health and improve

---

148. *Encyclopedia Britannica Online*, s.v. "Ukemochi no Kami," accessed February 23, 2021, https://www.britannica.com/topic/Ukemochi-no-Kami.

eyesight. Magickally, peppers hold positive energy to boost health and maintain energy. Each kind of pepper holds its own unique positive energy to boost and improve:

- Green peppers foster growth and prosperity.
- Red peppers boost vitality and strength.
- Yellow peppers inspire creativity.
- Hot peppers like cayenne can be added as an impetus to energize or get an action started.

For more, see cayenne pepper on page 235. Paprika is a spice made from dried and ground chili peppers. See paprika on page 254.

Pumpkin
Banishing, divination, health, prosperity, and revealing the unseen

The pumpkin is a winter squash native to the New World. It is the food attributed to keeping the pilgrims alive through their first years. A verse from 1630 reads, "We have pumpkins at morning and pumpkins at noon,/If it were not for pumpkins, we should all be undoon."[149] Pumpkins have a tough skin that allows them to be stored much longer than summer squashes. They are easy to prepare and can be cooked right in the shell, and then the tender flesh is scooped out and eaten or used in recipes.

Leave a pumpkin as an offering to wild energies. It is biodegradable and will not make any litter. Pumpkins are loved by many animals. The seeds are a favorite of many birds, squirrels, and mice.

The pumpkin is associated with the autumn festivals, Halloween, Samhain, and Thanksgiving. It is the symbol of the changing season. The fruit is used to decorate tables, windows, porches, and walkways. The flesh is used to make breads, cookies, muffins, soups, drinks, and other seasonal treats. Carving a jack-o'-lantern is a traditional Halloween activity. The pumpkin is associated with magick, the occult, the mysterious, and the unknown. It holds energy to both loosen the tongue and reveal what is unseen. Serve a pumpkin-flavored treat or toasted seeds to anyone you hope to garner information from. Serve pumpkin muffins during any meeting in which you hope to learn something hidden.

The pumpkin holds the power to banish habits, unwanted spirits, or abusive people from your life. Hollow out a pumpkin and write a note detailing what or who is to be ban-

------

149. Jack Staub, *Alluring Lettuces: And Other Seductive Vegetables for Your Garden* (Layton: Gibbs Smith, 2010), 164.

ished. Place it inside the pumpkin on a firesafe surface along with a handful of bay leaves, a spoon of cloves, a handful of garlic skins, and a sprig of rosemary. Nestle a candle inside and light. Let it burn until it burns out. The next morning, bury the remains. The scent of pumpkin drives away harmful energy and makes your home warm and inviting. Light a pumpkin-scented candle before guests arrive to make the gathering festive and fun.

Pumpkins also have the energy to draw prosperity. Place them on the altar, hearth, or doorstep to bring prosperity into the home. Pumpkin flesh holds energy to attract the positive. Make a batch of pumpkin cookies and give them to elicit fondness. Take 1 cup of cooked flesh, mix in honey, cinnamon, ginger, and nutmeg, and serve to anyone you want to sweeten. Mix a cup of cooked pumpkin with cardamom, cinnamon, and brown sugar to compel a favor.

Tomatillo
Instigating, powering up, and protection

The tomatillo is a relative of the Cape gooseberry and the Japanese lantern fruit. The plant produces small green fruit that grow wrapped in papery husks. Although they never caught on in Europe, the tart fruit is very popular in Mexican and Southwest cooking. Tomatillos are associated with Mars and the element fire. In Mexico, tomatillos are made into a remedy for fever, urinary tract infections, and diabetes.[150] Tomatillos are easy to grow, but at least two tomatillo plants are necessary for pollination. The fruit forms inside a husk that balloons out from the pollinated flower. When you harvest, choose fruit that have filled the husks. Remove the papery husks and save them to use in protection rituals. Burn them with onion and garlic papers to empower protection magicks. Use the fruit in soups, sauces, and jams to instigate action.

Tomato
Creativity, health, love, luck, prosperity, protection, and warding

The tomato is native to the Americas, and because it is a member of the nightshade family, Europeans thought it was poisonous and were very suspicious of it. They called it the "wolf's peach," citing that like other nightshades, ingesting it led to "licentiousness" and

150. Gail Forman, "Transforming Tomatillo," *Washington Post,* April 13, 1983, https://www.washingtonpost.com/archive/lifestyle/food/1983/04/13/transforming-tomatillo/d53c1fa5-2623-4b31-877a-30e976e73263/.

poisonings.[151] Eventually, the Spanish and the Italians adopted the fruit, and around 1554 a renowned botanist named Pietro Andrea Mattioli named it in print *pomi d'oro*, or the "golden fruits."[152]

The tomato is a food of love associated with Aphrodite, Hera, and Venus. Eat tomatoes to inspire creativity and draw love and good health into your life. Serve your lover a dish of sliced tomatoes drizzled with olive oil and a crumble of basil to inspire passion. Seduce your love with a dinner of spaghetti topped with a rich tomato-based sauce. Add some basil, marjoram, and oregano to win their affections.

Homegrown tomatoes burst with sweetness. Grow and indulge. Slow roast and serve them as a bruschetta topping to improve friendships. Tomatoes are chock-full of vitamins and minerals. They are a good source of calcium, magnesium, potassium, beta-carotene, and vitamins C, E, and K. They contain the carotenoids lycopene and lutein, which help maintain eye health. Add tomatoes to your diet to improve clear sight. Slice a ripe tomato, sprinkle it with salt, and eat to open perception. The tomato also offers energy for protection. Add it to your garden to draw prosperity and keep negativity away.

Yellow Summer Squash
Awareness, beauty, fertility, health, and luck

Yellow summer squash is native to the Americas. It is a favorite summer food as well as a food of Lammas. It is quick to grow and easy to cook. Unlike winter squashes, summer squashes are harvested while immature when the rind is still tender and edible. Squash is nutritious. It is a good source of fiber, folate, riboflavin, manganese, magnesium, phosphorus, potassium, and vitamins A, B$_6$, and C. Cook and add it to your diet for healthy skin and hair. Eat it to help treat skin conditions. Add it to soups and stir-fries to add positive energy for abundance. Add it to corn and potatoes for a hearty dish with energy to energize and heal.

Yellow squash is associated with wholeness of the spirit and activating the intuitive mind. Eat it to increase awareness. Add it to your diet to inspire spiritual enlightenment. Use it in recipes to increase fertility. Yellow squash is a faery favorite. Leave a squash in offering to garner favor.

....

151. Storl, *A Curious History of Vegetables,* 262–65.

152. David Gentilcore, *Pomodoro!: A History of the Tomato in Italy* (New York: Columbia University Press, 2012), 1–2.

Zucchini
Prosperity, protection, psychic awareness, sex, and spirituality

Zucchini is a long, green edible summer squash. Though squashes are native to the Americas, this Italian favorite traveled to Europe and was cultivated by the Italians who named it *zucchino*, or "immature squash." Zucchini gained favor and spread across Europe, where it became known as a courgette in France and a marrow in England and Africa.

Zucchini is a garden favorite. There is an old saying: "Teach a neighbor to grow zucchini, and she will grow it for your whole neighborhood." It is easy to grow and provides a quick and steady yield, producing summer through fall. And zucchini is easy to cook. You can boil it, bake it, roast it, or shred it and add it to other recipes. You can use it as a side dish, use it as a main dish, and bake it into delectable cakes, breads, and muffins. It is low in calories and loaded with significant amounts of vitamin C, B_6, riboflavin, folate, vitamin K, potassium, and manganese.

Zucchini is a food of Lammas. Add it to meals to boost health and enhance vision. It is associated with wholeness of the spirit and fruitfulness of the intuitive mind. Eat it to increase awareness and encourage spiritual enlightenment. Use it in spells for increase and fertility.

This year's garden produced a multitude of fruit. We had so much zucchini we had to keep coming up with different recipes to use it.

Other Vegetable Recipes
Butternut Squash with Brown Butter and Sage

Butternut holds a warm energy for clear sight, healing, and prosperity. In kitchen magick butternut squash can be baked and served to deepen relationships and influence others to see your view of things.

You will need:

1 large butternut squash, peeled, seeded, and chopped into 1-inch pieces

olive oil

2 Tablespoons butter

½ cup fresh sage leaves

salt and pepper

Preheat the oven to 400 degrees Fahrenheit. Put the squash pieces into a bowl, sprinkle with olive oil, and stir to coat. Spread the squash pieces in a single layer over a baking sheet. Roast for 15 to 20 minutes or until tender. Remove from the oven. In a small saucepan melt the butter. When the butter begins to foam, add the sage leaves. Only allow the butter to just begin to brown. Be careful not to burn it. Cook the sage leaves for about 30 seconds. Pour the butter and sage over the butternut squash. Season with salt and pepper and serve.

Roasted Potatoes

You will need:

salt

1 teaspoon white vinegar

4 potatoes, peeled and sliced into wedges about ¼ inch thick

2 cloves garlic, minced

1 teaspoon rosemary

olive oil

pepper

Preheat the oven to 400 degrees Fahrenheit. Boil a pan of water. Add a pinch of salt and the vinegar, then boil the potatoes for 6 minutes. Drain and dump the potatoes into a bowl. Add garlic and rosemary and toss. Drizzle oil over the potato mixture and toss to coat. Pour the potato wedges onto a baking sheet, arranging in a single layer, and season with salt and pepper. Bake for 15 minutes. Turn the potatoes and bake 10 minutes more or until they are sizzling and golden brown.

Roasted Tomatoes

Tomatoes resonate with loving energy to inspire creativity and fortify good health. Serve them as a side to draw positive energy into your life. Pile them on top of toasted bread to inspire romance or encourage affection.

You will need:

¼ cup olive oil

3 cloves garlic, crushed and chopped

2 teaspoons fresh rosemary

½ teaspoon sugar

¼ teaspoon salt

3 pounds tomatoes, sliced in half and seeded

In a large mixing bowl, add olive oil, crushed garlic, rosemary, sugar, and salt and mix together. Add the seeded tomatoes and stir until coated.

Arrange in a single layer on a baking sheet. Preheat the oven to 225 degrees Fahrenheit and bake for 3 hours until caramelized. This makes an amazing bruschetta topping.

Roasted Zucchini

Zucchini holds a wholesome, stable energy to boost health and enhance clear sight. When it is roasted with olive oil, it becomes a delicious treat to enhance all things spiritual. Eat it to increase awareness and encourage spiritual enlightenment. Serve it to increase creative thought and make endeavors fertile.

You will need:

4 or more zucchini sliced into narrow boats

olive oil

parmesan

thyme

salt and pepper

sprinkle chili flakes

Arrange zucchini boats on a baking sheet and drizzle with olive oil. Top them generously with shredded parmesan. Sprinkle with thyme and salt and pepper. Preheat the oven to 350 degrees Fahrenheit and bake for 30 minutes or until lightly caramelized.

Sprinkle with chili flakes and serve.

Salsa Verde

Tomatillos have a wonderfully tart flavor that adds a delightful zip to savory dishes. They are associated with Mars and have a clean energy to infuse foods and get actions started and ideas flowing.

You will need:

8 tomatillos

food-safe gloves

5 chiles de árbol

2 Tablespoons oil

½ white onion

2 cloves garlic

salt to taste

Remove the papery husks from the tomatillos and rinse well. Put on the gloves and cut the stem off each chile de árbol. Tap out the seeds and discard them. Set the chili pieces aside. Heat a frying pan. Add the oil, the onion, and the tomatillos in a single layer. Sear on one side, then flip them over and brown on the other side. Remove from heat. Place the garlic and chiles de árbol in the pan and brown while watching carefully, as they cook much faster. Place all the ingredients in a blender or food processor and pulse until finely chopped. Season to taste with salt. Cool the salsa in refrigerator.

Savory Eggplant Relish

Eggplant holds energy to attract the positive. This dish resonates with energy for good health and attraction.

You will need:

1 large eggplant

olive oil

1 onion, chopped

1 bell pepper, seeded and chopped

1 stalk celery, chopped

1 small zucchini, chopped

1 carrot, diced

2 tomatoes, seeded and chopped

2 cloves garlic, minced

2 Tablespoons fresh cilantro, chopped

1 teaspoon basil

salt

black pepper

1 teaspoon lemon juice

pita bread

Preheat the oven to 400 degrees Fahrenheit. Slice the eggplant into planks. Drizzle with olive oil and toss until coated. Arrange the planks on a baking sheet in a single layer and roast in the oven until tender. While the eggplant is roasting, sauté the onion until clear. Add pepper, celery, zucchini, carrot, tomatoes, and garlic to sauté and cook for 5 minutes. Stir in cilantro, basil, and cooked eggplant, stirring eggplant to bits. Season with salt, black pepper, and lemon juice. Serve the relish hot or cold with quartered pita bread. It can be prepared a day in advance.

Creamy Pumpkin Soup

Pumpkins carry energy for abundance, banishing, divination, health, prosperity, and revealing the unseen. Add the magickal energies of these complementary spices and the result is a creamy, comforting soup brimming with positive energy to lift moods and put everyone in a festive frame of mind. Allspice holds energy for wealth and healing; cinnamon for love, passion, and success; cloves for love and prosperity; ginger for positive energy for good health and success; and nutmeg for clarity of vision and luck. When infused with positive energy, this soup will draw the best to you.

You will need:

1 Tablespoon butter

1 onion, chopped

2 cups roasted pumpkin (see page 136)

3 cups chicken or vegetable broth

¼ cup maple syrup

1 cup half and half or cream

½ teaspoon ground ginger

¼ teaspoon ground cinnamon

⅛ teaspoon ground nutmeg

salt and pepper

In a large pot or dutch oven, heat the butter. Add onion and sauté until caramelized. Transfer the onion to a blender, add the pumpkin and the broth, and puree until smooth. Transfer the puree back to the pot and add the syrup and cream. Bring the soup to a simmer. Add spices and season with salt and pepper to taste. Remove from heat and serve. Dress it up with a dollop of sour cream and a sprinkle of cinnamon.

Chapter 10
FUNGI

Fungi are classified in a kingdom unto itself. There are more than a hundred thousand known species, including yeasts, molds, mushrooms, and truffles. They are the decomposers and recyclers working to absorb, dissolve, and digest dead plants and animals. They are vital to an ecosystem. Fungi are responsible for replenishing the soil. They break down organic matter and humus into nutrients, making them available for living plants to absorb. Some fungi contain deadly toxins. Some fungi can cause infections, while others, such as penicillin, we use as medicines.

Some fungi are helpful. We use yeast to make bread rise. We use yeasts to ferment wines and beers. We add cultures to milk to turn it into yogurt and cheese. Some fungi, such as mushrooms and truffles, we eat whole or add to recipes to improve the flavor. Fungi-based protein is used as a meat replacement.

Mushroom
Courage, healing, psychic awareness, strength, and truth

Just recently I learned that each mushroom is like a flower and is a spore-bearing fruiting body of a much larger fungus body, the mycelium, that lives under the soil. In fact, some of these fungus bodies are the largest living things on the planet. Here in Oregon lives a 2,400-year-old giant honey mushroom that is growing on over 2,300 acres and slowly killing off the forest trees. It is reputed to be the largest living organism on the planet.[153]

Mushrooms have a mixed reputation. The very word conjures thoughts of psychedelic trips or accidental poisonings. Mushrooms are notoriously hard to identify. Every year there is news of another "expert" getting poisoned. Even the symptoms vary. You can usually count on a violent bout of nausea, vomiting, and diarrhea after eating a bad mushroom (I know—I've been there stuck on the toilet, clutching a container to hold vomit in my lap), except in the case of the death cap mushroom. The death cap looks and tastes like a safe mushroom. Ingesting it produces none of the usual symptoms. Instead, it quietly ruins your liver and kidneys. Even at the market, mushrooms are a bit of a mystery. Did you know that portobello mushrooms, button mushrooms, and white mushrooms are all the same kind of mushroom just at different levels of maturity?

Mushrooms come in many shapes and colors. They pop up after the rain. The appearance of a ring of mushrooms can indicate faery activity. In ancient Egypt mushrooms were a royal delicacy associated with immortality. Shiitake and maitake mushrooms have been used for centuries in both China and Japan, where they are associated with longevity and strength. Science tells us that many mushrooms do boost the workings of the immune system.[154] They are high in antioxidants and selenium to help prevent inflammation. Mushrooms contain riboflavin for red blood cell production, niacin for healthy skin, and zinc for overall good health.

153. Anne Casselman, "Strange but True: The Oldest Living Organism on Earth Is a Fungus," *Scientific American*, October 4, 2007, https://www.scientificamerican.com/article/strange-but-true-largest-organism-is-fungus/.

154. Alena G. Guggenheim, Kirsten M. Wright, and Heather L. Zwickey, "Immune Modulation from Five Major Mushrooms: Application to Integrative Oncology," *Integrative Medicine: A Clinician's Journal* 13, no. 1 (February 2014): 32–44, https://www.ncbi.nlm.nih.gov/pmc/articles/PMC4684115/.

Truffle
Attraction, aphrodisiac, health, romance, and virility

The truffle is the fruiting body of a subterranean fungus prized for its distinctive flavor. Truffles are aphrodisiacs used in both ancient Greece and Rome.[155] They contain the pheromone androstenol that acts as an "effective sexual enhancer."[156] Serve them to heighten any romantic encounter. Indulging on truffles will make both parties seem more attractive. Note that truffle oil does not contain any amount of truffle or pheromone.

....

155. Amy Reiley, "Truffles: The Aphrodisiac Science and Lore," Napa Truffle Festival, January 8, 2012, https://www.napatrufflefestival.com/truffles-the-aphrodisiac-science-and-lore/.

156. Heayyean Lee, Kyungmin Nam, Zahra Zahra, and Muhammad Qudrat Ullah Farooqi, "Potentials of Truffles in Nutritional and Medicinal Applications: A Review," *Fungal Biology and Biotechnology* 7, no. 9 (June 2020): n.p., https://fungalbiolbiotech.biomedcentral.com/articles/10.1186/s40694-020-00097-x.

Chapter 11

FRUITS

Many of today's common ailments and chronic conditions are brought on and exacerbated by a bad diet. You can break the habit of snacking on junk food by reaching for a piece of fruit next time you are hunting for a snack. Fruits hold an uplifting energy to refuel and nourish, renew your life force, and protect your body from disease. Adding fruit to your diet reduces the risk of heart disease and stroke. When you buy fruit, don't hide it away; instead store it where you can see it so it will not go forgotten. Make an effort to eat what is in season. Fresh fruit purchased at the peak of its ripeness is at the height of its energy and has the best flavor. Often there will be a price drop due to overstock when a fruit is in season, so it will usually be cheaper. Take advantage of the bounty. Don't avoid the unfamiliar. See what is available in the produce aisle and try it. You may be surprised by what you've been missing.

Discover the local fruit. Check out what is growing in your community. Notice if your neighbors have an overabundance. Many fruit trees produce a large amount of fruit all at once, and many gardeners would rather share their bounty or trade their surpluses than having it rot. Visit a farmer's market and make some new discoveries. Not only does it support the local economy, but it gets you involved in your community, which is good for the body and soul.

Get out into nature. Make a day of berry picking or take a trip to a farm that allows you to pick your own selection. Not only will you return home with a box full of produce, but you will shore up memories as you forge a connection with the natural world.

Fruits

Açaí
Antiaging, health, stamina, and strength

Açaí is the berry of a palm that is a staple in the diet of tribes in the Amazon.[157] The berries are high in antioxidants. Eat freeze-dried berries or add açaí juice that has not been pasteurized for a feel-good elixir that will boost your energy and fortify strength. Add to smoothies and fruit salads to increase stamina. Consume to fortify yourself before any confrontation or hostile encounter. Mix with healing potions to hasten recovery.

Apple
Beauty, fertility, garden magick, healing, love, and youth

Since long ago, the apple has appeared as an ancient symbol of fertility and knowledge in folklore. It is associated with female deities, femininity, sexuality and seduction, Taurus, and Venus. The apple is an offering often left for the Goddess. Its magickal energy is linked to both the autumn equinox and Samhain.

The apple is a food of both the dead and divination. It was customary for girls to take an apple and cut the peel in one long strip, then throw it behind them to see if it would fall to form the first initial of the one they were to marry.[158] Bobbing for apples was also a form of divination, as the first person to grab an apple with their teeth would be the first to marry. But most notably, apples are a food of love fed to lovers to foster affection or baked with cinnamon to encourage a reluctant one.

Apricot
Attraction, beauty, and love

The apricot is a fruit of love associated with Taurus and Venus. It is known to sweeten the disposition and instill romance. Feed apricots to the one you desire, to instill feelings of

157. John Colapinto, "Strange Fruit: The Rise and Fall of Açaí," *New Yorker*, May 23, 2011, https://www.new
yorker.com/magazine/2011/05/30/strange-fruit-john-colapinto.

158. D. C. Watts, *Dictionary of Plant Lore* (Amsterdam: Elsevier, 2007), 11.

passion. Add them to recipes to boost attraction. Eat them to nourish and balance the skin as well as instill the glow of youth. Share a treat of dried apricots to encourage romance, or drop an apricot pit into your pocket to attract a lover. Serve apricot jam to the one you desire to sweeten their thoughts of you. Bake an apricot tart to woo.

Banana
Energy, fertility, love, prosperity, and spirituality

Banana trees are not really trees but large herbs. The bright yellow, phallic-shaped fruit symbolizes love, sexuality, and fertility. Bananas contain potassium, magnesium, and iron along with three types of sugar—sucrose, fructose, and glucose—which make them a power-packed source of quick energy. Add a banana to a smoothie to sweeten and boost your energy. Bananas can be eaten raw or baked in bread to stimulate spirituality. Banana chips are a tasty treat and will keep a journey free from accidents when carried by the traveler. Bananas are associated with Jupiter. They contain energy for fertility and love. To increase sexual stamina, crush dried chips into a powder and dust over the body.

Blackberry
Abundance, healing, protection, and sweetening

The blackberry bush is a bramble, an impenetrable, thorny shrub that grows like a weed here in Oregon. On the upside, it yields a bounty of tart berries that are a delight to animals, birds, and cooks who use them in baked goods, jams, and wines. The berries represent an abundant harvest and are traditionally baked into pies to celebrate the first harvest festivals. They contain an uplifting energy to empower and excel. Before your next business meeting, treat yourself to an empowering smoothie by blending a handful each of blackberries, raspberries, and strawberries with 1 cup of yogurt. Drink to engage and inspire.

Though blackberries are a favorite of the Fae, they hold energy for protection and, if planted around the home, will protect it from vampiric energies. Blackberry canes can be woven into wreaths with rowan and ivy for a protection that will even return a hex to the sender. Burn blackberry leaves to vanquish unwanted spirits. Hang a bough over your door to break a run of bad luck.

Young blackberry leaves are loaded with antioxidants. Blackberry tea is a traditional remedy for diarrhea, bleeding gums, and sore feet. Brew a cup of tea to alleviate digestive disorders.

Tradition holds not to harvest berries after September 29 (some references cite October 11; this is because the date of Michaelmas changed) because the devil, or depending which country you are in, the Puka, has tainted the berries, rendering them toxic.[159] This is good advice, as berries tend to mold when the weather changes.

Blueberry
Abundance, health, legal matters, luck, memory, money, prosperity, and protection

A perennial native to North America that produces small berries loaded with nutritional benefits, the blueberry has one of the highest antioxidant capacities among all fruits and vegetables. Blueberries contain compounds to reinforce the nervous system and boost brain health. Eat a cup daily to improve memory and expand spiritual awareness. Make a blueberry pie and eat a slice when you need some fortification. Some Native Americans in the Upper Midwest used tea brewed from the leaf and root to lower blood sugar, cure urinary tract infections, and treat cramps, hiccups, hysteria, epilepsy, colic, and labor pains, writes Kate Redmond at the University of Wisconsin–Milwaukee.[160] Burn dried leaves to instill calmness. Use in protection magick. Tuck blueberry leaves under the doormat to keep away undesirables. Add blueberry sprigs to a wreath to keep away unwanted visitors.

Cantaloupe
Beauty, beginnings, healing, love, and revive

An orange-fleshed summer melon that grows on a vine, cantaloupe is also called muskmelon and is associated with the sea, summer, the element water, and the moon. Cantaloupes contain vitamins and minerals to fortify health and beauty. The orange flesh is high in beta-carotene, a powerful antioxidant that fights free radicals that attack cells in your body. It is loaded with the antioxidant folate, which may help restore memory loss due to aging. Its high water content is hydrating to help restore energy and vigor. Wrap slices in prosciutto for a summer appetizer. Include cantaloupe in summer fruit salads to boost nutrients and hydrate cells. Whiz in a blender with ice and coconut water for a quick pick-me-up that will restore energy and revitalize your spirit. Blend cantaloupe with a spoonful of plain yogurt for a refreshing face mask that will soften and hydrate skin cells.

....

159. William Henderson, *Notes on the Folk-lore of the Northern Counties of England and the Borders* (London: The Folklore Society, 1879), 96.

160. Kate Redmond, "Browsing the Bog," University of Wisconsin Milwaukee field station bulletin 32 (2007): 26, https://dc.uwm.edu/cgi/viewcontent.cgi?article=1163&context=fieldstation_bulletins.

Cherry
Beauty, fertility, love, protection, and wisdom

The cherry tree is one of the first trees to flower. It is associated with spring, renewal, and the abundance of nature. The cherry tree is associated with Buddha and Venus. The blossom is a symbol of feminine beauty. The fruit represents fertility and youthfulness. Eat the fruit to boost attraction. Serve up a freshly baked cherry pie to win a man's affections. Begin a romantic interlude with a bowl of fresh cherries to infuse sexual energy. Tie a lock of hair around a blossoming branch to attract a new love. Cherry stones were used in divination. It is an old European tradition to count cherry stones after a meal, saying, "Tinker, tailor, soldier, sailor, richman, poorman, beggarman, thief" or "Silk, satin, muslin, rags," with the last stone predicting a future husband's profession.[161] Eat a handful of cherries as you contemplate an important decision. The fruit promotes rational action rather than emotional decisions. Float a handful of cherry blossoms in your bath to lift your spirits. Hang a blossoming bough over your threshold to keep negativity out.

Coconut
Beauty, clear thinking, confidence, healing, moon magick, protection, and purification

The coconut palm produces a large fruit that provides water, a sweet meat, and an aromatic oil. Coconut milk is the fat-rich cream removed from coconut meat. It is symbolic of mother's milk and holds nourishing energy to heal and nurture. It is used in cooking curries and Asian dishes. Coconut increases HDL (the good cholesterol), boosts thyroid function, and improves cognitive ability.

Magickally, coconut energy is associated with the moon and the element water. Its energy strengthens confidence and inner resolve. Fill a bowl with sliced apples, grapes, strawberries, raspberries, and watermelon to elicit feelings of romantic love. Sprinkle the fruit with shredded coconut to help overcome inhibitions. Add coconut to recipes for beauty, healing, and renewal.

Cranberry
Bonding, communication, cleansing, healing, love, and protection

The cranberry is a group of evergreen shrubs that produce a tart edible berry native to North America. To Native Americans the cranberry was a food, a dye, and a healing agent

---

161. Barnaby Rogerson, *Rogerson's Book of Numbers* (London: Picador, 2014), 148.

used to treat blood disorders, fever, dysentery, and scurvy.[162] Cranberry juice is a natural medicine that helps relieve many urinary tract discomforts. It is associated with Neptune, water, and the moon. The cranberry has a brightly tart, cleansing, yet festive energy that can be used for energy, celebration, and protection. Cranberry sauces are included in fall and winter holiday feasts. Serve them at gatherings to strengthen tribal bonds. Dried cranberries can be strung and added to holiday decor to add a festive protection. Make a seasonal garland by stringing cranberries with popcorn, walnut halves, and apple slices. Hang outdoors to feed wildlife.

Currant
Courage, thought, psychic sight, and spirituality

The currant is a fruit-bearing shrub in the genus *Ribes* native to most countries in the Northern Hemisphere. Currant varieties include red, black, white. White currents are quite rare. Red currants are often eaten fresh and baked into sweet tarts and pies, breads, and cakes. Black currants are tart and used to make jams, puddings, and sauces. Currants are loaded with antioxidants. They are a good source of vitamin C, potassium, fiber and iron. Magickally, currants have a courageous festive energy. They are baked into holiday breads and scones to fortify the spirit and remedy feelings of loneliness. Serve them to dismiss judgmental notions or align opposing viewpoints. Black currants hold energy to support vision quests and spiritual advancement. Use them to advance psychic ability or aid divination.

Fig
Abundance, blessings, enlightenment, divination, fertility, love, protection, strength, and wisdom

The fig is a small fruit native to the Middle East with a long history as a symbol of love. In ancient Greece "the arrival of a new fig crop elicited a copulatory ritual," writes culinary blogger Tori Avey.[163] The Romans believed the fig was a fruit of Bacchus and made love potions from it.[164] Cleopatra employed the fruit and often served it drizzled with honey to woo visiting dignitaries. Buddha found enlightenment meditating underneath the Bodhi

---

162. Kate Redmond, *Browsing the Bog* (Milwaukee: University of Wisconsin Milwaukee UWM Digital Commons, 2007), 25–26.

163. Tori Avey, "Learn Why These 10 Foods Are Edible Aphrodisiacs," the History Kitchen, PBS, February 10, 2014, https://www.pbs.org/food/the-history-kitchen/10-edible-aphrodisiacs/.

164. Robert Hendrickson, *Lewd Food* (Radnor, PA: Chilton Book Company, 1974), 243.

tree, a sacred fig tree.[165] It was tradition for Buddhist students to wear amulets made of fig bark to help them find wisdom. It is said that if you have a fig tree, you have the power to charm a person simply by offering them a fig from it, and they will remain bound to you for as long as they enjoy eating figs!

Figs are associated with Mars, Jupiter, Bacchus, and Saturn. Their energy attracts love and abundance. Serve them to guests to improve friendship. Mix figs, dates, and walnuts and serve to instill positive energy. Carry dried figs when traveling to avoid troubles and facilitate a safe return. Eat figs in the evening to gain a restful sleep.

Goji Berry
Beauty, communication, energy, happiness, healing, protection, and youth

The goji berry, also known as the wolfberry, is a small round, orange-red fruit with a long tradition as a medicine and food plant in East Asia. In China it is thought to be a superior tonic used to fortify well-being and foster longevity.[166] Goji berries are good for you. They contain compounds that protect eye health against disorders like macular degeneration.[167]

The goji berry holds a bright, uplifting energy to reverse aging and protect against disease. Goji berries help to regulate cholesterol. A 2015 study revealed the active polysaccharides in goji berries boost the immune system and may protect the body from cancer and fatigue.[168] Supercharge your health by eating a small amount of berries daily to increase vitality and endurance. Add them to cereals and smoothies to protect the body from environmental stresses. Nibble a handful of dried berries or drop some into a mug of hot water, let steep for 9 minutes, and drink for glowing skin, shining hair, and bright eyes. Goji has an uplifting energy and will lift your mood when eaten. Feed to someone to induce laughter. The berries facilitate communication and aid in rival parties coming to

165. "Ficus religiosa," Missouri Botanical Garden, accessed February 24, 2021, https://www.missouribotanical garden.org/PlantFinder/PlantFinderDetails.aspx?taxonid=282754&isprofile=0&.

166. Staff reporter, "China's First Provincial-Level Wolfberry Association Established," People's Daily Online, August 19, 2001, http://english.people.com.cn/english/200108/19/eng20010819_77685.html.

167. Shang Li, Na Liu, Er-Dan Sun, Jian-Da Li, and Peng-Kin Li, "Macular Pigment and Serum Zeaxanthin Levels with Goji Berry Supplement in Early Age-Related Macular Degeneration," abstract, *International Journal of Ophthalmology* 11, no. 6, (2018): 970–75, https://www.ncbi.nlm.nih.gov/pmc/articles/PMC6010398/.

168. Jiang Cheng, Zhi-Wei Zhou, Hui-Ping Sheng, et al., "An Evidence-Based Update on the Pharmacological Activities and Possible Molecular Targets of *Lycium barbarum* Polysaccharides," *Drug Design, Development and Therapy* 9 (2015): 33–78, https://www.ncbi.nlm.nih.gov/pmc/articles/PMC4277126/.

terms. Encourage quarreling couples to eat a bowl of berries together to lighten the mood and sort out differences. Serve to encourage friendship. Eat before meditation to deepen spiritual connection. Goji shrubs are a popular hedging plant in England used to encourage happiness and keep negative forces at bay.

Grape
Abundance, beauty, celebration, fertility, the harvest, luck, and success

A berry of the deciduous vines of the genus *Vitis*. Grapes are associated with Jupiter and were a favorite of Bacchus, Dionysus, Pan, and Zeus. Grapes symbolize abundance, luxury, wealth, and hedonism, as grapes are used to make the celebratory drink wine. Both grapes and wine are used to stimulate sexual energy and increase fertility. Kindle your love's affection by serving up a fresh fruit salad. Slice up some sweet summer fruits, such as apples, grapes, honeydew, kiwi, strawberries, raspberries, and watermelon, to elicit feelings of romantic love.

Grapes hold positive energy for good luck. It is tradition in Spain to eat a grape at each chime of the clock at midnight on New Year's and receive good luck all year long.[169] In the UK visitors bring grapes to hospital patients to wish them a quick recovery. Add raisins to trail mixes and baked goods for good luck when traveling. Usher abundance into your home by twisting a grapevine into a wreath and hanging it on the front door.

Grapes also hold energy to open the mind to inspiration and vision. Eat a handful to increase awareness. Serve a bowl at meetings to lighten the mood and get thoughts to flow.

Grapefruit
Cleansing, communication, energy, joy, and vitality

The grapefruit is a large hybrid tart fruit in the citrus family. It has long been touted as a diet food, as it is low in sugar and is consumed to detox and lose weight. Grapefruits are a good source of vitamins A and C to boost the immune system and promote healthy skin. They contain flavonoids, compounds that lower the risk of ischemic stroke among women, and potassium for heart health. However, grapefruit has been found to interact with certain heart and blood pressure medications.

....

169. Judy Cantor-Navas, "12 Grapes at Midnight: Spain's Great New Year's Eve Tradition, and Superstition," Food Republic, December 28, 2012, https://www.foodrepublic.com/2012/12/28/12 -grapes-at-midnight-spains-great-new-years-eve-tradition-and-superstition/.

The grapefruit is associated with the moon. It has a nurturing, lifting energy to soothe stress-related conditions, remedy fatigue, ease depression, and grant resilience in adversity. Add slices to water and serve at any meeting to keep feelings amicable. Add to bathwater to revive and energize. Soak tired feet in a grapefruit bath to restore spirit. Drink juice to detox. The joyful scent awakens the senses, promotes mental clarity, and encourages action. Breathe deeply as you cut a grapefruit to boost confidence and feel positive. The grapefruit has a refreshing energy with the power to lift the body, mind, and spirit. Eat a grapefruit or drink a glass of juice before a meeting to stimulate intellect and refresh ideas. Add to breakfast to energize the subconscious and open communication. Wear grapefruit essential oil during meditation to deepen spiritual connection and facilitate communication with the higher self. Add grapefruit essential oil to a spray bottle of water and spritz the air above you to remain fresh and awake.

Honeydew Melon
Beauty, friendship, love, and refreshment

The honeydew is a cultivar of the muskmelon. It is rich in fiber, vitamins, minerals, and plant polyphenols, compounds with anti-inflammatory qualities. It is a good source of vitamin C and potassium. Honeydews also contain superoxide dismutase, an antioxidant that may help alleviate the harmful effects of sun exposure.

The honeydew is associated with Venus, love, abundance, and fertility. It is used in food magick to encourage love and nurture beauty. Its mild, sweet flavor can be used in dishes to encourage fidelity, friendship, and kindness. Add balls of honeydew to a melon salad and serve to sweeten a friendship. Serve slices wrapped in prosciutto as an appetizer to charm and impress. Slice into thin slices and place them on your face to revitalize energy and freshen beauty. Cover each eye with a slice of cucumber and relax to rejuvenate.

Kiwi
Beauty, happiness, love, nourishing, prosperity, and relaxation

The edible berries of several species of woody vines in the genus *Actinidia*, also known as the Chinese gooseberry, kiwis are loaded with vitamins that rejuvenate cells and prevent disease. They have twice the amount of vitamin C as an orange and contain A, B_6, calcium, iron, and magnesium for beautiful skin and hair. The sweetly tart flavor will add a zip to fruits of love salads. Combine kiwi, apples, cantaloupe, and strawberries for a bright bowl of happiness that will nourish and fortify your family's health. Blend a kiwi with 1 cup of coconut water, a banana, and a handful of ice to make an energy-boosting smoothie with the power to open your mind and bolster your charisma.

Lemon
Brightening, clarity, confidence, friendship, happiness, love, and purification

A small yellow citrus fruit associated with the sun, the lemon has a stimulating, refreshing energy and a bright, cheery scent that lifts the spirit and encourages love and friendship. Add a lemon slice to a beverage when a friend is visiting to turn the friendship into a lasting one. Lemon energy can be used to cool emotions, lift mood, and cleanse the spirit, the body, and the home. Burn dried lemon peel with rose petals and lilac to soothe hurt feelings. The bright flavor of lemon enhances and brightens other flavors. Add it to dishes to brighten flavor and boost positive energy. Add lemon zest to dishes to add zest to your life.

Lemon juice is one of the important acids added to balance the salty-sweetness of a dish and improve the way it tastes. A dose of lemon juice brightens a bland dish into a tasty one. Lemon juice holds a purifying energy to enhance digestion. Use the cleansing energy of lemon to detoxify. Add slices of lemon to water and drink it in the morning to improve digestion and reset metabolism. Add it to bathwater to cleanse away the gunk of the world and emerge renewed. Add lemon juice to water and use it to wash magickal objects to clear away residual energy. Lemon washwater will make a room sparkle as it lifts the vibration.

Lime
Cleansing, healing, love, protection, and purification

A small green citrus fruit with a bright reviving scent, the lime is associated with Jupiter. Lime energy is refreshing. Energize your spirit with a lime spritz. Add lime juice to a spray bottle of water and spritz above you to alleviate fatigue and stimulate alertness. (Just be sure not to get it near your eyes.) Use it to combat energy vampires. Add lime slices to a footbath and soak to restore spirit. Lime juice can be added to drinks to promote calmness and strengthen love. Add lime zest to dishes to add zest to your life.

The lime tree is a favorite of nature spirits. If you live in a warm area, plant a lime tree as a gift to your garden energies. The lime also has energy for protection. To break a hex, drive two iron nails through a fresh lime and bury it. Carry a lime twig in your left pocket to find protection when walking through a wild place.

Mandarin Orange
Attraction, fertility, hospitality, love, and marriage

The mandarin orange is a small citrus fruit also called mandarine. While similar to the clementine, mandarin oranges are sweeter and are often found canned. In traditional Chinese medicine, the dried peel of the fruit is used to regulate chi.[170] The scent is worn to attract men. The fruit promotes fruitfulness, kindness, and happiness and instills hospitality. Add it to meals to foster feelings of welcome. Serve it with goat cheese, walnuts, and a drizzle of honey to sweeten a relationship and encourage easy conversation.

Mandarin orange energy is uplifting. Fill a bathtub and drink the juice of a mandarin while you soak to relax and recover. Pour mandarin juice into a footbath to alleviate depression and anxiety. Rub it into the bottoms of your feet to renew vigor.

Mango
Dream magick, fertility, love, and uplifting

The mango tree is related to the cashew and pistachio. It was domesticated between 4,000 and 6,000 years ago in Southeast Asia and became a sacred tree in India, its many uses referenced in the Hindu epic *Ramayana*.[171] It is associated with love, marriage, and fertility. Mango leaves and flowers are used to decorate Hindu temples. The flowers are used as offerings given to the moon and the love god Madan. Mango leaves are woven into garlands and used as marriage decorations. *Amchur*, or *amchoor*, is a citrus-flavored spice with a honey-like fragrance made by powdering the dried unripe fruit.

The mango is a wishing tree associated with Buddha and the Hindu god Ganesha, who is often depicted holding a mango as a symbol of spiritual attainment.[172] Eat it to raise personal vibration. Add it to dishes to add positive, joyous energy. Peel and seed a mango and drop the fruit into a blender. Add a couple of spoons of plain yogurt and blend until smooth. Pour the smooth liquid into a glass and visualize yourself being filled with love, becoming Madan, the goddess of love herself, as you drink it, intoning, "I am filled with love, I am filled with love, I am love." Make an amazing mango love sorbet by blending

170. "Chen Pi in TCM," ChineseNutrition.org, accessed March 24, 2021, http://chinesenutrition.org/view_image.asp?pid=45.

171. Kiple, *A Movable Feast*, 47.

172. Amit Gupta, "Mango & Its Spiritual Significance," Speaking Tree, April 25, 2013, https://www.speakingtree.in/allslides/mango-its-spiritual-significance.

1 cup frozen mango, ¼ cup sour cream, 2 Tablespoons maple syrup, and 2 Tablespoons water. Serve it to the one you love to deepen affection. Mango leaves are associated with dream magick. Pluck a leaf from a mango tree and put it under your pillow to induce prophetic dreams.

Nectarine
Abundance, happiness, health, and love

Like the plum and peach, the nectarine belongs to the Rosaceae family. This fruit is associated with Venus and promotes love, happiness, and fertility. It is a symbol of marriage, longevity, and wishes granted. For an old-fashioned love spell, choose an unblemished fruit. Pluck it from the tree and sit in its shade. Eat the fruit as you visualize the one you love. When you have finished eating the fruit, bury the stone to stimulate the growth of affection. Serve up some fruits of love by slicing up some nectarine, oranges, apricots, and apples. Squeeze some lemon over the top and serve it to the one you love to sweeten emotions. Nectarines are good for you. Add them to your diet to protect your health.

Orange
Abundance, clarity, divination, fertility, health, happiness, love, luck, money, and weddings

The orange is a member of the citrus family, with bright energy associated with the sun. Since the lovely fruit comes ripe in December, it was considered a godsend and became a traditional holiday gift to encourage wealth and happiness in the coming year. The scent alone has energy to lift the mood and inspire joy. In the thirteenth century, it was a French custom to make *pommes d'ambre*, or "amber apples," by taking an orange and sticking whole cloves into it.[173] It was then tied up with a decorative ribbon and hung to let the lovely, fresh citrus scent freshen the air. Add a combination of orange blossoms, orange peels, and orange seeds to a bridal sachet to ensure happiness in the marriage. Add the peel to potpourris to lift mood. Or burn the peel to be blessed with love, luck, and money.

Oranges are a good source of vitamin C to boost immune health and neutralize harmful free radicals. They contain compounds to alleviate harmful effects of sun exposure and reverse skin aging. Eat orange slices for healthy skin. Drink fresh orange juice to boost energy. Float orange blossoms in the bath to enhance attraction.

....

173. Catherine Boeckmann, "How to Make Pomander Balls," *Old Farmer's Almanac*, October 23, 2020, https://www.almanac.com/content/how-make-pomander-balls.

Sweet orange oil is ideal for self-purification, inspiring creativity, and lifting the spirit. Anoint a green candle with sweet orange oil and honey. Roll the candle in ground cinnamon and burn it to bring prosperity.

Peach
Abundance, fertility, happiness, health, love, luck, and wishes

A fruit native to China associated with innocence, spring, Venus, and good health, the peach is the symbol of immortality and, like the plum and nectarine, is a fruit of love. Serving up a fresh-baked peach pie is an old folk magick to win a man's affections. Share a peach with the one you love to inspire fond affection. Serve a salad made of sliced peaches, fresh mozzarella, and fresh basil. Drizzle with olive oil for a dish to turn a friendship flirty. Eat peaches to promote fertility, happiness, and abundance.

Peach blossoms are used to empower spells for beauty, love, and luck. Peach leaves hold energy to drive away negative energy. A branch of peach wood holds the power to find and is used in dowsing. Peach stones carry energy for protection and are often made into amulets that are carved and sealed in red wax.

Pear
Energy, enthusiasm, longevity, love, lust, and strength

A fruit tree native to Asia, Europe, and North Africa, the pear is associated with Venus, Aphrodite, Hera, and Pomona. It represents immortality and marital satisfaction. It was once customary in the Old World to plant a pear tree after the birth of each daughter to ensure her long life and fruitfulness.[174] Plant a pear tree to draw abundance and to attract faeries to your garden. Eat a pear to lift thoughts and inspire happiness. Serve your love a dish of pear slices to increase his enthusiasm. Add strawberries to make his affections sweeter. Serve pears poached in wine to make gatherings more festive. Add a sprinkling of anise and cinnamon to help clear away grudges and inspire fond memories. Use pear leaves and wood in money and prosperity spells. A wand made of pear wood will boost any positive working.

---

174. Fred Hageneder, *The Meaning of Trees* (San Francisco: Chronicle Books, 2005), 170.

Persimmon
Abundance, changing sex, healing, love, prosperity, and self-realization

The persimmon (*Diospyros kaki*) is an Asian fruit also known as divine fruit, God's pear, and Oriental persimmon. It is native to China and spread to Korea and Japan more than a thousand years ago. In the 1880s the Oriental persimmon traveled to the United States, and now hundreds of different varieties are grown in California.

In Japan persimmons are the national fall fruit. They are featured in celebrations and honored for their joyous, festive energy. Their very appearance symbolizes good health, wealth, longevity, and the reunion of extended family. In Buddhism the persimmon is symbolic of spiritual transformation.[175] In Chinese the characters for persimmon translate to a household blessing or that "many 100 things be as you wish them to be."[176]

Diospyros virginiana, or the common persimmon, is a species native to North America. The name *persimmon* is an Algonquian word meaning "dry fruit." Captain John Smith (1580–1631) wrote about them in his Jamestown interactions, "If it is not ripe, it will drive a man's mouth awrie with much torment. But when it is ripe, it is as delicious as an apricock."[177]

Persimmons are eaten raw like an apple, and they are cut into pieces and added to other fruit dishes. They are also dried and made into candy, breads, and puddings. Persimmons are rich in fiber, are a good source of vitamins A and C, and contain lutein and zeaxanthin, compounds that protect eyes against degeneration.

Magickally, the persimmon is associated with Libra, Venus, Mars, and Saturn and holds energy for love, luck, and abundance magick. Persimmons are a favored offering. Potted persimmons encourage the flow of wealth into the home. Set one on the doorstep to draw positive energy. The small gold fruits resemble golden coins and will grant prosperity. Eat a persimmon to gain insight and inspiration. Persimmons are said to aid the process of transition, especially when changing sexes, and have the ability to predict the coming winter. Take a fruit and cut it open. If the seed looks like a knife, the coming winter will be a cold one. If it looks more like a fork, it will be a dry, mild winter.

175. Shannon Wianecki, "The Constant Garden," *Hana Hou!* 17, no. 2 (April/May 2014), https://hanahou
.com/17.2/the-constant-garden.

176. Elizabeth Cha Smith, "Persimmon," Lan Su Garden, November 22, 2017, https://lansugarden.org
/content/CI_assets/Plant_Talk_4_Persimmon_web.pdf.

177. "Persimmons," Real Food Encyclopedia, Food Print, accessed February 25, 2021, https://foodprint.org
/real-food/persimmons/."

Pineapple
Chastity, hospitality, luck, money, protection, and welcoming

A sweet, juicy fruit produced by a plant in the family Bromeliaceae. The pineapple was named after the pine cone by European explorers in the Americas.[178] The Latin name *Ananas comosus* is more accurate, as *nana* in Tupí-Guaraní means "excellent fruit."[179] When pineapples were introduced to Europe, they became a symbol of royal privilege and wealth. Only the incredibly rich could afford to buy one. In the 1670s, when pineapples had reached the height of their popularity, a pineapple would "sell for as much as $8000 in today's money."[180] The pineapple became a symbol of hospitality, as a hostess's ability to produce a pineapple said much about her position and resourcefulness.[181] Oddly enough, the fruit was too expensive to be eaten and was used as a centerpiece or carried as an accessory.

Colonial America fell in love with the pineapple, and it became a symbol of prosperity and hospitality.[182] The pineapple became a fruit of homecomings, served to welcome a traveler back home. It became customary to place a pineapple outside the door to announce a sea captain's safe return and invite friends to visit.[183] Today the pineapple is also a secret symbol of swingers.[184]

Pineapples are associated with the element fire, the sun, abundance, attraction, growth, happiness, strength, and success. The pineapple is a wonderful party food. Not only does it promote feelings of hospitality, but it holds energy for enthusiasm. Add pineapple juice to party drinks to promote happiness. Bake pineapple rings into desserts to strengthen the bonds of friendship. Make a pineapple-infused vodka by filling a wide-mouth jar with

....

178. Stephen Block, "The History of Pineapple," the Kitchen Project, February 25, 2021, https://www.kitchen project.com/history/Pineapple/.

179. Gary Y. Okihiro, *Pineapple Culture: A History of the Tropical and Temperate Zones* (Berkeley, CA: University of California Press, 2009), 74.

180. Terry MacEwen, "King Pine, the Pineapple," Historic UK, accessed March 24, 2021, https://www.historic -uk.com/CultureUK/King-Pineapple/.

181. Loren Berg, "The Pineapple as Ornamental Motif in American Decorative Arts," paper for HIS 5330, Eastern Illinois University, 2009, 4.

182. Berg, "The Pineapple as Ornamental Motif in American Decorative Arts," 5.

183. "Pick of the Season," *The National Culinary Review* 25 (2001): 12.

184. Hayley Richardson, "Secret Signs Your Neighbor Might Be a Swinger," New York Post, June 2, 2017, https://nypost.com/2017/06/02/secret-signs-your-neighbor-might-be-a-swinger/.

chunks of pineapple. Top the jar with vodka, seal, and let steep in your refrigerator for several days. Serve it to encourage cheer.

Plum
Abundance, good luck, happiness, healing, love, and youth

The plum is a stone fruit like the cherry, peach, and apricot. There are three categories of edible plums: European, Japanese, and North American. They are a popular fruit eaten fresh and made into desserts, preserves, and jellies.

The plum is a symbol of marriage, longevity, and wishes granted. Serve plums when you need a boost of luck. Drop a plum pit into your pocket before any endeavor to ease the way and find fortune. Eat plums to promote health, fertility, happiness, and abundance. Pick a fresh plum and take a bite. Kiss the one you love with the juice upon your lips to deepen affection. Eat a plum in the shade of the tree while you dream about the one you desire. Bury the pit at the foot of the tree to have your feelings reciprocated. Pick a plum off a tree and offer it to someone you wish to see you in a positive light. Plant a plum tree in the northeast corner of your garden to keep misfortune away.

Prunes are dried plums. They are loaded with fiber to ease digestion. Eat them to stay regular. Carry them on trips to ease the way. Prunes are rich in beta-carotene for healthy eyes and skin.

Pomegranate
Beauty, creativity, divination, fertility, health, luck, wealth, and wishes

The fruit of a small deciduous tree cultivated since ancient times throughout the Mediterranean, the pomegranate is an ancient food with a biblical past. In fact, some believe it to be the forbidden fruit of Genesis.[185] Pomegranates are a symbol of feminine fertility, a fruit of both death and rebirth. It is associated with Persephone and her journey into the underworld, with Ceres, Demeter, Hathor, Ra, Saturn, and Samhain. The goddess of love Aphrodite is "credited in Greek mythology with planting the first pomegranate tree," writes culinary blogger Tori Avey.[186] It is sacred to Venus and is a food of both weddings and of funerals. Buddhists consider the pomegranate a blessed fruit. One story tells of

---

185. Tori Avey, "Learn Why These 10 Foods Are Edible Aphrodisiacs," the History Kitchen, PBS, February 10, 2014, https://www.pbs.org/food/the-history-kitchen/10-edible-aphrodisiacs/.

186. Tori Avey, "Learn Why These 10 Foods Are Edible Aphrodisiacs," the History Kitchen, PBS, February 10, 2014, https://www.pbs.org/food/the-history-kitchen/10-edible-aphrodisiacs/.

how the Buddha gave a pomegranate to Hariti, a demon who devoured her children, to cure her of her obsession.[187]

In art the pomegranate is a food of luck and love and, when pictured with a peach, represents long life and fertility. Eat to draw abundance and happiness. Eat the seeds to increase fertility. Wish upon the seeds as you eat them one by one to draw positive energy. Feed the seeds to your lover to encourage the affection to be returned. Split a pomegranate and leave the first portion as an offering to find favor. The juice of the pomegranate is highly nutritious and contains high amounts of antioxidants to help reverse aging. Pour some juice into a goblet and take a drink, then offer it to your love to strengthen your bond.

Raspberry
Healing, love, money, and protection

A perennial with an edible fruit that, along with the rose and the blackberry, is a member of the Rosaceae family. Here in the Pacific Northwest raspberries grow like crazy, producing crops of berries from mid-June to October. Raspberries are available in a wide variety of cultivars with berries in shades of white, gold, blue, red, and black. Though they were "brought West on the Oregon trail in the late 1800s," according to produce company Oregon Raspberries & Blackberries, raspberries have naturalized and now grow wild in many places along with their more recent hybrids: boysenberries, loganberries, tayberries, and olallieberries, which are often found at farmer's markets.[188]

Raspberries are one of my favorite fruits. Not only do raspberries taste good, but they are good for you. Of all the fruits, raspberries contain one of the highest concentrations of antioxidants to boost immune health and counter the aging process. Raspberries are associated with Venus and the elements earth and water. Use in food magick to add passion to relationships. Kindle your love's affection by serving a bowl of fresh berries topped with sweetened whipped cream. Want to succeed in business? Treat yourself to a smoothie made by mixing blackberries, raspberries, and strawberries. Drink it before your meeting to sweeten words, align views, and encourage teamwork.

187. Hugo Munsterberg, *Dictionary of Chinese and Japanese Art* (New York: Hacker Art Books, 1981), 241.

188. "Raspberry," Oregon Raspberries and Blackberries, accessed February 25, 2021, https://oregon-berries.com/variety/raspberry/.

Raspberry leaves also hold nurturing energy. In the Middle Ages, raspberries were a favored women's tonic used to encourage fertility. The leaves were brewed into infusions made to heal and protect. Drink as a tea to support menstrual health. Add a raspberry leaf infusion to washwater to encourage happiness and harmony. Add it to bathwater to encourage love. Anoint a candle with oil and roll it in bits of crushed dried raspberry leaves and dried periwinkle flowers. Burn it to empower love spells.

Rhubarb
Celebration, clear sight, fidelity, health, inspiration, and love

Rhubarb is a member of the buckwheat family also known as garden rhubarb and the pie plant. It is native to Asia, where it has been grown for over five thousand years for its medicinal qualities.[189] Today, in traditional Chinese medicine, rhubarb remains one of the most widely used medicinal herbs. The dried root and rhizomes of the plant are used to treat constipation, liver and gallbladder complaints, poor blood circulation, and senility. Rhubarb traveled to America in the late 1700s: according to folklore, it was Ben Franklin who brought the tart vegetable to American gardens.[190] Today as a garden escapee, it has naturalized in woodland areas.

Rhubarb leaves contain high levels of oxalic acid, a toxin that causes abdominal pain, convulsions, low blood pressure, shock, mouth and throat pain, and vomiting. Do not ingest the leaves. They can be used to make a natural insecticide.

The sweet-tasting stalks are good for you. They are high in vitamins and minerals. Studies have shown that it is rich in the healing antioxidants resveratrol, lutein, and zeaxanthin, beneficial compounds that may help fight cancer, lower cholesterol and blood pressure, reduce inflammation, and protect eye and brain health. Brew up a stimulating rhubarb infusion to encourage friendships and inspire creative thought. Cut 2 cups of trimmed stalks into 1-inch pieces. Put them in a saucepan and cover with water. Bring it to a boil and simmer for 40 minutes. Remove from heat. Stir in sugar to taste. Let it cool. Strain and serve the liquid as tea over ice with sliced strawberries.

Magickally, rhubarb is associated with Venus and can be used in love spells. Serve a piece of rhubarb pie to your love to strengthen your emotional bond. Make a jar of rhu-

---

189. Bell Library Staff, "Rhubarb," Bell Library, University of Minnesota, accessed February 25, 2021, https://www.lib.umn.edu/bell/tradeproducts/rhubarb.

190. Bell Library Staff, "Rhubarb," Bell Library, University of Minnesota, accessed February 25, 2021, https://www.lib.umn.edu/bell/tradeproducts/rhubarb.

barb jam and give it to anyone you want to sweeten toward you. To see your way to a decision, chew a piece of raw stalk or make a tea and sip it to gain clear sight.

Strawberry
Joy, love, luck, money, peace, prosperity, and success

The strawberry is a hybrid species of the genus *Fragaria,* and while store-bought berries are available year-round, their bland taste cannot compare to the lush, sweet homegrown fruit. If your grow zone allows, you can plant once for a crop that will increase each year.

Strawberries are a food of love associated with Venus. Use them in recipes for love, affection, friendship, and happiness. Add them to sweetening spells to make a person's attitude sweeten toward you. Serve the fruit to your love to initiate a zesty romance. Kindle affection with a summer fruit salad. Mix sliced apples, grapes, honeydew, kiwi, strawberries, raspberries, and watermelon to elicit feelings of romantic love. Mix orange segments with strawberries and eat to change your luck. Make a success smoothie by mixing blackberries, raspberries, and strawberries and drinking it before any business endeavor. Leave a strawberry as an offering to gain the favor of your garden fey. Carry a strawberry leaf for good luck.

Tangerine
Beauty, creativity, energy, hospitality, joy, love, strength, and vitality

A cultivar of the mandarin orange native to Tangier, Morocco, the tangerine has bright, cheerful energy to inspire confidence, joy, and love. The tangerine is associated with the sun. The scent grants creative inspiration. Serve a dish of segmented fruit to your guest to make them feel appreciated. Fill a dish with tangerine segments. Top it with crumbled goat cheese and chopped walnuts pieces. Add a drizzle of honey and serve to inspire friendship. Peel and eat a tangerine to lift your mood and ignite your creative spark.

Watermelon
Abundance, cleansing, healing, love, refreshment, and wishes granted

Watermelon is a vine-like flowering plant native to Africa that produces a large summer-favorite water-filled fruit. The sweet fruit has a refreshing, nurturing energy. Eat cold watermelon on a hot day to revitalize and restore. The restorative energy can lift and open. Drink a glass of watermelon juice to clear mental blocks. Add watermelon balls to summer salads to open to new possibilities. Use the fruit in recipes to heal and grow. Serve it at family picnics and barbecues to brighten emotions and sweeten memories. Serve it to a lover to kindle affection. Watermelons are associated with Cancer, Pisces, the moon, summer, July 4th (in America), and the element water.

Use watermelon seeds in abundance spells. Save the seeds and plant with a whispered wish to have the sprout energize its manifestation. Cut a watermelon into large slices and serve outdoors to children to sweeten their mood and foster fond memories. Have them call out a wish after spitting out a seed.

Fruit Recipes

Melon Salad

Combine the cool, uplifting energy of cantaloupe and honeydew with orange and mint for a sweet, refreshing dish that will restore and revitalize both the mood and thought. Serve it to lighten mood or instill a flirtatious energy.

You will need:

1 cup orange juice

¼ cup mint leaves, chopped

½ teaspoon cinnamon

1 Tablespoon of honey

2 cups each cantaloupe and honeydew, scooped into small balls

Mix together orange juice, mint, cinnamon, and honey and pour over melon balls. Serve cold.

Pear and Goat Cheese to Woo

This dish brims with amorous energy to encourage romance. Share it with a lover to stir passions or serve it to increase enthusiasm and instill marital satisfaction.

You will need:

2 ripe pears (if not in season, use figs)

4 ounces goat cheese

2 spoons chopped pistachios or walnuts

honey

For a hot-weather dish, slice and core the pears and arrange on 2 plates. Crumble goat cheese over the pear slices and top with a spoon of chopped nuts and finish with a drizzle of honey over the top. Serve to the one you desire to foster warm feelings or inspire romance.

When the weather turns cold, roast the pears to warm and soften them and bring out their natural sweetness. Heat oven to 375 degrees Fahrenheit. Slice and core the pears and arrange them on a baking dish. Dot with goat cheese. Sprinkle walnut pieces over the top and bake for 10 minutes. The cheese should just begin to brown. Remove the pan from the oven, drizzle with honey, and serve to the one you desire.

Decadent Marsala Poached Pears with Mascarpone Cream

This posh dish is easy to make and impressive to serve. Make to it pamper or to serve at a party to induce a festive mood. You can poach the pears whole or slice and core them. It's up to you and how you would like to present them. A whole pear takes longer to cook but creates an impressive display. If you are going to leave the pears whole, you might want to slice a bit off the bottom of each pear so that it sits flat. If you peel and slice them, you can serve the mascarpone in a dollop in the center and then spoon over the wine sauce and sprinkle with walnut pieces.

For the marsala pears, you will need:

5 or 6 firm ripe pears

1 cup marsala wine

3 Tablespoons butter, soft

3 Tablespoons sugar

honey

2 cinnamon sticks, broken

Preheat the oven to 350 degrees Fahrenheit. Arrange the pears in a baking dish and pour in the marsala. Dot the pears with butter. Sprinkle sugar over the top of each pear and give each a drizzle of honey. Break the cinnamon sticks roughly over the pears. Cover the dish loosely with foil and bake 15 minutes for sliced pears or 25 minutes for whole pears. Remove the foil and reduce the oven temperature to 325 degrees. Baste the pears with wine sauce from the pan by spooning the liquid generously over each pear. Bake for another 15 to 25 minutes, or until the pears are very tender and slightly shriveled. Serve warm or at room temperature, with the juices and a scoop of ice cream or mascarpone cream.

For the mascarpone cream, you will need:

⅓ cup mascarpone cheese

½ whipping cream

¼ teaspoon cinnamon

2 tablespoons honey

walnut pieces to finish

Whip the cheese and cream together. Mix in cinnamon and honey. Serve over fruits and top with walnut pieces.

Cantaloupe and Cucumber Salad

This energizing salad is brimming with cool, uplifting energy for health and beauty. Serve it to restore spirit and improve outlook.

You will need:

1 cucumber, thinly sliced

1 cantaloupe, rind and seeds removed, cut into 1-inch pieces

¼ cup fresh mint, chopped

2 Tablespoons red onion, finely chopped

½ cup roasted pepitas

1 Tablespoon lemon juice

2 Tablespoons olive oil

salt and pepper to taste

In a large bowl, toss together cucumber, cantaloupe, mint, and onion. Sprinkle pepitas, lemon juice, and olive oil over the top and season with salt and pepper.

Watermelon Salsa

This salsa has a cool, restorative energy to refresh and energize. Serve during the heat to lift your mood and inspire happiness.

You will need:

2 cups watermelon, seeded and chopped into small pieces

½ cup peeled and finely chopped cucumber

¼ cup finely chopped red onion

¼ cup finely chopped sweet red pepper

1 jalapeño pepper, seeded and finely chopped

¼ cup chopped fresh cilantro

juice of 1 lime

honey

pinch of salt

In a large bowl, combine the solid ingredients. In a small bowl, combine the lime juice, honey, and salt to taste. Pour the lime juice mixture over fruit and serve with tortilla chips.

Chapter 12

HYDRATION AND WHAT WE DRINK

Your body is a universe within itself, and when all systems are in sync and working properly, you will achieve optimum health. Your energy reserves will seem boundless. You will sleep well and you might even feel sparkly. I often do. It is in these moments when my energy soars, my perception opens, and I become a witness to the synchronicities at work all around me, that I am truly alive—not just a cog in the wheel but a resonating, expanding, contributing, and oh so vibrant part of the fabric of the universe.

We all know that fueling the body with the things it requires helps its performance. Unfortunately, we all have communities of bacteria in our gut that ping the brain with messages to fill it with junk like sugar and soda to fuel its bloom. When you are thirsty, drink water.

The Element Water

Water holds magickal energy to baptize, cleanse, heal, quench, and renew. Water ignites creativity and turns what is barren fertile. Water holds energy for life. It is necessary for good health. It grants satisfaction through quenching thirst. We should all drink lots of water. Not flavored water, not sweetened water, not caffeinated water. Just water. That so many people do not drink plain water shocks me. Don't be one of them. Your body is 60 percent water. Your cells require clean water to function. Not being hydrated affects your mood, your health, and your ability to concentrate. It affects your memory and even your ability to think. When you lose as little as 2 percent of your body's water content, both physical performance and brain performance are impaired and the frequency of head-aches, constipation, and kidney stones increases.[191] One of the very first things you should do when you wake each morning is drink a glass of water.

All water has magickal properties for health and cleansing, but it also carries energies from its source. Spring water holds energy for growth, manifesting, protection, prosperity, knowledge, and the vigor of the earth. Well or artesian water also contains earth energy and has properties to spark intuition and manifest wishes. True glacier water is old water, formed thousands of years ago and held frozen in glaciers. Moon water is water that has been left under the moon overnight to charge with lunar energy. To make a batch, simply pour water from a desired source (i.e., rain, storm, river, or spring) into a clean glass bowl, and at the full moon set it on a moonlit windowsill or place it outside under the light of the moon. You can even set a mirror under the bowl to make the moonlight stronger. Moon water holds lunar energy and will power all moon magick. Use it to bless healing rituals, intensify the mystical, empower intuition, inspire reconciliation, and consecrate initiations.

The Magickal Energies of Other Things We Drink

Coconut Water
Beauty, clear thinking, moon magick, healing, protection, and purification

Coconut water is the lightly sweet juice of immature, green coconuts. It is a refreshing drink that boosts hydration and aids digestion. It is a magnificent hangover remedy, as it settles the stomach and hydrates the cells as it replaces essential electrolytes. Drink coco-nut water to rehydrate and remedy battle fatigue. Use it as a base for smoothies or drink it alone to improve cognitive ability. Magickally, coconut energy is associated with the moon and the element water. Its energy strengthens confidence and inner resolve. Its rich nutri-ent compounds nourish hair and skin cells to give beauty a glowing boost.

---

191. Joe Leech, "7 Science-Based Health Benefits of Drinking Enough Water," Healthline, June 30, 2020, https://www.healthline.com/nutrition/7-health-benefits-of-water.

Tea

Clarity, communication, courage, divination, healing, meditation, protection, and riches

Tea is one of the world's most popular drinks. It is made from the plant *Camellia sinensis*, a species of evergreen shrub whose leaves and buds are used to produce white, green, black, and matcha tea. It is not related to the tree that produces tea tree oil.

Tea originated in China as a medicinal drink and today is the most popular drink, second only to water. A cup of tea will lift the spirit and calm anxiety. Tea contains the stimulant caffeine and L-theanine, a potent amino acid that acts as a relaxing agent. L-theanine interacts with brain receptors, increasing dopamine, the neurotransmitter gamma-aminobutyric acid, and glycine levels in various areas of the brain to produce a sense of calm. Tea is also loaded with antioxidants. It contains more catechin polyphenols (a flavonoid that may help inhibit the growth of cancer cells) than both red wine and chocolate.

Tea is associated with Mercury, the moon, and the element water. It has energy to soothe the spirit, sharpen awareness, enhance communication, and stimulate psychic abilities. Drink a cup to open awareness and inspire creative conversation. Brew up a rejuvenating spritz by filling a small spray bottle with cooled tea. Carry it with you and spritz the air above you to awaken clarity and manifest a fresh perspective. Add an infusion to your bathwater to combat boredom and encourage spirituality. Add a sprinkling of tea leaves to money-drawing rituals to empower the working.

Tea also holds energy for protection. Crumble a handful of tea leaves with salt and strew across a threshold to keep negative energy from entering. Wash mirrors with an infusion of tea to ward against a harmful energy coming through.

Reading tea leaves is an ancient art that has been practiced the world over. A cup of tea is brewed from loose leaves. The tea is sipped and then the cup flipped upside down, and the leaves left at the bottom of a cup are read

Herbal Teas

Comfort and medicine

Anytime after 3:00 p.m. I turn to herbal tea to skip the caffeine and still gain a cup of warm comfort. Herbal teas are not made from tea (*Camellia sinensis*) but from a variety of different herbs, flowers, and spices, and they are sometimes referred to as herbal infusions or tisanes. Popular herbal teas are often a blend of several different herbs and hold the energies of the plants they are made with.

There are hundreds of kinds of herbal teas. Some of my favorites are as follows.

Chamomile Tea
Abundance, communication, peace, rest, and water elementals

Chamomile is member of the daisy family, an Old World medicinal plant with use dating back thousands of years.[192] The name chamomile refers to *Chamaemelum nobile*, or Roman chamomile, and *Matricaria chamomilla*, or German chamomile, two plants belonging to different species but used to treat the same problems. The dried flowers are brewed into an infusion that is used both internally and externally. Chamomile tea has antiseptic powers to soothe the skin and calms the nerves and induces sleep when taken internally. Drink before bedtime to calm the nervous system. Pour an infusion into bathwater to soothe a frazzled mind. Drink a cup of chamomile tea to prepare the mind and body for magickal work.

Chamomile is a sweet-scented strewing herb. It was mixed into potpourris and stuffed into sachets to scent linens and clothes. Chamomile has a calm, grounding energy. It is associated with the sun and has energy to manifest abundance. An infusion of chamomile tea is a Hoodoo good luck fix used by gamblers to wash their hands to increase winnings. Use as a hand wash to attract opportunities. Chamomile also has energy for protection and is known as a "plant doctor" because it is said to revive a sickly plant when planted nearby.

Lavender Tea
Clarity, communication, healing, love, protection, sleep, and transformations

Lavender (*Lavandula angustifolia*) is a fragrant herb in the mint family. It is native to the Mediterranean and was used by the ancient Egyptians as perfume and the Greeks and Romans as medicine.[193] Lavender is associated with Mercury, Gemini, Virgo, and the element air, making it a good addition to any spell that requires fast, clear, communication. The scent of lavender is calming. The herb has been used to scent bathwater for centuries. In fact, the word lavender comes from the Latin word *lavare*, which means to wash.[194]

---

192. Moumita Das, *Chamomile Medicinal, Biochemical, and Agricultural Aspects* (New York: Taylor & Francis, 2014), 3.

193. Steven Foster and Rebecca L. Johnson, *National Geographic Desk Reference to Nature's Medicine* (Washington, DC: National Geographic, 2008), 144.

194. Foster and Johnson, *National Geographic Desk Reference to Nature's Medicine*, 144.

Lavender tea has a floral flavor with a hint of earthy sweetness. It holds a calm energy to clear the mind and open awareness. To brew a cup, add ½ teaspoon of dried lavender buds to a mug. Pour boiling water over it, allow it to steep for 5 minutes, strain, and drink. Drink a cup to end restlessness and calm a worried mind.

Lemon Balm Tea
Friendship, happiness, healing, love, peace, and success

Lemon balm (*Melissa officinalis*) is a fragrant and easy-to-grow lemony herb that is a member of the mint family. It is also called bee balm, common balm, and sweet melissa. Lemon balm energy heals emotions, supports good health, and improves outlook. Avicenna, an eleventh-century herbalist, wrote, "It causeth the mind and heart to become merry."[195] Lemon balm is associated with Diana, Jupiter, emotions, water and the moon. Lemon balm holds energy to encourage love and friendship. It is a bee favorite, and lemon balm honey holds energy to comfort the brokenhearted. The leaves, fresh or dried, brew up a calming tea that eases anxiety and soothes a frazzled spirit. Brew up an infusion and drink to ease mild depression, sharpen memory, and restore balance.

Licorice Root
Binding, fidelity, love, lust, protection, and psychic enhancement

If you like the flavor of licorice (*Glycyrrhiza glabra*) like I do, then you will appreciate the warm, gentle comfort of licorice root tea. It is made from the root of a perennial that has been used since ancient times as a medicine and a sweetener. Licorice root promotes happiness, as it contains natural antidepressant compounds. It is associated with Mercury and holds energy for compulsion. Brew up some licorice root tea and sweeten it with honey. Sip it to soothe a sore throat or quiet a cough. Serve it to sweeten your words and elicit a favorable reaction. In Hoodoo licorice root is added to love and lust potions to gain the power of compulsion and heat up passion. As a spiritual herb, licorice root aids in communication with your higher self. Brew an infusion of licorice root and mugwort and drink to enhance psychic ability. Make an astral infusion with equal parts licorice root, cardamom, cinnamon, and coriander. Bring 1 cup of water to boil. Pour over 1 Tablespoon of the astral mix. Let it steep for 9 minutes. Strain and add it to bathwater. Soak before bed to aid astral travels.

....

195. Martha Bockée Flint, *A Garden of Simples* (Boston: Charles Scribner's Sons, 1900), 13.

Rooibos Tea
Calming, courage, patience, and dream work

Rooibos is a pleasantly sweet, naturally caffeine-free herb native to South Africa. The bush is a member of the pea family, and its name simply means "red bush" in Afrikaans. Rooibos tastes similar to black tea but with a woody and slightly nutty flavor. Rooibos energy is calming and supportive. Drink it to slow wild thoughts or calm worry. Drink it before a tough undertaking for courage and perseverance. Drink it before sleep to enhance dream recall.

Coffee
Clear thoughts, communication, euphoria, and stimulation

The coffee bean is the fruit of a perennial evergreen native to Africa. It is loaded with the stimulant caffeine, making it a popular morning drink to boost energy and help millions get started daily. Coffee also contains antioxidants that enhance immune system function, and it is a natural laxative. A cup of coffee often clears the mind and helps one focus. Drink a cup or eat a handful of chocolate-covered espresso beans for an instant energy boost. Coffee is associated with Mercury the messenger god and holds energy to facilitate clear communications. Serve coffee at a meeting to get everyone on board with the same idea. Sweeten it with honey to sweeten someone to your idea.

Beware: too much coffee can lead to jitters, anxiety, frequent urination, and aggressive behavior. It exacerbates bladder problems and insomnia. The *British Journal of Pharmacology* reported consuming too much coffee can affect female fertility and hinder conception.[196] Coffee also hinders our ability to reach a meditative state. Coffee is one of the foods banned by Mormons, who hold that it hinders the ability to be spiritually attuned. I myself do not drink coffee. It empties my mind so that I am only good for working out or cleaning house after indulging in a cuppa. But as everyone is different, and everyone's body processes substances differently, this might not hold true for you. Next time you indulge, pay attention to how your mind and body respond. Coffee can sharpen the way you feel and cause you to react to things in a negative way. It often enhances the ability to feel while

---

196. R. E. Dixon, S. J. Hwang, F. C. Britton, K. M. Sanders, and S. M. Ward, "Inhibitory Effect of Caffeine on Pacemaker Activity in the Oviduct Is Mediated by cAMP-regulated Conductances," *British Journal of Pharmacology* 163, no. 4 (June 2011): 745–54, https://doi.org/10.1111/j.1476-5381.2011.01266.x.

robbing the mind of thought. Routinely drinking coffee can inhibit your ability to hear your inner voice, which hinders empathy and clairvoyance.

Beer
Banish worry, celebration, happiness, health, and relaxation

One of the oldest recipes in the world is part of a poem written in 1800 BCE by an anonymous poet to honor Ninkasi, the Sumerian goddess of brewing and beer.[197] Beer was ancient Mesopotamia's favorite drink. Some scholars believe that the original incentive for growing barley was not for making bread but for the brewing of beer.[198]

Here in Oregon, craft brewing is big business and homebrewing is a popular hobby. Unlike wine that must age, some beer recipes are drunk young and are ready just ten to fourteen days after brewing.

Beer is the ultimate party drink. It adds life and cheer to celebrations. Serve beer to a gathering of friends to lighten the mood, loosen tongues, and get conversation flowing. Buy a selection of different beers and serve them as tasters to add interest to a dinner party. A glass of cold beer is an excellent remedy for aching muscles after a day of outdoor work. I love to sip a cold beer while soaking in a bubble bath after a day spent working in my garden. Beer is a popular offering, the first of the bottle poured out as a libation to honor and show gratitude.

Wine
Abundance, celebration, relaxation, and romance

Wine is another ancient drink and a favored libation. The first wine we know of was made between 7000 and 6600 BCE by tribes from Jiahu in the Yellow River Valley of China. They made a fermented rice-honey-fruit wine and stored it in earthenware jars.[199] The oldest

197. Joshua J. Mark, "The Hymn to Ninkasi, Goddess of Beer," Ancient History Encyclopedia, March 1, 2011, https://www.ancient.eu/article/222/the-hymn-to-ninkasi-goddess-of-beer/.

198. Stephen Bertman, *Handbook to Life in Ancient Mesopotamia* (Oxford, UK: Oxford University Press, 2005), 292.

199. Patrick McGovern et al., "Fermented Beverages of Pre- and Proto-Historic China," *Proceedings of the National Academy of Sciences* 101, no. 51 (December 21, 2004): 17,593–98, https://www.pnas.org/content /101/51/17593?ijkey=045cde6ef4c520d545f639ff51d0b0b2a513d401&keytype2=tf_ipsecsha.

winery that we know of was founded around 4100 BCE in ancient Armenia.[200] Wine was popular in Asian, Jewish, Roman, Greek, and Egyptian cultures. Today there are more than ten thousand wineries in the United States alone.

Wine is often served with dinner to relax those dining and heighten the flavor of the food. It is served to celebrate events and honor guests. Glasses of wine are often raised to toast or commemorate an event. Wine is a popular evening drink to sip as one unwinds and releases the flurry of the past day. It is a magickal libation poured in offering.

Kombucha
Energy, health, longevity, restoration, and vigor

Kombucha is an ancient elixir with a history that dates back over two thousand years. To the Chinese it was known as the elixir of immortality, as it is brimming with probiotics and is taken to nourish gut health, which is the root of the health of all of the body's systems.[201] While some refer to the membrane as a mushroom, it is not a fungus but a symbiotic culture of bacteria and yeast, thus the name SCOBY.

Kombucha is made by growing a SCOBY in sweetened tea. The SCOBY eats the sugar, tea, and caffeine and turns the liquid into a fermented goodness that tastes a bit like slightly sweet and tangy, fizzy vinegar. Fermented foods nourish gut health and may help treat chronic issues like diarrhea and IBS. Drink it to fortify health.

Hot Cocoa
Gratitude, happiness, health, longevity, love, luxury, and riches

Hot cocoa is made from mixing milk, sugar, and the pulverized seeds of the cacao tree, a delicious, joyful food used to attract happiness, prosperity, and luxury. It is loaded with the psychoactive feel-good chemical anandamide and the love chemical phenylethylamine, which releases dopamine in the pleasure centers of the brain. Cacao also contains trypto-phan, an amino acid that converts into serotonin, a neurotransmitter known to promote a sense of well-being and relaxation. And it's good for your brain, as it contains the com-

200. James Owen, "Earliest Known Winery Found in Armenian Cave," *National Geographic*, January 12, 2011, https://www.nationalgeographic.com/news/2011/1/110111-oldest-wine-press-making-winery-armenia-science-ucla/.

201. Laura Zhang, "The Cloudy Origins of Kombucha," *Folklife*, April 15, 2019, https://folklife.si.edu/magazine/cloudy-origins-of-kombucha.

pound resveratrol, which has been found to slow cognitive decline.[202] Indulge in a cup of hot, rich, sweet chocolatiness to induce a sense of comfort and well-being.

Hot Cocoa

When it's cold outside, it's hard to match the comfort of a cup of hot cocoa. Cocoa and sugar both increase energy and lift mood. This recipe makes 4 servings.

You will need:

½ cup sugar

¼ cup unsweetened cocoa powder

pinch of salt

4 cups milk

1 teaspoon vanilla extract

In a saucepan, whisk together sugar, cocoa powder, and salt. Stir in milk and bring the mix to a simmer. Remove from heat, stir in the vanilla, and pour the cocoa into mugs. Finish with a dollop of whipping cream or a couple of marshmallows.

Hot Chai

Make a cup of hot chai and drink it in quiet contemplation to renew vigor and awaken magickal perception. Or brew a pot and share with a friend to renew bonds and meld shared ideas. The black tea holds energy to open the mind, while the spices bring energy for friendship, love, and renewed passion.

You will need:

2 cups water

2 star anise pods

½ teaspoon cardamom

½ teaspoon cloves

2 cinnamon sticks

5 teaspoons black tea leaves

202. Arrigo F. G. Cicero, Massimiliano Ruscica, and Maciej Banach, "Resveratrol and Cognitive Decline: A Clinician Perspective," *Archives of Medical Science* 15, no. 4 (July 2019), 936–43, https://www.ncbi.nlm.nih .gov/pmc/articles/PMC6657254/.

2 cups of milk

honey or sugar to sweeten

In a 2-quart saucepan, bring water to a boil. Add star anise, cardamom, cloves, cinnamon sticks, and black tea. Bring to a boil and boil for 1 minute. Turn heat down and add the milk. Watch the pan until the milk begins to simmer. When the milk mixture begins to rise in the pan, remove it from heat and set aside to steep for 5 minutes. Strain and pour into serving cups. Add honey or sugar to sweeten. Sip before divination to awaken the mind and open communication channels.

Sweet and Tangy Lemonade

The best homemade lemonade is made by mixing equal amounts of fresh lemon juice and sugar. In this recipe the bright enthusiastic energy of lemon is sweetened to make a refreshing drink to lift mood and encourage happiness. This recipe makes about 2 quarts.

You will need:

2-quart pitcher

1 cup water, plus 3 cups

¾ cups sugar

¾ cups freshly squeezed lemon fresh juice

2 cups ice or more

Pour 1 cup of water into a saucepan and heat. Stir in sugar to dissolve. Bring it to a simmer and then set aside to cool to room temperature.

Pour the remaining water and lemon juice into the pitcher then add the cooled sugar syrup. Stir to combine. Add ice and serve.

Add a few sprigs of fresh peppermint to each glass for a refreshing lift, some sliced strawberries to add energy for love and abundance, or stevia to encourage shared vision.

Smoothies

While I shy away from using the microwave for anything magickal, I will on occasion use other conveyances. Recently, my husband bought me a fantastic little food processor that whizzes up smoothies in a snap. I was quick to discover that any fruit whizzed with a handful of ice and some coconut water becomes a sweet, cool delight to energize on a hot summer day.

Green Drink

This smoothie is my go-to drink to energize after a morning of hard work. The energy of spinach and coconut water work together to boost energy for enhanced health and vitality.

You will need:

2 cups ice

1 cup fresh spinach leaves

1 to 2 cups coconut water

Blend the ingredients together until the ice and spinach have been turned into small bits. Drink while the drink is slushy.

Date Shake

This decadent milkshake holds energy to foster love and friendship and support expansion and growth.

You will need:

2 cups ice

1 cup milk

9 Medjool dates, pits removed

Blend the ice, milk, and dates together until they have been turned into small bits. Serve while the drink is slushy.

Mango Lassi

This drink is brimming with refreshing energy to foster feelings of well-being and self-love.

You will need:

2 cups ice

1 cup fresh mango, peeled, pitted, and sliced

½ cup Greek yogurt

Blend together the ice, mango, and yogurt until smooth and creamy. Serve while the drink is frozen.

Make a Batch of Moon Water

Moon water is water that has been blessed and left overnight to charge in the light of the full moon. It is infused with lunar energy to boost work for healing, clearing, and blessing. Moon water is used to empower moon magicks. It is brimming with healing energy and can be added to magickal baths and used to water ailing plants. It is used in rituals to anoint and consecrate and is drunk to intensify the mystical and increase intuition.

To make a batch of moon water, select a source. If you plan on drinking it, use artesian or spring water. Pour the water into a clear jar and seal it with a lid. Set it in a moonlit windowsill to charge in the moonlight.

If you are using the moon water for magickal work, you may want to choose a natural source, as it will carry its own brand of energy.

- Artesian water (well water drawn up from an aquifer) holds elemental earth energy, which will boost workings for good health, knowledge, and wishes.
- Spring water (water that flows up to the surface naturally) will boost work for health, healing, renewal, and acquiring knowledge.
- Rainwater contains energy from the element air. It will benefit spells for abundance, communication, fertility, inspiration, and clear thought.
- Morning dew will boost work for beauty, sight, glamour, luck, and faery magick.
- River water will boost work for communication, moving forward, opportunity, protection, renewal, setting things in motion, freeing yourself, or getting rid of something.
- Seawater will boost work for healing, manifesting, renewal, strength, and power.

Choose your water and pour it into a clean glass bowl. Set the bowl on a moonlit windowsill. You can even set a mirror under the bowl to make the moonlight stronger. If you have an outdoor place where it will not be disturbed, you may set it outside under the light of the moon, but you may want to cover it to keep out night visitors. Retrieve it before sunrise and use it to fuel your magickal workings.

Chapter 13
SPICES AND HERBS

There is nothing like a well-stocked spice cabinet to bring out your inner witchiness. Since the dawn of time, herbs and spices have been valued for their medicinal and magickal properties. Stories attribute our knowledge of their use as being given by angels, Nephilim, faeries, and even the gods themselves. Herbs and spices are powerful allies for the magickal practitioner. Each holds its own unique brand of magickal energy that corresponds with a magickal working.

Abundance: Cinnamon, fenugreek, ginger, poppy seeds, sesame seeds

Banishing: Basil, bay leaf, black pepper, caraway, clove, horseradish, juniper berries, sage, star anise

Beauty: Celery seed, cilantro, fenugreek, parsley, poppy seeds, rosemary, sesame seeds, turmeric, vanilla

Comfort: Clove, juniper berries, marjoram, vanilla

Communication: Caraway, fennel seeds, lavender, mint, rosemary, thyme, turmeric

Creativity: Basil, chervil, coriander, lemongrass, mint, paprika, savory

Expansion/Increase: Allspice, fenugreek, ginger, tarragon

Happiness: Basil, celery seeds, chervil, cilantro, coriander, marjoram, mint, nutmeg, oregano, parsley, pineapple sage, saffron, vanilla

Health: Allspice, caraway, cayenne pepper, cilantro, cinnamon, coriander, fennel seeds, ginger, lavender, marjoram, mint, peppermint, saffron, sage, spearmint, turmeric

Hex Removal: Bay leaf, chamomile, dill, paprika

Love: Allspice, basil, cardamom, cilantro, cinnamon, cloves, coriander, cumin, dill, ginger, lavender, mace, juniper berries, nutmeg, marjoram, mint, oregano, paprika, parsley, peppermint, rosemary, saffron, savory, sesame seeds, spearmint, star anise, vanilla

Luck: Allspice, basil, bay leaf, chamomile, chervil, cinnamon, cloves, coriander, dill, ginger, horseradish, juniper berries, mace, nutmeg, poppy seeds, star anise, thyme, turmeric, vanilla

Money: Allspice, basil, chamomile, cinnamon, dill, fenugreek, ginger, mace, mint, nutmeg, parsley, poppy seeds, sesame seeds, thyme

Power/Vitality: Bay, black pepper, cayenne pepper, chervil, cinnamon, cumin, fennel seeds, horseradish, oregano, saffron

Prosperity: Basil, celery seed, cinnamon, cloves, ginger, juniper berries, marjoram, mint, nutmeg, parsley, sage, sesame seeds, spearmint, thyme

Protection: Anise, basil, bay leaf, black pepper, caraway, cayenne pepper, cinnamon, cloves, cumin, dill, fennel, ginger, horseradish, juniper berries, lavender, marjoram, mint, mustard, oregano, paprika, parsley, rosemary, sage

Psychic Ability: Anise, bay leaf, cinnamon, juniper berries, lemongrass, nutmeg, peppermint, poppy seeds, savory, star anise, thyme

Rest: Chamomile, lavender, peppermint, poppy seeds, rosemary

Success: Bay leaf, cinnamon, fenugreek, ginger, parsley, thyme

Wisdom: Bay leaf, cardamom, sage, savory

Some Common Herbs and Spices and Their Magickal Properties

Each herb and spice in your cabinet has its own unique store of energy that can be used to empower your magickal practice. Some herbs, such as basil, can be used for almost anything. Basil holds the power to lift the soul, clear the mind, and inspire. Basil will empower abundance, love, and attraction recipes, but its soothing, uplifting energy will also end quarreling. I always keep a stock supply of basil on hand. Its gentle energy resonates with my magickal work. Bay leaves are another. Bay's victorious energy can be used to purify, increase vitality, encourage psychic development, and even break curses. Cinnamon has energy to empower. It has a wonderful aroma that will scent an entire room and can be used in recipes for love, lust, healing, riches, success, and protection. The empowering energy of cinnamon will also add power to other herbs. Nutmeg is another favorite. It holds power for growth and expansion. It is associated with Jupiter and is used to draw luck and riches and encourage opportunities.

As you begin to work with your herbs and spices, you will come to find some work for you better than others. Start getting familiar with them one by one. Choose a spice and read up on its history and its uses. Start experimenting with recipes and keep track of your results. Note them down in detail. It is through the action of record keeping that you will begin to understand which recipes work and which fizzle. Fresh leaves can be chopped and sprinkled over dishes. Whole leaves can be dropped in to infuse soups and sauces. Seeds are more flavorful when they are first toasted and then cracked to release their fragrant oils. Unless directed, herbs should be added near the end of cooking to retain their flavor.

Allspice
Health, healing, increase, love, luck, and money

Allspice is the berry of the pimento tree (*Pimenta dioica*), also known as the Jamaica pimento and myrtle pepper. It is a New World spice and is called allspice because the English who named it thought its flavor tasted like "a combination of clove, juniper berries, cinnamon, and pepper," explains the Herb Society of America.[203]

Allspice is a healing herb associated with Mars and the element fire. Its energy is very uplifting. Use it in recipes to increase health, lift spirits, and improve energy. The berries hold a warming energy that will energize recipes to draw money, luck, or spice up relationships.

....

203. "Allspice History and Fun Facts," the Herb Society of America, 2016, https://herbsocietyorg.presence host.net/file_download/inline/ad769e0a-5a34-455a-956d-55630399a66b.

Allspice is one of the gambler's herbs. The berries are ground and dusted over hands to influence luck. Drop a few berries into your pocket to find favor when you have to face a testy situation. Add it to recipes with cinnamon to attract new opportunities.

Allspice is used ground and whole to flavor puddings, cakes, and biscuits. It is a holiday spice used in mulled wine, chutneys, and mincemeat dishes. It is often combined with cinnamon, ginger, and nutmeg.

Anise
Preventing nightmares, protection, and psychic abilities

Anise (*Pimpinella anisum*) is a flowering annual also known as aniseed and sweet cumin. It produces a small fruit/seed with a licorice flavor. The flavor is similar to star anise (*Illicium verum*), fennel (*Foeniculum vulgare*), and caraway (*Carum carvi*), so much so that there is a lot of confusion over which is which even though none are related.

Anise is one of the oldest-known spices. "Egyptians were reportedly the first to cultivate anise for use as a spice," writes the Herb Society of America.[204] Early Romans served anise cakes that were baked in bay leaves, precursors to our modern wedding cakes.[205] Anise was cited by Hippocrates as a remedy for many ills.[206] He recommended it to soothe the stomach, dispel gas, ease pain, clean the teeth, and sweeten breath. King Edward I taxed the valuable anise seeds, and King Edward IV perfumed his clothes with it.[207]

Anise is associated with the moon, Apollo, Hermes, and Mercury, and like licorice root, anise has energy to soothe and open. A tea made from anise will open perception and deepen intuition. Before divination, make an infusion by pouring 1 cup of boiling water over 2 teaspoons of anise seed. Cover and steep for 10 minutes. Strain and sip the tea to increase psychic abilities and raise vibration. Serve it to quarreling parties to dispel hostility and see past hurt feelings. Take it before bed to prevent nightmares. Add an infusion to

204. "Anise History and Fun Facts," the Herb Society of America, 2016, https://herbsocietyorg.presencehost.net/file_download/inline/02911f74-0bf8-4875-810d-94dbea72de95.

205. Joel S. Denker, *The Carrot Purple: And Other Curious Stories of the Food We Eat* (Lanham, MD: Rowman & Littlefield, 2015), 10.

206. Laurence Marie Victoria Totelin, "Hippocratic Recipes; Oral and Written Transmission of Pharmacological Knowledge in Fifth- and Fourth- Century Greece," PhD diss., University College London, 2013, https://core.ac.uk/download/pdf/29410529.pdf.

207. Denys J. Charles, *Antioxidant Properties of Spices, Herbs and Other Sources* (New York: Springer, 2013), 159.

bathwater and soak to safeguard your dreams or to grant protection when traveling the astral realm.

Anise is traditionally used to flavor goat cheese and lamb dishes, but it pairs well with carrot, citrus, fig, melon, and mint. Anisette is an anise-flavored liqueur made by distilling the seeds. It is a favorite in many Mediterranean countries, traditionally served as a Christmas cordial with a toast to usher in goodwill and happiness.

Basil
Cheer, creativity, exorcism, happiness, harmony, love, luck, protection, and wealth

Basil (*Ocimum basilicum*) is a culinary favorite with a distinctive scent and a pungent flavor. The French called basil *herbe royale*, as it is known for its lovely fragrance.[208] In India basil was an emblem of hospitality.[209] In Tudor England small pots of basil were given to guests as tokens of welcome and hospitality.[210] It was a symbol of love in Italy.[211] Today a healthy basil plant is a popular housewarming gift given to bring good luck to the new home and foster harmony to those within.

Basil is associated with Krishna, Lakshmi, Mars, and Scorpio. It holds an uplifting peaceful energy. Use it to soothe emotions, ease anxiety, and end quarreling. Add it to recipes to promote a happy family life. Brew an infusion of basil leaves. Allow the infusion to cool and then strain and pour it into a spray bottle. Spritz a room to dispel anger after a hostile encounter. Spray yourself to improve your mood and restore peace. A tea made from basil leaves will aid in spirit communication. Sip it before meditation to deepen intuition. Basil is also an herb of prosperity and can be carried to attract money or used to boost sales. Keep a small pot of basil in your kitchen window to keep your larder full. Spritz a room with a basil infusion to draw opportunities or increase business. Keep a plant near the till to increase sales or near the door to draw customers and win their favor. Basil is also an herb of the harvest festival Samhain and is used in rituals of the dead.

Basil is used both fresh and dried. Fresh basil is made into pesto and served with tomato and cheese dishes. It is an ingredient in many Italian, Mediterranean, Thai, and Vietnamese recipes, often used to flavor sauces, salad dressings, soups, and entrées. Basil pairs well

....

208. Charles, *Antioxidant Properties of Spices, Herbs and Other Sources*, 173.

209. Michael T. Murray, Joseph E. Pizzorno, and Lara Pizzorno, *The Encyclopedia of Healing Foods* (New York: Atria Books, 2005), 468.

210. Watts, *Dictionary of Plant Lore*, 25.

211. Murray, Pizzorno, and Pizzorno, *The Encyclopedia of Healing Foods,* 468.

with onions, garlic, and olives. It combines well with oregano, summer savory, rosemary, and sage.

Bay Leaf
Glory, luck, psychic vision, protection, strength, victory, vitality, wisdom, and wishes

The bay (*Laurus nobilis*) is an aromatic evergreen tree also known as the laurel, bay laurel, sweet bay, bay tree, and true laurel. The California bay (*Umbellularia californica*) is a different genus and has noticeably more menthol and eucalyptol, giving the leaves a more medicinal flavor that mellows as the leaves dry. Both are used as a cooking herb to flavor soups and sauces. The oil of the bay leaf has antibacterial, antifungal, and antiviral properties. It has been used down through the centuries as an external treatment for some bacterial and fungal infections. Laurel soap, also called Aleppo soap, is the first known soap, made a thousand years ago in Syria.[212]

Magickally, the bay is associated with the sun, Leo, Daphne, Delphi, Apollo, victory, and visions. The laurel crown and wreath date back to ancient Greece, where they were given to celebrate a triumph.[213] Use bay energy to invigorate athletes and inspire the creative. Fill a spray bottle with a bay leaf infusion and spritz the air above you to awaken creativity. The positive energy will fuel recipes for victory and success. Greek priestesses in the temples of Apollo chewed bay leaves to receive visions.[214] Use it in clairvoyance and wisdom brews. The scent of bay clears away confusion to allow for clairvoyance and wisdom, and when burned, the smoke has a calm awakening effect. Burn it to open the mind and stimulate psychic powers.

Bay leaves have a strong menthol flavor that simmers down into a more complex tea-like essence that gives body to the other flavors. They contain enzymes that help to break down proteins and digest food faster. Bay leaf tea is a digestive aid drunk to calm indigestion. It also has properties to induce sleep. Bay leaf is used to flavor chicken and fish dishes, stews, and soups. It is combined with cumin to flavor bean, lentil, and split pea recipes. Bay

....

212. Cathy Hanson, "Aleppo Soap," Historical Research Update, December 19, 2016, https://www.historical researchupdate.com/news/aleppo-soap/.

213. NIIR Board of Consultants & Engineers, *The Complete Book on Spices & Condiments* (Delhi: Asia Pacific Business Press, 2006), 48.

214. Jennifer Peace Rhind, *Fragrance and Wellbeing: Plant Aromatics and Their Influence on the Psyche* (London: Singing Dragon, 2014), 82.

is also used to add complexity to sweet custards, ice creams, and crème brûlée. Bay leaf pairs well with cloves and allspice.

Black Pepper
Banishing, fearlessness, lust, motivation, protection, purification, and strength

Black pepper (*Piper nigrum*) is the fruit of a flowering vine native to India also known as peppercorn. The fruit produces peppercorns that are green, white, or black depending on its ripeness. Pink peppercorns come from the Peruvian pepper tree (*Schinus molle*).

Black pepper is one of the world's most beloved spices. Its sharp aroma and earthy flavor pair well with many spices. Pepper is a lover's spice known for its aphrodisiac properties. In nineteenth-century Normandy it became fashionable for affluent men to take their female companions to bistros for a late supper of *steak au poivre* to heat passions.[215] Pepper holds a fiery healing energy to clarify thoughts, lift anxiety, and alleviate mild depression. It is associated with the warrior energy of Mars, the element fire, and potent male energy to initiate action. It is added to recipes to activate or heat things up and get them moving. Add its lusty energy to encourage action and stimulate flow. Pepper fuels recipes for protection magick, both defensive and offensive.

Pepper, along with salt, is the most common food flavoring used to heat and add flavor to dishes from meats to desserts. And it's good for you. The peppercorn holds piperine, an anti-inflammatory that helps stimulate digestive enzymes to increase absorption of nutrients, and compounds like curcumin, making it available at a cellular level. For the best flavor, choose whole peppercorns and mill as you need it. Add it to recipes just as they finish cooking.

Caraway
Anti-theft, banishing, clarity, communication, health, and protection

Caraway (*Carum carvi*) is a spice plant also known as meridian fennel and Persian cumin. Caraway is a member of the carrot family. Caraway is one of the world's oldest culinary spices. The seeds were found in Mesolithic food remains, which dates their use as a cooking spice to about five thousand years ago.[216] The pungent anise-like flavored seeds have

215. Bruce Wallis, "A French Dish of Love," *Duluth (Minnesota) News Tribune*, February 10, 2016, https://www .duluthnewstribune.com/lifestyle/food/3944138-bruce-wallis-french-dish-love.

216. Andi Clevely, Katherine Richmond, Sallie Morris, and Lesley Mackley, *Cooking with Herbs and Spices* (Leicester, UK: Anness Publishing, 1997), 289.

been used down through the ages to spice up breads, cheeses, desserts, and flavor liquors. A bread flavored with caraway seeds was favored by the Roman soldiers, and caraway's popularity spread across Europe as they conquered the land, reported Domenica Marchetti for NPR. Since the Middle Ages caraway has been cultivated from Sicily to Scandinavia and was referenced in German medical books from the 1100s as a treatment for stomachache, flatulence, and colic.[217] In Britain seed cakes were "baked by farmers' wives to celebrate the end of wheat sowing and given to farm workers."[218]

Caraway seeds possess carminative properties to soothe the stomach and relieve gas pains. A tea made from steeping the seeds may help clear thoughts, strengthen memory, restore appetite, and remedy digestive disorders. Measure a spoonful of caraway seeds into a cup. Fill it with boiling water and steep to make a pleasant, calming tea that may help a new mother increase her milk production. Mix with an infusion of chamomile and a spoon of honey to soothe frazzled nerves. Chew the seeds to freshen both insight and breath. Caraway is associated with Mercury and the harvest festivals. It holds energy for protection. Drop a handful of seeds into your pocket and carry them to repel negative energy. The seeds work especially well when you have to deal with hectic energy, as you can take a few out of your pocket to chew while waiting in line to keep your thoughts stress-free and help them from turning negative.

Caraway seeds are baked into breads and used to flavor carrot, potato, cauliflower, and cabbage recipes. Caraway's pungent anise flavor intensifies when the seeds are roasted. Place caraway seeds in a pan on low heat and stir for 3 minutes or until seeds become fragrant. Add them to beef, lamb, or pork dishes to heighten flavor. Caraway pairs well with cumin, dill, and parsley.

Cardamom
Clarity, enthusiasm, lust, and love

Cardamom (*Elettaria cardamomum*) is a member of the ginger family prized for its sweet, pungent-flavored seedpods. Cardamom seeds are the world's third most expensive spice,

217. Domenica Marchetti, "The Caraway Seed Is a Spice Worth Meeting," NPR, March 6, 2013, https://www.npr.org/2013/03/05/173529055/the-caraway-seed-is-a-spice-worth-meeting.

218. Hugh Fearnley-Whittingstall, "Hugh Fearnley-Whittingstall's Caraway Recipes," *Guardian*, November 11, 2011, https://www.theguardian.com/lifeandstyle/2011/nov/11/caraway-recipes-hugh-fearnley-whittingstall.

saffron being first and vanilla second. The Egyptians chewed cardamom for fresh breath. The Greeks and Romans used it for perfumes.[219]

Cardamom is associated with Venus. It has an enthusiastic energy that is used for both commanding and compelling. The seeds are added to wine to stir feelings of passion. End a meal with baked apples seasoned with cardamom, cinnamon, and brown sugar to encourage romance. Cardamom can be added to spells as a catalyst to encourage the action of other herbs. Cardamom is an ingredient of chai, which can be served to strengthen relationships. Add milk and honey and serve when doing negotiations to encourage generosity.

Cardamom is a warm spice like cinnamon and nutmeg. Its aromatic blend of spicy and sweet flavors complements cakes, muffins, and pastries. It is a staple in Indian and Middle Eastern spice blends. Cardamom is an ingredient in many curries and chai teas. It pairs well with cinnamon, ginger, cloves, and paprika.

Cayenne Pepper
Cleansing, energy, healing, heating, strength, and protection

Cayenne pepper is a cultivar also known as the red hot chili pepper. Not much is known about its origin. The hot spice powder is made by grinding the flesh and seeds of *Capsicum frutescens*.

Cayenne pepper is associated with fire, Mars, potent male energy, and the impetus of creation. Add a pinch of ground cayenne pepper as a catalyst to recipes to add a burst of energy to get things moving or heat things up. Cayenne pepper promotes a faster recovery. Add a pinch of ground pepper to a cup of tea with lemon and honey to fight off a cold. Make a cleansing tonic by adding ¼ cup of lemon juice, 3 Tablespoons of maple syrup, and ⅛ teaspoon of ground cayenne pepper to a quart of water and drink to fortify when fasting. Sprinkle crushed pepper over dishes to energize. Toast a slice of organic bread and top it with crushed avocado pieces. Drizzle olive oil over the top, add a sprinkle of salt and crushed cayenne pepper, and serve it to warm a relationship. Cayenne is used in protection magick for both defensive and offensive spells.

Cayenne heats up chili, curries, sauces, and stews. It brightens deviled eggs, dips, and salsas.

....

219. Clevely, Richmond, Morris, and Mackley, *Cooking with Herbs and Spices,* 299.

Celery Seed

Beauty, cheerfulness, communication, lust, mental powers, prosperity, and rest

Modern celery (*Apium graveolens*) was cultivated from a small wild celery called small-age. Smallage is the plant we get celery seed from. Smallage grew in river estuaries across ancient Europe. Celery seeds were found in the tomb of Tutankhamen, and the Romans used the strongly flavored seeds as flavoring.[220] Celery seed has energy to calm and restore. In the past it was taken in England in spring as a tonic for the blood.[221] Pour 1 cup of boiling water over 1 teaspoon of celery seeds. Let steep for 10 minutes. Strain out the seeds and sip the tea to soothe the nerves and calm troubled thoughts. Drink before bed for a restful sleep.

Celery seed is associated with Mercury. It holds energy to boost communication and increase mental powers. Make an infusion of celery seed and star anise to sharpen focus. Drink before meditation to open channels with the higher self. Sprinkle over food and eat to strengthen concentration and expand awareness.

Celery seed has a strong flavor that goes well with eggs, tomatoes, and chicken. It is popular in Scandinavian and Eastern European cooking. Both the seeds and leaves are used to flavor sauces, soups, stews, and salads. Celery seed is used in recipes for coleslaw, pickles, and potato dishes and to season soy sauces and vinegars. It pairs well with cumin, ginger, sage, and turmeric.

Celery salt is made by grinding celery seeds with salt in a 1 to 2 mixture. It is sprinkled over chicken, coleslaws, deviled eggs, macaroni, potatoes, and tuna salads.

Chervil

Creativity, happiness, inspiration, joy, luck, renewal, and youth

Chervil (*Anthriscus cerefolium*) is an herb of antiquity also known as garden chervil. It is believed that Moses used chervil to "bless the vessels of the Tabernacle," and it was an herb of joy to the ancient Greeks.[222] The Strawberry Banke Museum staff write that it can be used medicinally as an eyewash.[223] In the language of flowers chervil means sincerity.

....

220. Richard Craze, *The Spice Companion* (London: Quintet Publishing, 1997), 36.

221. E. Lewis Sturtevant, "History of Celery," *The American Naturalist* 20, no. 7 (July 1886): 602, https://www.journals.uchicago.edu/doi/abs/10.1086/274288.

222. Leslie Honaker, "Plant of the Week: Chervil (Herb)," *East Valley (Arizona) Tribune*, last modified, October 7, 2011, https://www.eastvalleytribune.com/get_out/at_home/plant-of-the-week-chervil-herb/article_9cf1ae7f-5625-5b15-a4ca-3115646cd5d7.html.

223. Strawberry Banke Museum staff, *The Herb Garden at Strawberry Banke Museum* (Portsmouth, NH: Strawberry Banke Museum, n.d.), 8.

Chervil is associated with Jupiter. It holds a positive energy to encourage joy and creative thought. Add it to foods to restore vigor. Brew an infusion and use it as a face wash to diminish wrinkles and appear younger. Use to ease the itch of insect bites. Brew a chervil infusion and sip to find inspiration or lift mood.

Chervil has a mild anise or tarragon-like flavor. It is an ingredient in the classic French herb seasonings known as *fines herbes,* in which it is combined with parsley, chives, and tarragon. Use it to flavor fish, eggs, poultry, salads, soups.

Cilantro
Beauty, cleansing, enthusiasm, happiness, healing, longevity, and love

Cilantro (*Coriandrum sativum*) is a small annual also known as Chinese parsley. It grows wild across the Mediterranean. The leaves are used in cooking and added to salsas. Cilantro seed is the cooking spice coriander.

Cilantro is associated with Mars, Aries, Scorpio, and the element fire. It holds energy to boost love spells, stimulate attraction, provoke lust, and bind offenders. It is used in love magicks and fertility rites. In China it is believed to be an herb of immortality.[224] Medicinally, cilantro has phenomenal cleansing abilities, as it helps rid the body of toxins and may even remove mercury from cells. The leaves can be torn and applied to soothe insect bites. Add it to recipes to restore or reset. Blend it with pineapple sage, coconut water, and ice for a refreshing icy drink with energy to cleanse and revitalize. Cilantro holds energy for beauty and can be added to bath spells and beauty regimens for radiant, youthful skin.

Some think that cilantro has a soapy taste. "These people have a variation in a group of olfactory-receptor genes that allows them to strongly perceive the soapy-flavored aldehydes in cilantro leaves," writes Melissa Petruzzello for Encyclopedia Britannica.[225] Despite this, cilantro is one of the most widely eaten herbs in the world. It dominates Mexican, Indian, Thai, Chinese, Caribbean, Mediterranean, North African, and Eastern European cooking. Its versatile flavor complements avocado, beans, cheese, chicken, eggs, fish, lamb, lentils, mayonnaise, peppers, pork, rice, salads, shellfish, tomatoes, and yogurts. It is a staple in recipes for salsas, guacamole, burritos, and chili.

....

224. Marian Burros, "Coriander: Pungent Herb Grows Popular," *New York Times*, August 17, 1983, https://www.nytimes.com/1983/08/17/garden/coriander-pungent-herb-grows-popular.html.

225. Melissa Petruzzello, "Why Does Cilantro Taste Like Soap to Some People?" Encyclopedia Britannica, accessed March 1, 2021, https://www.britannica.com/story/why-does-cilantro-taste-like-soap-to-some-people.

Cinnamon
Healing, love, luck, protection, strength, spirituality, success, and wealth

Cinnamon is a spice that comes from the inner bark of trees that belong to the genus *Cinnamomum*, and though there are hundreds of types of cinnamon, only four are used for commercial purposes: *Cinnamomum verum*, sometimes referred to by its old botanical name *C. zeylancium*, is known as Ceylon cinnamon, real cinnamon, and true cinnamon; *C. cassia* is Chinese cinnamon; *C. burmannii* is known as Korintje or Indonesian cinnamon; and *C. loureiroi* is Vietnamese cinnamon or Saigon cinnamon.

Ceylon cinnamon from Sri Lanka is the more valued of the four. However, it is also the most delicate and therefore less easy to distribute. Ceylon cinnamon has a low coumarin content, unlike the other three. Coumarin is a naturally occurring toxin that may cause liver failure when taken in high doses. Cinnamon leaf essential oil is made by distilling the leaves.

Cinnamon has been prized not only for its warm scent and sweet flavor but also for its medicinal and healing properties. It is one of the oldest recorded herbal medicines, listed in the Bible and in four-thousand-year-old Chinese texts.[226] Cinnamon is a stimulant, astringent, and carminative. It is used to soothe digestive ills and treat diarrhea.

Cinnamon is associated with the sun and Uranus. It holds energy to draw money, stimulate psychic abilities, kindle love, boost attraction, and increase magickal energy in general. Use a pinch of cinnamon to energize an intention. It will act as a spark of energy to get the manifestation moving. The scent of cinnamon registers deep within us to sharpen focus and open doors. Dress a candle in olive oil and roll it in ground cinnamon to raise energetic vibrations and deepen concentration.

Cinnamon is used ground and whole to flavor foods and mull syrups, wines, and punches. It is a popular holiday spice used in cookie, cake, pastry, and biscuit recipes. In Mexico it is added to hot chocolate and mole recipes.

Cloves
Comfort, exorcism, friendship, love, prosperity, protection, and romance

Cloves (*Syzygium aromaticum*) are the aromatic flower buds of an evergreen native to the Malukas, or Spice Islands. They are also known as a winter spice. Like cinnamon, cloves are associated with feasts and celebrations. It was customary for the people of the Spice

---

226. Charles, *Antioxidant Properties of Spices, Herbs and Other Sources*, 231.

Islands to plant a clove tree at the birth of a child. The child would wear a necklace made of strung cloves as a protection amulet from evil and illness.[227] Cloves are used to calm the stomach, relieve gas, and treat toothaches, as they have a numbing effect. Clove oil is loaded with eugenol, which has both antiseptic and anti-inflammatory properties. It is a common ingredient in mouthwashes, toothpastes, soaps, and insect repellents.

Cloves are associated with Uranus and Aquarius and have a warming energy to activate other energies. Add them to recipes to stimulate forward action. Clove energy is a psychic enhancer. The scent lifts the spirit and heightens positive emotions. Use it to empower recipes for love. At your next dinner party, dress a candle in olive oil, roll it in ground cloves, and burn it to deepen affection and friendships. Mix ground cloves with olive oil and wear it as a perfume to draw love to you. Sew dried cloves into a friendship gift to strengthen a bond. Cloves are also an herb of protection with a cleansing vibration and can be used to dispel negative energy and bind those who think ill toward you. Stud a candle with whole cloves and burn it to drive away hostility, dispel negative energy, or stop gossip.

Cloves are one of the holiday spices used to stud holiday hams. They are pressed into oranges and hung to make a scented pomander ball. Cloves love meat. Mix cloves with red wine and basil for a succulent marinade. Or used the French technique called an *onion cloute*, or "nailed onion," by studding half an onion with a dozen cloves and then dropping it into a broth or braise. Since cloves hold energy for protection with a cleansing vibration, this can be served to dispel negative energy or bind those who think ill toward you. Cloves pair well with allspice, basil, cinnamon, nutmeg, orange peel, star anise, and vanilla.

Coriander
Adaptation, creativity, enthusiasm, healing, love, and luck

Coriander (*Coriandrum sativum*) is the seed of the annual herb known as cilantro or Chinese parsley. The leaves are used in cooking and added to salsas, while the seed is a cooking spice. In Ayurvedic medicine, coriander is combined with fennel seeds and cumin to soothe digestion, reduce stomach acid and act as a restorative.[228] Coriander is mentioned in Sanskrit texts dating back almost seven thousand years.[229] It was found in the tombs of

---

227. Clevely, Richmond, Morris, and Mackley, *Cooking with Herbs and Spices,* 300.

228. Rumin Jehangir, "CCF: Ayurvedic Detoxifying & Rejuvenating Tea," Chit.Chaat.Chai., March 24, 2021, https://chitchaaatchai.com/food/recipes-ayurveda/drinks/ayurvedic-cumin-coriander-fennel-tea/.

229. Andi Clevely and Katherine Richmond, *The Complete Book of Herbs* (London: Smithmark Publishers, 1998), 85.

the pharaohs, and the Roman legions carried coriander through Europe using it to flavor their bread.[230] In the *Arabian Nights*, coriander is cited as a love potion.[231] To the Chinese it was an herb that bestowed immortality.[232]

Coriander is associated with Mercury, the moon, and Mars. It is used to draw luck and new love and is added to food to encourage passion. To make your partner lusty, add a sprinkle of ground coriander to a glass of wine. Anoint candles with olive oil and roll in crushed coriander to empower love spells. Burn to promote positive energy flow. Add coriander to recipes to encourage a new way of thinking. Coriander energy lifts and inspires. It eases fear and facilitates a change. Use it in meditation to gain insight when facing a crossroads or adapting to change. Chew a handful of coriander to bolster your spirit and make your thoughts receptive when facing a new job or an interview.

Coriander is used to flavor foods all over the world, from Moroccan harissa to Indian curries. It is toasted and crushed with equal parts cumin and fennel seeds and used as a rub on chicken, fish, beef, and pork. Coriander instills a light citrus flavor to European cookies, gingerbread, apple pie, and bread pudding.

Cumin
Anti-theft, exorcism, protection, and virility

Cumin (*Cuminum cyminum*) is the seed of a flowering plant in the parsley family native to Egypt. It has an ancient history and "has been found in 4,000-year-old excavations in Syria and in ancient Egypt, where it was used both as a spice and as an element in preserving mummies," reports chef and culinary writer Danilo Alfaro. "It appears in the Bible in both the Old Testament and the New Testament."[233] Cumin made its way to India and South America with the Spanish explorers, where it became part of the national cuisines.[234] Today cumin is used in Indian curries and many Latin American recipes.

Cumin is associated with Mars and Taurus. It holds a warm earthy energy to fuel protection magicks. Sprinkle it over onion and pepper dishes to empower them. Add cumin

....

230. Clevely, Richmond, Morris, and Mackley, *Cooking with Herbs and Spices,* 292.

231. Picton, *The Book of Magical Herbs,* 89.

232. Picton, *The Book of Magical Herbs,* 89.

233. Danilo Alfaro, "What Is Cumin?" the Spruce Eats, May 18, 2020, https://www.thespruceeats.com/what-is-cumin-995638.

234. Deborah Madison, *The Illustrated Encyclopedia of Fruits, Vegetables, and Herbs* (London: Book Sales Inc., January 26, 2017), 283.

to love recipes to encourage fidelity. Dress a candle with olive oil and roll it in ground cumin. Set it in the center of the table at any gathering and light it to keep the conversation amicable.

Cumin's strong earthy flavor adds depth to Southwestern, Greek, Indian, Middle Eastern, and North African dishes. It is an ingredient in curries, kebabs, and stews. It is added to taco, bean, and chili recipes. It pairs well with cinnamon, coriander, ginger, and turmeric.

Dill
Concentration, love, luck, lust, money, and protection

Dill (*Anethum graveolens*) is an annual herb in the celery family native to northern Europe and Russia. Dill has both carminative and sedative properties. It is referenced in the Papyrus Ebers in 1550 BCE as a medicinal herb and has been used for centuries as a soothing tonic and an aphrodisiac.[235] The Romans believed dill drew good fortune and made wreaths from its leaves to honor athletes and heroes. Dill is mentioned in Matthew as being a tax payment, "ye pay tithe of mint and dill and cumin, and have omitted the weightier matters of the law."[236] To the medieval world, dill was a medicinal herb and a magickal one, used to counter witchcraft.[237] Dill traveled to the New World, and the seeds became known as "meeting house seeds," as they were given to children to chew during long sermons to keep them from feeling hungry.[238]

Magickally, dill is associated with the element fire, Mercury, and Gemini. It is used to attract prosperity and good luck and valued for its powers of protection. Eat bread flavored with dill before job hunting to improve prospects. Dill seeds hold a warming energy that can be sprinkled on rolls to activate wheat's energy to draw prosperity. Add a pinch to any money spell to activate and empower. Dill holds positive, affirming energy. Add sprigs to a vase of flowers and use it as a table centerpiece to boost optimism, inspire conversation, and discourage disagreements. Use dill to garnish deviled eggs and serve them to elevate a negative outlook or counter envy.

Dill is a traditional herb used in German and Scandinavian cooking to flavor salads, white sauces, and meats. Fresh dill adds a pleasant brightness to egg, seafood, and fish

235. Carol Schiller and David Schiller, *The Aromatherapy Encyclopedia: A Concise Guide to Over 385 Plant Oils* (Laguna Beach, CA: Basic Health Publications, 2008), 105–6.

236. Matthew 23:23 (New American Standard).

237. James Moseley, *The Mystery of Herbs and Spices* (Bloomington, IN: Xlibris, 2006), 118.

238. Picton, *The Book of Magical Herbs*, 69.

dishes. Chop a handful of fresh dill and mix it into a cup of plain yogurt. Add a clove of minced garlic and a squeeze of lemon for a zesty sauce to serve over fish. Dill seed is well known as a pickling spice. It goes well on carrots, potatoes, spinach, and zucchini. Dill pairs well with basil, coriander, cumin, ginger, mustard, paprika, parsley, and turmeric.

Fennel Seeds
Communication, healing, perception, protection, purification, and strength

Fennel (*Foeniculum vulgare*) is a perennial herb in the carrot family. Fennel is one of the nine sacred herbs recorded in the tenth-century *Lacnunga*: when used in combination with mugwort, betony, lamb's cress, plantain, chamomile, nettle, crabapple, and thyme, it had the power to drive off the devil.[239] The sweet scent of fennel made it a popular strewing herb. In the Middle Ages fennel was hung over doors and the seeds were stuffed into keyholes to ward off evil spirits.[240] In Germany, fennel was used to ward off illnesses attributed to being "elf-shot."[241] In the New World the seeds were chewed during the long sermons to stave off hunger, and fennel became known as one of the "meeting house seeds."[242]

Chew fennel seeds to relieve gas pains or make an infusion by bringing 1 cup of water to a boil. Add 1 teaspoon of crushed fennel seeds and reduce the heat to a simmer. Strain out the seeds and sip. Fennel has antianxiety properties. Its energy can open perception. Sprinkle fennel seeds over your food to refresh your outlook. Chew a handful to sweeten your words so they will find favor. Anoint a candle with grape-seed oil and roll it in fennel seeds. Burn it to overcome obstacles, find clarity, and grant solutions. Drop fennel seeds into a pocket or sew them into the hem of your clothes to enliven your personality and become more charismatic. Fennel is associated with Mercury. It has energy for magickal protection. Sprinkle fennel seeds across windowsills and thresholds to ward house of negative energy.

Fennel seeds add a subtle fragrant sweetness to breads and cookies and are used to flavor soups, sauce, and marinades. Add them to dressings or mayonnaise and use them to spice up macaroni and potato salads. Their flavor complements broccoli, brussels sprouts,

---

239. Storl, *A Curious History of Vegetables*, 132.

240. Small, *Culinary Herbs*, 371.

241. Storl, *A Curious History of Vegetables*, 132.

242. Andrew Weil, *National Geographic Guide to Medicinal Herbs* (Washington, DC: National Geographic, 2010), 149.

seafood, and cheese dishes. Fennel seeds pair well with allspice, anise seed, caraway seed, cardamom, chervil, cinnamon, cumin, fenugreek, lemon balm, mint, parsley, and thyme.

Fenugreek
Abundance, beauty, increase, and money

Fenugreek (*Trigonella foenum-graecum*) is used as an herb, a tea, a spice, and a vegetable called *methi* that is popular in Indian cuisine. It is an herb of increase. Women in the Middle East, North Africa, and India have used the seeds and leaves of fenugreek since ancient times to stimulate menstrual flow and increase milk flow.[243] In the Middle Ages fenugreek was used as a cure for baldness.[244] A fenugreek infusion makes a nicely scented hair rinse. Fenugreek is an herb of increase. It was taken by men to improve libido and by women to bring on childbirth, increase breast milk production, and add to a fuller breast size.[245] Fenugreek is an aphrodisiac. It contains diosgenin, a saponin similar to human sex hormones.[246] Fenugreek stimulates metabolism and aids gastrointestinal and stomach ailments. The seeds are rich in iron and, when eaten, cause perspiration and urine to smell like maple syrup, which might be why fenugreek is known as an herb of allure and magnetism. Fenugreek is associated with Mercury and Apollo. It holds energy to increase charisma. Fenugreek is highly aromatic. The herb can be found in Asian markets while the seeds are available as spice. Add ground fenugreek seeds to curries for a savory dish that will inspire ideas to increase wealth. Stuff a white cotton pouch with 2 Tablespoons of fenugreek seeds, 2 Tablespoons of dried basil, and ¼ cup of chamomile. Place the pouch under your pillow and keep track of your dreams to reveal a missed opportunity. Fenugreek complements cardamom, cinnamon, cloves, coriander, cumin, fennel seed, garlic, dried lime, pepper, and turmeric.

Ginger
Abundance, courage, energy, health, love, luck, prosperity, and success

Ginger (*Zingiber officinale*) is a hot, fragrant spice that comes from the root of a plant native to China. The Chinese have used ginger since the sixth century for its therapeutic effects

....

243. NIIR Board of Consultants & Engineers, *The Complete Book on Spices & Condiments*, 93.

244. Clevely, Richmond, Morris, and Mackley, *Cooking with Herbs and Spices*, 325.

245. Craze, *The Spice Companion*, 117.

246. Anna Kruger, *The Pocket Guide to Herbs* (London: Parkgate Books, 1992), 40.

and its flavor.[247] Dioscorides, the Greek physician, recommended ginger to aid digestion, and in the sixteenth century, "Henry VIII recommended ginger root as a remedy for the plague," write aromatherapists Carol Schiller and David Schiller.[248]

Ginger is a warming spice associated with the moon and Mars. It holds energy to protect and to increase or heat up the action of any luck, money, or love recipe. Add a pinch of ground ginger to recipes, brews, and potions to boost the working. Use it to empower prosperity work. An infusion made from ginger will give a pleasant lift and increase stamina and well-being. Peel and chop a 1-inch piece of ginger root. Bring 4 cups of water to a full boil. Turn down the heat. Add the ginger root and simmer for 15 minutes. Strain and drink. Add lemon, honey, and cayenne pepper to fight a cold, boost your immune system, or increase your personal power.

While fresh ginger root is a staple for Asian cooking, in the Unites States it is well-known as a powdered holiday spice used to make sweets like ginger snaps and gingerbread. Its lovely peppery flavor blends well with many spices, making it a component of many blends, from pumpkin pie spice, chai, and curry, to Old Bay and garam masala. Use ginger to heighten the flavor of cardamom, cinnamon, cloves, dried fruits, honey, nutmeg, paprika, pepper, and saffron.

Horseradish
Exorcism, luck, protection, purification, and strength

The perennial horseradish (*Armoracia rusticana*) is a member of the mustard family. The young leaves can be used to flavor foods, but it is the spicy root that has been valued for its sharp, hot flavor. Horseradish has been used for over 3,000 years "as an aphrodisiac, a treatment for rheumatism, [and] a bitter herb for Passover seders."[249] As reported in *The Encyclopedia of Healing Foods*, "According to legend, the Delphic oracle told Apollo, 'The radish is worth its weight in lead, the beet its weight in silver, the horseradish its weight in gold.'"[250]

Horseradish is associated with Mars and Scorpio. It is loaded with stimulating energy, vitamins, and natural antibiotics. A tea made from boiling the grated root is good for treat-

---

247. NIIR Board of Consultants & Engineers, *The Complete Book on Spices & Condiments*, 93.

248. Schiller and Schiller, *The Aromatherapy Encyclopedia*, 117.

249. "Horseradish History," Horseradish Information Council, Horseradish.org, accessed March 1, 2021, https://horseradish.org/horseradish-facts/horseradish-history/.

250. Murray, Pizzorno, and Pizzorno, *The Encyclopedia of Healing Foods*, 488.

ing flu and urinary tract infections. Pour 1 cup of boiling water over 1 teaspoon of grated horseradish and steep for 5 minutes. Strain and drink it for a stimulating infusion that will help heal and rejuvenate. Eat horseradish to enhance strength and gain the fortitude to accomplish something difficult. Add it to food to boost endurance.

The hot and spicy flavor of horseradish is often added to yogurt and sour creams and served with beef or made into a cocktail sauce and served with seafood. Make a comforting casserole by adding horseradish sauce to steamed broccoli and cauliflower. Mix it into root mashes or use it to spice up potatoes. It also combines well with ketchup, ginger, and soy sauce.

Juniper Berries
Antitheft, banishing, comfort, exorcism, love, protection, and visions

Juniper berries are small cones of a genus of conifers in the cypress family native to Europe, South Asia, and North America. The juniper is referenced in the Old Testament as being a refuge, and the berries were used in the Middle Ages for protection against evil and to keep snakes away.[251] The Egyptians used juniper berries as medicine, as cooking spice, and to embalm the dead.[252] The ancient Greeks fed their athletes juniper berries to boost their stamina.[253]

Juniper is associated with Mars, Saturn, and Aries. Juniper has a long history as a magickal fumigator. In France it was burned as a disinfectant; in Italy, to ward off the evil eye. Hippocrates recommended burning the berries as fumigant to purify sickrooms.[254] Today the wood and berries are burnt as incense to cleanse, to protect, and to coax spirits to become visible. Burn juniper berries on a charcoal disk on the New Year to bless and add protection for the coming year. Drop three berries into your left pocket when traveling to avoid accidents and stay safe. Juniper also has energy for love. Three berries dropped into a glass of wine will warm affections. Add the berries to love sachets to increase potency. Add them to bathwater to increase attraction.

While juniper berries are aromatic and bitter and known for their role in flavoring gin, in the kitchen the peppery-piney flavor is used to complement poultry and venison and

....

251. Clevely, Richmond, Morris, and Mackley, *Cooking with Herbs and Spices*, 305.

252. Andrew Dalby, *Dangerous Tastes: The Story of Spices* (Berkeley: University of California Press, 2000), 133.

253. Stephanie Gailing, *Planetary Apothecary* (Berkeley: Crossing Press, 2012), 166.

254. Marcello Pennacchio, Lara Jefferson, and Kayri Havens, *Uses and Abuses of Plant-Derived Smoke* (Oxford, UK: Oxford University Press, 2009), 107.

add a Scandinavian flavor to jams, jellies, and relishes that use orange, lime, and rhubarb. Juniper berries can be used fresh or dried. Crush 2 Tablespoons of dried juniper berries and 3 dried bay leaves into ½ cup of red wine and use it as a marinade to flavor venison, beef, and duck. Juniper berries combine well with bay, caraway, celery, garlic, marjoram, pepper, rosemary, savory, and thyme.

Lavender
Calm, clarity, communication, healing, love, protection, and sleep

Lavender is a fragrant Old World herb in the mint family. Early Romans used lavender to scent washwater.[255] In fact, the word lavender comes from the Latin word *lavare*, which means to wash. "In the Middle Ages, lavender was a strewing herb," writes Nancy Hajeski in *National Geographic Complete Guide to Herbs and Spices*.[256] The scent of lavender is calming. In sixteenth century England lavender was quilted into hats to "comfort the braines."[257] In 1640 English herbalist John Parkinson wrote that lavender was "especiall good use for all griefes and paines of the head and brain," notes Penelope Ody in *The Complete Medicinal Herbal*.[258]

Lavender is associated with Mercury, Gemini, Virgo, and the element air, making it a good addition to any recipe for fast, clear communication. The scent of lavender holds a calming energy to clear the mind and open awareness. Lavender tea is made by pouring boiling water over dried lavender buds. Bring 1 cup of water to a boil. Measure a teaspoon of lavender into a mug. Pour the hot water over the buds and allow it to steep for 5 minutes. Strain and serve to aid communication or make a closed mind more receptive. Add a teaspoon of chamomile to induce restfulness and relieve worry. Lavender buds are used in love magicks and added to wedding cakes to ensure fertility. Add lavender buds to recipes to attract and protect relationships or to promote harmony in the home. Sprinkle over muffins or cakes to add positive energy. Add candied violets to attract love.

Culinary lavender is available both fresh and dried. English lavender (*Lavandula angustifolia*) has the sweetest fragrance of all lavenders and is the most commonly used to add a floral nuance to cookies, breads, and even ice cream. Lavender is a component in the

255. Reader's Digest, *Magic and Medicine of Plants* (New York: Reader's Digest, 1986), 233.

256. Nancy J. Hajeski, *National Geographic Complete Guide to Herbs and Spices: Remedies, Seasonings* (Washington, DC: National Geographic, 2016), 184.

257. Reader's Digest, *Magic and Medicine of Plants*, 233.

258. Penelope Ody, *The Complete Medicinal Herbal* (London: Dorling Kindersley, 1993), 73.

famous blend *herbes de Provence* (with marjoram, oregano, rosemary, and thyme). Lavender-infused sugar is a posh treat made by layering flowers and sugar in a jar and letting it sit for several weeks. The sugar is used to sweeten lemonades and teas. It is mixed into batters, pressed into sugar cookies, and sprinkled over fruit. Lavender pairs well with lemon, oregano, rosemary, sage, and thyme.

Lemongrass
Inspiration, mental clarity, psychic powers, purification, and wakefulness

Lemongrass (*Cymbopogon citratus*) is a scented grass native to Southeast Asia. The fragrant leaves are used in cooking and brewed into tea. The oil is a traditional insect repellant used to repel mosquitoes and fleas.

Lemongrass holds an inspiring energy to lift and open. Drop a stalk into a glass of iced tea and sip it to restore energy and awaken the senses. Make an infusion of lemongrass and sip it to brighten your outlook. Add a lemongrass infusion to a spray bottle and spritz the air above you to open communication channels and inspire creativity. Lemongrass is a Hoodoo herb used to wake lust. Brew an infusion and sip it with your lover to heighten awareness of each other. Add a sprig of lemongrass to glass of white wine and sip to heighten pleasure. Lemongrass holds energy to boost positive emotions and clear away negative energy. It can rid a room of a haunting or end a hex. Pour boiling water over a handful of lemongrass, a spoonful of chopped burdock root, and a sprig of rosemary. Let it steep for 9 minutes and strain. Add it to your washwater and use it to wipe down the threshold, doorways, floors, and countertops to banish negative energy and lift vibration.

Lemongrass is a component of Thai cuisine. Its lemony ginger flavor brightens soups, marinades, salads, and desserts. The leaves are also good for infusing lemon flavor into teas, soups, marinades, and sauces, but the more flavorful part is the pale green base of the stem. Use it to flavor teas, poultry, seafood, and vegetable dishes. Lemongrass pairs well with garlic, lemon, lime, coconut, chili peppers, pears, and shallots.

Mace
Love, luck, money, and truth

Both mace and nutmeg come from the fruit of a tree (*Myristica fragrans*) native to the Banda Islands. The fruit is the size of an apricot. The flesh splits to reveal a red mesh-covered seed. Mace is the red mesh outer coating and the seed is nutmeg. Mace is removed by hand and dried and then sold in whole pieces called blades. It is a highly aromatic warming spice with a flavor that is sweeter and subtler than nutmeg.

Mace and nutmeg were "first brought to Europe from the Banda Islands by Portuguese sailors in 1512," where it "gained the reputation as a cure-all," writes Penelope Ody.[259] Mace is associated with Jupiter, Pisces, the element air, and the celebration of Samhain and Yule. Magickally, it holds positive energy to attract luck and abundance. Charge candles with positive energy by anointing them with oil and then rolling them in ground mace. Use them in spells to draw love, luck, and money. Grind mace with equal parts cardamom, clove, and ginger to make a prosperity-drawing powder. Sprinkle ground mace over a cappuccino and serve it to encourage a lasting friendship. Make a truth powder with mace, dried rose petals, and mint. Grind it into a powder and dust it on your hands. Touch a person you think is lying to compel them to tell you the truth.

The flavor of mace is slightly more peppery than nutmeg. It is used to make curries, meat marinades, and creamy sauces. It is a flavoring for cocoas, eggnog, milkshakes, cakes, and pastries. Mace complements fruit, custards, and cheese dishes. It heightens the flavor of creamed soups and chicken pies. A pinch will bolster the flavor of pumpkin, potato, and sweet potato dishes. Mace combines well with cardamom, cinnamon, cloves, coriander, cumin, ginger, nutmeg, paprika, pepper, and thyme.

Marjoram
Comfort, happiness, healing, joy, love, prosperity, and protection

Marjoram (*Origanum majorana*) is a tender perennial native to Cyprus and southern Turkey. Its name means "joy of the mountain."[260] To the Greeks and Romans marjoram symbolized happiness. It was woven into crowns and wreaths and worn by wedding couples for happiness.[261] In Greece, marjoram was planted on graves to bring peace to those who have died.[262] It "was listed as one of Tusser's strewing herbs scattered over floors to freshen, disinfect and ward off disease," writes the Herb Society of America. "Marjoram

....

259. Ody, *The Complete Medicinal Herbal*, 73.

260. Reader's Digest, *Magic and Medicine of Plants*, 243.

261. Reader's Digest, *Magic and Medicine of Plants*, 243.

262. Gabriel Mojay, *Aromatherapy for Healing the Spirit: Restoring Emotional and Mental Balance* (Rochester, VT: Healing Arts Press, 2000), 94.

(*Origanum* sp.) was grown in English knot gardens as bee and butterfly plants in the Tudor and Stewart periods, and was planted in mazes during the 16th century."[263]

The scent of marjoram is calming. Today it is used to restore joy to the grief-stricken. Sip an infusion made from the leaves or flowers to treat depression. Add it to your bath to lift your mood and foster joy or soothe muscle spasms, aching joints, and sprains. Rub it on the forehead to relieve a headache. Marjoram is associated with the moon, Diana, Juno, Mercury, Jove, Osiris, Thor, and Samhain. It holds energy for love, healing, protection, and prosperity. Use marjoram in love recipes. Stir it into pasta sauces to improve flavor and lift your outlook. Add it to vegetables and tomato-based dishes to boost positive energy. Sip marjoram tea to calm spirit and renew appreciation for life.

Marjoram has a long history as a "meat herb." Its pleasant aromatic flavor works fantastically with a wide range of meats both roasted and cooked in stews. Use it to flavor chicken, lamb, and tomato-based dishes. It combines well with basil, bay, chili, cumin, mint, paprika, parsley, rosemary, sage, and thyme.

Mint
Communication, healing, inspiration, motivation, prosperity, protection, travels, and uplifting

There are over thirty varieties of mint (*Mentha*) that grow throughout the world. Spearmint and peppermint are two of the most popular. Spearmint is a symbol of hospitality.[264] Mint is very aromatic. The ancient Hebrews used it as a strewing herb in their temples, while in Greece it was customary to rub crushed mint into tables as a symbol of hospitality.[265] Folks in the Middle Ages used mint to whiten teeth, cure cold sores, soothe wasp stings, and keep milk from curdling," shares the Herb Society of America.[266]

Mint is associated with Hecate, Venus, Mercury, and the element air. It holds a refreshing, uplifting energy that can be used in health, motivation, and money-drawing recipes. Mint is a popular strewing herb and releases a sweet scent when walked upon. It holds positive energy to lift the spirit and improve outlook. Crumble dried mint leaves and sprinkle them around a room after an argument to restore feelings of peace. Strew mint to change

263. The Herb Society of America, *Oregano and Marjoram* (Kirtland, OH: The Herb Society of America, 2005), 12.

264. NIIR Board of Consultants & Engineers, *The Complete Book on Spices & Condiments,* 118.

265. James Moseley, *The Mystery of Herbs and Spices,* 122.

266. "Mint History and Fun Facts," the Herb Society of America, accessed March 2, 2021, https://herbsociety org.presencehost.net/file_download/inline/df74f754-852e-4680-bf3d-bc8d25fa8bf9.

the atmosphere of a room or appease the spirits of a place. Toss a handful into a fire to enhance focus and induce calm clarity before rituals. Stuff mint leaves into a mesh bag and drop it under running bathwater to revive and restore. Brew a mint infusion and use as a hair rinse to refresh outlook, lift the spirit, and inspire creative thought. Add an infusion to a footbath to relax the anxious and refresh the weary. Tuck a sprig of mint into your left pocket to draw positive energy and avoid being cursed. Grow it along the front path to keep negative energy away. Stuff mint leaves in your front left pocket when you must face something that makes you anxious. Touch the pocket and draw a deep breath to keep a level head. Like pepper, mint holds energy to "heat things up"; use it to stimulate business. Pour an infusion of mint into a spray bottle with spring water and mist your place of business to attract customers. Spritz the threshold when selling your home to make prospective buyers feel positive. Mint tea grants restorative energy and clarity of mind and enhances psychic abilities. Add a mint sprig to a glass of iced tea and sip with a friend to infuse relationship with cheerful energy.

Fresh mint adds a lovely cool flavor to a number of sweet and spicy drinks and dishes. It is a traditional seasoning for lamb, stews, and marinades. It cools watermelon and brightens rice. Add chopped mint to revitalize worn chicken, pea, and bean dishes. It combines well with lemon, chili peppers, basil, and oregano.

Mustard
Courage, faith, fertility, and protection

The mustard family (Brassicaceae) is a huge family, some of whose members are grown for the spicy flavored seeds that are ground to produce the popular condiment mustard. Mustard is an ancient herb found in prehistoric caves from Europe to China.[267] The ancient Greeks believed mustard was given to mankind by Asclepius, the god of healing, and a plaster of mustard paste has been used down through the ages to treat a variety of ailments.[268] In herbalist John Gerard's 1597 *The Herball*, he recommends mustard to aid digestion, warm the stomach, and stimulate the appetite.[269] Mustard seed is a healing spice with properties to stimulate the immune system and relieve pain. The seeds have an anti-

267. James Moseley, *The Mystery of Herbs and Spices*, 79.

268. Moseley, *Herbs and Spices*, 79.

269. John Gerard, *The Herball: or the Generall Historie of Plantes* (London: John Norton, 1597), 190, https://books.google.com/books?id=pgZfAAAAcAAJ.

inflammatory effect on sore muscles. A teaspoon of mustard taken at bedtime will help relieve leg cramps. Mustard also may also help with fertility. Mix a spoon with olive oil and honey and take daily to improve chances of conception.

The mustard seed is a symbol of faith representing both opportunity and change. Carrying a mustard seed is one of the oldest-known good luck amulets. As a child, I had a pendant, a tiny mustard seed enclosed in glass. Sprinkle mustard seeds across your doorway to protect your house from intruders. Fill a bag with mustard seeds and bury it beneath your doorstep to deter spirits, prevent hauntings, and protect against accidents. Before working with a dark energy, string mustard leaves and wear them on your head to conceal your identity or staple or glue mustard leaves to a plain Halloween mask. Add mustard greens to meals to promote courage and valor.

After loads of spring rain, the wild hills along the southern highways turn yellow with a black mustard superbloom. It grows as high as six feet to cast the hills in a yellow hue. The seed of black mustard (*Brassica nigra*) is also known as eye of newt and is said to aid flying spells and formulas to open perception. In Hoodoo it is ground with graveyard dirt and sulfur to make a defensive powder to disrupt the activities of a meddler or to thwart a troublemaker. Mix a pinch of ground mustard seed with sea salt and add it to bathwater to end bad luck or remove a hex. Use mustard to ward the body before facing a jealous rival. Dip a finger into a jar of mustard and trace a protective symbol over your belly to ward against the evil eye.

As a condiment, mustard brightens tired dishes, giving life to everything from chili to toasted cheese. Mustard seeds can be found in white and black varieties. White mustard seeds are toasted to add to dishes and used for pickling. Black mustard seed is a common ingredient in Indian cooking often added to stir-fries. Mustard seeds can be ground to make homemade mustard condiments. It pairs well with bay, chili, coriander, cumin, dill, fennel, fenugreek, garlic, honey, parsley, pepper, tarragon, and turmeric.

Nutmeg
Clarity of vision, confidence, divination, friendship, love, luck, and prosperity

Nutmeg (*Myristica fragrans*) is the seed of an evergreen tree that has long been prized for its medicinal properties. It was carried whole for its protective powers. Culinary author James Moseley relates that in 1147 Saint Hildegard wrote that "whoever received a nutmeg on New Year's Day and carried it in his pocket would be unharmed by any fall, would suffer no broken bones, would be immune to strokes, hemorrhoids, scarlet fever, and boils."[270] By the sixteenth century, nutmeg became so popular in Europe the wealthy took to carrying personal silver graters, "which they pulled out at mealtimes to season their meat and wine," and physicians in Elizabethan London prescribed nutmeg pomanders as a cure for the bubonic plague, explain Michael Murray and Joseph and Lara Pizzorno in *The Encyclopedia of Healing Foods*.[271]

Nutmeg is associated with Jupiter and the element fire and is known for its ability to draw luck. It is an ingredient in wealth and fast-money magicks. Sprinkle it over candles to empower prosperity spells. For quick money, take a green candle and carve the amount you desire into it. Anoint the candle with oil, roll it in ground nutmeg, and place it on a firesafe dish. Arrange 4 silver coins around the candle and light. Visualize the money making its way to you. Use a nutmeg seed as a protective amulet. Drop a nutmeg seed into your left pocket for safe travel or to help you navigate a tricky situation.

Nutmeg most notably is a holiday spice used along with cinnamon, ginger, and allspice. It can enliven both sweet and savory dishes. Add it to puddings and to pumpkin, pear, and apple pastries. It pairs well with allspice, cardamom, cinnamon, cloves, coriander, cumin, ginger, mace, pepper, and thyme.

Oregano
Energy, dreams, joy, legal issues, love, protection, strength, and vitality

Oregano (*Origanum vulgare*) is a flowering perennial herb in the mint family also known as wild marjoram. The Greeks and Egyptians both use oregano as a culinary spice to flavor food and wine.[272] In the Middle Ages, oregano was a popular strewing aid and a charm to ward against magick. Oregano is a close relative to sweet marjoram (*Origanum majorana*) and like marjoram, it symbolizes joy and happiness. It was tradition in Greek and Roman marriages ceremonies for the bride and groom to be crowned with marjoram.[273] Add an infusion to a footbath to revive the weary. Add a few drops of oregano oil to a diffuser to fight the flu. Oregano oil is a potent antifungal remedy. Dilute it with olive oil and apply topically to help treat infection.

....

270. Moseley, *The Mystery of Herbs and Spices*, 83.

271. Murray, Pizzorno, and Pizzorno, *The Encyclopedia of Healing Foods,* 497.

272. NIIR Board of Consultants & Engineers, *The Complete Book on Spices & Condiments*, 133.

273. Maud Grieve, *A Modern Herbal*, vol. 2 (New York: Dover Publications, 1971), 521.

Oregano is associated with the moon, Juno, Venus, Aphrodite, and Diana. It is an herb of love reputed to bring passion to your life. Add it to dishes to sweeten affections and encourage freedom of expression. Anoint a candle in olive oil and roll it in dried oregano to empower a love spell. Use it in food magicks to encourage peace and tranquility or find comfort when separated from a loved one. Drink oregano tea to induce psychic dreams. Oregano also holds energy for protection. Tie a bouquet of oregano with a red string and hang it in a doorway or crumble and scatter it over the threshold to ward a room. Use it in magickal work to repel a meddling neighbor or stop the interference of a troubling coworker.

Oregano is a popular cooking herb. It is a feature in many Greek and Italian recipes. The sweet minty flavor complements tomato-based sauces, pizzas, pastas, and bruschetta toppings. It pairs well with basil, bay, chili, cumin, garlic, paprika, parsley, rosemary, sage, sumac, and thyme.

Paprika
Creativity, energy, enthusiasm, hex removal, love, and passion

Paprika (*Capsicum annuum*) is a deep red spice made from ground dried peppers. Though native to the New World, this spice is now celebrated the world over. It was introduced to Europe via Spain, and then in the 1500s paprika migrated to Hungary, where it became the national spice.[274] There are many types of paprika. The most popular are hot, sweet, smoked, plain, Hungarian, and Spanish.

Paprika is made from capsicums; it too is associated with the element fire and Mars. Paprika holds energy to remove obstacles, power things up, and break hexes. Sprinkle over hummus and serve to friends to gel relationships. Serve it with pita at gatherings to get over differences.

Paprika is a staple in Hungarian, Portuguese, and Spanish cooking. It is a key ingredient in Hungarian goulash and is often made into a sauce served over seafood. The vibrant color makes paprika a lovely garnish to sprinkle over hummus, deviled eggs, and potato salads. It adds a sweet peppery flavor to chicken, fish, and roasted potatoes. Stir it into sour cream or yogurt for a bright dip. Paprika pairs well with allspice, caraway, cardamom, garlic, ginger, oregano, parsley, pepper, rosemary, saffron, thyme, and turmeric.

---

274. Storl, *A Curious History of Vegetables*, 46–47.

Parsley
Beauty, death, love, protection, purification, romance, victory, and wealth

Parsley (*Petroselinum crispum*) is a versatile garden herb native to the Mediterranean. Lore holds that it "sprang from the blood" of the ill-fated baby Archemorus, killed by a serpent.[275] Parsley was an herb of champions worn by Hercules as a symbol of his success.[276] It was a symbol of male potency to the Romans. To the Greeks it was a funeral herb laid on tombs.[277] "Parlsey was used in [the] Hebrew celebration of Passover as the symbol of spring and rebirth," writes Dr. Victor Kuete in *Medicinal Spices and Vegetables from Africa*.[278]

Parsley is associated with the element air, Mercury, Mars, Aphrodite, Persephone, Venus, and the liminal states in life. It is an herb of the dead used to facilitate spirit communications. It symbolizes both victory and death, the coming of spring, and redemption. Anoint candles in olive oil and roll them in dried parsley bits to boost spirit communication. Parsley is used in purification baths, in meditation, and to cheer. It holds energy to heal and protect. Plant it around ponds and fountains to maintain a healthy environment. Plant walkways with parsley and rue to ward entry and keep negative energy from entering. Fresh parsley tea with a bit of honey may calm an upset stomach. A parsley poultice will soothe insect bites and stings. Parsley is reputed to stop rowdy drunken behavior. Add an infusion of parsley to bathwater to cleanse away negative energy or break a negative cycle.

Parsley isn't just a garnish. Many restaurants serve a sprig of parsley with their dish because it freshens breath, aids in digestion, and stimulates the appetite, and parsley has a reputation for keeping food fresh as it guards it from contamination. Parsley has a versatile, bright, slightly peppery flavor and will boost the taste of just about any dish. It is a staple in European and Middle Eastern cuisine. It is used to make tabbouleh, green sauces, and pesto. It is added to soups, sauces, and salads. It pairs well with basil, bay, capers, chervil, chili, chives, garlic, lemon balm, marjoram, mint, oregano, pepper, rosemary, sorrel, sumac, and tarragon.

....

275. Dublin University Magazine editors, "A Dinner of Herbs," *The Dublin University Magazine* 42 (July–December 1853): 44, https://books.google.com/books?id=Zl4ZAAAAYAAJ.

276. Storl, *A Curious History of Vegetables*, 312.

277. Moseley, *The Mystery of Herbs and Spices*, 124.

278. Victor Kuete, ed., *Medicinal Spices and Vegetables from Africa* (Lonon: Academic Press, 2017), 527.

Peppermint
Purification, sleep, love, healing, and psychic powers

Peppermint (*Mentha ×piperita*) is a hybrid mint native to Europe and the Middle East, but it is now naturalized across the world. Peppermint is prized for its refreshing taste and pleasant aroma. It holds a refreshing, uplifting energy and is associated with Venus, Zeus, Pluto, and the underworld. Peppermint tea improves energy and grants clarity of mind. Sip it to inspire creative thought and enhance psychic abilities. Brew an infusion and add it to bathwater to revive yourself. Pour it over your head for a refreshing mental lift. Add it to a footbath to revive after a tiring ordeal.

Like pepper, peppermint energy is good for heating things up. Use it to empower health and money recipes. Add leaves to your wallet to attract money. Grow a bed of peppermint near the door to keep negative energy away. Add peppermint to a spray bottle filled with spring water and mist your place of business to attract customers. Stuff a handful of peppermint leaves into your pocket to avoid being cursed. Protect yourself from the wrath of a jealous neighbor by mixing peppermint with equal parts cinnamon, galangal, rue, and vervain. Sprinkle the mixture across your windowsills and thresholds to repel negativity energy.

Add a few sprigs of fresh peppermint to iced teas, lemonades, and cocktails during the heat of summer for a refreshing lift. Add chopped leaves to a vinaigrette to enliven a salad. Add torn leaves to fruit dishes or top deviled eggs, omelets, and scrambles. Cheer up tired bean, beef, and fish soups and stews with a sprinkling of peppermint. Use it to flavor carrots, green beans, peas, and spinach dishes. It pairs well with lemon, chili peppers, basil, and oregano.

Pineapple Sage
Faery flower, happiness, and hospitality

Pineapple sage (*Salvia elegans*) is a perennial shrub native to Mexico and Guatemala with red tube flowers that are a favorite of hummingbirds. It was introduced as an ornamental garden plant around 1870. In the language of flowers, pineapple sage represents hospitality.

The red tubular flowers attract hummingbirds and faeries. The leaves and flowers are edible and are often added to salads, blended into smoothies, and dropped into iced teas to infuse their sweet, uplifting flavor. Add the leaves and flowers to sachets and charm bags to promote harmony. Plant it in your garden to draw positive energy for happiness and cheer.

Pineapple sage boasts a lovely pineapple and sage flavor that complements chicken and pork dishes. Its bright flavor complements green drinks and salads. Crush a few fragrant leaves over chicken or pork and serve with chunks of pineapple to turn a party festive. Chop the leaves into batters to flavor cakes, cookies, and muffins. Blend a few sprigs with ice and pineapple juice for a lovely, refreshing green drink with energy to pamper and cheer. Pineapple sage pairs well with basil, mint, lemon thyme, rose petals, and nasturtium blossoms.

Poppy Seeds
Abundance, beauty, fertility, invisibility, luck, money, remembrance, and sleep

Poppy seeds (*Papaver* spp.) are the seeds of a colorful flower cultivated as an ornamental plant, for its oil-rich seeds that are used as food, and for a drug made from the sticky white substance that oozes from immature flower heads when they are slit. The ooze hardens into a brown substance as it dries, which is then pulled off the flower and processed into the opiates opium, codeine, morphine, and heroin. As the flowers mature, they lose their narcotic properties. Poppy seeds have been valued since ancient times. They were used as spice by the Sumerians 4000 BCE.[279] "In the Ebers Papyrus, the Egyptians described them as a sedative," according to *The Complete Book on Spices & Condiments*.[280] "Ancient Greeks thought that poppies were a symbol of fertility and placed garlands of poppy blossoms at the shrines of Demeter, goddess of fertility, and [Artemis], goddess of the hunt," explains Laura Martin in *Garden Flower Folklore*. They baked the seeds into bread as a love charm and fed their athletes a mixture of poppy seeds, honey, and wine for strength.[281] The red poppy is an emblem of remembrance.

Poppies are associated with sleep and rest, forgetfulness and confusion, the moon, Saturn, Hecate, Hypnos, Morpheus, Persephone, and the underworld. The fresh flowers have a lovely scent and can be floated in bathwater to revive and comfort. Dried poppy flowers can be added to dream pillows to boost their power and can be used in love spells and enchantments. Grow poppies in the garden to add color and invite faery energies. Grow them to keep negative energies away. Bake the seeds into sweet breads and mix them into salad dressings to encourage affection. In Hoodoo poppy seeds are stuffed into a poppet and used to cause a delay and to dominate and confuse your enemy.

....

279. Craze, *The Spice Companion*, 96.

280. NIIR Board of Consultants & Engineers, *The Complete Book on Spices & Condiments*, 333.

281. Laura C. Martin, *Garden Flower Folklore* (Guilford: Globe Pequot Press, September 12, 2009), 59.

Poppy seeds are used to give texture to rolls, breads, and cakes. They have a distinct flavor and an irresistible crunch that elevates muffins, cakes, cookies, and sweet salad dressing. Poppy seeds complement grapefruit, lemon, orange, and onion flavors.

Rosemary
Beauty, communication, friendship, love, protection, purification, remembrance, and rest

Rosemary (*Salvia rosmarinus*) is a fragrant evergreen perennial native to the Mediterranean. It has been valued for its scent and used in medicine and cooking for more than two thousand years.[282] Romans offered rosemary sprigs to their household gods.[283] The Greeks wore crowns made of rosemary to enhance brain function and strengthen memory.[284] Rosemary has long had an association with love and death. It is both a wedding and a funeral herb added to bridal bouquets and funeral flowers. Rosemary sprigs were distributed to mourners and tossed into the grave of the deceased in fond remembrance.[285] Rosemary was revered for its energy to restore and protect. It was burned in sick rooms and carried by travelers. In the Middle Ages it was tucked under pillows to chase demons away. In times of plague rosemary was worn in neck pouches. In Victorian times it was stuffed into the hollowed handles of walking sticks for its protective powers.[286]

Rosemary is associated with the sun and Leo. Its versatile energy can be used for many workings. Rosemary has properties to heal, to clear and purify, to instill good thoughts and dreams, to improve memory, and to draw good luck and love. Steep a sprig of rosemary in spring water and drink it to enhance mental ability. The scent of rosemary eases headaches and calms the psyche. Snap off a sprig and breathe in the scent to ease a headache and calm racing thoughts. Float sprigs in bathwater and breathe in the steam when a stubborn thought persists. Fill a muslin bag filled with thyme, hops flowers, and rosemary and tuck it under a pillow to keep nightmares at bay. Combine a handful of rosemary with bachelor's button, basil, and lavender to make a floor wash that promotes peace. Add rosemary to white wine and use it as a facial rinse to tighten skin and make it glow. Add rosemary to a meal when you

....

282. Nancy Burke, *The Modern Herbal Primer* (New York: Time-Life, 2000), 123.

283. Picton, *The Book of Magical Herbs*, 73.

284. Burke, The *Modern Herbal Primer*, 123.

285. Picton, *The Book of Magical Herbs*, 74.

286. Picton, *The Book of Magical Herbs*, 73.

want it to be remembered. Rosemary is also a love oracle, and when a silver coin and a sprig of rosemary are placed under the pillow, it will grant dreams of a future love.

Rosemary has a woodsy lemon flavor that is used to flavor teas, poultry, lamb, pork, and fish. It complements mushrooms, peas, potatoes, spinach dishes, and tomato sauces. Pair it with bay, chives, garlic, lavender, lovage, mint, oregano, parsley, sage, savory, and thyme.

Saffron
Fertility, happiness, healing, love, lust, strength, psychic abilities, renewal, and wind raising

Saffron (*Crocus sativus*) is the red stigmas, or threads, plucked from the crocus, one of the first flowers to bloom each spring. It breaks through the snow, a reminder of spring even while winter still has a grip on the world. Saffron is the most expensive spice in the world. It takes over two hundred thousand handpicked saffron threads, or about a football field full of flowers, to make just one pound of saffron. Saffron has been used for medicine and magick for thousands of years. It is mentioned in a Chinese book of medicine from 2600 BCE.[287] Phoenicians revered saffron for its fertility properties and made cakes flavored with saffron to honor the goddess Ashtoreth.[288] The Egyptians grew saffron in their sacred gardens at Luxor. Cleopatra used it to increase her sex appeal.[289] Saffron also holds powers of protection. In Morocco saffron was used to drive away the djinn and thwart the evil eye. Ink made from saffron was used to empower Hebrew amulets.[290]

Saffron is associated with Venus, Aphrodite, the sun, Mars, Leo, the element fire, wealth, power, and singularity. It holds an uplifting, healing energy. An infusion of saffron is taken to help relieve depression, help treat alcoholism, and help enhance the body's healing powers. Mix saffron with rosewater to make a sunny-colored ink that will empower love spells.

Saffron is used in Indian cooking, Spanish *paella*, French *bouillabaisse*, and Italian risotto. It is used to make the traditional Swedish bread *Lussebullar*. The threads are crushed and added to soups, stews, and salad dressings. A pinch is added to rice and chicken recipes to infuse the dish with a subtle honeyed flavor and a lovely deep yellow color. Saffron pairs

287. Hajeski, *National Geographic Complete Guide to Herbs and Spices*, 260.

288. Small, *Culinary Herbs*, 332.

289. Ravi K. Puri and Raman Puri, *Natural Aphrodisiacs* (Bloomington, IL: Xlibris, 2011), 57.

290. D. C. Watts, *Dictionary of Plant Lore*, 336.

well with cardamom, cinnamon, citrus fruits, honey, milk and cream, white wine, vinegar, and rosewater.

Sage
Cleansing, fertility, health, longevity, protection, warding, wisdom, and wish magick

Sage (*Salvia officinalis*) is a cooking herb also known as garden sage, common sage, and culinary sage. Medicinally, sage holds stimulant properties to aid digestion and accelerate wound healing. The Greeks and Romans recognized its healing properties. Arab physicians believed it could grant immortality and increase intelligence.[291] This led to the Arabic saying, "Why should a man die who has sage in his garden?"[292] And for centuries people drank sage tea to bolster health, enhance memory, and improve mood.[293]

Sage is an herb of protection valued since ancient times to ward against evil. It is a component of four thieves vinegar, a medieval remedy to ward off the plague, and since sage is a natural flea repellant, it kept the wearer healthy.[294] Sage is famously used in Native American ceremonies to purify and protect. White sage (*Salvia apiana*) and desert sage (*Artemisia tridentata*) are two of the traditional smudging sages.[295]

Magickally, sage is a plant of power associated with Venus, Jupiter, Leo, Zeus, and Consus. A sage infusion will sharpen concentration and improve attention. Its energy can be used to open communications. Drink a cup to enhance overall cognition. Crumble dried sage and rub it over your hands when meeting someone for the first time to ease communication. Sage smoke will act as a bridge for communication. Burn sage while meditating on the name of someone you have lost touch with to occupy their thoughts and instigate contact. Write their name on a piece of paper and place it in an envelope. Crumble a bit of sage and rosemary into the envelope and seal it. Mail the envelope to yourself. The person you wish to be remembered by will be encouraged to reach out to you as the letter makes its way to you. Sage is associated with Jupiter and will boost recipes for abundance. Keep a small pot of sage in your kitchen window to keep your larder full.

....

291. Hajeski, *National Geographic Complete Guide to Herbs and Spices*, 69.

292. Picton, *The Book of Magical Herbs*, 116.

293. Burke, *The Modern Herbal Primer*, 125.

294. Picton, *The Book of Magical Herbs*, 116.

295. Michelle Gruben, "Sage Advice: An Illustrated Guide to Smudging Herbs," Grove and Grotto, January 10, 2016, https://www.groveandgrotto.com/blogs/articles/100896071-sage-advice-an-illustrated-guide-to-smudging-herbs.

Sage is a poultry spice rubbed into turkey and used to make stuffing for Thanksgiving feasts. It is fried and served with butternut squash and torn and added to bean dishes, tomato sauces, omelets, polenta, and pesto. Sage is used to infuse oils and flavor butter. It is a highlight of northern Italian cuisine used in bean and potato dishes, stuffed meats and sausages, savory breads, and pasta dishes. Sage complements bay leaf, caraway, marjoram, oregano, parsley, pineapple sage, savory, and thyme.

Salt
Cleansing, healing, and protection

While salt is a mineral and not an herb, it is one of the most popular food flavorings added to almost every dish to enhance its flavor. Salt concentrates other flavors, making food taste better. It is one of the oldest food preservers. Early cultures used salt to dry foods. It kills bacteria and is a natural desiccation agent.

Salt is magickal. It is an age-old protective aid strewn across thresholds and windowsills, cast over the shoulder, thrown over footprints, and added to baths and washwaters. It is used to set a magickal barrier and to absorb, break down, and neutralize negative energy. It is both a purifier and protector that will cleanse and banish negative energy that may cling to an object, person, or place. To clear a room of negative energy, sprinkle salt across the floor or add it to water and asperge. Aspersing is the act of sprinkling with liquid in order to affect spiritual and magickal cleansing. This is an ancient rite, just like burning incense. Aspersing rituals enlist the elemental power of both water and earth. To cleanse a room of negativity, simply dissolve sea salt in rain or spring water and sprinkle it around the perimeter of the room or rooms that need to be cleansed.

Today there are many types of salt availed to the cook. Sea salt, kosher salt, pink salt, flaky salt, finishing salts. Some flaky, some coarse, some fine, and though they vary slightly in flavor and texture, all are salty. When using flaky salts in a recipe, always use a little more than the recipe calls for.

Savory
Aphrodisiac, cheer, creativity, mental powers, passion, and psychic ability

Satureja is a genus of highly aromatic herbs, two of which are cherished as garden herbs: the annual, summer savory (*Satureja hortensis*), also called garden savory, and the perennial winter savory (*Satureja montana*). Both are widely cultivated cooking herbs with warm energy and a minty-peppery flavor. Pliny the Elder called it *satureia*, derivative of the word satyr, as it was thought that the satyrs acquired some of their friskiness from eating this herb.[296]

Savory is associated with Venus, Mercury, Pan, and the element air. It has a soothing, jovial energy. Sip a cup of savory tea to calm an upset stomach or ease a cold. Crush the leaves and apply it as a poultice, or brew an infusion and apply it to bites and stings for instant relief. Savory is known for its ability to strengthen mental powers. Stuff it into pockets, eat it, or burn it to stimulate creativity. Pick a sprig and rub the leaves between your fingers to draw out essential oils. Breathe in the scent to enliven thoughts. Drink savory tea while studying to aid memory. It will sharpen observations and heighten psychic ability. Sip to gain wisdom to say the right thing or make the right decision. Sprinkle savory over food and serve it at dinner to add life to any gathering.

Savory herbs are very aromatic and are cherished for their ability to warm dull dishes with their minty-thyme flavor. In Germany savory is called the "bean herb" because its peppery flavor adds to the complexity of bean, pea, and lentil dishes.[297] Add it to cold bean salads. Summer savory is milder than winter savory, but both are used to season beans, vegetables, pork, lamb, stuffing, and sauces. Savory blends well with basil, bay, cumin, garlic, lavender, marjoram, mint, oregano, parsley, rosemary, and thyme.

Sesame Seeds
Abundance, beauty, money, love, lust, and opening

Sesame seeds (*Sesamum indicum*) are edible, oil-rich seeds of a flowering plant in the genus *Sesamum*. They have been cultivated for thousands of years for their nutrient-rich oil that has a distinctive nutty aroma and taste. Sesame is mentioned in Assyrian, Hindu, and Babylon texts as food, medicine, perfume, and beauty oil.[298] A wine of the seed is credited in an Assyrian creation story as being drunk by the gods before they created the earth, and the oil is mentioned in the Vedas as being excellent for humans.[299] In the Mediterranean, the toasted seeds are crushed to make the flavorful paste tahini, used in hummus and halva.

Magickally, sesame energy is associated with Ganesha, the sun, and the element fire. The seeds are known for their legendary powers to open opportunities and discover hidden

....

296. Henry Flowers and Sara Holland, eds., *The Herb Society of America's Essential Guide to Savory* (Kirtland, OH: The Herb Society of America, 2015), 5.

297. Moseley, *The Mystery of Herbs and Spices*, 130.

298. Murray, Pizzorno, and Pizzorno, *The Encyclopedia of Healing Foods*, 456.

299. Murray, Pizzorno, and Pizzorno, *The Encyclopedia of Healing Foods*, 456; DK, *The Story of Food: A History of the Everything We Eat* (London: DK Publishing, 2008), 41.

treasures. As the seeds mature, they cause the pod to burst. The seeds scatter out with *pop!*—a small explosion that casts them out over the ground.

Sesame seeds are used in Middle Eastern cuisines. They have a nutty, slightly sweet flavor that is enhanced by toasting, and they come in white and black varieties, with the black seeds being a bit more bitter. Their flavor complements many kinds of baked goods, both sweet and savory. They are sprinkled on soups and stir-fries to add crunch and flavor. They blend well with garlic, lemon, honey, beans, ginger, carrots, green beans, and broccoli.

Spearmint
Healing, love, mental powers, and prosperity

Mint (*Mentha spicata*) is loved for its refreshing qualities and extolled for its healing powers. Sixteenth-century herbalist John Gerard wrote that it was "marvellous wholesome for the stomacke," and in Russia it was said to be a remedy for the heart.[300] Spearmint, also known as common mint, garden mint, lamb mint, and mackerel mint, is a species of mint native to Europe and Asia but now naturalized all over the world. Its oil is gentler than peppermint's, which makes it easier to use. Spearmint is an ingredient in many healing formulas. Spearmint tea soothes the stomach and alleviates flatulence. When massaged into muscles, it has an antispasmodic effect to soothe cramps and spasms.

Spearmint is associated with Venus and Virgo and holds properties to draw prosperity and heighten awareness. The scent is refreshing. Inhale to sharpen concentration and expand awareness. Spearmint is an ingredient in a popular Hoodoo love magick smoking blend that uses damiana, lobelia, passionflower, and skullcap to inspire relaxation and boost affection. And spearmint holds powers of protection. Make a protective powder by grinding dried spearmint with cinnamon, galangal, rue, and vervain. Roll your candles in the mix to empower protection magicks. Take a handful to your front door and blow it out of your open palm in the direction of a malicious neighbor to end their attentions, or stuff it into a mojo bag and carry it to neutralize negative energy.

Spearmint is sweeter than peppermint and has a more delicate flavor. It works well in both sweet and savory dishes. It is used to make jellies and jams and to flavor sweets like grasshopper pie. Mix a handful of mint with strawberries and basil. Sprinkle it with balsamic vinegar and serve with a crusty bread and goat cheese for a sweet treat that is sure to

---

300. Gerard, *The Herball*, 553; Watts, *Dictionary of Plant Lore*, 361.

intrigue and impress. Use spearmint to dress up watermelon, or add a sprig to a cold glass of tea to make it more refreshing.

Star Anise
Banishing, funerals, love, luck, and psychic powers

Star anise (*Illicium verum*) is a star-shaped pod of an evergreen tree native to Vietnam and China. It has a licorice flavor and is used as a spice to flavor desserts and savory dishes. It is a holiday spice baked into apples and pumpkin dishes and often blended with cinnamon, cloves, ginger, and nutmeg. Though the flavor of star anise is similar to anise (*Pimpinella anisum*), also known as aniseed, because both contain the essential oil anethole, which gives both anise and star anise their licorice flavor, the two are not related. And Japanese star anise (*Illicium anisatum*) is toxic.

In Asia, star anise is a sacred temple incense. It "has been used in China for flavoring and medicine for over three thousand years," shares the Herb Society of America.[301] In Italy, Germany, and France its oil is used to flavor liqueurs. Star anise is associated with Jupiter, Pisces, Sagittarius, and the element air. Its positive energy is used to drive away negativity and draw good luck. Grind and use it as incense to invoke your deities or banish negative energy. Burn it to increase psychic abilities. Star anise has energy to repel negativity. Grind and sprinkle it on holiday fare to help clear away grudges. Combine with cinnamon to inspire fond memories. Carry a pod in your pocket when you go into negotiations to gain favor. Burn it to dispel negative energy after an argument. Stuff a bath sachet with 3 star anise and a handful of bay leaves for a purifying bath that will balance emotions. String star anise pods with whole cloves to make a cheerful yet protective amulet. Wear it as a charm. The appealing scent is activated by body heat to inspire affection while warding against jealousy and malicious thoughts. A star anise with more than eight points is considered a good luck amulet in China and can be worn to protect against the evil eye.[302]

Star anise is a component in the popular five-spice powder (with cloves, cinnamon, fennel, and Sichuan peppercorns). It has a sweet licorice-peppery flavor, and it is used whole to mull wine and cider and ground to flavor baked goods like gingerbread and pumpkin pie. Add star anise to stews and broths to heighten the flavor. It goes well with

---

301. "Star Anise—Illicium verum," the Herb Society of America, 2018, https://herbsocietyorg.presencehost .net/file_download/inline/462b2f20-9e3a-40a6-b64d-76f53ed3dd18.

302. "Star Anise—Illicium verum," the Herb Society of America, 2018, https://herbsocietyorg.presencehost .net/file_download/inline/462b2f20-9e3a-40a6-b64d-76f53ed3dd18.

onions, peppercorns, and soy sauce. Use it in holiday baking with allspice, cinnamon, clove, ginger, and nutmeg for a holiday spice.

Tarragon
Banishing, compassion, dragons, expansion, rebuilding, secrets, and welcoming

Tarragon (*Artemisia dracunculus*) is a perennial herb in the sunflower family that is also known as dragon's wort and little dragon. Lore holds that tarragon was a gift from Artemis to Chiron, who employed it to develop his first medicines.[303] Tarragon holds a restoring energy and was used by the Romans to prevent exhaustion. In India it was mixed with fennel to make a restorative drink.[304] In the Middle Ages a sprig of tarragon was placed in a shoe to ward against exhaustion.[305]

Tarragon is associated with Aries, Mars, the element fire, Artemis, Diana, and Venus. It has mild tranquilizing properties and can be taken as an infusion to promote calmness, restore the weary, and encourage confidence. It is an herb of hospitality brimming with a positive energy that can be used to expand or build. The scent of tarragon is strongly inviting and encourages compassion for others. Tarragon also gives an excellent boost to spells for destiny and finding one's life path. It can be added to love charms and spells to instill peace, kindness, and good luck. Tarragon is known for its ability to banish negativity and will protect the home from thieves and malevolent spirits when grown on windowsills and near entries.

French tarragon is well known for adding flavor to eggs, poultry, and fish. Use the grassy anise flavor to empower your cooking and make your guests feel special. Tarragon is a favored herb in French kitchens, where it is used both fresh and dried to complement the flavors of asparagus, chicken, egg dishes, fish, peaches, and rabbit. Its anise-sweetness is combined with mustard and used to flavor poultry dishes and desserts. It pairs well with basil, bay, capers, chervil, chives, dill, and parsley. Tarragon is an ingredient in béarnaise sauce. It pairs well with strawberries, with mustard in salad dressings, or on chicken.

....

303. Picton, *The Book of Magical Herbs*, 35.

304. Picton, *The Book of Magical Herbs*, 35.

305. Murray, Pizzorno, and Pizzorno, *The Encyclopedia of Healing Foods*, 515.

Thyme
Communication, courage, dreams, healing, love, luck, psychic powers, purification, sight, and success

Thyme (*Thymus vulgaris*) is an aromatic perennial herb with a long history of culinary, medicinal, and magickal uses. In Assyria, Babylon, Greece, and Rome it was used to flavor liquors, meat, cheese, and honey. The Egyptians used thyme to embalm the dead.[306] The Romans and the Greeks used it as an offering and burned it on the altars of their gods.[307] It is one of the nine sacred herbs recorded in the tenth-century in the Anglo-Saxon *Lacnunga*: when used in combination with mugwort, betony, lamb's cress, plantain, chamomile, nettle, crab-apple and fennel, thyme had the power to protect from evil spirits.[308] And according to a recipe from 1600, thyme is used in an ointment to see the faeries.[309] The Greek word *thymus* means courage and in the Middle Ages thyme was a symbol of valor.[310] Knights were given sprigs of thyme and the image was embroidered on their scarves as a sign of their bravery.[311] For the Romans thyme was an herb of comfort brewed as an infusion to treat a hangover and melancholia.[312] Today thyme has a reputation of clearing the mind, calming the nervous system, and encouraging courage, creativity, intuition, and psychic abilities.

Thyme is associated with Mercury and Venus, water, Taurus, and Libra. Fill a muslin bag with thyme, hops flowers, and rosemary and tuck it under your pillow to keep nightmares at bay. Tuck 3 bay leaves and a sprig of thyme into a small white or orange muslin or cotton bag. Carry it in your left pocket to draw luck to you. Wear a sprig of fresh thyme to aid in seeing faeries. Carry a sprig in your pocket to aid in seeing clearly, to increase the power of attraction, or to fortify confidence. Brew a tea of 1 spoon each of thyme and marjoram. Sweeten it with honey and sip to draw true love.

Thyme is a staple in Southern European and Mediterranean cuisines used for centuries to flavor meat, stews, and soups. It is used fresh and dried, alone and bound with other herbs, tied up with cooking twine, and suspended in stocks, soups, and sauces to simmer

....

306. Picton, *The Book of Magical Herbs*, 103.

307. Burke, *The Modern Herbal Primer*, 127.

308. Storl, A Curious History of Vegetables, 131–32.

309. H. G Adams, ed., *Flowers: Their Moral, Language, and Poetry* (London: H. G Clarke, 1844), 111.

310. Burke, *The Modern Herbal Primer*, 127.

311. Picton, *The Book of Magical Herbs*, 104.

312. Picton, *The Book of Magical Herbs*, 106.

in flavor and aroma. Thyme is a component of the classic herb blends *bouquet garni* and *herbes de Provence*. It combines well with allspice, basil, bay, chili, clove, garlic, lavender, marjoram, nutmeg, oregano, paprika, parsley, rosemary, sage, and savory.

Turmeric
Beauty, communication, healing, luck, purification, and the sun

Turmeric (*Curcuma longa*) is a member of the ginger family. The rhizome is ground to make the bright yellow powder that has been celebrated as a dye, spice, and medicine since ancient times. Turmeric has a long history in traditional cultures throughout the East, and "it is still used today in rituals of the Hindu religion and as a dye for holy robes," according to the *Encyclopedia of Healing Foods*.[313] "Turmeric is the dye most often used to create the traditional saffron-colored robes worn by Buddhist monks," writes Bethany Foster.[314] It is an important ingredient in both Chinese and Indian medicine and is used to treat a range of illnesses from inflammation to chest pain to gastrointestinal troubles.[315] Recent studies have confirmed that it is good for both your body and brain.[316] Turmeric holds properties that may help fight cancer, Alzheimer's disease, and other chronic illnesses. It is loaded with curcumin, a healing ingredient that gives it its vibrant color.

Turmeric has a warming energy and is associated with Ganesha, Mercury, Jupiter, the sun, and the element fire. It holds energy for attraction and is used as a beauty treatment in many traditional Indian ceremonies in which family members apply a paste of turmeric to the bride and groom.[317] The Hindus refer to turmeric as "the golden spice" and believe it holds auspicious energy.[318] Add it to your beauty regimen to enhance your complexion, but be careful, as it stains! Turmeric is ground and made into a paste used as an offering in Indian temples.[319]

....

313. Murray, Pizzorno, and Pizzorno, *The Encyclopedia of Healing Foods*, 521.

314. Bethney Foster, "The Religious Significance of Turmeric," Classroom, September 29, 2017, https://classroom.synonym.com/the-religious-significance-of-turmeric-12086453.html.

315. Murray, Pizzorno, and Pizzorno, *The Encyclopedia of Healing Foods*, 521.

316. Honor Whiteman, "Turmeric Compound Could Boost Memory and Mood," *Medical News Today*, January 25, 2018, https://www.medicalnewstoday.com/articles/320732.

317. Watts, *Dictionary of Plant Lore*, 392.

318. Hajeski, *National Geographic Complete Guide to Herbs and Spice*, 264.

319. Bethney Foster, "The Religious Significance of Turmeric," Classroom, September 29, 2017, https://classroom.synonym.com/the-religious-significance-of-turmeric-12086453.html.

Make a magickal powder by grinding 3 bay leaves and mixing them with 1 Table-spoon of turmeric and 1 Tablespoon of cinnamon. Anoint a yellow or orange candle with almond or sunflower oil and roll it in the powdered bits to empower spells for fertility, prosperity, and success. Use it to empower rituals for advancement.

Turmeric has a dusty, slightly bitter flavor and a deep golden color. It is a stock herb in Indian and Caribbean cooking, where it is often used to flavor chicken and rice dishes. Turmeric combines well with coconut, poultry, eggs, kale, lemon, lime, pineapple, rice, and yogurt. It also pairs with chili, cilantro, cloves, coconut milk, coriander, cumin, curry leaf, fennel, galangal, garlic, ginger, lemon grass, mustard seeds, paprika, and black pepper.

Vanilla
Affection, beauty, comfort, love, luck, lust, mental powers, and trust

Vanilla (*Vanilla planifolia*) flavoring comes from the bean pod of an orchid native to Mexico but today is grown all around the world. When the pollinated *Vanilla planifolia* orchid fades, a long slender fleshy pod develops. Vanilla is one of the world's most-beloved flavors. Both vanilla and chocolate were foods of the Aztecs, writes Richard Craze in *The Spice Companion*.[320] The Spanish brought vanilla to the Old World and introduced it to Europe in the 1520s, and it became one of food's most popular flavorings.[321]

Vanilla is associated with Venus, Libra, Pisces, and the element water. The scent of vanilla induces feelings of affection, making it an empowering element in love charms and beauty spells, and when worn, it is an aphrodisiac. Vanilla also holds energy to calm the spirit, grant clear thinking, increase good luck, and inspire friendship and affection. Make an attraction amulet by taking a sharp tool and making a small hole in the end of a vanilla bean. Thread a string through the hole and wear it to boost charm to draw affection. The heat of your body will activate the pod's scent and make you smell irresistible. If you have a pod that has dried out, grind it into a powder and use it in rituals to bring clarity to a situation. Dust it over your hands and touch someone when you wish to gain their trust. Add a bit of ground cinnamon and use it to dress candles to empower magick for success.

To use a vanilla pod, split it lengthwise and scrape the seeds out. Add the seeds to recipes for flavoring. If you are using a vanilla bean, don't discard the pod. Instead, use it to infuse milk or cream or drop it into a jar of sugar to make a posh treat that will sweeten even the

....

320. Craze, *The Spice Companion*, 119.

321. Hajeski, *National Geographic Complete Guide to Herbs and Spice*, 230.

most difficult houseguest. Vanilla sugar is sugar that has been infused with vanilla scent and flavor. To make a batch just drop the pod in a container of sugar and seal. You can add additional pods as you use them. Pods can remain in the sugar indefinitely. Vanilla sugar is an ingredient used to make many European desserts and adds a lovely sweet vanilla flavor to baked goods. Use vanilla sugar to foster positive emotions and feelings of kindness.

Vanilla extract is made by adding vanilla seedpods to alcohol. Commercial vanilla extract is made by macerating and percolating vanilla pods in a solution of ethanol and water. You can make your own vanilla extract by pouring 1 cup of vodka, bourbon, gin, or whiskey into a jelly jar. Add three whole vanilla beans. Seal tightly and let it sit in a cool, dark place for at least two months. Give the jar a gentle shake whenever you happen to notice it.

Herbal Seasoning Blends

Start with these basic recipes to discover your preference. Make up small batches and experiment, adjusting the amounts to craft your own signature blends.

Tuscan Herb Mix

This is a love blend of Italian herbs that pair well with garlic and parmesan.

You will need:

3 Tablespoons dried basil

1 Tablespoon dried rosemary

1 Tablespoon dried oregano

1 Tablespoon dried thyme

Combine the ingredients and store the mix in an airtight container. Use it in pasta dishes or over toasted bread.

Herbes de Provence Mix

This famous blend is popular in the South of France and holds a charming, welcoming energy.

You will need:

2 Tablespoons dried basil

2 Tablespoons dried rosemary

2 Tablespoons dried savory

2 Tablespoons dried thyme

1 Tablespoon ground fennel seed

1 Tablespoon dried tarragon

Combine the ingredients and store the mix in an airtight container. Use it to add a savory flavor to stews, egg dishes, and sauces.

Fines Herbes

This is a classic French spice mixture with cheerful energy.

You will need:

1 Tablespoon dried chervil

1 Tablespoon dried parsley

1 Tablespoon dried chives

1 Tablespoon dried tarragon

Combine the ingredients and store the mix in an airtight container. Use it to season chicken, fish, and egg dishes.

Bouquet Garni

Bouquet garni is a generic term for fresh herbs tied into a bundle and used to infuse soups, stews, and stocks. The string-tied bundle of herbs is then removed prior to serving. The spice bundle often contains basil, marjoram, thyme, rosemary, bay leaf, or sage. Submerge it in broths and soups to bless a relationship.

You will need:

sprig of parsley

sprig of rosemary

sprig of thyme

2 whole dried bay leaves

Bind the herbs together with cooking twine. Submerge it in broths and soups. Removed prior to serving.

Quatre Épices

Quatre épices is a spice mixture favored in French charcuterie and Arabian cooking with energy for prosperity and growth.

You will need:

3 Tablespoons white pepper

1 Tablespoon grated nutmeg

2 teaspoons ground ginger

1 teaspoon ground cloves

Mix the spices together and use the mix to flavor bean and pork dishes.

Greek Herb Mix

This herbal blend supports happiness.

You will need:

2 Tablespoons Greek oregano

1 Tablespoon dried dill

1 Tablespoon dried marjoram

1 Tablespoon dried mint

1 Tablespoon dried thyme

Grind the ingredients together and store the mix in an airtight container. Use it to season meatballs, chicken, fish, vegetable dishes, and sauces.

Chinese Five Spice

This blend has a lucky energy to encourage good things in life.

You will need:

2 teaspoons toasted Sichuan peppercorns

5 star anise, ground

1 Tablespoon ground cinnamon

1 Tablespoon ground fennel seeds

½ teaspoon ground cloves

Grind the ingredients together until very fine. Use the mix in marinades, rubs, and stir-fries and to season braised or roasted fatty meat, fish, and poultry dishes with a delicate sweetness.

Poultry Seasoning

This is a classic seasoning mix used to flavor chicken and turkey dishes with energy to banish the blues and instill cheer.

You will need:

2 teaspoons dried sage

1½ teaspoons dried thyme

1 teaspoon dried marjoram

½ teaspoon dried rosemary

½ teaspoon ground black pepper

¼ teaspoon ground nutmeg

Grind the ingredients together until very fine and store the mix in an airtight container.

Curry Spice Blend

This is a warming spice blend with energy to facilitate communication and warm relationships.

You will need:

2 Tablespoons ground coriander seeds

1 Tablespoon ground cumin

2 teaspoons ground turmeric

1 teaspoon ground black pepper

1 teaspoon ground allspice

1 teaspoon chili powder

Grind the ingredients together until very fine and store the mix in an airtight container. Use it to curry meats or vegetable dishes.

French Chicken Broth Seasoning Mix

This is a savory blend of herbs with energy to lift your mood and encourage creative passion.

You will need:

1 Tablespoon dried marjoram

1 Tablespoon dried savory

1 Tablespoon dried thyme

1 teaspoon dried basil

1 teaspoon dried rosemary

1 teaspoon dried sage

½ teaspoon ground fennel seed

Combine all the ingredients and store the mix in an airtight container.

Pumpkin Pie Spice

This is a festive blend with energy for happiness and prosperity.

You will need:

3 teaspoons ground cinnamon

1 teaspoon ground cloves

¾ teaspoon ground ginger

½ teaspoon ground allspice

½ teaspoon ground nutmeg

Mix all the ingredients together. Store the mix in a small jar and use 1 sprinkle or 1 spoon at a time.

Spicy Pumpkin Pie Spice

You will need:

4 teaspoons ground cinnamon

2 teaspoons ground ginger

1 teaspoon ground allspice

½ teaspoon ground cloves

½ teaspoon ground cardamom

pinch of ground black pepper

Combine all the ingredients and store in an airtight container.

Mix Up a Batch of Black Salt

Salt and pepper go hand in hand. Both are famous for their protective powers. This recipe mixes the two to make a protective powder that is not to be eaten. Black salt is a strewing aid poured across thresholds to prevent unwanted people and spirits from trespassing. Black salt works effectively to absorb negative energy from a new home, haunted house, or any space with aggravated energy. Set a dish filled with black salt in the center of the room or spread it over the area that needs to be cleared. (Salt is harmful to plants as it hinders their ability to draw water, so avoid using in areas with soil.) Leave it overnight. Sweep it up the next morning and dispose of it away from the property. Black salt will empower binding rituals and neutralize negative intent. It is an effective aid in dealing with negativity at the office. Hide a small bag of black salt in your workplace to absorb anger and frustration and end gossip. Strew between you and a hostile coworker to compel them to leave you alone. Pour a handful of black salt into an envelope and tape it under the chair of a difficult coworker. Toss a handful of black salt across the path of someone who has been bothering you to encourage them to go away. When an unwanted person is leaving your home, throw a handful in their footsteps to impede their return.

You will need:

1 part black pepper

1 part ash from a ritual fire

pinch of iron scrapings from your cauldron or cast-iron pan

2 parts salt

Grind the pepper and ash into a fine powder before mixing in the iron scrapings and salt. Store the black salt in an airtight container. Sprinkle black salt across the floor to remove negativity from your home. Sweep it out the front door, toward the street. Strew a line of black salt across your thresholds and windowsills to keep out evil or deflect gossip. Use it to banish anything you want out of your life, be it depression, negativity, a restless spirit, other magic workers, unwanted guests, roommates, or coworkers. Strew it across your threshold to keep unwanted guests from showing up. Place a handful under your doormat to encourage an intruder to leave. Toss a handful over the footsteps of someone as they leave to discourage them from coming back. Sprinkle black salt over a trespasser's footsteps to encourage them to move on. Discreetly toss a handful toward an unwanted roommate when they turn their back to encourage them to move. If you are under personal attack, fill a pouch with black salt and carry it to boost protection. Sew a pouch into the hem of a loved one's coat to protect them from bullies. Place a handful in your pocket when going into a confrontation.

Fancy Flavored Oils

Herb-infused olive oils are easy to make and are lovely for dipping bread, drizzling over pasta, or making a special salad dressing. Use a good-quality olive oil. And don't forget to set an intention. Write it out on a label to affix to your oil jar. Consider the other energies present. Consult the moon. Is it waxing or waning? This will determine the words you use. If the moon is waxing, you should call what you desire. If it is waning, you should push away what you wish to banish. Your actions must be done mindfully as you channel your intent into the ingredients you are working with. So as you measure, add, and mix, focus and intone your intent, channeling it into the process with your actions, thoughts, and words. Tell the mixture what you want it to do. When you have finished, fix the label to the jar to reinforce your intention. You can even add an ingredient list with each herb and spice and the quality you wish for them to add to your magickal mixture.

For best results, use organic herbs and spices. Make sure that any plant matter you use is clean and dry. Any water introduced into your oil will encourage mold to grow in the airspace of your jar. Use a clean, dry jar with a tight-fitting lid. Fill it to the top so there is no airspace. Keep in mind that when oil oxygenates, it becomes rancid, so choose a jar to fit your batch. If you are making a small batch, use a small jar; this will reduce the oil's exposure to oxygen, allowing it to last longer. Small canning jars are four ounces and hold ½ cup of oil. Half pint jars hold 8 ounces, or 1 cup, of oil.

I recommend that you start small and see which oils you like and how much you use so you don't waste ingredients. Infused oils have a real potential to become unsafe if not properly prepared and stored. Make sure your jars are clean and completely dry. Gently bruise your fresh herbs to release their oils. Place the herbal matter in the jar, top with oil, and allow the jar to sit in a cool, dark place for the indicated time. Strain and use the oil immediately, or store it in the refrigerator for up to 2 weeks. The moment you notice any change in color, scent, clarity, or taste, discard it for safety.

Rosemary-Infused Olive Oil

The single oil I always have on hand is rosemary. It is a lovely aromatic oil with a savory taste and a versatile energy that can be used to heal and protect, clear and purify, instill good thoughts and dreams, improve memory, and even draw good luck and love. Use it as a dipping oil for pizza and bread. Drizzle it over salads and pasta. Use it as a blessing oil to anoint candles or massage into skin.

You will need:
¼ cup fresh rosemary leaves, woody stems removed

olive oil

Put your dry, clean rosemary springs into a small canning jar or bottle with a tight-fitting lid. Top with oil and seal. Reinforce your intention as you roll the jar back and forth in your hands, making sure that the herbs are completely submerged in the oil. Label the jar, noting both the ingredients and the bottling date. Place it on a dimly lit shelf. Allow the oil to steep for 2 weeks. Be sure to check on it every few days and give it a gentle shake as you reinforce your intention. After 1 week, open your bottle and taste. Use it up within a week or refrigerate it for up to 1 month.

Sweet Spice Blessing Oil

This oil holds a positive, stimulating energy to amplify psychic awareness and encourage spiritual enlightenment. Use it to draw positive influences into your life. It will support uplifting intentions for growth. Use it to anoint, bless, or consecrate.

You will need:
1 cinnamon stick
1 Tablespoon whole cloves
2 Tablespoons fennel seeds
olive oil

Place the spices into the jar and cover with oil. Seal and reinforce your intention as you roll the jar back and forth in your hands, making sure that the herbs are completely submerged in the oil. Label the jar, noting both the ingredients and the bottling date. Place it on a dimly lit shelf. Allow the oil to steep for 2 weeks. Be sure to check on it every few days and give it a gentle shake as you reinforce your intention. Use it to make dressings and mayonnaises.

Cold-Infused Calendula Oil

Calendula is an edible flower with a flavor similar to saffron. This recipe uses solar energy to empower the flower's natural healing energy.

You will need:
1 handful calendula blossoms
olive oil

Pick your flowers. Wash and dry them and set them on a clean kitchen towel to wilt. Allow the flowers to wilt for 12 hours or more to remove most of the moisture. The next day, fill a glass jar halfway with your clean, dry calendula flowers. Pour oil over the flowers.

Seal the jar and shake. Set the jar on a sunny shelf and shake it daily for 4 weeks. When it's ready to use, strain out plant matter, reserving the oil for magickal use. Rub the oil into your hands to bring good luck to your dealings. Rub it into skin and touch someone you wish to influence to open them to your point of view. Rub it into dry skin or apply it to scrapes and wounds to encourage healing. Rub it into sore muscles to remedy aches.

Sweet and Spicy Courage Oil

This oil resonates with fiery energy to encourage courageous yet opened-minded communications. Use it to soothe your psyche before engaging in any tough interaction. It will support public speaking, managing crowds, or interacting with someone new.

You will need:
1-inch section ginger root, shredded

1 Tablespoon black peppercorns

1 Tablespoon cloves

olive oil

Grind the ginger, peppercorns, and cloves together. Put the spices into a bottle with a lid, or fill a small canning jar. Add oil to the top and seal. Turn the jar to mix and store it in a cool, dark place. Every couple of days, pick up the jar and roll it back and forth in your hands as you reinforce your intention. After 2 weeks, strain out the spices and bottle the oil. Wear it on your pulse points to increase courage and keep your thoughts cool and clear when you must meet a rival or go head-to-head with someone.

Tarragon Drizzling Oil

This oil holds a friendly energy to welcome and make someone feel appreciated.

You will need:
1 cup fresh tarragon leaves

1 cup fresh parsley

1 cup olive oil

Fill a medium saucepan with water and bring it to a boil. Add tarragon and parsley to the water and blanch until herbs turn bright green, about 8 or 9 seconds. Remove the herbs from the water, pat dry, and puree until smooth. Slowly whisk in 1 cup of olive oil. Use it immediately to finish dishes and cultivate a warm feeling of welcome. Drizzle over chicken or steak to soothe ruffled feathers or make a guest feel comfortable.

Parsley, Thyme, and Tarragon Infused Olive Oil

Mix up a batch of this beautiful green oil to celebrate a special guest.

You will need:

¼ cup each fresh parsley, thyme, and tarragon

1 cup olive oil

1 Tablespoon granulated garlic

1 teaspoon red chili flakes

coarse salt

Put a pot of water on to boil. Rinse the herbs, then blanch them by dropping them into the boiling water for 10 to 15 seconds. Dump the herbs into a colander. They should now be bright green. Turn the blanched herbs onto a clean kitchen towel and blot dry before dropping them into a blender. Add the oil and puree until smooth. Pour the mixture into a medium-size caning jar and add garlic, red chili flakes, and coarse salt. Seal tightly. Reinforce your intention as you roll the jar back and forth in your hands to mix. Use it as a dipping oil for bread or toast. Serve it as salad dressing, or drizzle it over an egg disk or cheese and serve to make a guest feel special. Store in the refrigerator for up to 1 week.

Ginger, Garlic, and Shallot Oil

This oil contains what is known in Asian cooking as the trinity of flavors. The water in the ingredients is prone to mold, so this blend should be kept in the refrigerator to macerate. It is brimming with energy to protect health and happiness.

You will need:

2-inch piece ginger root, peeled

2 cloves garlic, peeled

3 small shallots, peeled

wide-mouth glass jar with a lid

olive oil

Put ginger root, garlic, and shallots into the jar and add oil to the top. Seal tightly and label the jar, making note of both the ingredients and the bottling date. Leave it in the refrigerator for 2 weeks. Strain the oil into a clean bottle. Pour it over seafood and chicken dishes.

Chapter 14
DAIRY AND EGGS

Milk, butter, cheese, and other dairy products are made from the nutrient-rich liquid produced by mammalian mothers to nourish their infants. They hold nurturing energy and are associated with Imbolc, the moon, Hathor, Venus, Mercury, and pure mother's love. Milk was once considered a mystical gift. In *Stirring Waters: Feminist Liturgies for Justice* Diann Neu writes, "Milk is one of the earliest sacred foods throughout the world, equivalent to our present-day communion," representing purity and nourishment.[322]

Cow's milk, butter, ghee, and cheese hold magickal energy to nurture love, enhance beauty, and fuel rituals for prosperity and protection. Rich, fatty goat's milk, yogurt, and cheese hold delicious energy for health, vitality, and success. While extra creamy and easy to digest, sheep's milk and cheese carry nurturing energy for healing, riches, and wealth. Lore claims cheese was created thousands of years ago when milk was poured into a lamb's stomach to contain it during a journey by camel. The enzymes in the stomach combined with the camel's movement caused the milk to curdle and become the first cheese, explains Jerry Johnson in *Old-Time Country Wisdom & Lore*.[323] Today there are a multitude of varieties made around the world. Cheese is a valuable source of vitamins, minerals, and protein and unlike milk it can be kept for months.

....

322. Diann L. Neu, *Stirring Waters: Feminist Liturgies for Justice* (Collegeville, MN: Liturgical Press, 2020), 13.

323. Jerry Johnson, *Old-Time Country Wisdom & Lore* (Minneapolis, MN: Voyageur Press, 2011), 260.

Dairy is a favored offering to deity, faery folks, and household gods. The first portion of an unopened carton of milk or cream is poured out in offering or mixed with honey and left to garner favor. When buying milk, spend the extra money to get organic full-fat products. Animals that produce certified organic milk are happy and healthy and much more like the livestock of the past. They are fed 100 percent organic feed. They are never given antibiotics or added growth hormones, and they usually have access to the outdoors.

Milk has energy to pamper. It is used in beauty baths and bars to nourish skin and indulge the spirit. Cleopatra is famed for soaking in her fragrant milk and honey baths. Add a cup of whole milk to your bathwater for soft, supple skin. Add a cup to moon bath rituals or blend with honey to boost attraction magicks. Combine with the soothing energy of chamomile or lavender for a healing bath that will calm the spirit and quiet the mind.

Béchamel Sauce

Béchamel is a versatile white sauce that brims with energy to comfort. Pour it over vegetables, pastas, and even mac and cheese to add creamy richness.

You will need:

4 Tablespoons butter

¼ cup onion, minced

⅓ cup flour

¼ teaspoon ground nutmeg

3 cups whole milk

½ teaspoon salt

white pepper to taste

Melt butter in a saucepan. Add onion and sauté until clear. Stir in flour and nutmeg. Add milk and cook, stirring constantly to keep the sauce smooth until it becomes thickened. Season with salt and pepper and serve.

Mornay Sauce

Béchamel is one of the mother sauces of French cuisine. It is a base for making other sauces, such as this cheesy mornay sauce. Serve over wilted spinach for a Florentine-style dish or pour over macaroni for a rich and cheesy mac and cheese.

You will need:

1 batch of béchamel (see page 282)

2 ounces gruyère cheese

2 ounces parmesan cheese

Melt the cheeses into the béchamel sauce and serve.

Alfredo Sauce

This creamy rich pasta sauce is a simple way to dress up a pasta dinner and multiply the comfort factor. It comes together very quickly, so make sure to start your pasta before you begin the sauce.

You will need:

4 Tablespoons butter

1 clove garlic, minced

1 cup heavy cream

1 cup parmesan cheese, grated plus more for finishing

salt and pepper to taste

In a medium saucepan, heat butter. Add garlic and sauté, stirring when needed until the garlic just begins to turn golden. This happens quickly as the butter heats, so don't turn your back. Minced garlic can go from golden to brown in seconds if it is not stirred. Add cream and bring it to a simmer. Cook for 3 minutes, then stir in the cheese. Cook only 1 to 2 minutes, then remove the pan from heat and stir until the cheese is melted and the sauce is smooth. Season the sauce with salt and pepper. Pour it over fettuccine and toss. Top the dish with a generous handful of grated parmesan and serve.

The Decadent, yet Incredibly Simple, Baked Brie

This is a party recipe to add to your repertoire. It is incredibly simple to put together, and it delivers a scandalously rich treat brimming with positive festive energy. Brie is a holiday cheese, and when it is dressed with raspberry jam and wrapped in pastry, it becomes a decadent treat to rival any dish on the feast table.

You will need:

1 sheet thawed puff pastry

wheel of brie cheese in the 8-to-12-ounce range (You can use a larger wheel, but you will then need 2 sheets of puff pastry.)

good apricot or raspberry preserves

1 egg, beaten

Preheat the oven to 400 degrees Fahrenheit. Set the brie in the center of the pastry and top it with a couple spoons of jam. Fold the corners over the brie, gently pressing the edges to form a neat package. Transfer the wrapped brie to the baking sheet or pie plate. Brush with egg and bake until golden-brown, about 35 minutes. Serve warm so that cheese remains gooey.

The Magick Egg

Eggs are one of the oldest symbols of creation. They are a living food. Eggs are good for you. They are loaded with high-quality proteins, vitamins, minerals, and good fats. Throughout history, the egg has symbolized the hope of life renewed. In the winter, chickens will stop laying unless a heat lamp is installed. In the past, egg production stopped in the dark months and resumed in the spring with the growing daylight hours, thus renewing a food source.

The egg is associated with the Goddess, the sun, and the elements earth, air, and water. It is a symbol of spring, rebirth, fertility, abundance, beginnings, and life itself. During their spring festivities, the ancient Chinese, Egyptians, Greeks, and Romans gave gifts of eggs, symbolizing nature's resurrection.[324] Even the Hebrews have a traditional boiled egg they eat at Passover.[325] Eggs are painted at Easter. In Ukraine hollowed eggs are still elaborately

324. "Eggs as a Symbol of Life," Alimentarium Museum, accessed March 5, 2021, https://www.alimentarium .org/en/knowledge/eggs-symbol-life; Toni Tipton, "Egg Personified the Coming of Spring: A Universal Symbol of Life—Eggs Have Long History," *Los Angeles Times*, March 31, 1988, https://www.latimes.com /archives/la-xpm-1988-03-31-fo-1022-story.html.

325. Peggy Trowbridge Filippone, "Traditional Passover Seder Foods," the Spruce Eats, last modified September, 24, 2019, https://www.thespruceeats.com/traditional-passover-seder-foods-1807638.

painted and given as gifts to preserve the health of the recipient, while in Mexico confetti-filled *cascarones*, rumored to have origins in ancient China, are popular holiday items.[326]

Down through history, the egg has symbolized life renewed. Eggs were left at family altars and gravesites as offerings to the dead. The Greeks left baskets of eggs and pomegranates for the departed, while Ukrainians saved eggshells to toss into moving waters so the dead can join the celebration.[327] Eggs have been used to instill good luck and impart protection down through the ages. In Germany, an egg was dyed green and carried for good luck.[328] In Italy, they were buried in vineyards to protect against bad weather. In Mexico it is customary to break an egg on someone's head at Easter for good luck![329] The act of egging, or throwing eggs at people or property, is a well-known form of protest.

Eggs are used in countless rituals. They are an aid in the divination known as oomancy and are often used to cleanse energy. In some traditions of Hoodoo, rootwork, and Romani magick, eggs are rolled over the body to absorb sickness, curses, and negative energy. Eggshells contain the egg's protective powers. Powdered eggshell, or cascarilla powder, is a powder that has been used down through the ages to set barriers and wards for protection against negativity, hexes, and malicious spirits. You can purchase cascarilla powder or save your eggshells and make your own.

Homemade Cascarilla Powder

You will need:
shells of 6 eggs

Collect the empty shells from at least 6 eggs. Wash them and pull out the membrane. Set the shells out to dry. When they are completely dry, take them in your hand, raise

326. James Taylor, "9 Egg-cellent Easter Eggs from around the World," Travel Associates, April 14, 2017, https://www.travelassociates.com/luxury-holidays-news/9-egg-cellent-easter-eggs-from-around-the-world.

327. Orysia Paszczak Tracz, "The Things We Do …," *The Ukrainian Weekly* 47, no. 66 (November 22, 1998), http://ukrweekly.com/archive/pdf3/1998/The_Ukrainian_Weekly_1998-47.pdf.

328. Elizabeth Wood, *Pancakes and Plum Pudding* (Leicester, UK: Troubador Publishing, 2020), 69.

329. "A Smashing Twist on Easter Egg Hunts: Getting a Confetti-Filled Egg Broken over Your Head Means Good Luck," *(Canada) National Post*, March 21, 2016, https://nationalpost.com/life/a-smashing-twist-on-easter-egg-hunts-getting-a-confetti-filled-egg-broken-over-your-head-means-good-luck.

them to your lips, and tell them what you want them to do. Blow over them, then crumble the shells into a mortar. Crush them into a fine powder.

You can speed the process by setting the washed eggshells on a baking sheet and baking at 350 degrees Fahrenheit for 10 minutes. You might want to do this process when you are alone, as hot eggshells smell awful. The aroma does dissipate quickly, leaving the cooled shells scentless.

When the eggshells have cooled, grind them as you focus on what they are going to be used for. In Hoodoo, blessings are often said at this point. This is also the point where you might add a pinch of herb, a bit of black salt, red brick dust, or iron scrapings to boost the powder's protection power.

Dust cascarilla powder across your threshold and windowsills to keep ghosts and negative energies away. Add it to washwater to power up your cleaning. Eggshell contains properties to negate negative emotions, so this works especially well to remove the hostile atmosphere from a room after an argument. Add a pinch of cascarilla powder to a protection amulet to empower the working. Strew cascarilla powder to form a circle of protection instead of salt when doing ritual work outdoors. Not only does it set a barrier of protection, but it will add a calcium boost to the soil. (Salt is detrimental to the soil and harmful to all the inhabitants of your garden.) Dust cascarilla on your body for protection when you know you have to go into a confrontation or face a jealous rival. The powder will shield you from psychic or magickal attacks. Mix in a few drops of water to make a paste, and use it to paint symbols on your skin. Sprinkle it around the perimeter of your home to ward against gossip, jealousy, or trespassers. Pour a mound and draw symbols in it when doing ritual or spellwork.

Homemade Mayonnaise

Mayonnaise is a sauce made from whipping together eggs and oil. It holds energy to bless, smooth, and enhance. Once you master a basic mayonnaise, you will be able to vary it to make any number of dips and sauces.

You will need:

1 egg yolk, at room temperature

1 teaspoon lemon juice

½ teaspoon dijon mustard

½ olive oil

salt and pepper to taste

Whisk the yolk until thick and yellow. Whisk in the lemon juice. Add the mustard and whisk until thick. Slowly add the oil, whisking it in bit by bit, so as to not break the emulsion. If the mayonnaise separates after the oil is added, add another yolk and start the process again. Whisk the mayonnaise until thick and creamy. Season with salt and pepper. Cover it with plastic wrap and chill until ready to use.

Homemade Aioli

This fancy mayo can be used as a dip or spread over chicken or vegetables. Serve with roasted potatoes, boiled egg dishes, or spread on bread for a spicy mayonnaise alternative brimming with energy to protect health and encourage a positive outlook.

You will need:

1 batch homemade mayonnaise (see above)

2 cloves garlic, peeled and chopped

Mash the garlic into a paste. Whisk the paste into the mayonnaise and serve.

Honey Mustard

This delicious dipping sauce combines mayonnaise and mustard into a sweet and creamy sauce with energy to lift and sweeten.

You will need:

½ cup mayonnaise

2 Tablespoons mustard, dijon, yellow, or a combination

3 Tablespoons honey

1 teaspoon apple cider vinegar

¼ teaspoon cayenne pepper

⅛ teaspoon garlic powder

⅛ teaspoon salt

In a small bowl whisk together the ingredients.

Creamy Poppy Seed Dressing

This sweet and creamy dressing holds energy to gel friendships and empower intentions for love and enchantment.

You will need:

½ cup mayonnaise

2 Tablespoons milk

2 Tablespoons sugar

1 Tablespoon apple cider vinegar

2 Tablespoons poppy seeds

pinch of salt

Place the ingredients into a canning jar. Fix the lid on tight and shake to mix. Serve it as a salad dressing.

Vanilla Custard

Eggs, milk, and sugar come together for a sweet, creamy treat that is good in a pastry shell, over fruit, or served alone. Custard holds comforting mother's love energy to placate the spirit after a difficult day. Serve it to someone feeling low. Serve it to sweeten or add cheer to festivities.

You will need:

4 egg yolks

3 cups milk

½ cup sugar

⅓ cup cornstarch

¼ teaspoon salt

¾ teaspoon vanilla

In a large bowl, beat the egg yolks well. Gradually stir in milk until blended. In a large heavy saucepan, mix together sugar, cornstarch, and salt. Gradually stir in the milk mixture until incorporated. Cook over low heat, stirring constantly, until the mixture thickens and comes to a boil (about 10 minutes). When the mixture begins to simmer, time for 1 minute, stirring constantly, then remove it from heat and immediately cool the pan quickly by setting it in an ice bath. Stir in vanilla. Serve when the custard has cooled.

Spinach Goat Cheese Frittata

The rich tang of goat cheese sets off the spinach in this frittata for a lovely meal served alone or with a side salad. It is loaded with delicious energy for health, vitality, and success. Serve it to bolster health or to gain clear sight before making an important decision.

You will need:

8 eggs

1 cup half and half

¼ cup parmesan, plus ¼ cup

1 Tablespoon butter

1 onion, chopped

1 clove garlic, minced

1 pound of fresh spinach

4 ounces of goat cheese

salt and pepper

Heat oven to 400 degrees Fahrenheit. In a large bowl, whisk eggs, half and half, and ¼ cup of parmesan. In a cast-iron skillet, melt butter and sauté onion and garlic until caramelized. Add spinach and cover. Cook until the spinach is wilted. Add the egg mixture and cook until partially set. Add goat cheese and stick the skillet into a hot oven. Bake for 15 minutes, until the top is brown. Remove from oven, top with remaining parmesan, and season with salt and pepper.

Serve with a helping of fresh greens to boost energy.

Chapter 15
RECIPES FOR THE SEASONS

Earth is a moving planet. It revolves around the sun, creating a year from one full rotation, and as it revolves, it also spins so that the light of the sun falls upon different parts of the planet at different times, creating night and day. Because the axis of the planet is at a tilt, the energy of the sun strikes Earth more intensely at some times than at others. To someone on the planet, this resulting effect is felt as seasonal change. Not only do we get the year and night and day, we get summer and winter, a season of growing and a season of dormancy, or the season of bounty and the season of want.

Earth moves and we experience this movement as time. We witness it each day as the sun rises to travel across the sky before it descends, casting the world into darkness. We feel it in the seasons as Earth both circles the sun and turns upon its axis. One full rotation and another year has passed. Earth moves and time is created.

Neolithic societies across the world observed these changes as natural units for timekeeping and created calendars based on the solar year and the lunation. One of the most famous may be England's Stonehenge. It is possible that "not only did Stonehenge act as a solar calendar, similar to the western calendar used today, but it also acted as a lunar calendar and was important for a developing agricultural society to successfully plan for the seasons," writes James Matthews for Ancient Origins.[330] Old societies marked the seasonal change with festivals. The Celts celebrated the seasonal divisions with various fire festivals. The Anglo-Saxons celebrated the solstices and equinoxes. Today many Pagans observe the Wheel of the Year, celebrating the solstices and equinoxes with harvest and fire festivals. For the modern Pagan, the Wheel is a handy tool to observe an annual cycle and keep in sync with the natural world.

The Wheel of the Year calendar marks the sun's annual death and rebirth in a cycle of growth and dormancy that corresponds to the solstices and equinoxes. The equinoxes occur every six months, first around March 21 then again around September 22. These are the days of "equal night." Between these equinoxes the hours of daylight lengthen, and then diminish, so that between each equinox is the longest and then the shortest day. These are the solstices, or the period when the sun reaches its farthest northern and then southern declinations. This declination creates the shortest and longest period of daylight. The summer solstice falls in mid-June, marking the first day of summer with the longest period of sunlight. The winter solstice falls mid-December and marks the first day of winter with the longest period of darkness. The calendar is further divided into "cross-quarter" days that mark the midpoints between the solstices and equinoxes. These are the festival days held to honor and observe the cycle of the seasons.

The Tides of the Year

While modern people may live disconnected from the natural world, for most of our existence, survival was dependent upon understanding and living in harmony with the fluxes and tides of the seasons. The agricultural year naturally divides into four quarters based on the action of the solstices and equinoxes. Each quarter holds its own tide of energy, one season flowing into the next like a great wheel, an ever-turning seasonal phenomenon of promise, fulfillment, harvest, and want. A practitioner of natural magick wakes to the world aware of the energies of the ever-changing tides of the year and works to harmonize with them and reflect them within. When one wakes to the world, it becomes a place of magick and wonder.

The following table describes the tides of the year as experienced in the Northern Hemisphere.

....

330. James Matthews, "Prehistoric Calendar Revealed at Stonehenge," Ancient Origins, last modified June 18, 2016, https://www.ancient-origins.net/news-history-archaeology/prehistoric-calendar-revealed-stonehenge-006119.

The Tides of the Year		
The Growing Tide	Vernal equinox to Midsummer	March to June
The Harvesting Tide	Midsummer to the autumn equinox	June to September
The Resting Tide	Autumn equinox to Yule	September to Yule
The Cleansing Tide	Midwinter to the vernal equinox	December to March

Yule and the Winter Solstice

December 20 to 21, quarter day, solar festival

This solstice marks the birth of the sun child, as on this darkest night of winter, light returns to the world. For on this morning, after the year's longest night, darkness relinquishes its reign, and from this day forward, the hours of daylight increase.

Yuletide is a time for new beginnings, as we each aspire to be better. It is a time to gather and feast. With joy we come together and relationships are renewed. The celebration holds a magic for us all as bonds of friendship and family ties are strengthened and we look ahead with hope.

The Symbols of the Season

For millennia Yule has been a time of feasting and merriment, and many of its old customs are still practiced in our modern celebrations. Traditions such as greening the home with pine, holly, and mistletoe; decorating a tree; wassailing; baking specialty cakes, cookies, and breads; and the baking of the Yule log all can be traced back to antiquated solstice customs. Even Santa, the bearded, jolly old soul, parallels stories of the god Odin and the Norse Yule Elf, who leaves gifts on the solstice to those who give him offerings. In England he is Father Christmas, in Germany Kris Kringle, in Holland St. Nick, and in Russia Father Winter. Gathering together for the feast, giving gifts, putting up lights, and hanging wreaths are all symbols of the Yuletide, and these symbols of the season have origins dating back more than five thousand years.

The Yule Log

The winter solstice marks the shortest day of the year and the first day of winter. This solstice is also referred to as Yule, which is derived from the Norse word *jól*, pronounced "yohl," and is the name of an ancient Norse fire celebration marking the rebirth of the sun god and the lengthening hours of light. *Jól* lasted for twelve days. The Yule log cake originated from an actual log burned to strengthen the sun.[331] It was important that the log was found on one's own property, as it was designated to bring luck into the household for the coming winter. A piece of the log was often kept as a lucky talisman, stored under the bed to protect the home from lightning and accidental fires until it was retrieved the next solstice and used to kindle the next Yule log fire. After the Yule log was burned down to ash, handfuls were strewn on the fields to ensure fertility. Some of the ashes were also kept to use in various charms.[332]

As the kitchen stove replaced the hearth as the heart of the home, the Yule log also evolved. While today's Yule logs are still symbols of luck and good fortune for the coming year, most are made from sheet cakes, filled, rolled, and frosted to look like a log or stump, some even decorated with mushrooms made from meringue.

Yule Log Cake

You will need:

4 eggs

1 cup white sugar

⅓ cup milk

1 teaspoon vanilla extract

¼ cup unsweetened cocoa

1 cup flour

1 teaspoon baking powder

½ teaspoon salt

filling of choice

---

331. Mihai Andrei, "Yuletide Is Almost Upon Us! But What's 'Yule' Anyway?" ZME Science, last modified January 21, 2021, https://www.zmescience.com/other/feature-post/yule-history-christmas-paganism-25112020/.

332. Stephanie Butler, "The Delicious History of the Yule Log," History.com, August 31, 2018. https://www.history.com/news/the-delicious-history-of-the-yule-log.

Preheat the oven to 375 degrees Fahrenheit. Spray a 15 × 10-inch half sheet pan with cooking spray and line with parchment paper, then spray the parchment paper. Beat the eggs until they turn thick and foamy. Add the sugar, milk, and vanilla extract and mix.

In a separate bowl, combine the dry ingredients. Gently fold the flour mixture into the egg mixture. Stir only until incorporated. Spread the batter evenly into the prepared pan and bake for 15 minutes or until a wooden pick comes out clean. Lightly sift an even layer of powdered sugar over a dish towel. Turn the cake out of its pan onto the prepared cloth while it is still warm.

Carefully peel away parchment paper. Trim away crisp edges and immediately roll the cake up in the cloth, jellyroll style, to cool. When cool, unroll the cake carefully and spread with filling. This swiss roll is a dry cake, and whipped cream, Nutella, and chocolate ganache (see page 122) work well as filling. Roll it up again and chill. When the cake is cold, frost it with your favorite frosting.

Chocolate Buttercream Frosting

This creamy, rich frosting goes well with the dryness of the swiss roll.

You will need:

⅓ cup unsweetened cocoa

½ cup butter, softened

2 cups powdered sugar

2 teaspoons vanilla

2 to 3 Tablespoons milk

Mix together until smooth.

Imbolc or Candlemas

February 2, cross-quarter day, earth festival, the year's first fire festival

Before modern life, being human was a difficult thing. To survive took planning. Communities relied on each other and worked together to ensure the group survived. They saw the year, marked with its seasonal change, as a great turning wheel that shifted the world from light to darkness; from spring to summer, fall, then winter; from bounty to want. And they created calendars by the waxing and waning of the moon, dividing the year into quarters by the solstices and equinoxes. Imbolc, also known as Candlemas, is held on February 2, halfway between the winter solstice and the spring equinox, making it a cross-quarter day on the Wheel of the Year calendar. Imbolc celebrates the waking of nature, as Imbolc is thought to mean "in the belly," which referred to the pregnant ewes who were about to birth their lambs, replenishing the food stores with milk and meat that were depleted from the barren winter months.

Life in the past was reliant upon hard work and stocking up for the winter. Crops were grown and kept in storage for the months when the ground would be barren. With the receding light, poultry stopped laying and the livestock stopped producing milk. A community's food supply began to dwindle as the cold winter months stretched on. Life was tied so closely to nature she became deity, the gods and goddesses each an expression of her many aspects. After surviving the hardships of winter, human hearts swelled with joy and relief. The sun was returning to break the hold the cold long nights held on the world. Life and bounty would soon return with the warming earth.

Imbolc is an earth festival celebrating the return of life to the world, for not only are the daylight hours noticeably growing longer, but now nature is waking, as many of the animals are pregnant and their udders are filling with milk, marking the return of nature's bounty and the end of a long, dark winter.

Imbolc Is a Fire Festival

This cross-quarter day is not just an earth festival but the first of three fire festivals as we celebrate the return of light to the world. This is the feast day of Brigid, the Celtic goddess of fire, healing, childbirth, inspiration, and creativity. Imbolc is about making changes and setting goals for success in the coming year. It is about recharging our own personal power. Now is the time to shake off the winter blues and rekindle your passions. Gather around the hearth fire and revel in its warmth as you come up with plans for the coming spring. Draw up that project you've been longing to start. Now is the time to breathe life into the ideas that were only dreams during the long winter months.

Long ago it was a Celtic custom to light sacred fires on hilltops to encourage the return of light to the world. Today we can greet the returning light by turning on a light in every room on the eve of the holiday. Or better yet, start this day with a sunrise ritual. Get up and greet the dawn. Quietly watch the sun as it rises, or sing it up into the sky. Make this a day rich in ritual. When we are children, our lives are sprinkled with small, magickal rituals, including nightly prayers, singing skipping songs, blowing dandelion heads, and blowing out birthday candles. When we are adults, practicing daily ritual allows us to experience a more magickal life. Through ritual, we can reprogram the unconscious mind so we have a different set of expectations about how the world will respond to us. Through ritual, we can find our way to the places in our lives that exist in between the tick-tock of everyday living and the luscious places of dreaming, the magickal places that connect us to the Divine. The power of ritual comes from heritage, tradition, and, most of all, something being emblazoned in your brain over time. Set aside part of this lovely day to create your own personal ritual, something filled with meaning to you that will mark this as a sacred day.

Milk, Butter, and Cheese

As the very name Imbolc refers to "ewe's milk," referring to the sheep who by themselves replenished the family's depleted food stores, it is not surprising that dairy would have a focus at this festival. Sheep cheese and herbed and honey butters were served with freshly baked breads. Gifts of milk, butter, and cheese were left out for Brigid and a bed was made up for her by the hearth in exchange for a blessing on the household, in the form of prosperous herds and abundant crops.[333] Milk, butter, and cheese hold magickal energy to nurture love, enhance beauty, and fuel rituals for prosperity and protection.

Honey Butter

You will need:

½ cup butter, softened

½ cup honey

Mix the butter and honey together to form a creamy spread.

Sally Lunn or Sun and Moon Bread

This recipe is adapted from a tall muffin-size bun or teacake hawked by street vendors in Bath, England. The origins of this sweet, golden, buttery breakfast bread are lost, but

---

333. Morgan Daimler, *Brigid: Meeting the Celtic Goddess of Poetry, Forge, and Healing Well,* Pagan Portals (Alresford, UK: Moon Books, 2016), 44–46.

according to lore, it is both the creation of an eighteenth-century baker named Sally Lunn and a pastry named from the French *soleil et lunn,* or "sun and moon."[334]

You will need:

2 6-cup muffin tins or 1 tube pan

¼ cup warm water

¼ cup sugar, plus a pinch for the yeast

1 Tablespoon yeast

1 cup milk

½ cup butter

4 cups flour

2 teaspoons salt

1 Tablespoon lemon zest

3 eggs, room temperature

1 Tablespoon vanilla extract

Pour the warm water into a small bowl. Add a pinch of sugar and sprinkle the yeast over the top. Stir to dissolve. Set the bowl aside for 10 minutes.

In a medium saucepan, warm the milk. Add the butter and melt. Stir and cool. In a mixing bowl, whisk together flour, sugar, salt, and lemon zest. Add the milk mixture, eggs, vanilla, and yeast mixture and mix until smooth (about 3 minutes). The batter will be soft and sticky. Spray a piece of plastic wrap with cooking spray and cover. Set it aside to rise until doubled, about 2 hours.

Butter your cooking pan and spoon in the batter. If you are using muffin tins, fill each cup halfway. Cover with oiled plastic wrap and let the batter rise a second time, about 1 hour.

Preheat the oven to 350 degrees Fahrenheit. Remove the plastic wrap and bake the buns for 30 minutes or until golden brown. Test one with a wooden pick. It should come out clean. Turn out the buns to cool. Serve them slathered with honey butter spread.

....

334. *Merriam-Webster,* s.v. "Sally Lunn," accessed March 24, 2021, https://www.merriam-webster.com /dictionary/Sally%20Lunn; Amanda Fiegl, "Colonial Recipes: Sally Lunn Cake," *Smithsonian Magazine,* March 11, 2010, https://www.smithsonianmag.com/arts-culture/colonial-recipes-sally-lunn -cake-82438919/.

Ostara and the Spring Equinox

March 20 or 21, quarter day, solar festival

The cold of winter is over and now the earth is waking as spring returns. Life all around us is beginning to stir as the land begins to warm. The landscape begins to change. Frozen waters held captive all winter begin to release in melted drips and small running streams. Seeds that slept in the frozen ground wake and rise in tentative shoots as the sun warms the earth. Bulbs bloom and wildflowers appear. Fruit trees erupt in showy blossoms, the promise of sweet fruit soon to come.

Spring was a wonder to behold as the once cold and muddy earth became blanketed in green shoots and colorful blossoms. Spring was venerated, worshiped, and named as goddess. Our modern holiday is named after Oestre, Eastre, or Estre, the Teutonic fertility goddess of dawn and light, a name that stuck even when in 595 CE Pope Gregory mandated the conversion of the Anglo-Saxon peasants. He sent a group from Rome to England with instructions to convert the pagan inhabitants to Christianity, and by "superimpose[ing] Christian ceremonies and philosophy" on the existing festivals, we ended up with a holiday named after a pagan goddess and symbols of the hare and egg.[335]

Ostara, or the spring equinox, is a time of balance as opposing forces come together at a point of equal strength. Ostara marks the beginning of the growing period. The dark, cold days have given way to light with the return of the sun. From this point until the summer solstice, the hours of daylight gradually increase, flooding the world with life energy. Now is the season of manifestation as unions of all kinds merge to create new life. This is the time when the energy of the universe transfers from spirit into matter, bringing what is within to manifest without. For just as the sun is reborn at Yule, so is the earth reborn at Ostara.

Holiday Breads

Down through the ages, feast days were heralded by a flurry of holiday baking. As long ago as 627 BCE Jeremiah wrote, "The children gather wood, the fathers light the fire, and the women knead the dough and make cakes of bread for the Queen of Heaven."[336]

....

335. "Eostre and Easter: What Are the Origins of This Spring Festival?," the *(UK) Field*, April 9. 2020, https://www.thefield.co.uk/country-house/easter-eostre-24035; "The Pagan Goddess behind the Holiday of 'Easter,'" Times of Israel, April 5, 2015, https://www.timesofisrael.com/the-pagan-goddess-behind-the-holiday-of-easter/.

336. Jeremiah 7:18.

Ostara is no exception, and there are recipes around the world that were baked as a tribute to the end of winter's wrath. In Ukraine and Poland, you will find *babka*, a rich, buttery egg bread filled with raisins. In the Netherlands it's *paasbrood*, a traditional Easter loaf filled with a sweet almond paste and studded with golden raisins and candied lemon peel. From Portugal comes the lightly sweet saffron bread *pão doce*. For the Greeks and Italians, it was the braided egg bread *tsoureki*. The Czechs baked *houska*, a sweet, eggy braided loaf. In Armenia it was the *choereg*, in Bulgaria *kozunak*, and in Lithuania *velykos pyragas*. *Kulich* is an Easter bread that is often baked in a coffee can. It is popular in Russia, Belarus, Bulgaria, and Serbia. In the United Kingdom, the hot cross bun, a sweet, lightly spiced yeast bun studded with currants or raisins and marked with a cross on top, either piped in icing or etched into the dough, was the favored treat.

Just as the symbols of the egg and the hare worked their way into modern practice, the bun crossed over into Christian tradition, believed to be a magickal treat with the power to protect the home and improve relationships. According to an old Irish rhyme, splitting a bun with a friend will strengthen your relationship, as it brings luck to both. It became a custom to save a bun as a protective talisman that, if hung in the kitchen, would protect the home from fire and make sure dough made throughout the year would rise.[337] Sailors from the British Isles believed that if the bun were taken to sea, it would protect against shipwreck.[338] In fact, the hot cross buns were held to be so powerful that during the reign of Elizabeth I, the London Clerk of Markets issued a decree forbidding the sale of spiced buns except at burials, at Christmas, or on Good Friday, shares Fraser McAlpine for BBC America.[339]

Hot Cross Buns

A hot cross bun is a spiced sweet bun made with currants or raisins and marked with a cross on the top, and it is traditionally eaten on Easter. This recipe makes 18 buns.

....

337. Rachel Nuwer, "5 Great Historical Myths and Traditions about Hot Cross Buns, a Pre-Easter Pastry," *Smithsonian Magazine*, April 17, 2014, https://www.smithsonianmag.com/smart-news/five-great -myths-about-hot-cross-buns-traditional-pre-easter-pastry-180951130/.

338. Fraser McAlpine, "Let's Make Some Hot Cross Buns for Easter," BBC America, 2003, https://www .bbcamerica.com/anglophenia/2013/03/lets-make-some-hot-cross-buns-for-easter.

339. Fraser McAlpine, "Let's Make Some Hot Cross Buns for Easter," BBC America, 2003, https://www .bbcamerica.com/anglophenia/2013/03/lets-make-some-hot-cross-buns-for-easter.

For the bun, you will need:

¼ cup dried currants or raisins

juice of 1 orange

¾ cup warm milk

¼ cup sugar, plus a pinch for the yeast

2¼ teaspoons yeast

½ cup butter, melted

1 egg

zest of 1 orange

1 teaspoon salt

½ teaspoon cardamom

1 teaspoon cinnamon

½ teaspoon nutmeg

3 cups flour

frosting

For the glaze, you will need:

¼ cup water

3 Tablespoons sugar

Place the currants in a small bowl and pour the orange juice over the top to soften them. Cover and let them sit about 2 hours.

In a large mixing bowl, whisk warm milk with a pinch of sugar and yeast. Set it aside for 15 minutes. Add sugar, melted butter, egg, zest, salt, cardamom, cinnamon, and nutmeg and mix until smooth. Add flour a cup at a time, reserving last ½ cup to see if it is needed. Knead the dough until it is shiny and slightly elastic, about 10 minutes. Transfer the dough to a lightly floured work surface. Shape the dough into a ball, then flatten it until it is a disk ½ inch in thickness. Drain the currants and spoon them evenly over surface of dough. Fold the dough into thirds. Turn it and fold into thirds again. Reshape dough into a ball again. Transfer it to a lightly oiled mixing bowl. Cover and let the dough rise until doubled in size, about 2 hours.

Place the dough on a lightly floured work surface. Roll the dough to form a ball, and then divide the dough into 16 equal golf-ball size pieces. Roll each piece of dough into a ball. Spray a baking sheet with cooking spray and arrange the balls in rows. Let them rise for 30 minutes. Preheat the oven to 400 degrees Fahrenheit. Bake until golden brown, about 20 minutes.

While the rolls are baking, make a simple sugar glaze by heating ¼ cup of water and 3 Tablespoons of sugar on medium to a simmer. Simmer 3 minutes. Remove the glaze from heat and set it aside. When the buns are golden brown, cool them on a rack. Brush the glaze over the tops. Then using frosting, mark the top with a cross.

Caraway Seed Cake

Seed cakes are small pound cakes made with caraway seeds and spices baked to mark the end of the sowing of the spring wheat crop. They were handed out to farmhands to thank them for their efforts and mark the end of the planting.[340] Seed cakes were popular teacakes in Victorian England, and they are sweet and lovely when served with a nice cup of tea.[341]

You will need:

6-inch cake pan or small loaf pan

½ cup butter, softened

⅔ cup sugar

2 eggs, beaten

1 Tablespoon caraway seeds

1¼ cups flour

3 Tablespoons almond flour

1 teaspoon baking powder

½ teaspoon salt

1 teaspoon cinnamon

¼ teaspoon cloves

Preheat the oven to 350 degrees Fahrenheit. Spray the pan with cooking spray, then dust it with flour. In a mixing bowl, cream together butter and sugar until light and fluffy. Beat in the eggs. In a separate bowl, stir together the remaining ingredients. Fold the flour

340. Small, *Culinary Herbs*, 277.

341. Andrea Broomfield, *Food and Cooking in Victorian England* (Westport, CT: Praeger Publishers, 2007), 78.

mixture into the wet mixture and stir to form a soft dough. Do not overmix. Spoon the dough into the prepared pan. Bake for 50 minutes or until a wooden skewer comes out clean.

Beltane and May Day

May 1, cross-quarter day, earth festival, second fire festival

The first of May, or May Day, is the remnant of Beltane, an ancient spring festival celebrating the fertility of nature. It is one of the year's four cross-quarter days, falling midway between an equinox and solstice. Long ago the Celtic festival of Beltane, or "bright flame," signaled the end of the dark half of the year, and the people who had survived the hardships of winter rejoiced, celebrating with a great fire festival that honored the sun's life-giving energy, vitality, and the act of creation.

Passions ran high and romance bloomed on Beltane eve, and as a result, many babies were born the following year. You only have to look out your window to note that May is a sensual month. The world is alive and it is celebrating the fact. Celebrate life by joining in the dance of creation and let your spirit soar. Put on some music and give into the lure of rhythm by abandoning yourself to dance. Embrace the energy and allow it to awaken your senses.

The May Day Basket

Back when neighborhoods were rural and everyone knew each other, friendships were celebrated with the giving of a May Day basket.[342] The making of the baskets was a family activity. On the eve before the first of May, family members would gather with scissors, glue, and paper to make pretty baskets. Then early the morning of May 1, flowers were picked and candy sorted to fill the baskets, which were then left anonymously on a friend's front steps. Though the tradition has faded, it still lingers in small towns and rural areas. Families still labor over homemade baskets, fill them with treats, and then sneak out to slip the basket on the neighbor's doorknob, ring the bell, and run, because tradition holds that if you are caught, you will receive a kiss.

Start your own tradition by creating a May Day basket. It can be as fancy or as simple as you want it to be. If you are working with your children, you can simply fold colorful pieces of construction paper to form a cone basket. Secure the side with tape or glue and

342. Eric Stone, *The Seasons of America Past* (Mineola, NY: Dover Publications, 2005), 52.

add a handle at the top. Decorate it with ribbon, stickers, or paper flowers. Fill your basket with candy, baked treats, or flowers and leave it anonymously on a friend's, neighbor's, teacher's, or loved one's doorstep. To keep it safe from marauding animals, if the handle allows, you can also tie it to the door handle.

The Sunny Energy of Honey

Early civilizations honored the bees. The Sumerians, Babylonians, Indians, and Egyptians wrote about the miracle cures of honey, while the Greeks considered it "the food of the gods."[343] Honey is one of the earliest known offertories. "One jar of honey to all the gods, one jar of honey to the Mistress of the Labyrinth" was written on a Knossos tablet from 1300 BCE.[344]

Magickally, honey has energy to empower work for beauty, fulfillment, love, and happiness. Honey can be used to compel someone to speak the truth. It is the key ingredient in sweetening spells and Cleopatra's famed milk and honey bath.

Honey Cake

For thousands of years versions of honey cakes have been offered up as a gift to the gods to both appease them and garner favor. The Egyptians, Greeks, and Romans all had a version.[345] Honey cakes were a traditional food of the holy land and are still a modern Rosh Hashanah favorite. In *Letters from the Hive*, Stephen Buchmann writes, "German pilgrims to the Holy Land acquired a passion for it and copied the recipe at home, where superstitious peasants believed it offered protection against evil spirits."[346]

This recipe makes a sweet and spicy cake that is delicious served warm or cold.

You will need:

10- or 11-inch cake pan

2 cups flour

343. Susan Scheinberg, "The Bee Maidens of the Homeric Hymn to Hermes," *Harvard Studies in Classical Philology,* vol. 83, ed. Albert Henrichs (Cambridge, MA: Harvard University Press, 1979), 5.

344. Michael Ventris, *Documents in Mycenaean Greek*, 2nd ed. (Cambridge, UK: Cambridge University Press, 1973), 310.

345. Alan Davidson, *The Oxford Companion to Food* (Oxford, UK: Oxford University Press, 2014), 395.

346. Stephen Buchmann, *Letters from the Hive: An Intimate History of Bees, Honey, and Humankind* (New York: Bantam Books, 2005), 181.

2 teaspoons baking powder

½ teaspoon baking soda

½ teaspoon salt

1 teaspoon coriander

1 teaspoon ground cinnamon

½ teaspoon ground cloves

½ teaspoon ground allspice

½ cup olive oil

1 cup honey

½ cup sugar

2 eggs

1 teaspoon vanilla extract

½ cup strong black or earl grey tea

Preheat the oven to 350 degrees Fahrenheit. Lightly grease and flour a cake pan. In a large bowl, whisk together the flour, baking powder, baking soda, salt, and spices. Make a well in the center and add the oil, honey, sugar, eggs, vanilla, and tea. Mix to combine ingredients into a thick batter. Pour the batter into the prepared pan. Bake for 30 minutes or until the cake springs back when gently pressed. Let it stand for 15 minutes, and then invert the cake onto a wire rack to cool completely. Place it on serving dish and drizzle generously with honey. You can dress it up with pansy, violets, lavender, or any edible flower.

Make a Batch of Candied Flowers

Candied flowers, or sugared flowers, add a delicate floral flavor and a beautiful appearance to any dessert. Edible flowers are coated with a thin layer of egg white and sugar to preserve their shape and color. This recipe calls for superfine sugar. If you do not have any, you can make a batch by whizzing granulated sugar in a small food processor.

You will need:

1 to 2 cups organic edible flowers (see pages 306–8 for ideas)

½ cup superfine sugar

1 teaspoon water

1 egg white, at room temperature

tweezers

small paintbrush

Wash and dry your flowers. Pour sugar in a small bowl and set a spoon beside it. In another small bowl, whisk the water with the egg white until a few bubbles appear. Pick your first flower up with a pair of tweezers. Dip the paintbrush in the beaten egg white and gently paint all the surfaces on the front, top, and back of the flower to coat. Set aside the paintbrush and hold the flower over the bowl of sugar. Spoon up a small amount of sugar and delicately sprinkle it over the flower. Set the flower on a sheet of parchment paper to set. Repeat the process until all flowers have been candied. Set them aside to dry. The flowers are ready when they are stiff. This could take 4 hours or overnight.

Some of My Favorite Edible Flowers
Elder Flowers

These blossoms come from a fruit-bearing deciduous shrub or small tree known as elderberry and lady elder. The elder blooms in the spring, producing large umbrella-shaped clusters of small white flowers. Each cluster can measure up to ten inches across. Elderflowers are used to make elderflower water, elderflower cordial, and elderflower syrup.

The elder is a faery tree associated with Venus and love magick. The flowers have energy to support blessing, healing, and seduction recipes. The tiny flowers should be picked in the morning to avoid the catty fragrance some varieties produce as the day warms. The flowers mature into small dark berries that can be made into jams, syrup, and ink. The raw stems, leaves, and unripe berries contain a toxic compound that can be harmful when consumed in large amounts.

Lavender

A fragrant herb in the mint family, lavender was cultivated by ancient Egyptians in Thebes, where it was used to perfume both the living and the dead. Lavender is associated with Mercury, Gemini, Virgo, and the element air, making it a good addition to any recipe seeking fast, clear communication. Lavender also holds energy to calm emotions, attract love, protect a relationship, and promote harmony in the home.

Nasturtium

Nasturtium has a bright orange or yellow flower with a peppery flavor, a lot like watercress. The flowers are often added to salads to add energy for cheer, health, and vigor. Nasturtiums are reputed to make one pure of heart. Add them to recipes to find destiny, realize life's purpose, or become more authentic. Nasturtiums are associated with the sun, Ostara, and Neptune.

Pansy

A garden flower in the genus *Viola*, the pansy is also known as heartsease and Johnny-jump-up. According to lore, the god Eros accidentally shot one of his love-inducing arrows into the pansy, causing it to smile. It is a cheerful flower brimming with positive energy. Add it to recipes to spread cheer. Pansies are an ingredient in many love spells and are associated with Eros, Cupid, Pluto, Saturn, and Venus. In the language of flowers, pansy means "happy memories." It has a mild slightly grassy-wintergreen flavor and can be used in salads or served with soft cheese.

Rose

The rose is one of the oldest-known perennial shrubs. Today there are thousands of varieties and colors. It is associated with Venus, Aphrodite, Bacchus, Dionysus, the moon, Taurus, peace, empowerment, attraction, and love and is steeped in lore. Each color of the rose has its own meaning:

Red: Passion

White: Purity

Pink: Happiness

Yellow: Friendship

Roses have a subtle floral flavor that lends well to desserts, jams, salads, and teas. The rose is one of Juno's favorite flowers. The sweet scent encourages both acceptance and affection. Rose energy is nurturing. Add it to recipes to lift vibration, to add energy for well-being and happiness, or to enhance beauty and attract love.

Sage Flowers

Blossoms of a cooking herb also known as garden sage, common sage, or culinary sage, sage flowers have a subtle sweet-savory flavor. Their beautiful color adds a festive touch to a variety of dishes. They work equally well as a garnish for baked goods, meat dishes, and teas. Sage is associated with Venus, Jupiter, Leo, Zeus, and Consus. Sage energy can be used to protect employment, open communications, find opportunities, and attract prosperity.

Violets

The traditional candied flower (not the African variety, which is inedible), *Viola* is a genus of spring-flowering plants in the family Violaceae, also known as heartsease, as they hold a calming energy to ease anxiety and soothe anger. Violets have a sweet and floral flavor and make an elegant garnish on cakes, muffins, cookies, custards, ice cream, and other desserts. Use them in recipes to encourage affection, promote harmony, and boost spirituality.

Litha and the Summer Solstice

June 20 to 22, quarter day, solar festival, fire festival

Litha is an ancient solar celebration also known as Midsummer, Alban Hefin, Sun Blessing, Gathering Day, Feill-Sheathain, and St. John's Day. It marks the longest period of daylight and the shortest night. It occurs between June 20 and 22, when the sun reaches its farthest point north of the equator, marking the height of summer. Early agricultural societies celebrated this ancient solar event with feasts and festivals celebrating light and the power of the sun, for every day past this point, the sun begins to lose its strength as the hours of darkness once again begin to grow. But for now, nature revels in its abundance.

It is a time to celebrate summer in all its fertility, for the Wheel is turning, the season shifting, and though the time of light will begin its descent into the season of cold and darkness, for now we have light, and warmth, and bounty. Rejoice. For this is the joyous high point of summer and all the riches of nature are in full bloom. Now is the time to sing and dance. It is a day for picnics and a night for parties as we celebrate summer in all of its fertility. Use this energy to empower yourself. Join in the celebrations of handfasting, weddings, and births. Host a barbecue or a bonfire and use the party to renew your connection to your tribe. All social gatherings should be a hit when infused with the energy flowing through this magickal time. Picnic at the park. Shop the farmer's market. Attend a local tulip, wine, craft beer, or salsa festival. Look at your community calendar and participate, and when you see a familiar face call out a hello, stop for a chat. Walk your neighborhood and greet your neighbors. Let the nice weather draw you outside, and as you come in contact with your neighbors once again, as they work in their yards or lounge in the sun, let it make you more social. Appreciate the beauty you encounter. Smile. Let your heart open as you rejoice in the magick of the season.

Lemon Olive Oil Friendship Cake

Lemon has a stimulating, refreshing energy to encourage love and friendship and instill clarity and happiness. Its bright, cheery scent revives the weary and lifts the spirit. The tart flavor of lemon enhances and brightens other flavors. Its energy brightens mood and energizes conversation.

You will need:

springform pan

1¾ cups flour

1 teaspoon baking powder

¾ teaspoon salt

4 eggs

1 cup sugar, plus more for sanding the cake top

1 teaspoon lemon zest, finely grated

1 Tablespoon fresh lemon juice

¾ cup olive oil

¾ cup milk

Heat the oven to 350 degrees Fahrenheit. Lightly grease a springform pan. In a small bowl, whisk together flour, baking powder, and salt. In a mixing bowl, whip eggs until foamy. Add sugar, lemon zest, and juice, and whip the mixture with a hand mixer until it is fluffy and pale yellow. Reduce the mixer's speed and slowly pour in oil. Mix until the oil is fully incorporated. Add half of the flour mixture and mix until incorporated. Mix in the milk. Mix in the remaining flour mixture. Pour the batter into the prepared pan. Sand with sugar by sprinkling a Tablespoon or two over the surface. Bake for 45 minutes, until a knife inserted into the center comes out clean and the cake is golden brown.

Lughnasadh and Lammas ("Loafmass")
August 1, cross-quarter day, earth festival, fire festival

Lammas is the first of the three harvest festivals in the season of ripening, for now our backyard gardens burst with fruit. There is corn to pick. Eggplant and peppers hang heavy, waiting for use, while an endless supply of tomatoes and squash mature. Watermelons and dozens of small pumpkins grow on vines that have escaped their plots and now trail across the yard. The blackberry bramble is loaded with berries to yield a harvest to make jams, pies, and treats every weekend from now until the end of September.

Lammas, or first fruits day, was when the ancient people of Britain and France harvested the first of their cereal crops (wheat, barley, oats, rye, and flax) and celebrated the first harvest of the year.[347] The sun is strong this time of year. The summer days are warm and long with light that stretches well into the evenings, but the Wheel of the Year is turning, and though nature's energy now surges into the harvest tide, we look ahead, knowing the growing darkness of winter is coming. In Old English the word *hærfest* meant "harvest" and "autumn," and this month our gardens yield a cornucopia of vegetables. Berry bushes are heavy with ripe berries, for this is the season of ripening and all of nature bursts with abundance.

Lammas marks the beginning of the harvest season. The Wheel of the Year turns, the seeds have sprouted to grow and fruit, and we are mindful that now is the time for gratitude, as we celebrate, not only the abundance of the season but also transformation, rebirth, and the ever-turning Wheel. It is a time to take note of the abundance and give thanks for all that we have in our lives.

Lammas is also known as Loaf Mass Day as the liturgical year adapted to agrarian life, recognizing the importance of giving thanks for the seasonal abundance and all the blessings in our lives. In the past when village life revolved around the growing of the grain, this was the day the first sheaves of grain were brought in from the field and baked into the first loaves from the new grain crop. These loaves were blessed, broken into quarters, and left to guard the grain that had been gathered. Today we give thanks for the first grains as

---

347. John Y. Koch, *The Celts: History, Life, and Culture* (Santa Barbara, CA: ABC-CLIO, 2012), 551.

we honor the spirit of the field, the grain gods, and the Corn Mother, being mindful that this is a time of death and rebirth as the cycle of the harvest comes full circle.

The Lammas Loaf

The art of baking is as old as the first civilizations. "Researchers working in the desert in Jordan actually found the charred remains of a flatbread baked 14,400 years ago," writes Karen Bachmann for *The Daily Press*. "The British Museum has on display actual loaves that were baked over five thousand years ago."[348] Food played a pivotal role in celebrations honoring the harvest and the changing seasons. Celebration breads were skillfully made and ornately decorated. This year engage in the tradition of making a Lammas loaf. It can be as simple or as extravagant as you wish it to be. Some bakers craft loaves in the image of a wheat sheaf, some in the shape of a man, and some in the shape of a sun wheel to symbolize the god of the harvest. Choose a recipe and update it or adapt it by including local ingredients. Be mindful as you work the dough. Remember, intention is everything. As you shape the dough, intone what energy you want it to hold. Vocalize to increase the energy. You can say something like one of these:

- *From the fields to the table, as the Wheel turns, the grain is ripe for reaping. But what falls will rise again. So we celebrate our bounty.*
- *With thankful hearts we honor this grain and its gifts. By its body, we are connected to the earth and sky, to the sun and rain, and to one another.*
- *As the Earth Mother grants the grain, the God lies down to be born again.*

Let your spirit lift with joy and thankfulness for the bounty of the seasons. Give thanks for the abundance in your life by giving a loaf of fresh bread to a friend along with the recipe and pass along a lineage that weaves back to the beginning of time.

Wheat brims with earth energy. It symbolizes the Goddess, rebirth, and renewal and holds energy for abundance, beginnings, fertility, protection, and wealth. Yeast holds energy for activating. When we combine the two and infuse it with our intent through mindfully working the dough, we create a magickal loaf to nurture our body and our spirit.

....

348. Karen Bachmann, "History: Baked Bread a Food Staple of Earliest Civilizations," *The Daily (Timmins, Ontario) Press*, September 13, 2019, https://www.timminspress.com/opinion/columnists/history-baked-bread-a-food-staple-of-earliest-civilizations.

The Split Loaf

This recipe makes 1 loaf.

You will need:

7 × 4-inch loaf pan

5 cups flour

2 teaspoons salt

2¼ teaspoons yeast

1 cup water

¼ cup milk, warm

Spray a loaf pan with cooking spray and set it aside. Sift the flour and salt together. In a small bowl, mix the yeast with half the water and let it sit for 10 minutes. Make a well in the flour and pour in the water mixture. Stir in remaining water. Let it sit to sponge. After 20 minutes, add the milk and mix. Move the dough to a lightly floured work surface and knead it until smooth and elastic, about 10 minutes. Place the dough in an oiled bowl. Spray a piece of plastic wrap with cooking spray and cover the dough. Let it rise for 2 hours, or until doubled in size.

Punch down the dough and turn it out onto a lightly floured work surface. Shape the dough into a rectangle and roll it up lengthwise, tucking the ends to form a loaf. Set the dough in the loaf pan, seam-side down. Cover and let it rise for 30 minutes. The dough should rise over the top of the pan.

Use a sharp knife to score the top of the loaf. Let the loaf sit for 10 minutes while the oven preheats to 450 degrees Fahrenheit. Bake for 25 minutes, or until the loaf is golden and sounds hollow when thumped on the bottom.

Party Bruschetta

This is inspired by Postino, a lovely restaurant in Phoenix where I often shared an order of bruschetta with friends. The order comes with three slices of toast, each cut into three sections, arranged on a serving board, and topped with a different choice of toppings, to provide the table with a total of nine portions.

Slice three ¼-inch thick slices from your favorite rustic loaf and toast them under the broiler for 3 minutes on each side until golden brown. You will want to time this and keep an eye on it, as every broiler cooks at a different rate. When the toast is golden, slice each piece into 3 segments, from top to bottom. Reassemble the toast on a serving tray into 3 pieces of bread with the portions not quite touching, and top each with your choice of toppings.

Roasted Red Pepper and Goat Cheese

Serve this bruschetta topping to boost mood, inspire creativity, or improve a friendship. This recipe tops 3 portions.

You will need:
1 red or yellow pepper
1 clove garlic, minced
salt and pepper
olive oil
1 ounce goat cheese

Preheat the oven to 400 degrees Fahrenheit. Slice and seed the pepper. Put pepper slices in a small bowl. Add garlic and a pinch of salt and pepper. Drizzle with olive oil (1 teaspoon or so) and stir to coat. Pour the mixture out onto a baking sheet and bake for 10 to 15 minutes until pepper has cooked through.

Prepare 1 piece of toast as instructed on pages 312–13. Spread goat cheese over each portion of toast, then top with a heaping of the pepper mixture and serve.

Sliced Pear, Gorgonzola, and Candied Walnuts

Serve this topping to encourage enthusiasm or inspire affection. This recipe tops 3 portions.

You will need:
1 pear
1 ounce gorgonzola
honey
candied walnuts

Slice the pear into paper-thin slices. Prepare 1 piece of toast as instructed on pages 312–13. Fan pear slices over each portion and then top generously with gorgonzola. Drizzle with honey. Chop several candied walnuts and spoon the nut bits on top of the gorgonzola.

Candied Walnuts

This recipe tops 3 portions.

You will need:

1 Tablespoon butter

¼ cup sugar

1 cup walnuts

salt

Heat a small nonstick pan. Add butter, sugar, and walnuts and stir together. When the mixture begins to sizzle, turn the heat down and stir for 5 minutes. The sugar mixture should turn into a brown caramel. Pour it out onto a sheet of parchment paper. Sprinkle it with a pinch of salt, and then spread it in a single layer and allow to cool.

Tomato, Basil, and Mozzarella

Serve this topping to strengthen friendship or inspire romance. This recipe tops 3 portions.

You will need:

1 tomato, chopped into small pieces

2 or 3 basil leaves, finely chopped

olive oil

balsamic vinegar

salt and pepper

1 ounce mozzarella, sliced

Put the tomato bits and basil into a small bowl. Sprinkle them with olive oil and vinegar and season with salt and pepper. Stir to coat.

Prepare 1 piece of toast as instructed on pages 312–13. Arrange the mozzarella over each portion. Spoon the tomato mixture over the mozzarella and serve.

It's Berry-Picking Season

If you live in an area where berries are abundant, pack up the family and head to a U-pick farm, or if forest hikes are more your thing, pack a nature guide and go foraging for wild berries. Here in the Pacific Northwest, you will find blackberries, blueberries, boysenberries, loganberries, marionberries, and raspberries ripe and ready for the picking.

Berries represent an abundant harvest and are traditionally baked into pies to celebrate the first harvest festivals. I have a resident blackberry bush that is both a blessing and a curse, as it is an invasive thorny bramble that grows like a weed, and throughout the early spring and summer, I have to dig out shoots every weekend to keep it contained. On the upside, it yields a bounty of small, soft, tart berries that are a delight to use in baked goods, jams, and wines. Blackberries carry energy for abundance, healing, and protection.

Blackberry Crumble

For the fruit filling, you will need:

5 cups fresh blackberries

4 eggs

2 cups sugar

1 cup sour cream

1 bar of cream cheese

¾ cup flour

pinch salt

zest of ½ lemon

1 teaspoon lemon juice

½ teaspoon cinnamon

1 teaspoon almond extract

For the crumble, you will need:

3 cups flour

1½ cups sugar

¼ teaspoon salt

1½ cups cold butter, cut into 1 inch pieces

Preheat the oven to 350 degrees Fahrenheit. Grease a 9×13-inch baking pan. Mix the filling ingredients together in a large bowl. In a separate bowl or a food processor, combine the crumble ingredients. Press half of the crumble mixture into the bottom of the pan. Pour the fruit filling over the crumble and top with the remaining crumble mixture. Bake 45 to 55 minutes.

Mabon and the Fall Equinox
September 21 to 22, quarter day, solar festival

On this day, when the hours of light and the hour of darkness are equal, we give thanks for the fruits of the earth during this second harvest festival. The autumnal equinox, the time of Mabon, marks the second harvest of the Pagan year. This is the second of the three harvest festivals, the first being Lammas or Lughnasadh and the third being Samhain.

On Mabon the hours of light and darkness become equal. From this point forward, the days begin to shorten as the nights cool and lengthen reminding all of winter's approach. Now is the time when the warmth is behind us and cold lies ahead. In the past, this was a time to take stock and be grateful for the gifts of the earth, knowing that soon the crops would wither and the fields would grow dormant.

At Mabon we give thanks to the harvest deities, such as the Middle Eastern goddess Astarte, the Greek Demeter, the Egyptian Renenutet, the Roman Saturn, and honor the aging deities such as the Crone, the Irish Morrígan, and the Greek Hecate or Persephone, as we turn our eyes to the dying sun, acknowledging the growing nights and coming cold. Now is a time of remembrance, a time to honor our ancestors and align with the natural energies for protection, balance and harmony, wealth, prosperity, and security.

The Magick Apple

Local apple crops are now ripe for picking. Many farms today entertain guests as part of their business. Check your area and see if there are any family farms that allow U-pick. Then load your family into the car and head off for a farm adventure, where you will pick fresh fruit right off the tree, maybe even go on a hayride, or load up on fresh baked goods or jams and jellies.

The apple is an ancient symbol of fertility and knowledge. It is associated with love and Venus and is often left for her in offering. An apple can be used as a poppet to compel another. Apple slices, when sprinkled with cinnamon and eaten, encourage a reluctant lover. The apple is also a food of the dead and holds magickal energy linked to both the autumn equinox and Samhain.

French Apple Cake

You will need:

9-inch springform pan

4 large apples

¾ cup flour

¾ teaspoon baking powder

¼ teaspoon salt

2 eggs

¾ cup sugar

3 Tablespoons rum

1 teaspoon vanilla

8 Tablespoons butter, melted

Heavily butter a 9-inch springform pan. Peel, core, and dice the apples into 1-inch pieces. In a small bowl, whisk together the flour, baking powder, and salt. In a mixing bowl, beat the eggs until foamy and then whisk in the sugar, rum, and vanilla. When combined, whisk in half of the flour mixture. Slowly stir in half of the melted butter. When incorporated, stir in the remaining flour mixture and then the rest of the butter. Add the apple pieces and mix with a spoon until they're well-coated with the batter. Pour the batter into the prepared cake pan and smooth the top a little with a spatula.

Bake at 350 degrees Fahrenheit for 50 minutes to 1 hour, or until a knife inserted into the center comes out clean. Let the cake cool for 5 minutes, and then run a knife around the edge to loosen the cake from the pan. Carefully remove the sides of the cake pan, making sure no apples are stuck to it.

Apple Crisp

You will need:

enough peeled, cored, and sliced apples to fill a 2-quart baking dish

2 Tablespoons lemon juice

salt

½ cup brown sugar

cinnamon to taste

1 cup flour

1 cup sugar

1 cup butter

more butter to dot

In a large mixing bowl, add apple slices. Sprinkle with lemon juice and a pinch of salt and stir to mix. Dump the apples into a deep baking dish and top with brown sugar and cinnamon. In a mixing bowl, stir together flour, sugar, and cinnamon. Cut in butter until the mixture is crumbly. Pour it over the apples and dot it generously with butter. Bake at 375 degrees Fahrenheit for 50 minutes or until the apples are tender and crust is brown.

Samhain and Halloween

October 31, cross-quarter day, fire festival, final harvest festival

Samhain, celebrated the same day as Halloween, is a cross-quarter day and the final harvest festival, marking the beginning of the dark half of the year. This is both the end and the beginning of the Celtic year. The year is turning to the resting tide, and all of nature is responding. We decorate our houses in orange and black and set out jack-o'-lanterns to glow in the dark as we hover around fires telling ghostly stories, drink mugs of cider, and give candy to children who dare to trick-or-treat. Yes, it's Halloween, but just what did this odd holiday evolve from?

The history of Halloween goes back to pre-Christian Europe, when in Ireland it was known as Samhain or summer's end, and for the Celts, this was the time when the world stood outside of ordinary time as the veil between the worlds grew thin, allowing for the dead to cross between. Feasts were held, and places were set at the table not only for the living but also for the dead as they were remembered and honored.

Samhain marks the final harvest and the beginning of the darker half of the year. Samhain was both the end and the beginning of the Celtic year. It was a fire festival known for misrule, much like Saturnalia, and was associated with death, for this was not only the death of the year but also the time when the surplus livestock were butchered for winter's meat.

Samhain is known as a time when both faery and spirit activity increases, as on this night the veil between the world grows thin so that the dead may return to warm themselves at the hearths of the living, and some of the living slip through doorways to visit the *sídhe* in the Otherworld. On this night we honor those who died in the year before.

Winter is coming. We feel it in the cooling air. Sense it in the shortened days. The nights lengthen and cool, for the tides have shifted into the resting tide and the realm of ancestors. Samhain is a time of purification as we give up things we do not need, replacing bad habits with good ones. It is time to purge ourselves of things we are better off without.

Samhain and the Dead

Halloween is associated with death. Not only did this day mark the time when the surplus livestock were butchered for winter's meat, but for the ancient people of Britain, Ireland, and Northern France, it marked the death of the old year and the beginning of the new, and on this night both faery and spirit activity increased.[349] The veil between the worlds grew thin so that the dead could return to warm themselves at the hearths of the living, and some of the living slip through doorways to visit the sídhe in the Otherworld. The eve and day of Samhain were characterized as a time when the barriers between the human and supernatural worlds were broken. "Not a festival honoring any particular Celtic deity, Samhain acknowledged the entire spectrum of nonhuman forces that roamed the earth during that period," writes Mircea Eliade.[350] This included the dead, the spirits of the land, nature spirits, and all the Fae, which made the night a truly frightful one. Candles were lit and set in windows and placed on graves. Food and drink were left out and fires were kept burning so a visiting spirit could warm their cold bones.

Samhain's association with death persists today as modern cultures across the world take time this month to remember their ancestors. The Czech Republic celebrates the Commemoration of All the Departed on November 2. On this day individuals visit the gravesites of their relatives and decorate the graves with flowers and candles in their memory.[351] In the evening a chair is placed beside the fire for the dead to warm themselves. In Austria, a plate of bread and a glass of water are left out overnight on a tabletop, while in Poland the windows and doors of the home are opened to welcome in the spirits of the

----

349. John W. Allen, *It Happened in Southern Illinois* (Carbondale: Southern Illinois University Press, 2010), 254.

350. Mircea Eliade, *Encyclopedia of Religion*, vol. 6 (New York: Macmillan, 1987), 176.

351. "Dusicky—Czech Halloween," Prague.net, accessed March 9, 2021, http://www.prague.net/blog/article/29/dusicky-czech-halloween.

dead.[352] In Mexico *el Día de los Muertos*, or the Day of the Dead, is celebrated to remember and honor the dead as their spirits return to the family homes. Many families make altars and decorate them with candy, photos, flowers, and food. Candles are lit to help the dead find their way back to their homes, and family graveside feasts are held.[353]

Breads of the Dead

Through the ages, food has played an important role in Halloween celebrations. The practice of trick-or-treating spun out of the European Christian tradition of going from home to home, asking for soul cakes, or currant buns, on All Souls' Day. When the treat was given, the beggar would, in return, offer up a prayer for the soul of the homeowner's relative.[354]

Soul cakes, also known as farthing cakes or Saumans loaves, are small cakes filled with allspice, nutmeg, cinnamon, or currants, and they originated in England during the Middle Ages.[355] In Scotland, the soul cakes were made of oat flour and known as the "dirge-loaf, while in Italy, the food of choice for All Saints' Day celebrations is a cookie called *ossi dei morti*, "bones of the dead."[356] In the Americas the Aztecs believed that the souls of the dead returned with the migration of the monarch butterfly each fall, and during Día de los Muertos, sugar skulls and *pan de muerto*, or "bread of the dead," an anise-flavored brioche, are made to honor the dead on altars and at graveside feasts in Mexico.[357]

Soul Cakes

Soul sakes were small scone-like cakes that were baked on Halloween to commemorate the dead. Traditionally, the small cakes were decorated with a cross cut into the top or

352. Crowder Sentry Staff, "International Students Celebrate Different Halloween Traditions," *Crowder Sentry*, October 11, 2013, https://www.crowdersentry.net/international-students-celebrate-different-halloween-traditions/.

353. Caryl-Sue, "Dia de los Muertos," *National Geographic*, October 17, 2012, https://www.nationalgeographic.org/media/dia-de-los-muertos/.

354. Maggie Black, "Saints and Soul-Caking," *History Today* 31, no. 11 (November 1981): n.p., https://www.historytoday.com/archive/saints-and-soul-caking.

355. Nicholas Rogers, *Halloween: From Pagan Ritual to Party Night* (Oxford, UK: Oxford University Press, 2002), 28–30.

356. T. F. Thiselton-Dyer, *British Popular Customs, Present and Past* (London: G. Bell, 1900), 410; Deborah Mele, "All Saints Day Cookies—Ossa Dei Morti," Italian Food Forever, November 1, 2019, https://www.italianfoodforever.com/2019/11/all-saints-day-cookies-ossa-dei-morti/.

357. Silver RavenWolf, *Halloween!: Customs, Recipes, Spells* (St. Paul, MN: Llewellyn Publications, 1999), 59.

pressed into dough with currants and were given out to soulers, or singers who went door to door singing and saying prayers for those who had died in the year before.

You will need:

1 cup butter

1 cup sugar

2 eggs

3½ cups flour

1 Tablespoon baking powder

1 teaspoon salt

2 teaspoons cinnamon

2 teaspoons ginger

1 teaspoon allspice

¼ teaspoon nutmeg

½ cup of dried currants

4 to 6 Tablespoons milk, to mix

Preheat the oven to 375 degrees Fahrenheit. In a large mixing bowl, cream the butter and sugar together. Beat in the eggs. In a separate bowl, sift together the flour, baking powder, salt, and spices. Add the flour mixture to the sugar mixture and mix until incorporated. Stir in currants, adding enough milk to make a biscuit-like dough.

Roll the dough out and cut out rounds with a biscuit cutter. Mark the top of each biscuit with a cross and place them on a greased baking sheet. Bake for 12 to 15 minutes or until golden brown.

Leave a Dish of Colcannon for the Faeries

The veil between the worlds is thin this night, and just as the dead slip through, the puka, banshees, faeries, and other spirits freely come and go, some causing destruction and making mischief if they feel slighted. Colcannon is a traditional Irish dish made on Samhain from mashed potatoes, cabbage or kale, and leeks to appease the wandering spirits.[358] Recipes vary region to region with some specifying finely shredded savoy cabbage, while others use chopped kale or chard. The variety of onion also changes from leeks to green

....

358. Jennifer Billock, "A Brief History of Ireland's Fortune-Telling Mashed Potato Dish (Recipe)," *Smithsonian Magazine*, October 26, 2018, https://www.smithsonianmag.com/travel/colcannon-fortune-telling-mashed-dish-recipe-180970492/.

onions to shallots or a combination, and others still add parsnips to the mash. One thing that is constant is that colcannon is a traditional potato mash eaten on Samhain. Sometimes trinkets were hidden inside to predict the coming year. According to *Smithsonian Magazine* writer Jennifer Billock, "A coin meant wealth in the coming year, a rag meant poverty and a stick meant your spouse was going to beat you."[359] It is customary to scoop out a serving, dress it with a chunk of butter, and set the bowl on the front step as an offering to appease any roaming ghosts or faeries.

Colcannon

You will need:

4 large potatoes

6 Tablespoons butter, plus more for serving

½ cup chopped leeks, white parts only

3 cloves garlic, minced

3 cups finely chopped cabbage, kale, or other leafy green

½ cup chicken broth

½ cup heavy cream

salt and pepper to taste

Peel, cube, and boil the potatoes until tender. Drain and set them aside. Add butter to a stockpot or dutch oven and heat. Add the leek pieces and garlic. Sauté for several minutes. Add the chopped cabbage and chicken broth to the leek mixture and sauté for 5 more minutes. Add the cream and heat to a simmer. Remove from heat and mash in the potatoes. Add salt and pepper to taste and serve the colcannon hot, with a slice of butter on top. Set out a serving to feed any hungry spirit that may be passing by.

359. Jennifer Billock, "A Brief History of Ireland's Fortune-Telling Mashed Potato Dish (Recipe)," *Smithsonian Magazine*, October 26, 2018, https://www.smithsonianmag.com/travel/colcannon-fortune-telling-mashed-dish-recipe-180970492/.

Bibliography

Books

Adams, H. G., ed. *Flowers: Their Moral, Language, and Poetry*. London: H. G Clarke, 1844.

Alcock, Joan P. *Food in the Ancient World*. Westport, CT: Greenwood Press, 2006.

Allen, John W. *It Happened in Southern Illinois*. Carbondale: Southern Illinois University Press, 2010.

Ardinger, Barbara. *Pagan Every Day: Finding the Extraordinary in Our Ordinary Lives*. Newburyport, MA: Weiser Books, 2006.

Baker, Margaret. *Folklore and Customs of Rural England*. Lanham: Rowman & Littlefield, 1974.

Barnett, Robert A. *Tonics: More Than 100 Recipes That Improve the Body and the Mind*. New York: Harper Perennial, 1997.

Berger, Pamela. *The Goddess Obscured: Transformation of the Grain Protectress from Goddess to Saint*. London: Robert Hale, 1988.

Beyerl, Paul. *A Compendium of Herbal Magick*. Ashland, WA: Phoenix Publishing, 1998.

Bible. New American Standard. La Habra, CA: Lockman Foundation, 1995.

Blake, Deborah. *Everyday Witchcraft: Making Time for Spirit in a Too-Busy World*. Woodbury, MN: Llewellyn Publications, 2015.

———. *The Goddess Is in the Details: Wisdom for the Everyday Witch*. Woodbury, MN: Llewellyn Publications, 2009.

Buchmann, Stephen. *Letters from the Hive: An Intimate History of Bees, Honey, and Humankind*. New York: Bantam, 2005.

Buhner, Stephen Harrod. *Sacred and Herbal Healing Beers*. Boulder, CO: Siris Books, 1998.

Butler, Simone. *Moon Power: Lunar Rituals for Connection with Your Inner Goddess*. Beverly: Fair Winds Press, 2017.

Burke, Nancy. *The Modern Herbal Primer*. New York: Time-Life, 2000.

Charles, Denys J. *Antioxidant Properties of Spices, Herbs and Other Sources*. New York: Springer, 2013.

Child, Lydia Maria. *The History of the Condition of Women, in Various Ages and Nations*. Vol. 2. London: J. Allen & Company, 1835.

Clevely, Andi, and Katherine Richmond. *The Complete Book of Herbs*. London: Smithmark Publishers, 1998.

Clevely, Andi, Katherine Richmond, Sallie Morris, and Lesley Mackley. *Cooking with Herbs and Spices*. Leicester, UK: Anness Publishing, 1997.

Craig, Timothy J. *Japan Pop!: Inside the World of Japanese Popular Culture*. London: Taylor & Francis, 2015.

Craze, Richard. *The Spice Companion*. London: Quintet Publishing, 1997.

Crowley, Vivianne. *The Magickal Life: A Wiccan Priestess Shares Her Secrets*. London: Penguin Books, 2003.

Culpeper, Nicholas. *The Complete Herbal*. Manchester, UK: J. Gleave and Son, 1826.

Cumo, Christopher, ed. *The Encyclopedia of Cultivated Plants*. Santa Barbara, CA: ABC-CLIO, 2013.

Cumo, Christopher. *Foods That Changed History*. Santa Barbara, CA: ABC-CLIO, 2015.

Cunningham, Scott. *Cunningham's Encyclopedia of Magickal Herbs*. St. Paul, MN: Llewellyn Publications, 1985.

———. *Earth Power: Techniques of Natural Magic*. St. Paul, MN: Llewellyn Publications, 1983.

Daimler, Morgan. *Brigid: Meeting the Celtic Goddess of Poetry, Forge, and Healing Well*. Pagan Portals. Alresford, UK: Moon Books, 2016.

Dalby, Andrew. *Dangerous Tastes: The Story of Spices.* Berkeley: University of California Press, 2000.

Das, Moumita. *Chamomile Medicinal, Biochemical, and Agricultural Aspects.* New York: Taylor & Francis, 2014.

Daniels, Cora Linn, and C. M. Stevens. *Encyclopaedia of Superstitions, Folklore, and the Occult Sciences of the World.* Chicago: J. H. Yewdale & Sons, 1903.

Davidson, Alan. *The Oxford Companion to Food.* Oxford, UK: Oxford University Press, 2014.

Deerman, Dixie, and Steven Rasmussen. *The Goodly Spellbook: Olde Spells for Modern Problems.* New York: Sterling Ethos, 2014.

Denker, Joel S. *The Carrot Purple: And Other Curious Stories of the Food We Eat.* Lanham, MD: Rowman & Littlefield, 2015.

Dioscorides, Pedanius. *De Materia Medica.* Translated by Tess Anne Osbaldeston. Johannesburg: Ibidis Press, 2000.

DK. *The Story of Food*: A History of the Everything We Eat. London: DK Publishing, 2008.

Earle, Rebecca. *Potato.* London: Bloomsbury Academic, 2019.

Eliade, Mircea. *Encyclopedia of Religion.* Vol. 6. New York: Macmillan, 1987.

Farmer, Steven. *Sacred Ceremony: How to Create Ceremonies for Healing.* Carlsbad: Hay House, 2002.

Flint, Martha Bockée. *A Garden of Simples.* Boston: Charles Scribner's Sons, 1900.

Flowers, Henry, and Sara Holland, eds. *The Herb Society of America's Essential Guide to Savory.* Kirtland, OH: The Herb Society of America, 2015.

Foster, Steven, and Rebecca L. Johnson. *National Geographic Desk Reference to Nature's Medicine.* Washington, DC: National Geographic, 2008.

Franklin, Anna. *The Hearth Witch's Compendium: Magical and Natural Living for Every Day.* Woodbury, MN: Llewellyn Publications, 2017.

Frazer, James George. *The Golden Bough.* Vol. 2. New York: Macmillan, 1900.

Gailing, Stephanie. *Planetary Apothecary.* Berkeley, CA: Crossing Press, 2012.

Gawain, Shakti. *Creative Visualization: Use the Power of Your Imagination to Create What You Want in Your Life.* Novato: New World Library, 2002.

Gentilcore, David. *Pomodoro!: A History of the Tomato in Italy.* New York: Columbia University Press, 2012.

Gerard, John. *The Herball: or the Generall Historie of Plantes*. London: John Norton, 1597.

Girard, James E. *Principles of Environmental Chemistry*. Sudbury, MA: Jones & Bartlett Learning, 2013.

Gregg, Susan. *The Complete Encyclopedia of Magical Plants*. Beverly, MA: Fair Winds Press, 2008.

Grieve, Maud. *A Modern Herbal*. Vol. 2. New York: Dover Publications, 1971.

Hageneder, Fred. *The Meaning of Trees*. San Francisco: Chronicle Books, 2005.

Hajeski, Nancy J. *National Geographic Complete Guide to Herbs and Spices*. Washington, DC: National Geographic, 2016.

Hamrick, Julia Rogers. *Choosing Easy World: A Spiritual Guide for the Suburbanite*. New York: St. Martin's Griffin, 2011.

Health Research Staff. *Garlic*. Pomeroy, WI: Health Research Books, 1983.

Hendrickson, Robert. *Lewd Food*. Radnor, PA: Chilton Book Company, 1974.

Henrichs, Albert, ed. *Harvard Studies in Classical Philology*. Vol. 83. Cambridge, MA: Harvard University Press, 1979.

Hensperger, Beth. *Bread for All Seasons: Delicious and Distinctive Recipes for Year-Round Baking*. San Francisco, CA: Chronicle Books, 1995.

The Herb Society of America. *Oregano and Marjoram*. Kirtland, OH: The Herb Society of America, 2005.

Hutton, Ronald. *The Stations of the Sun: A History of the Ritual Year in Britain*. Oxford, UK: Oxford University Press, 2001.

———. *The Triumph of the Moon: A History of Modern Pagan Witchcraft*. Oxford, UK: Oxford University Press, 2001.

Iacobbo, Karen, and Michael Iacobbo. *Vegetarian America: A History*. Westport, CT: Praeger, 2004.

Johnson, Jerry. *Old-Time Country Wisdom & Lore*. Minneapolis, MN: Voyageur Press, 2011.

Kindred, Glennie. *Earth Wisdom: A Heart-Warming Mixture of the Spiritual and the Practical*. London: Hay House UK, 2011.

Kingsolver, Barbara. *Animal, Vegetable, Miracle: A Year of Food Life*. New York: HaperCollins, 2007.

Kiple, Kenneth F. *A Movable Feast: Ten Millennia of Food Globalization*. Cambridge, UK: Cambridge University Press, 2007.

Kiple, Kenneth F., and Kriemhild Coneè Ornelas, eds. *The Cambridge World History of Food*. Vol. 1. Cambridge, UK: Cambridge University Press, 2000.

Koch, John Y. *The Celts: History, Life, and Culture*. Santa Barbara, CA: ABC-CLIO, 2012.

Kowalchik, Claire, and William Hylton. *Rodale's Illustrated Encyclopedia of Herbs*. Emmaus, PA: Rodale Press, 1987.

Kruger, Anna. *The Pocket Guide to Herbs*. London: Parkgate Books, 1992.

Kuete, Victor, ed. *Medicinal Spices and Vegetables from Africa*. London: Academic Press, 2017.

Mars, Brigitte. *Dandelion Medicine: Remedies and Recipes to Detoxify, Nourish, and Stimulate*. Pownal, VT: Storey Publishing, 1999.

Martin, Laura C. *Garden Flower Folklore*. Guilford, CT: Globe Pequot Press, 2009.

Mickaharic, Draja. *A Century of Spells*. Newburyport, MA: Weiser Books, 2001.

Moseley, James. *The Mystery of Herbs and Spices*. Bloomington, IN: Xlibris, 2006.

Mojay, Gabriel. *Aromatherapy for Healing the Spirit: Restoring Emotional and Mental Balance*. Rochester, VT: Healing Arts Press, 2000.

Munsterberg, Hugo. *Dictionary of Chinese and Japanese Art*. New York: Hacker Art Books, 1981.

Murray, Michael T., Joseph E. Pizzorno, and Lara Pizzorno. *The Encyclopedia of Healing Foods*. New York: Atria Books, 2005.

National Research Council. *Lost Crops of the Incas: Little-Known Plants of the Andes with Promise for Worldwide Cultivation*. Washington, DC: National Academy Press, 1989.

Neu, Diann L. *Stirring Waters: Feminist Liturgies for Justice*. Collegeville, MN: Liturgical Press, 2020.

NIIR Board of Consultants & Engineers, *The Complete Book on Spices & Condiments*. Delhi: Asia Pacific Business Press, 2006.

Ody, Penelope. *The Complete Medicinal Herbal*. London: Dorling Kindersley, 1993.

Okihiro, Gary Y. *Pineapple Culture: A History of the Tropical and Temperate Zones*. Berkeley, CA: University of California Press, 2009.

Om, Mya. *Energy Essentials for Witches and Spellcasters*. Woodbury, MN: Llewellyn Publications, 2010.

Padulosi, S., K. Hammer, and J. Heller, eds. *Hulled Wheat: Proceedings of the First International Workshop on Hulled Wheats*. Rome: International Plant Genetic Resources Institute, 1996.

Pagrach-Chandra, Gaitri. *Warm Bread and Honey Cake*. London: Pavilion Books, 2012.

Panda, H. *Handbook on Spices and Condiments*. New Delhi: Asia Pacific Business Press, 2010.

Pendell, Dave. *Pharmako/Poeia*. San Francisco: Mercury House, 1995.

Pennacchio, Marcello, Lara Jefferson, and Kayri Havens. *Uses and Abuses of Plant-Derived Smoke*. Oxford, UK: Oxford University Press, 2009.

Pennick, Nigel. *History of Pagan Europe*. London: Routledge, 1997.

———. *Pagan Magic of the Northern Tradition: Customs, Rites, and Ceremonies*. Rochester, VT: Destiny Books, 2015.

Phillips, Roger, and Nicky Foy. *The Random House Book of Herbs*. New York: Random House, 1990.

Picton, Margaret. *The Book of Magickal Herbs: Herbal History, Mystery, and Folklore*. London: Quarto, 2000.

Pitrat, Michel, and Claude Foury. *Histoires de legumes*. Paris: Institut National de la Recherche Agronomique, 2003.

Puri, Ravi K., and Raman Puri, *Natural Aphrodisiacs*. Bloomington, IL: Xlibris, 2011.

Radin, Dean. *Real Magic: Ancient Wisdom, Modern Science, and a Guide to the Secret Power of the Universe*. New York: Harmony Books, 2018.

RavenWolf, Silver. *Halloween!: Customs, Recipes, Spells*. St. Paul, MN: Llewellyn Publications, 1999.

Reader's Digest. *Magic and Medicine of Plants*. New York: Reader's Digest, 1986.

Reynolds, Mary. *Garden Awakening: Designs to Nurture Our Land & Ourselves*. Cambridge, UK: UIT Cambridge, 2016.

Rhind, Jennifer Peace. *Fragrance and Wellbeing: Plant Aromatics and Their Influence on the Psyche*. London: Singing Dragon, 2014.

Richard, Gladys A. *Navaho Religion: A Study of Symbolism*. Princeton, NJ: Princeton University Press, 1977.

Riley, Gillian. *The Oxford Companion to Italian Food*. Oxford, UK: Oxford University Press, 2007.

Roediger, Virginia More. *Ceremonial Costumes of the Pueblo Indians: Their Evolution, Fabrication, and Significance in the Prayer Drama.* Berkeley: University of California Press, 1991.

Rogers, Nicholas. *Halloween: From Pagan Ritual to Party Night.* Oxford, UK: Oxford University Press, 2002.

Rogerson, Barnaby. *Rogerson's Book of Numbers.* London: Picador, 2014.

Rowling, Marjorie. *Life in Medieval Times.* New York: TarcherPerigee, 1973.

Rüpke, Jörg, ed. *A Companion to Roman Religion.* Malden, MA: Blackwell Publishing, 2011.

Rutledge, Sarah. *The Carolina Housewife.* Reprint, Columbia: University of South Carolina Press, 1979.

Sargent, Claudia Karabaic. *A Gift of Herbs.* New York: Viking Studio Books, 1991.

Schiller, Carol, and David Schiller. *The Aromatherapy Encyclopedia: A Concise Guide to Over 385 Plant Oils.* Laguna Beach, CA: Basic Health Publications, 2008.

Schlegel, Rolf H. J. *History of Plant Breeding.* Boca Raton, FL: CRC Press, 2018.

Shurtleff, William, and Akiko Aoyagi. *History of Soynuts and Soynut Butter.* Lafayette, CA: Soyinfo Center, 2012.

Silverblatt, Irene. *Moon, Sun, and Witches.* Princeton, NJ: Princeton University Press, 1987.

Simrock, Karl Joseph. *Handbuch der deutschen Mythologie.* Bonn, Germany: Adolf Marcus, 1887.

Small, Ernest. *Culinary Herbs.* Ottawa: NRC Research Press, 2006.

Staub, Jack. *Alluring Lettuces: And Other Seductive Vegetables for Your Garden.* Layton, UT: Gibbs Smith, 2010.

———. *75 Exciting Vegetables for Your Garden.* Layton, UT: Gibbs Smith, 2005.

Starhawk. *Dreaming the Dark: Magic, Sex, and Politics.* Boston: Beacon Press, 1997.

Starhawk. *The Earth Path: Grounding Your Spirit in the Rhythms of Nature.* San Francisco: Harper San Francisco, 2004.

Stone, Eric. *The Seasons of America Past.* Mineola, NY: Dover Publications, 2005.

Stone, Merlin. *When God Was a Woman.* San Diego: Harcourt Publishing, 1978.

Storl, Wolf D. *A Curious History of Vegetables.* Berkeley, CA: North Atlantic Books, 2016.

Telesco, Patricia. *How to Be a Wicked Witch: Good Spells, Charms, Potions and Notions for Bad Days.* New York: Simon & Schuster, 2001.

Thiselton-Dyer, T. F. *British Popular Customs, Present and Past.* London: G. Bell, 1900.

Ventris, Michael. *Documents in Mycenaean Greek*. 2nd ed. Cambridge, UK: Cambridge University Press, 1973.

Wardwell, Joyce A. *The Herbal Home Remedy Book: Simple Recipes for Tinctures, Teas, Salves, Tonics, and Syrups*. Pownal, VT: Storey Communications, 1998.

Warner, Melanie. *Pandora's Lunchbox: How Processed Food Took Over the American Meal*. New York: Scribner, 2013.

Warren, John. *The Nature of Crops: How We Came to Eat the Plants We Do*. Wallingford, UK: CAB International, 2015.

Watts, D. C. *Dictionary of Plant Lore*. Amsterdam: Elsevier, 2007.

Weil, Andrew. *National Geographic Guide to Medicinal Herbs*. Washington, DC: National Geographic, 2010.

Wilkins, John M., and Shaun Hill. *Food in the Ancient World*. Malden, MA: Blackwell, 2006.

Woodfield, Stephanie. *Dark Goddess Craft: A Journey through the Heart of Transformation*. Woodbury, MN: Llewellyn Publications, 2017.

Journal Articles

Adgent, Margaret A., David M. Umbach, Babette S. Zemel, Andrea Kelly, Joan I. Schall, Eileen G. Ford, Kerry James et al. "A Longitudinal Study of Estrogen-Responsive Tissues and Hormone Concentrations in Infants Fed Soy Formula," *Journal of Clinical Endocrinological Metabolism* 103, no. 5 (May 2018): 1899–909. https://pubmed.ncbi.nlm.nih.gov/29506126/.

Aris, Aziz, and Samuel Leblanc. "Maternal and Fetal Exposure to Pesticides Associated to Genetically Modified Foods in Eastern Townships of Quebec, Canada." *Reproductive Toxicology* 31, no. 5 (May 2011): 528–33. https://pubmed.ncbi.nlm.nih.gov/21338670/.

Bais, Souravh, Naresh Singh Gill, Nitan Rana, and Shandeep Shandil. "A Phytopharmacological Review on a Medicinal Plant: *Juniperus communis*." *International Scholarly Research Notices* 2014 (2014): 1–6. https://www.ncbi.nlm.nih.gov/pmc/articles/PMC4897106/.

Barański, Marcin, Dominika Średnicka-Tober, Nikolaos Volakakis, Chris Seal, Roy Sanderson, Gavin B. Stewart, Charles Benbrook, et al. "Higher Antioxidant and Lower Cadmium Concentrations and Lower Incidence of Pesticide Residues in Organically Grown Crops: A Systematic Literature Review and Meta-analyses." *British Journal of*

Nutrition 112, no. 5 (September 2014): 794–811. https://pubmed.ncbi.nlm.nih
.gov/24968103/.

Battaglin, W. A., M. T. Meyer, K. M. Kuivila, and J. E. Dietze. "Glyphosate and Its Degradation Product AMPA Occur Frequently and Widely in U.S. Soils, Surface Water,
Groundwater, and Precipitation." *Journal of the American Water Resources Association* 50,
no. 2 (April 2014): 275–90. https://onlinelibrary.wiley.com/doi/10.1111/jawr.12159.

Bernbaum, Judy C., David M. Umbach, N. Beth Ragan, Jeanne L. Ballard, Janet I. Archer,
Holly Schmidt-Davis, and Walter J. Rogan. "Pilot Studies of Estrogen-Related Physical
Findings in Infants." *Environmental Health Perspectives* 116, no. 3 (March 2008): 416–20,
https://pubmed.ncbi.nlm.nih.gov/18335112/.

Black, Maggie. "Saints and Soul-Caking," *History Today* 31, no. 11 (November 1981): n.p.
https://www.historytoday.com/archive/saints-and-soul-caking.

Borek, Carmia. "Garlic Reduces Dementia and Heart-Disease Risk." *Journal of Nutrition*
136, no. 3, supplement (March 2006): 810s–12s. https://pubmed.ncbi.nlm.nih.gov
/16484570/.

Borresen, Erica C., Kerry A Gundlach, Melissa Wdowik, Sangeeta Rao, Regina J. Brown,
and Elizabeth P. Ryan. "Feasibility of Increased Navy Bean Powder Consumption for
Primary and Secondary Colorectal Cancer Prevention." *Current Nutrition and Food Science* 10, no. 2 (May 2014): 112–119. https://www.ncbi.nlm.nih.gov/pmc/articles
/PMC4082309/.

Cheng, Jiang, Zhi-Wei Zhou, Hui-Ping Sheng, et al. "An Evidence-Based Update on the
Pharmacological Activities and Possible Molecular Targets of *Lycium barbarum*
Polysaccharides." *Drug Design, Development and Therapy* 9 (2015): 33–78. https://www
.ncbi.nlm.nih.gov/pmc/articles/PMC4277126/.

Chonpathompikunlert, Pennapa, Phetcharat Boonruamkaew, Wanida Sukketsiri, Pilaiwanwadee Hutamekalin, and Morakot Sroyraya. "The Antioxidant and Neurochemical
Activity of *Apium graveolens* L. and Its Ameliorative Effect on MPTP-Induced Parkinson-like Symptoms in Mice." *BMC Complementary Medicine and Alternative Medicines* 18,
no. 1 (March, 2018): 103. https://www.ncbi.nlm.nih.gov/pmc/articles/PMC5859653/.

Cicero, Arrigo F. G., Massimiliano Ruscica, and Maciej Banach. "Resveratrol and Cognitive Decline: A Clinician Perspective." *Archives of Medical Science* 15, no. 4 (July 2019):
936–43. https://www.ncbi.nlm.nih.gov/pmc/articles/PMC6657254/.

Cooper, Raymond. "Re-discovering Ancient Wheat Varieties as Functional Foods." *Journal of Traditional and Complementary Medicine* 5, no. 3 (2015): 138–43. https://www.ncbi.nlm.nih.gov/pmc/articles/PMC4488568/.

Dixon, R. E., S. J. Hwang, F. C. Britton, K. M. Sanders, and S. M. Ward. "Inhibitory Effect of Caffeine on Pacemaker Activity in the Oviduct Is Mediated by cAMP-Regulated Conductances." *British Journal of Pharmacology* 163, no. 4 (June 2011): 745–54. https://doi.org/10.1111/j.1476-5381.2011.01266.x.

Dublin University Magazine editors. "A Dinner of Herbs." *The Dublin University Magazine* 42 (July–December 1853): 44. https://books.google.com/books?id=Zl4ZAAAAYAAJ.

Earle, Alice Morse. "Sabbath-Day Posies and Noon-House Fare." *The Congregationalist and Christian World* 88, no. 37 (September 12, 1903): 361.

Gill, Jatinder Pal Kaur, Nidhi Sethi, Anand Mohan, Shivika Datta, and Madhuri Girdhar. "Glyphosate Toxicity for Animals." *Environmental Chemistry Letters* 16 (December 2017): 401–26. https://www.researchgate.net/publication/321822115_Glyphosate_toxicity_for_animals.

Guggenheim, Alena G., Kirsten M. Wright, and Heather L. Zwickey. "Immune Modulation from Five Major Mushrooms: Application to Integrative Oncology." *Integrative Medicine: A Clinician's Journal* 13, no. 1 (February 2014): 32–44. https://www.ncbi.nlm.nih.gov/pmc/articles/PMC4684115/.

Kwiatkowska, Marta, Edyta Reszka, Katarzyna Wozniak, Ewa Jabłonska, Jaromir Michałowicz, and Bozena Bukowska. "DNA Damage and Methylation Induced by Glyphosate in Human Peripheral Blood Mononuclear Cells (In Vitro Study)." *Food and Chemical Toxicology* 105 (July 2017): 93–99. https://pubmed.ncbi.nlm.nih.gov/28351773/.

Kwiatkowska, Marta, Jarosiewicz Pawel, and Bozena Bukowska. "Glyphosate and Its Formulations—Toxicity, Occupational and Environmental Exposure." *Medycyna Pracy* 65, no. 5 (2013): 717–29. https://pubmed.ncbi.nlm.nih.gov/24502134/.

Lee, Heayyean, Kyungmin Nam, Zahra Zahra, and Muhammad Qudrat Ullah Farooqi. "Potentials of Truffles in Nutritional and Medicinal Applications: A Review." *Fungal Biology and Biotechnology* 7, no. 9 (June 2020): n.p. https://fungalbiolbiotech.biomedcentral.com/articles/10.1186/s40694-020-00097-x

Lee, Jaehee, and Kyongshin Cho. "Flaxseed Sprouts Induce Apoptosis and Inhibit Growth in MCF-7 and MDA-MB-231 Human Breast Cancer Cells." *In Vitro Cellular & Develop-*

mental Biology—Animal 48 (2012): 244–50. https://link.springer.com/article/10.1007%2Fs11626-012-9492-1.

Li, Shang, Na Liu, Er-Dan Sun, Jian-Da Li, and Peng-Kin Li. "Macular Pigment and Serum Zeaxanthin Levels with Goji Berry Supplement in Early Age-Related Macular Degeneration." *International Journal of Ophthalmology* 11, no. 6, (2018): 970–75. https://www.ncbi.nlm.nih.gov/pmc/articles/PMC6010398/.

Lin, Xu, Jeffrey R. Gingrich, Wenjun Bao, Jie Li, Zishan A. Haroon, and Wendy Demark-Wahnefried. "Effect of Flaxseed Supplementation on Prostatic Carcinoma in Transgenic Mice." *Urology* 60, no. 2 (November 2002): P919–24. https://www.goldjournal.net/article/S0090-4295(02)01863-0/fulltext.

Lowcock, Elizabeth C., Michelle Cotterchio, and Beatrice A. Boucher. "Consumption of Flaxseed, a Rich Source of Lignans, Is Associated with Reduced Breast Cancer Risk." *Cancer Causes & Control* 24, no. 4 (April 2013). https://pubmed.ncbi.nlm.nih.gov/23354422/.

Lynch, Rhoda, Eileen L. Diggins, Susan L. Connors, Andrew W. Zimmerman, Kanwaljit Singh, Hua Liu, Paul Talalay, and Jed W. Fahey. "Sulforaphane from Broccoli Reduces Symptoms of Autism: A Follow-Up Case Series from a Randomized Double-Blind Study." *Global Advances in Health and Medicine* 6 (October 2017), n.p. https://journals.sagepub.com/doi/full/10.1177/2164957X17735826.

Mathew, B. C., and R. S. Biju. "Neuroprotective Effects of Garlic." *Libyan Journal of Medicine* 3, no. 1 (March 2008): 23–33. https://www.ncbi.nlm.nih.gov/pmc/articles/PMC3074326/.

McGovern, Patrick E, Juzhong Zhang, Jigen Tang, Zhiqing Zhang, Gretchen R. Hall, Robert A. Moreau, Alberto Nuñez, Eric D. Butrym, et al. "Fermented Beverages of Pre- and Proto-Historic China." *Proceedings of the National Academy of Sciences* 101, no. 51 (December 21, 2004): 17,593–98. https://www.pnas.org/content/101/51/17593?ijkey=045cde6ef4c520d545f639ff51d0b0b2a513d401&keytype2=tf_ipsecsha.

Mokhtari, Reza Bayat, Narges Baluch, Tina S. Homayouni, Evgeniya Morgatskaya, Sushil Kumar, Parandis Kazemi, and Herman Yeger. "The Role of Sulforaphane in Cancer Chemoprevention and Health Benefits: A Mini-Review." *Journal of Cell Communication and Signaling* 12, no. 1 (March 2018): 91–101. https://www.ncbi.nlm.nih.gov/pmc/articles/PMC5842175/.

Noda, Y., T. Kneyuki, K. Igarashi, A. Mori, and L. Packer. "Antioxidant Activity of Nasunin, an Anthocyanin in Eggplant Peels." *Toxicology* 148, no. 2–3 (August 2000): 119–23, https://pubmed.ncbi.nlm.nih.gov/10962130/.

"Pick of the Season." *The National Culinary Review* 25 (2001): 12.

Redmond, Kate. "Browsing the Bog," University of Wisconsin Milwaukee field station bulletin 32 (2007): 1–56.

Ren, Feiyue, Kim Reilly, Joseph P. Kerry, Michael Gaffney, Mohammad Hossain, and Dilip K. Rai. "Higher Antioxidant Activity, Total Flavonols, and Specific Quercetin Glucosides in Two Different Onion (*Allium cepa* L.) Varieties Grown under Organic Production: Results from a 6-Year Field Study." *Journal of Agricultural and Food Chemistry* 65, no. 52 (June 2017): 5,122–32. https://pubs.acs.org/doi/10.1021/acs.jafc.7b01352.

Samsel, Anthony, and Stephanie Seneff. "Glyphosate, Pathways to Modern Diseases III: Manganese, Neurological Diseases, and Associated Pathologies." *Surgical Neurology International* 6, no. 45 (March 2015): 45. https://www.ncbi.nlm.nih.gov/pmc/articles/PMC4392553/.

Stolarczyk, John, and Jules Janick. "Carrot: History and Iconography." *Chronica Horticulturae* 51, no. 2 (2011): 1–6. http://www.carrotmuseum.co.uk/finaljournal.pdf.

Sturtevant, E. Lewis. "History of Celery." *The American Naturalist* 20, no. 7 (July 1886): 602. https://www.journals.uchicago.edu/doi/abs/10.1086/274288.

Tian, Ming, Xiaoyun Xu, Hao Hu, Yu Liu, and Siyi Pan. "Optimization of Enzymatic Production of Sulforaphane in Broccoli Sprouts and Their Total Antioxidant Activity at Different Growth and Storage Days." *Journal of Food Science and Technology* 54, no. 1 (January 2017): 209–18. https://www.ncbi.nlm.nih.gov/pmc/articles/PMC5305717/.

Acknowledgments

This book would not have been possible without the amazing team at Llewellyn Worldwide. Thank you first and foremost to the talented Heather Greene. Thank you for your keen insight, kind words, and personal support. You were a true doula through the entire publishing process. It was your advice and guidance that turned a troubled manuscript into a work fit to publish. Thank you for having faith in me throughout all of the revisions. I am eager to begin our next project.

Thank you to Lauryn Heineman, production editor extraordinaire. Thank you for your time and effort. Thanks to your outstanding writing skills and sharp eyes, this book shaped up into something to be proud of. Thank you for helping to make it the best it could be.

It takes a village to publish a book. Thank you for everyone in production who helped transform a manuscript into this beautiful book. A special thanks to Donna Burch-Brown and Shira Atakpu for the brilliant book design and cover art.

Thank you to the ladies of my psychic circle. It was your friendship and exposure to your ideas and viewpoints that grew my spirituality and allowed my knowledge and awareness to expand. Thank you for making my world a fascinating and magickal place filled with limitless possibilities.

Thank you to Stephani Stephens. Your input was invaluable. Your inspiring thoughts helped form the foundation of this book. I often think back on our amazing conversations and am inspired to reach for more.

Thank you to my new friend Britta Nicholson. Thank you for your input and enthusiasm over this project. It was your cheerful words that helped me stay on track.

Thank you to my husband, without whose support this book would not have been possible.

INDEX

C